ALLIES AT ODDS

ALLIES AT ODDS

The Andean Church
and Its Indigenous Agents, 1583–1671

JOHN CHARLES

UNIVERSITY OF NEW MEXICO PRESS

Albuquerque

LIBRARY OF CONGRESS CATALOGING-IN-PUBLICATION DATA

Charles, John, 1970-
Allies at odds : the Andean church and its indigenous agents, 1583-1671 / John Charles.
p. cm.
Includes bibliographical references and index.
ISBN 978-0-8263-4831-9 (pbk. : alk. paper)
1. Indians of South America—Andes Region—Religion. 2. Catholic Church—Missions—
Andes Region—History. 3. Indians of South America—Languages—Social aspects.
4. Literacy—Social aspects—Andes Region—History. 5. Spanish language—Social aspects—
Andes Region—History. 6. Andes Region—Religious life and customs.
7. Conversion—Christianity. 8. Syncretism (Religion)—Andes Religion—History.
9. Spain—Colonies—America—Administration. I. Title.
F2230.1.R3C534 2010
282'.809032—dc22
2010023991

DESIGN AND COMPOSTITION
Barbara Haines

TEXT IS MINION PRO 10.25/14.25

Contents

Figures

The Archbishopric of Lima in colonial times.
Drawn by Giulia Curatola and Sandro Makowski.

Acknowledgments

A great number of people and institutions contributed to the making of this book, and I am pleased to be able to thank them for their generosity. My first debt of gratitude is to Rolena Adorno, who advised the project in its initial phase as a Yale doctoral dissertation and who provided much-needed encouragement and counsel throughout later steps of the research and writing process. It has been my remarkable fortune to study under the guidance of a scholar as dedicated as she to the teaching of the humanities. Rolena and the late Professor David S. Adorno were my first intellectual role models, and I will always feel blessed for the privilege of their friendship. This book also profited immensely from the mentorship of Roberto González Echevarría, who provided thorough feedback early on and gave me confidence in my topic's potential. Josefina Ludmer and Noël Valis read first drafts with great care and pushed me to keep my focus on the "lengua." During my graduate work, Georgina Dopico Black and Miruna Achim shared with me their brilliant scholarship and excitement for old books. Their encouragement did more to inspire my decision to study the early modern past than they can ever know.

I gratefully acknowledge the comments my work received from some of the best in Spanish colonial history. Kenneth Mills passed along clarifications and timely reminders to keep sight of the human dimensions of the archival record. Karen Spalding read drafts of my work, pointed me toward new sources, and taught me by example the importance of getting the facts of the trial docket straight. Kathryn Burns thoughtfully showed me her unpublished work on Andean scribes, which compelled me to rethink my approach to native literacy in colonial times. Sinclair Thomson, Thomas Abercrombie, and NYU's Atlantic World Workshop gave me insight on the cord keepers, as did Galen Brokaw, Bill Evans, and Colette de la Burde. Paul Firbas invited me to present my research at Princeton and pointed my thoughts in new and fruitful directions. I am especially appreciative of the friendship and support of Osvaldo Pardo. My turn to the issue of colonial religion began with my reading of Osvaldo's work on Mexican Catholicism, and ever since I have followed his lead for the right topics and questions.

In Peru, I have also had the opportunity to learn in the company of first-rate scholars. José Antonio Rodríguez Garrido kindly facilitated my studies at the Pontificia Universidad Católica and Instituto Riva-Agüero in 2001 and 2002 under the auspices of the Fulbright Program. Pedro Guibovich not only taught me how to read colonial manuscripts, but also told me where to find the ones most relevant to my study; there is no better guide to Peru's historical sources than Pedro. To Alan Durston I owe many thanks for teaching me about native languages and pointing me to their traces in the archives. The generosity of ideas and suggestions from José Cárdenas Bunsen, Marco Curatola, Rodolfo Cerrón-Palomino, Carlos Gálvez, Fernanda Macchi, Jeremy Mumford, and Cristóbal Aljovín opened my eyes to the fascination and complexity of pre-Hispanic and viceregal history as it is studied in the U.S. and Lima. I would also like to recognize the many archivists and librarians who helped me navigate the Peruvian collections, especially Laura Gutiérrez and Melecio Tineo of the Archivo Arzobispal de Lima, Elinos Caravasi of Lima's Biblioteca Nacional, Lothar Busse of the Archivo del Cabildo Metropolitano, and Ana María Vega of the Archivo de San Francisco de Lima. Donato Amado greatly assisted my research itineraries in Cuzco at the Archivo Arzobispal and the Archivo Departamental. My enormous thanks to Graciela Sotil and family, Eva Zighelboim, and Ricardo Pereira and Susana Baca for opening their homes to me during my extended stays in Peru.

This book was also aided by grants from various entities and institutions. Early funding was provided from 2000 to 2003 by the Graduate School of Yale University, the Beinecke Rare Book and Manuscript Library, and the J. William Fulbright Scholarship Board. The National Endowment for the Humanities awarded a postdoctoral fellowship in the fall of 2005 at the John Carter Brown Library at Brown University. I would like to thank Norman Fiering, José Amor y Vázquez, Nicolás Wey-Gómez, Michael Hammerly, and Susan Danforth for helping to make my time in Providence so enjoyable and productive. My thanks also to the School of Liberal Arts, Department of Spanish and Portuguese, Roger Thayer Stone Center for Latin American Studies, and the Faculty Enhancement Fund of Tulane University for assisting my overseas research in 2006 and 2007, which included summer research periods at the Biblioteca Nacional de España and the Archivo Histórico Nacional in Madrid and the Archivo General de Indias in Seville. A welcome grant to support the reproduction of illustrations was provided by the office of Dean Carole Haber of Tulane's School of Liberal Arts. Jessica Desany of Harvard's Peabody Museum of Archaeology and Ethnology; Ivan Boserup of The Royal Library, Copenhagen; and Curry O'Day of Tulane University assisted with last-minute preparation of images, as did Hortensia Calvo and David Dressing of Tulane's Latin American Library. Thanks go to them and many other colleagues at Tulane for making my studies of Spanish American history prosper below sea level. I am pleased to acknowledge, in particular, Laura Bass and Ari Zighelboim for their special contributions to this book, not the least of which was the idea for its title.

I am grateful to the staff at the University of New Mexico Press for guiding the transformation of my manuscript into published form. Thank you to Clark Whitehorn for his enthusiasm and stewardship, Elise McHugh and Brian Stauffer for their assistance in the manuscript's preparation and revision, and Annie Barva for copyediting the text with care. I am indebted also to the anonymous readers whose useful suggestions helped me to catch sight of the broader implications of my argument. Abbreviated versions of chapters two and three appeared in *Colonial Latin American Review* 16, no. 1 (2007) and *The Americas* 64, no. 1 (2007), respectively. I thank the editors of both journals for the permission to draw on this material.

And finally, deep appreciation goes to many friends and family, from uptown New Orleans to upstate New York, for seeing this book through to completion. The Charles, Martin, Rice, and Milot families provided countless types of material and moral support during the many years of my academic wanderings. Chief thanks in this regard belong to my mother, Elizabeth Duffy Charles, my first and toughest teacher, who always respected without question my pursuit of advanced study. This book is dedicated with great affection to her and to my late father, W. Norman Charles (1929–1994). It is the memory of his tireless devotion to work and exceptional human decency that imparts the most valuable lessons to this day.

Voices from the Archive

The Vantage Point of the Native *Fiscal*

On 2 May 1644, the native villagers of the remote highland town of Huaraz, in the central Peruvian Andes, assembled in the public square to witness a momentous event: the investiture of Don Gonzalo Guaman Cochachin as *fiscal mayor de la doctrina,* or chief indigenous official of the parish. Atop the steps of the church stood the community's leaders, including the parish priest and coadjutant clergy, the royal administrator of the district, Spanish *encomenderos,* Andean ethnic lords, and the officers of the native municipal council. For Guaman Cochachin to become fiscal mayor by appointment of Lima's archbishop, with the support of Huaraz's secular and church authorities, was the culmination of his schooling in Castilian letters and Christian doctrine. Loyal to the parish in which he was born, and versed in the language and customs of his people, he was found to be ideally suited for the tasks of pastoral service. Guaman Cochachin would teach literacy and catechism to Indian children, interpret the priest's Spanish homily for Quechua-speaking parishioners, collect fees for the parish, and watch for ritual behaviors that the Church deemed contrary to the faith. One can imagine his arrival at the doors of the church amid congratulatory greetings and expectant stares. Attired in Spanish dress, before the town's ruling elite, Guaman Cochachin took an oath to God that he would fulfill his office with diligence and integrity. He received the title of his appointment, signed by the vicar general, and the staff of justice, which symbolized his authority to govern and police the town. Looking out over the entire community, his newly invested powers in hand, he was, quite literally, at the center of parish life.[1]

Given the traditional historiography of the Peruvian Church, it is easy to ignore the power that indigenous officials had in the management of parish affairs. Canonical histories of New World "spiritual conquest" mostly omit native church assistants, aside from brief discussions of their dutiful and anonymous presence alongside missionary priests, a story line that derives largely from the self-regarding statements of the original clergy themselves. Though Guaman Cochachin assumed responsibilities that countless Indians like him shared, no full account exists of the leading role that native intermediaries played in Christianity's spread throughout the Andes or the impact that indigenous society and culture had on missionary thinking and methods.[2] Familiar with Spanish language and customs, native church assistants made up a select group whom the clergy called *indios ladinos:* native interlocutors who communicated the will of Catholic authorities to the indigenous peoples. The contributions of indios ladinos to the making of Andean Christian society and the ways in which they used the Spanish language to describe their experience constitute the two main pillars of the present investigation of European-Andean interaction in the sixteenth and seventeenth centuries.

The term *indio ladino* was an abstract, catch-all category that captured many social types: Andean men and women; the *curacas* (native lords) who mediated the contact between Spanish officials and local communities; *yanacuna,* Indians who worked as servants in Spanish homes; *donados,* minor associates of religious convents; and *lenguas,* native guides and interpreters of the early Spanish explorations and campaigns of military conquest (Adorno 1991, 234; Solano 1975, 266–77).[3] What united this diverse group of individuals was their common experience as intermediaries who used the Spanish language to bridge the divide between two cultures. To be sure, Spain was not alone in enlisting locally powerful allies to assist in the governance of its colonies. Throughout history, global regimes have relied upon colonized agents to instruct subjugated peoples in a new language and religion, communicate the empire's laws, and oversee native commerce and labor. In Peru, local native authorities served myriad colonial institutions, but the Church was perhaps their leading source of employment. Most learned Spanish from missionary priests and influenced the course of Christianity at the parish and district level as much as the priests who initiated them in the language.

Intermittent references in missionary literature confirm that indios ladinos were vital to Andean evangelization. Shortly after the historic Third Provincial Council of Lima (1582–1583), which codified missionary practices throughout the Peruvian viceroyalty, the Jesuit provincial José de Acosta supervised the publication of a standard collection of thirty native-language sermons that parish priests were obliged to use when preaching to Indian neophytes. Sermon 9 of the *Tercero catecismo y exposición de la doctrina christiana por sermones* (1585) portrayed indios ladinos as model Christians whom beginners in the faith should aspire to imitate: "Have you not seen how the Viracochas [Spaniards] worship? And the many indios ladinos? They are good sons and pray and confess many times during the year and discipline themselves. They are blessed by God and the padres love them very much. Why would you not do the same?"[4] According to the *sermonario*'s prescriptive formulation, native church assistants exemplified for all Indians the swift and transparent assimilation of Hispanic language and Catholic practice.

Yet other missionary accounts told a less edifying story of native intermediaries of the Church. In 1608, the parish priest of San Damián de los Checa, Francisco de Ávila, charged that church assistants not only neglected their pastoral obligations but even perpetuated forbidden cults: "[T]he [indios ladinos] teach [the parishioners] to worship idols and they take them to make sacrifices, just as Christians take their own to church."[5] Ávila's contemporaries, the Jesuit priest Pablo José de Arriaga and the Quechua linguist Juan Pérez Bocanegra among them, offered equally damning portraits of the indigenous middlemen who undercut the clergy's efforts so as to enable their own political and spiritual influence over Andean parishioners. Given the endless shortage of qualified clergy, priests depended on native church assistants, but theirs was often an alliance marked by rivalry and distrust.

The conventional terms that applied to bicultural Indians thus grouped around two inconsistent notions: indios ladinos were at once the obedient servants of evangelization and the underhanded plotters of its demise. What reliance on these contradictory European viewpoints neglects, however, are the perspectives that native church assistants themselves offered on the challenges of their experience as delegates of evangelizing agendas. Did indios ladinos recognize themselves in the colonialist logic of Acosta's or Ávila's formulaic descriptions? How did they respond to the conflicting models of identity that Spanish priests assigned to them? Making native intermediaries the centerpiece of investigation provides initial answers to these questions as well as a more historically specific perspective on the types of linguistic and cultural interactions that the evangelization process involved. From the vantage point of Andean parish officials, the clash between Christian and Andean values acquires complex meanings that call into doubt the abiding image of the Indians' slow but eventual submission to Christianity or, conversely, that of a colonial society of European and native contenders separated into opposing and mutually exclusive cultural groups.[6] While the details of this study are specific to highland parishes of the Lima archdiocese, its consequences extend broadly to the literary practices of indigenous agents throughout the colonial Americas and to the conflictive dialogues and uneasy relationships that their mediating activity produced.[7]

Uncovering the Archival Past

Conducting affairs in both Spanish and native society was routine for indigenous officials, but it also produced inevitable conflicts between their obligation to enforce colonial laws and their customary obligation to protect native communities from the colonizers' abuses. Scholars of the colonial Andes have long studied the two-sided function of native leaders in the Spanish Crown's commercial enterprise and exploitation of native tributary labor and resources, which brought them opportunities for economic profit, yet diminished their standing among indigenous peoples understandably resentful of colonial exactions.[8] Similarly, as local religious authorities, Andean authorities mediated between the Catholic demands of missionary priests and the competing desires of native communities to venerate traditional divinities without Spanish interference. Because of their extraordinary power and uncertain loyalties in both the cultural and political domains, Andean church assistants inspired fear and suspicion in all directions. They came to embody for Europeans as well as for indigenous groups the ambivalent partnership that existed between missionary priests and native peoples.

To move beyond the external view of their activity, however, requires examination of the stories that indios ladinos told about parish officialdom, which differ from the European accounts found in pastoral literature, ecclesiastical correspondence, and missionary histories. Crucial precedents of this line of investigation exist in Francisco de Solano's identification of native interpreters as an "axial" but mostly underdeveloped issue in colonial historiography and in Rolena Adorno's studies of how two Andean literati,

Felipe Guaman Poma de Ayala and Juan de Santacruz Pachacuti Yamqui Salcamaygua, perceived their role as assistants in the ecclesiastical campaigns to stamp out traditional native beliefs and ritual practices (Solano 1975; Adorno [1986] 2000, 1991).[9] Partial answers to the mystery of indigenous missionary service do, in fact, appear in the historical works of Peru's native historians, especially Guaman Poma's chronicle, whose lengthy chapters devoted to parish priests and native assistants verify the central place that indios ladinos occupied in Andean Catholic society (Guaman Poma [c. 1615] 1980, 575–688). But these chapters also raise the additional question: What other indigenous voices of that time existed that might test and enrich this vivid firsthand testimony?

The archives of Peru and Spain contain myriad native accounts, largely unknown, as well as crucial data on the institutional and historical frameworks within which Guaman Poma and other indios ladinos expressed their views. Indigenous takes on parish life surface in various kinds of legal papers that originated in ecclesiastical tribunals: sworn declarations of parish inspection reports, idolatry trial testimony, and, most significant, legal petitions that native church officers authored to express concerns about the state of missionary affairs. The enormous quantity of indigenous writings and transcribed statements, though passed through notarial formulae and expressed in a Spanish language not the Indians' own, contains valuable insights on the tasks and challenges of religious pedagogy and parish employment and the official church policies that governed the two. Such everyday documentation provides added details about native society that are missing from the far-reaching narratives of the Andean chroniclers and shows where Spanish literacy among the indigenous peoples achieved its greatest influence.[10]

In other words, the surviving record that bears most directly on the activities of native church assistants originated at the points of the Indians' encounter with Spanish colonial law. The year 1583 therefore constitutes an ideal starting point of research, when the Third Council issued canon decrees that codified missionary practices and the duties of native church assistants throughout the Peruvian viceroyalty. From that date, the investigation charts how native intermediaries acted and reacted within the legal constraints placed upon their ecclesiastical authority, until roughly 1671, the final year of Archbishop Pedro de Villagómez's tenure in the metropolitan see. In this way, the study benefits from the abundant legislation and pastoral literature of the influential Lima council as well as from the trial documentation that came out of the archbishop's and his predecessors' commitment to extirpate native ritual practices, which included petitions of grievance that Andean officials of the central highlands filed in response to the repressive methods of *visitadores* (ecclesiastical inspectors) and parish priests. The goal of this periodization is to focus attention on the quotidian and often conflictive engagements of indigenous agents with the legal policies and missionary practices of the Lima Church during its first century of systematic attempts to evangelize. Consolidation of church authority in native parishes was a gradual process of trial and error that entailed the interaction of missionary policies, locally established religious practices, and legal mechanisms for negotiating and resolving disputes. What native intermediaries had to say about royal and canon law and its implementation in native parishes illuminates the complex process by which Christianity took shape on the Spanish Empire's South American periphery.

Archival testimonies corroborate the account of Guaman Cochachin: indios ladinos assumed primary roles in the conduct of secular and ecclesiastical administration, and expressed opinions on church policy that Lima's high clergy and royal officials took seriously. From the documents, key players emerge whose reputations spread from the villages of the central highlands to the halls of the see and *audiencia*: Rodrigo Flores Caja Malqui, the embattled Andean noble and political activist of Santo Domingo de Ocros, owner of a sizeable collection of books; Juan Tocas, the fiscal mayor of San Pedro de Ticllos, who repeatedly prosecuted suspected idolaters in the parish of San Pedro de Acas; Agustín Capcha, the *cabildo* scribe-cum-sacristan of Nuestra Señora de la Asunción de Ambar, who indicted curacas as well as priests for religious crimes; and Rodrigo de Guzmán Rupay Chagua, the native governor of Huamantanga and legal advocate who studied Castilian letters and Christian doctrine under the tutelage of Jesuit priests yet remained devoted to the ancestral divinities. The dichotomy of exemplary Christians versus scheming operators loses its meaning in view of the multifaceted experiences of native parish officials, as does the tired cliché that, with rare exceptions, Indians could neither read nor write. Literate Andeans of noble and common heritage not only managed local parish affairs, but also advocated individual and collective rights to the top reaches of the royal audiencia and church establishment. In this sense, the legal papers of the ecclesiastical tribunal reveal the understudied, litigious side of native parish service and cast Guaman Poma's and Pachacuti Yamqui's accounts of evangelization into new light.

Judicial records contain the history of the Spanish-Andean encounter as glimpsed in the legal confrontations that characterized life in native parishes. The intensity of conflict between and among parish priests and native advocates shows that the march of Christianity through the Andes rested on the imposition and maintenance of new relations of legal and extralegal authority, not merely on the spread and assimilation of new religious beliefs and customs. Lawsuits tell the knotted story of colonial political culture in which priests and parishioners could be allies one day and adversaries the next, depending on the ever-changing dynamics of the church policies born outside the parish and the local arrangements of power within. Indios ladinos seldom called into question the rights of the Church and Crown to govern; rather, the polemical objectives of their writings tied to concerns about the local exercise of Spanish colonial authority. A literate Andean society emerged, in other words, out of the combative legal setting of native parishes that afforded the opportunities and at times the imperatives for seeking privileges or redress.

From *Lengua* to Litigant

Many scholars have examined the role of native lenguas as mediators of the first contacts between Europeans and Americans, taking the figures of Doña Marina, Hernán Cortés's interpreter during the conquest of Tenochtitlán, and Felipillo, who likely translated the words of the Dominican friar Vicente de Valverde at Cajamarca, as starting points for understanding the historic confrontation of empires.[11] Colonial narratives of the conquest of Peru generally depict Felipillo as an incompetent pawn of the Spanish whose translation of Valverde's religious address sowed confusion and anger, hastening the violence that led to the defeat of Inca Atahualpa and his army. In keeping with such accounts, modern observers have fixated on the initial miscommunication between victors and vanquished, and the subsequent chaos and trauma, from an indigenous perspective, of life in a "world turned upside down."[12] Bygone representations of first encounters contain greater or lesser degrees of truth about the native peoples' original reactions; certainly, not all Indians adapted successfully to the arrival of the Europeans. But researchers have only begun to examine the historical process by which Andean intermediaries negotiated Spanish rule in the more settled colonial culture that followed Peru's drawn-out period of military conquest and civil wars. Ecclesiastical court records of later times contest the assumption that native church assistants were as benighted as the chroniclers declared Felipillo to be.

Scholarship of the past two decades has posited colonial Andean history not as a frozen snapshot of Spanish domination and native misunderstanding, but rather as a heterogeneous process of Spanish and Andean initiatives that coexisted, inflected each other, and transformed over time. Highly innovative research in this vein has examined the subject of religious change, using the Archivo Arzobispal de Lima's vast records of Peru's extirpation-of-idolatries campaigns of the seventeenth and eighteenth centuries.[13] Stories of Indians who stood before ecclesiastical tribunals on charges of witchcraft and sorcery hold undeniable ethnographic value and stir the imagination in ways different from the accounts of those who outwardly assimilated the Spaniards' language and cultural values. Yet testimonies of native ministers facing judicial prosecution are somewhat extreme cases that obscure the everyday forms of indigenous social action that appear in lawsuits against priests and records of pastoral and fiscal management. Lawsuits, in particular, constitute a relatively untapped field of cultural encounter and offer data on the plurality of social positions and cultural perspectives that merged in native pueblos. The marking of cultural and political boundaries took place in various kinds of legal conflicts, at times revealing surprising answers about what mattered most to priests and parishioners.

A crucial aspect of the testimonies under consideration is that as arguments directed to church authorities, they exhibit rhetorical and thematic features appropriate to the expectations of Spanish audiences. Andeans knew church law and court procedure, and legal writings gave them the rhetorical models and means of initiation into the rules of colonial lettered society. Native litigants denounced the actions of priests, royal administrators, and fellow Indians within legally established procedures, but never questioned the tenets of Christian doctrine or the ultimate legitimacy of Spanish colonial rule. The point is not to suggest that Andean church assistants "spoke for themselves," independent of the mediating filters that attended juridical testimony and verbal expressions of all types. Rather, interest centers on how indios ladinos came to terms with the forces of colonialism by mastering the linguistic tools that allowed them to respond as subjects to the European institutions and imperatives that ordered their lives.

Scholars of Peru's indigenous chroniclers have made it possible to see native Andeans as authors, or producers of discourses, familiar with native modes of thinking and expression as well as Spanish ideologies and narrative genres.[14] Viewing native writings in terms of their discursive features, and not solely in terms of the ethnicity of their authors, discloses fresh information about the relationship between the Spanish and the Andean in colonial culture and society. In the legal papers of the archive especially, new questions arise about the range of literary practices that were available to Indians, the Spanish-Andean collaborations that led to the creation of legal documents, the public fora that informed the production of native writings and testimonies, and the interface of native literacy and Spanish law. Such a focus has implications for understanding the acquisition of Christianity and legal knowledge as well as the social practices of literacy in native parishes. How did native intermediaries use written documents to learn the rules of the Church and challenge the clergy's autonomy in the ordering of religious and political affairs?[15]

This book puts forward a basic idea that unites the various parts: while theoretically literacy was essential for bringing Andean peoples into the Christian fold, its practice in the hands of native subjects thwarted the Church's efforts to evangelize on its own terms. An opening chapter assesses early modern theories of writing, the reach of Spanish literacy in Andean society, and the Indians' polemical uses of written documents in the religious and legal domains. Four middle chapters present a series of legal case studies to examine how Spanish theorists, parish priests, and native officials approached the following highly contentious aspects of missionary practice and parish officialdom: catechesis in native languages, the use of traditional Andean devices (cord records) in Catholic ritual practice, the role of coercion in parish fiscal management and policing, and the prosecution of religious error. Analysis of each legal conflict reveals the personal and political interests involved, the areas where European and Andean values came together or collided, and the local import of colonialist ideas with regard to legal jurisdiction, linguistic practice, sacral rites, clerical violence, and native religiosity. The final chapter explicates the ways in which native litigants forged discursive and political alliances with Spanish attorneys and measures the impact of Andean advocacy on the conduct of evangelization as a whole. Authorities of the Lima see and royal audiencia engaged in charged polemics over the source of native lawsuits. Was pastoral failure to blame? Did Andean accusers pursue seditious agendas?

The active and conflictive engagement of literate Andeans with the empowered denizens of the "lettered city" and the public adoption of Spanish laws and customs refute the idea of a colonial culture in which relations between Europeans and Andeans were at all times hostile.[16] To stem the negative consequences of cultural interaction, and sustain the hierarchies of a regime dependent on native tributary labor, royal law defined Spanish and indigenous societies as distinct "republics" subject to the Crown and with complementary roles in the colonial system (*Recopilación de leyes [RLI]* 1841, 2:230–31). However, legislation affirming social divisions clouded the reality of literate Andeans, such as Guaman Cochachin, who moved freely between ethnic groups and challenged the Spaniards' control over written records. Native legal writings show that common ideas traversed jurisdictions and cultural boundaries, and touched the hands of Indians, Spanish agents, and even the archbishop himself. All participated in a shared discourse about missionary procedures, even if risks were decidedly higher for native petitioners than for the judges deciding their case. Making native literary activity and social action the focus of attention posits a history of colonialism in which Spanish and Andean actors appear more connected than ever before. A fuller grasp of Andean contributions to the missionary polemics of colonial times therefore calls for uniting Spanish and indigenous viewpoints into a single framework of analysis.

The existence of an educated class of indios ladinos was undeniable, yet until the final years of the seventeenth century, royal and church law never admitted the possibility of their religious ordination. As early as 1567, the high clergy excluded native Andeans from the priesthood based on the so-called neophyte status of the indigenous peoples.[17] Occasionally, dissenting voices emerged among the high clergy on the topic of Indian priests, but it was not until 1697 that Charles II ordered that the native subjects of the Indies "be admitted in the religious orders, educated in the schools, and promoted according to their merit and capacity to the ecclesiastical dignities and public offices."[18] Still, denying holy orders to indios ladinos did not keep them from assembling parishioners for Sunday Mass or interpreting the daily litany at the side of the parish priest. They continued to watch for the crimes of native parishioners and corrupt priests and to assert their legal rights as members of the local community and the universal Church that extended beyond its walls. The goal is to understand better how they accomplished this, while keeping in mind the many linguistic and ideological constraints that accompanied indigenous cultural survival in a postconquest world.

Voided Presences

Historical sources on native Andean interactions with European written culture largely remain to be examined. A few Indians, Guaman Poma and Pachacuti Yamqui among them, left records of their experience in Spanish- and Quechua-language writings of their own composition. Another, the near-last surviving Inca prince, Diego de Castro Titu Cusi Yupanqui, dictated in Quechua his account of current and past affairs to an Augustinian friar; the only existing version is its Spanish translation. But in no sense were they the only Andeans of colonial times who set down personal testimonies in writing. The challenge for scholars has been to locate the many others, and to do this requires a turn to the archive. In a literal sense, the "archive" means the repositories of the Peruvian state, the Archbishopric of Lima, and Spain's Archive of the Indies—the seemingly infinite collections of books and manuscripts in which the origin of colonial indigenous history is stored. It also refers to "the Archive" that Roberto González Echevarría has conceptualized, with a nod to Foucault, in reflecting on the authority of writing and law in the Spanish colonial period. González Echevarría writes: "Power, secrecy and law stand at the origin of the Archive; it was, in its most concrete form, the structure that . . . housed the dispensers of the law, its readers, the magistrates; it was the building that encrypted the power to command" ([1990] 1998, 31).

The Archive's power to command in the Indies arose from Spain's need to regulate dealings between Europeans and native peoples through the official papers of the colonial administration. Its guardians determined not only what could be said, but also the rules by which words could be set down in writing. At the same time, the ordering of written texts involved undocumented suppressions and censorship—that is, a series of "cancellations and substitutions, of gaps . . . a process of repeated combinations, of shufflings and reshufflings ruled by heterogeneity and difference" (González

Echevarría [1990] 1998, 24). Scouring the archives for native voices, the process of giving meaning to the testimonies, and the writing down of them confirm González Echevarría's words. The attempt to elicit stories from the papers of Spain's colonial bureaucracy shows that indigenous testimonies are elusive: the statements of Indians were mediated by circumstances they did not control and were fragmented in their effort to tell their stories, make heard their demands, or avoid sentences of corporal punishment. González Echevarría also makes reference to the Archive as containing the previous discursive mediations through which Latin Americans narrated, which he describes as "voided presences": "They are both erased and, at the same time, a memory of their own demise" (25). Native voices were, too, in a sense "erased," yet at the same time the physical, institutional archive carries on as a "memory of their demise."

The appeal of the memory of that demise makes the archives of Spain and Peru the ideal place for investigating the Andean subjects who mastered their dominant forms in the pursuit of legitimation.[19] Recovering evidence of that mastery leads inescapably to the Andeans' interactions with the Catholic Church, for it was by this institution that they learned Spanish and joined the campaigns to identify and eradicate traditional Andean ritual beliefs and practices. For a few, this training was the means by which they came to write far-reaching historical narratives of the Inca past and colonial present. However, the outlook of most literate Andeans appears more fleetingly, in documents that were legally binding and literally bound. To transcribe their words is just one part of the task; to make them understood requires attention to the institutional conditions, social milieus, and political cultures that allowed for their emergence. Each of the kinds of instances brought forth—the role of the Andean assistant as church fiscal stands out as a prominent example—requires an understanding of what the documents communicate as well as the everyday forces with which native intermediaries interacted. Only in this broader context is it possible to assess the possibilities and constraints that shaped indigenous verbal conduct and symbolizing behaviors. In this regard, the archive and the Archive are fora that make high demands on scholars of the history of indigenous experience under Spanish rule. The pages that follow are an attempt to meet the challenge of bringing one untold aspect of that history to life.

Chapter 1

The Making of a Literate Andean Society

Images of Andean Literacy

In 1588, Bartolomé Álvarez, the *padre doctrinero* of the pueblo of Aullagas in the southern diocese of los Charcas, penned a lengthy *memorial* to Philip II in which he decried the havoc that literate Indians were creating in the native parishes of his district. Álvarez stated that "indios ladinos" did not apply their Spanish-language skills and positions of authority to teach Christian doctrine to native parishioners, as royal law had prescribed. Instead, they used their knowledge of Spanish writing and colonial law to bring complaints against parish priests:

> To grasp the [ladinos'] bad intentions look no further than to the designs of the Indian who wants to be a "letrado," but only to make lawsuits, without having the proper studies. If you were to ask him about Christian doctrine, he wouldn't know the law of God, or understand the catechism, or how to recite it. . . . The ladinos have not profited from the Spanish language or the Christian doctrine they have learned in the homes of priests, except to be worse than the other Indians and interpreters of their own aims and our ruin.[1]

In the priest's formulation, "their aims" meant the commitment to lawsuits rather than to Christian doctrine, and "our ruin," the destroyed reputations of good priests and, by extension, the survival of the Andean idolatries that the ladinos and native church personnel were supposed to combat. Álvarez invoked a colonialist form of reasoning, according to which the souls of innocent neophytes were at stake and should be protected from the bad example of ladino Indians no matter what the cost.

Álvarez was not alone in expressing unease about the spread of Hispanic language and customs in the Indies and about the Indians who were familiar with the ways of the Spanish. Andeans educated in colonial law and Spanish letters had special powers both to aid the cause of Christianity and to advance personal or anticlerical agendas. Contests for supremacy between priests and literate Andeans were an everyday part of native parish life, in which native literacy of the religious domain came into dramatic conflict with that of the political. The clergy's concern about how to direct the linguistic and social action of indios ladinos toward the goal of evangelizing Indians and away from litigious pursuits formed part of a heated polemic in missionary writings of the sixteenth and seventeenth centuries. The recurring trope of the acculturated yet disloyal native intermediary hints at an elusive problem at the core of Spanish missionary drives: alphabetic literacy and its uncertain place in the evangelization program.

Álvarez's condemnation of the ways educated Andeans used Spanish and written documents recasts the story of evangelization as one in which Indians were historical agents and not simply passive victims of Spanish designs. His account also points out a contradiction in colonial writings on the topic of native literary practice. Generally speaking, historical sources of the period did not represent Indians as writers, however incompetent or misguided they might have been in the eyes of some. In fact, missionary chroniclers attributed the Andeans' so-called delayed evolution and immorality to the absence of an alphabetic writing system. The Jesuit historian Bernabé Cobo summed up this view: "[The Indians'] capacity of understanding is so dull and clouded . . . because they lack the letters, sciences, and fine arts that tend to cultivate, perfect, and make it quicker and livelier in its operations and reasoning powers."[2] Spanish historians of the South American conquest belabored the Indians' puzzlement when they confronted written words, the canonical instance being Inca Atahualpa's confusion at Cajamarca and ultimate rejection of the authority contained in holy books. The native peoples' supposed repudiation of literacy empowered Europeans to assert the relative "barbarism" of Andean cultures against the standard of Christian Europe and therefore the legitimacy of Spanish military and spiritual conquest.

Consistent with colonial reports of this type, today's histories of early modern communication have emphasized the "tyranny of the alphabet": the role of alphabetic literacy in the erasure of traditional native forms of representation, the transformation of indigenous cultural domains, and the consolidation and maintenance of Spanish power.[3] The idea that Indians perceived writing as foreign has prompted gainful research on alternative native literacies or ways of encoding memory through "writing without words," such as pictorial histories, ceramic imagery, cartographic representations, and knotted strings (Boone and Mignolo 1994). But for the Andes, only a small number of studies have addressed the historical process by which Indians learned Spanish writing and utilized it within the institutional frameworks of colonial society.[4] Colonial-era narratives continue to support the retrospective account that Indians adapted poorly to the onslaught of writing and that just a select few could read and write.

Álvarez's contempt for literate Indians points in another direction that suggests Spanish schooling had gone too far. In theory, teaching Christian doctrine went hand in hand with the acquisition of Spanish language and book culture; though indoctrination took place in Quechua and other widely disseminated Andean languages, the Church's evangelizing mission drew from the conviction that standards of civility and goodness would find their maximum expression through the Indians' exposure to Spanish and written texts.[5] However, in the doctrinero's view, the license that parish officialdom gave Indians educated in the language of the colonizers made Andean intermediaries an obstacle to the constitution of local church and secular authority. To view native uses of alphabetic literacy in such broad and incompatible sketches as these obscures, of course, crucial details in the history of the indios ladinos' path from novice lenguas to legal advocates: namely, by what specific processes did native church assistants learn to read and write in Spanish? And where did the Europeans' thinking on Spanish and written documents connect to or diverge from the ways in which Indian officials came to terms with the language?

To be fair, the relative scarcity of known writings by Indians has nurtured contradictory assumptions about indigenous uses of alphabetic literacy. Aside from the bi- and trilingual grammars, lexicons, and pastoral complements for Indian ministry, the cycle of traditional myths from Huarochirí, and the rare notarial manuscript, colonial authorities did not cultivate Quechua and other native languages as written forms, which contrasts with the abundance of written records in Mesoamerican languages.[6] For the early colonial period, no Spanish-language histories by Indian authors survive apart from Guaman Poma's and Pachacuti Yamqui's chronicles and

Titu Cusi Yupanqui's translated account. However, a more complete picture of written culture in the Andes—the capture of literacy in native parishes, the methods of teaching reading and writing to Indians, and the production of Indian-authored manuscripts—emerges through analysis of religious texts as well as sources that came out of native interactions with Peru's ecclesiastical tribunals. Native writings scattered throughout the judicial dossiers of the Church (criminal and civil denunciations, lawsuits against priests, petitions for clemency or favors, and other legal genres) form a key part of what James Lockhart (1992, 7) has called the "mundane" documentation of the Spanish colonial bureaucracy. Legal documents were the Indians' primary type of written communication and provide a direct source for assessing the degree to which Indians learned Spanish in the area of the Lima archdiocese and the ways in which native writers put it to use.[7] An examination of the archive thus points to the specific forms of lettered Andean culture that Álvarez so virulently condemned.

Mediators of the Word

Native historical sources document that Indians quickly grasped the social and ideological significance of alphabetic literacy in Spanish. Even as they challenged European ideas about Inca history and society, Peru's indigenous chroniclers exalted writing's edifying powers as an instrument of religious conversion and equated barbarism with lack of letters. Pachacuti Yamqui ([c. 1613] 1993, 227–28) affirmed the authority of sacred books and written culture in his account of Inca history. His chronicle recounted the delivery of a "large book" in ancient times to the aged Pachacuti Inca Yupanqui, who, ignorant of its value, passed it on to a servant. Because the Inca cast off writing and with it religious truth, he made Andean peoples vulnerable to the deceptions of false idols: "The demons and devils, being ancient tyrants, overpowered the simple, ignorant people, without letters and judgment, . . . and became absolute lords."[8] Likewise, Guaman Poma condemned Indian "barbarians," who took no interest in learning Spanish, and affirmed the power of books to combat false worship. His idealized portrait of the "good Christian lord" who reads a holy book emphasized the vital role he believed reading should play in the cultivation of good religious customs (Guaman Poma [c. 1615] 1980, 775). The chronicler provided limited information, however, about the long history by which such acculturated figures

FIGURE 1. Exemplary Christians. Guaman Poma, *El primer nueva corónica y buen gobierno*, 775. Courtesy of the Royal Library, Copenhagen, Denmark.

learned how to read and write, and the types of books and documents they might have read or written.

The first South Americans to learn Castilian mediated the initial contacts between Spanish invaders and indigenous groups on the military battlefield and in the religious domain. Enlisted by force near Tumbes, on the northwest coast of the continent, they assisted the conquerors as agents and informants on the long and perilous march through Cajamarca to the Inca capital. Soon after the group's arrival in the Andes, the Crown addressed the missionaries' urgent need for native interpreters by ordering Francisco Pizarro to entrust one of his three lenguas to Vicente de Valverde (Lisson Cháves 1943–1948, 1:54). Without the linguistic and cultural knowledge of these hastily recruited lenguas, it is doubtful that the Europeans' initial victories, let alone their survival, would have been possible.

Not surprisingly, teaching Christian ideas amid opposing factions of Spanish soldiers and native chieftains proved to be an arduous task, and the first lenguas soon became scapegoats for the errors and misunderstandings that characterized early religious dialogue. The most famous depiction of the incapacity of native lenguas was El Inca Garcilaso de la Vega's retrospective censure of the linguistic performance of the go-between Felipillo, the alleged cause of Atahualpa and Valverde's fateful misunderstanding at Cajamarca in 1532 (Garcilaso [1617] 1960, 3:48). Ten years after that first encounter, the licentiate Martel de Santoyo reported to Charles V on evangelization's haphazard course and blamed the "faithless" native functionaries who were ill equipped for the task of communicating doctrine. His blanket depiction of the lenguas repeated the stereotype of linguistic and cultural ignorance that had begun to emerge: "The words of the native interpreter have no authority, even if he is baptized, because he lacks the faith and the fear of God and the fervor and discernment of the Spaniard."[9]

After the conquest of Andean settlements, the Spaniards' goal was to develop a literate class of native intermediaries who could ably teach the Spanish language and Christian doctrine to indigenous groups and assist the Church in the fight against the Indians' traditional beliefs and ritual customs. In 1545, Lima's first archbishop, Jerónimo de Loayza ([1545] 1951–1954, 2:146), instructed the clergy to gather the sons of the local nobility and train them for work as lay catechists.[10] At first, this duty fell to mendicant friars, who taught them Castilian literacy and the basic catechism, as well as sacred music and Latin liturgy for assisting Mass and other holy celebrations. By 1551, the Dominican order had inaugurated sixty schools in convents throughout the central and southern Peruvian Andes, including a seminary in the coastal town of Chincha that enrolled as many as seven hundred students (Vargas Ugarte 1953–1962, 1:328).[11] As a condition of their right to manage the tributary workforce, Spanish encomenderos also created schools of religious instruction and trained the sons of notables to teach Andean laborers.[12]

Still, the preparation of native church assistants was far from systematic. Occasionally, the Crown authorized the enlistment of native catechists, but most served informally, without official titles, depending on the variable needs of missionary priests. Loayza took added steps toward the creation of a literate intermediary class, however, when he called on missionary priests to uproot indigenous groups from their places of origin and repopulate them in *doctrinas* (parish districts). These parish settlements were to be governed by local native authorities, who would gather parishioners for Mass and instruct them in Spanish and the catechism, and receive in return exemptions from labor and tribute obligations and, in some instances, modest salaries. Loayza informed Viceroy Diego López de Zúñiga y Velasco that the new settlements would provide the *policía* (civil order) necessary for the Indians' religious education following the volatile early years of military and political unrest (Leuridan Huys 1997, 48).

In union with the archbishop's initiatives, the leaders of the First Provincial Council of Lima (1551–1552) set guidelines for the recruitment of "indios de confianza y razón" to assist in local governance. Missionary priests would appoint native parish hierarchies consisting of the following core members: one or two fiscales (or *alcaldes*) and their attendant *alguaciles*, to assist missionary priests with their sacramental duties, keep written records of the sacraments, and enforce public observance of the faith; the *sacristán*, responsible for maintaining the church building and its ornaments, and assisting Mass; the *cantor*, or choir leader, to lead sung celebrations of the Eucharist and other forms of public worship, such as holy processions, baptisms, and burials; and the *maestrescuela*, to teach Spanish literacy and Christian doctrine to Indian youth.[13] While in theory the council's decrees proposed a division of labors, the duties of parish officials along with those of native governors and municipal council authorities routinely overlapped.

In practice, native leaders of all ranks monitored Catholic ritual, informed priests of crimes, carried out punishments, and taught Spanish language and Christian doctrine.

The clergy enlisted lay assistants from all segments of Andean society. Native officials could be hereditary elites *(caciques principales* or *segundas personas)* or common Indians chosen from the local community; there was no overarching set of rules for churchmen to follow when selecting parish officials.[14] Some parish rosters consisted entirely of Andean notables and others of Indians without noble lineage or status. Typically, the caciques principales occupied positions of higher authority, such as fiscal or alcalde, whereas common Indians worked in subordinate roles, such as alguacil or sacristan. Given the traditional influence of native elites, it was advantageous for the clergy to adopt existing indigenous hierarchies in assembling parish teams. However, these occupational divisions sometimes broke down, to the consternation of indigenous nobles, as persons without hereditary rank ascended to positions of leadership by virtue of their Spanish-language skills and knowledge of doctrine and church law.

In 1569, Viceroy Francisco de Toledo issued ordinances to strengthen Loayza's resettlement program and vision of a literate Andean society. Following the advice of the jurist Juan de Matienzo ([1567] 1967, 122), the viceroy renewed calls for the founding of doctrinas, reminded the clergy of its obligation to enforce Spanish-language doctrinal instruction, and mandated the establishment of schools for Indian youth, especially the sons of caciques, in each native settlement. Priests would hire the most capable and "ladino" Indians of the parish to teach children up to the age of fourteen how to speak, read, and write in Spanish (Levillier 1921–1925, 8:359–60).[15] In addition, the Third Council of Lima (1582–1583), under the direction of the new archbishop, Toribio de Mogrovejo, mandated the teaching of reading and writing in Spanish to all native children.[16] The Indians' proficiency in the language and adoption of other markers of *ladinidad,* such as Spanish dress and customs, were the council's long-term aims.[17]

Schools for the sons of caciques were also an ongoing priority. Bringing the indigenous nobility under Spanish influence was essential given its role in upholding colonial laws, facilitating the collection of tribute, and assisting missionary priests. For José de Acosta, in order to uproot traditional Andean religiosity, it was necessary "to remove it first from the hearts, above all those of the kings, curacas, and principales to whose authority the rest cede freely and without delay."[18] Starting in the 1570s, Viceroy Toledo and the metropolitan see ordered the creation of boarding schools for the sons of the caciques principales and segundas personas of the Lima archdiocese and regions of Cuzco and Huamanga, which the Jesuits eventually administered. The year 1618 marked the inauguration in Lima of El Colegio del Príncipe, the royal boarding school for the sons of the indigenous nobility of the archbishopric, and, three years later, a homologous institution, El Colegio de San Borja, opened its doors in Cuzco to educate the sons of Andean ethnic lords of the dioceses of Cuzco and Huamanga.[19] At El Príncipe, adolescent notables of the Pacific Coast and central highlands enrolled in a six-year course of Castilian literacy and Christian doctrine, and then returned to their parishes to assist *corregidores* (royal administrators) and the clergy.[20]

Learning Primary Letters

In the sixteenth century, Roman Catholic pedagogy shifted gradually from an oral method of catechesis through lectures and sermons to the study and reading aloud of written texts. Doctrinal learning now involved a training of mind through literacy that was not limited, as before, to basic initiation into the rules of Christian practice.[21] Native Andeans learned the ABCs from *cartillas de leer* (reading primers) that mendicant friars brought from Spain to Peru (Torre Revello 1960, 215–16). The books included problems of simple arithmetic, reading and writing exercises in the Romance vernacular, and the basic prayers and articles of the Catholic faith.[22] Eager to consolidate teaching methods, Loayza ([1545] 1951–1954, 2:142) ordered the clergy to use these printed catechisms from Spain or face excommunication.[23]

Teaching Spanish literacy together with doctrine had practical advantages. Students repeated aloud the catechists' reading of the prayers and transcribed the words in catechisms before advancing to other types of texts. Indian children received catechesis daily, and adults on Wednesdays, Fridays, Sundays, and feast days following Mass. "Doctrina" consisted of reading and reciting the basic catechism (articles of the faith, Ten Commandments, seven sacraments, theological and cardinal virtues, and seven deadly sins) and the chief Catholic prayers (Lord's Prayer, Ave Maria, Apostles' Creed, and Salve Regina). Lessons also covered ideas such as the belief in one God, the eternity of the soul, and the meaning of the sacraments (see Armas Medina 1953, 269–305).

The Third Council held that instruction by catechism was the best way to establish doctrinal uniformity. In 1582, Archbishop Mogrovejo and the council's bishops placed Acosta in charge of a team responsible for the creation of a unified Spanish-Quechua-Aymara catechism, confession manual, and sermon collection for Indian ministry.[24] The council then hired the printer Antonio Ricardo to relocate from Mexico to Lima and supervise the publication of the *Doctrina christiana y catecismo para instrucción de indios* (1584), *Confessionario para los curas de indios* (1585), and *Tercero catecismo y exposición de la doctrina christiana por sermones* (1585). These were the first books printed in South America. Parish inspection reports confirm the Lima see's commitment to making the Christian texts universal. Visitadores asked *curas de indios* (parish priests) to exhibit these books, together with the decrees of Trent and of Lima's Second and Third Councils, the titles of their ordination and benefice, the bull of the Lord's supper, some *sumas de conciencias,* and, in later decades, the synods of Archbishops Bartolomé Lobo Guerrero and Hernando Arias de Ugarte. Priests sometimes lacked the catechisms or used borrowed copies, but most seem to have complied with the directive.

The *Doctrina christiana* consisted of two catechisms, the first for neophytes and the second for advanced students, and contained a syllabary to assist in the teaching of reading and writing in Spanish. As its title suggests, the *Catecismo breve para los rudos y ocupados* provided beginning students with a simplified exposition of the Catholic precepts in question-and-answer format:

Q. What do you understand the Holy Church to be?

A. The congregation of all the Christian faithful, whose leader is Jesus Christ, and His vicar on Earth, the Holy Pope of Rome.

Q. And if you are baptized and have sinned again, what must you do to avoid condemnation?

A. Confess your sins to the priest, repenting for them.

Q. And doing that, you will be saved?

A. Yes, you will, if you keep in fulfillment of the Commandments of God and the Holy Church, which are to love God above all things and one's neighbor as oneself.[25]

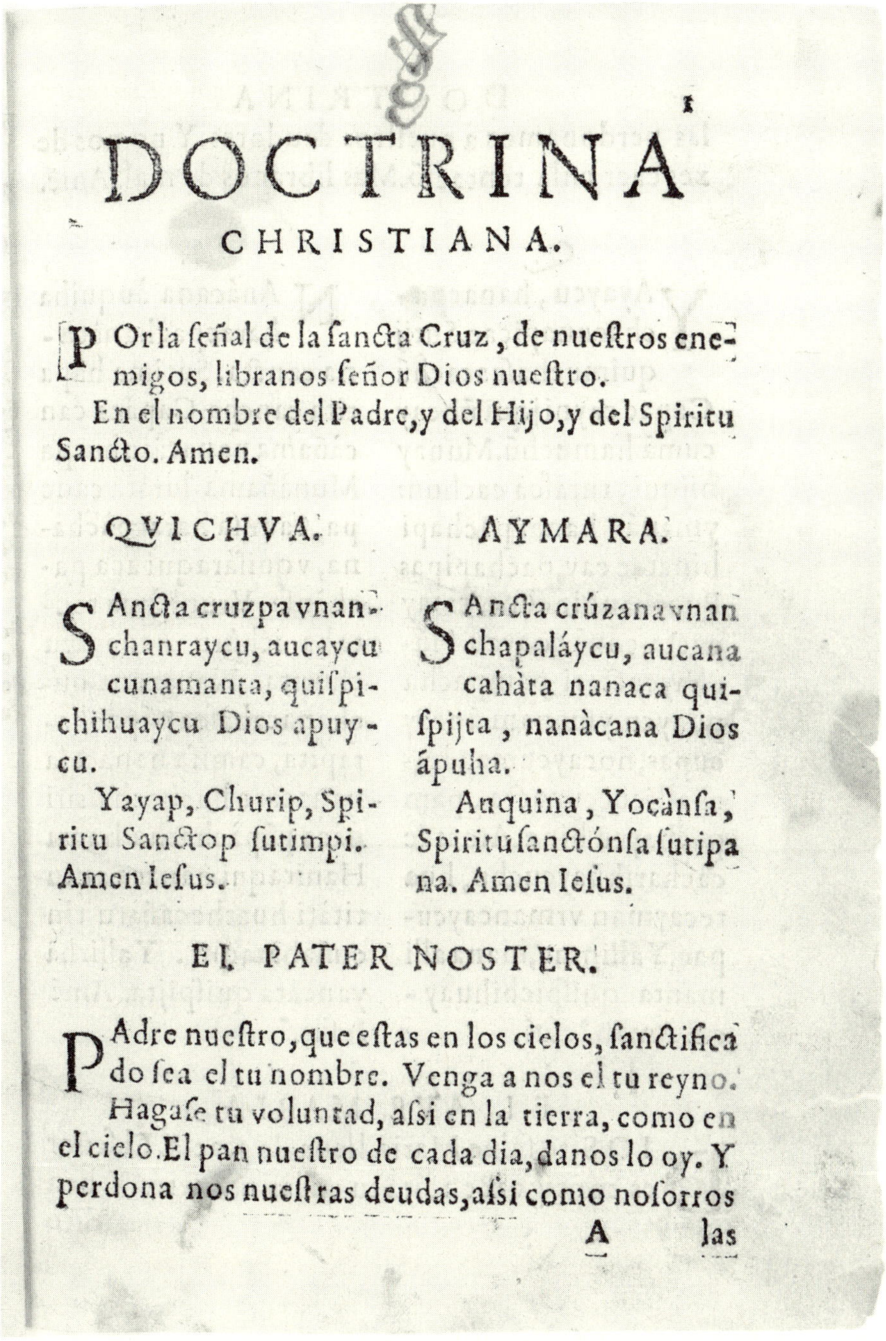

DOCTRINA
CHRISTIANA.

Por la señal de la sancta Cruz, de nuestros enemigos, libranos señor Dios nuestro.
En el nombre del Padre, y del Hijo, y del Spiritu Sancto. Amen.

QVICHVA.

Sancta cruzpa vnanchanraycu, aucaycu cunamanta, quispichihuaycu Dios apuycu.

Yayap, Churip, Spiritu Sanctop sutimpi. Amen Iesus.

AYMARA.

Sancta crúzana vnanchapaláycu, aucana cahàta nanaca quispijta, nanàcana Dios ápuha.

Auquina, Yocànsa, Spiritu sanctónsa sutipana. Amen Iesus.

EL PATER NOSTER.

Padre nuestro, que estas en los cielos, sanctificado sea el tu nombre. Venga a nos el tu reyno. Hagase tu voluntad, assi en la tierra, como en el cielo. El pan nuestro de cada dia, danos lo oy. Y perdona nos nuestras deudas, assi como nosotros

A   las

FIGURE 2. *Doctrina christiana y catecismo para instrucción de indios,* published in Spanish, Quechua, and Aymara (Lima: Antonio Ricardo, 1584). Courtesy of the John Carter Brown Library at Brown University.

At doctrina, students could ask questions about the meaning of the Holy Trinity, the communion of the saints, and other points of doctrine, which advanced students could explore further in the *Catecismo mayor para los que son más capaces*. Lectures on moral conduct, public crimes (illicit cohabitation, public drinking, blasphemy, theft of property), and the need for good works likely took place as well. The aim was to have students begin with the basic tenets of the Catholic faith and then graduate to more abstract points of doctrine.

Evangelization relied on printed catechisms but still took place mainly through the spoken word. The Spanish lexicographer Sebastián de Covarrubias Orozco defined *leer* (to read) as "to pronounce with words that which is written in letters" and "to teach a subject publicly, [as in] to read the catechism to someone," which foregrounds the oral dimension of written texts and a notion of literacy as more than purely alphabetic.[26] Markers of orality (exclamation points, colons to indicate pauses, word markers for continuing text) filled the pages of catechisms. Visitadores oversaw compulsory readings of sermons before assembled villagers. Priests and native assistants directed collective recitations of the *Doctrina christiana*. In this way, preaching and other forms of religious instruction in native parishes fostered what Brian Stock (1983, 90–91) has called "textual communities," or local societies based on collective uses of writing and a shared body of knowledge. Through catechesis, Indians recognized the primacy of writing as an instrument of colonialism and responded to it whether they knew how to read or not.[27]

At first, the clergy urged Andean neophytes to learn fixed prayers and avoid improvised and unsafe spiritual practices, such as conscious meditation. Decrees of the Second and Third Councils stated that Indians should be asked to recite the catechism and common prayers from memory, which would thereby give priests a standard by which to certify the "conversion" of native students.[28] This strategy followed the theory that the oral repetition of prayers could fortify the believer's relationship with God regardless of the believer's understanding of the concepts behind them (Nalle 1992, 105). Toledo criticized native catechists whose students "parroted" their lessons without true grasp of the words that they spoke.[29] But such rote performance of the catechism probably derived from the call-and-response methods used in doctrina. The indigenous peoples' status as converts in the eyes of visitadores and other magistrates depended on their capacity to recall the text of the *Doctrina christiana*.[30]

The Huarochirí manuscript (c. 1608) of Checa oral traditions confirms that Indians grasped the potential force of the prayers they learned in books. Chapter 20 of the anonymously authored *relación* describes the experiences of Don Cristóbal Choque Casa, who defied a local *huaca* (holy site or object) that had returned in colonial times to reclaim its authority over the native parishioners of San Damián. Choque Casa overpowered the divinity Llocllay Huancupa and saved the parish from spiritual ruin by reciting the basic catechism:

> Cristóbal invoked God, shouting out at the top of his voice all the prayers he knew, saying the *doctrina* from beginning to end over and over again. As midnight passed, the demon was overpowering him. He thought that nothing could save him, the demon was making him sweat so. Then he invoked our mother Saint Mary. . . . After finishing this, he prayed saying the *Salve Regina Mater Misericordiae* in Latin. While he was reciting it, just as he was in the middle of reciting it, that shameless wicked demon shook the house and, calling "Chus!" in a very deep voice, went out of it in the form of a barn owl. (Salomon and Urioste [c. 1608] 1991, 105)

Twenty-five years later, in the province of Canta, an Indian wanderer by the name of Juan Bautista told church investigators that his training in doctrina had brought similar protection. Accused of sponsoring a cult of the Virgin Mary without the Church's sanction, Bautista appeared before an ecclesiastical judge in the parish of Huamantanga and claimed his innocence. To prove his Catholic faith, he described his recent encounter with the devil, who had confronted him on the road to Canta in the form of a fire-breathing deer: "[The witness] saw [the devil] throw fire from his mouth, which caused him to fear, and then he recited the Apostles' Creed and the devil fled and left him alone."[31]

Uneven Language Spread

Nevertheless, few Indians assimilated Spanish letters to the degree that the Church and Crown had envisioned, especially in the first postconquest period. Lockhart (1968, 209, 213) has documented that by the 1550s, the ethnic lords of Lima and Huarochirí Province had adopted the colonizers' dress but had not learned the Spanish language, and that Cuzco's nobility of the period resisted outside linguistic and cultural influence as well.[32] Garcilaso recalled that none of his childhood peers in Cuzco, with the exception of Paullu Inca's son Don Carlos, attempted to learn more than basic Castilian: "[T]here was so little curiosity for learning the Spanish language, and neglect on the Spaniards' part in teaching it, that no one ever thought to teach it or learn it."[33] Three decades after the Spanish invasion, vast segments of the native population, from the Lima Valley to the former Inca capital, remained ignorant of Spanish. Bartolomé Álvarez ([1588] 1998, 267) charged that in remote highland areas, Indians refused to speak Castilian even when they knew how, which he attributed to subversive motives.

Regional, social, and historical factors conditioned the range of Castilian forms spoken among the native populace. As a general rule, by the early 1600s most Indians of Lima and the coastal plain knew some degree of Spanish. During a 1619 inspection of the Franciscan parish of Santiago de Surco, near Lima, the native leaders testified to the universal knowledge of Spanish in the parish,[34] and thirteen years later Father Francisco Pacho Herrera of Ica told church inspectors that "on the coast the *Doctrina christiana* should be taught in Romance because nearly all the Indians are ladinos and ignorant of the Quechua language."[35] In 1623, in the coastal pueblo of Nasca, the municipal scribe Pedro Guaxi stated that the parishioners rejected traditional customs, such as ceremonial dances, huaca devotions, and ritual drunkenness, "because almost all the Indians are ladinos, having been brought up among Spaniards."[36] Bernabé Cobo witnessed a similar degree of acculturation among the native residents of Santiago del Cercado (Lima's Indian district): "They are so well educated in terms of civility and Christian customs . . . and so Hispanized that in general all men and women speak our language, and in their bearing and decoration of their homes, they appear to be Spanish."[37]

These pockets of Spanish impact contrasted with the linguistic situation in highland parishes, where ignorance of the language persisted. In 1673, Fray Bernabé González of the parish of Huamantanga reportedly beat his native parishioners in order to force them to speak Spanish. Other documents of the period show that some Indian leaders of Cajatambo could not sign legal declarations and that others in the province of Chancay, though declared to be "ladino," could not read Spanish or give oral testimony without the aid of an interpreter.[38] Testimonies from the Cuzco region expressed similar ignorance of the language. Juan Pérez Bocanegra (1631, 34) noted that few Indians of the Cuzco diocese could recite the Apostles' Creed in Spanish. In the late seventeenth century, Quechua prevailed as the primary language of commercial, religious, and domestic interaction between Spaniards and the native peoples of the region (Cerrón Palomino 2003, 146 n. 14), and records of the Cuzco diocese contain examples of Andean ethnic lords and parish assistants who struggled to put their names in writing.[39]

A divide existed between lettered Andeans, such as Guaman Poma, who exalted the virtues of Castilian literacy, and the general population, which resisted its advance. When in 1650 Juana Ycha, an Indian woman from the parish of Huamantanga, faced charges of sorcery, her interrogators were surprised to find that, though baptized, she could not say the catechism in her own language, not to mention Spanish, or form the sign of the cross. When asked why she had neglected her catechism, Juana replied "that her father and her mother did not know how to pray and that they told her not to pray because there was no reason for praying."[40] Illiterate and cut off from any Christian education or apparent desire to learn, she nevertheless carried a rosary, a sort of amulet, she explained, that the archbishop had given her years before on his inspection tour of the parish.

Spanish-speaking Indians with little knowledge of Christianity were also a reality, which raises questions about the theoretical link between the acquisition of Spanish, on the one hand, and the purchase of Catholic doctrine, on the other.[41] In 1676, Father Joseph Morán Collantes of the province of Chancay denounced the seventy-year-old cacique principal of Huaral, Don Juan Soclac, and his wife, Doña María Chumpi, for idolatry, witchcraft, and pastoral negligence. Morán Collantes's legal complaint included the declaration of the *presbítero* Gregorio Antonio de Zepeda, who on a visit to the parish had found the Indians unprepared for Mass. "Although very ladino," the prosecution explained, "the Indians were totally ignorant of doctrine, and when this witness told the said Don Juan to begin to teach them [the catechism], he responded that he did not know how."[42] Soclac floundered under Zepeda's examination, stating that God was the sky and the earth and that the Virgin Mary was the consecrated host. Further testing exposed the cacique's inability to explain the Holy Trinity or recite the basic prayers, excepting parts of the Hail Mary in Quechua. When the judge asked Soclac and Chumpi's son to show his grasp of the catechism, he could only repeat the Hail Mary and parts of the Our Father and Apostles'

Creed, and acknowledged that this he had learned not from his parents, but on the fly, from an African prisoner he had met when visiting his father in jail.[43]

Religious instruction was at times sporadic, and in some parishes Andean students avoided Mass and doctrina altogether. During parish inspections, native witnesses told visitadores they objected to the punishments that came with daily Catholic observance.[44] While ecclesiastics, such as the Franciscan friar Luis Jerónimo de Oré ([1598] 1992, 188), endorsed the "humane and charitable rigor" of routine discipline, students no doubt resented the church officials who submitted them to floggings. Opposition to doctrina also came from parents, who resented having to pay the maestrescuela's salary from community income,[45] especially when they needed their children's help to meet the household's tribute quotas. Corregidores took students to work for the royal haciendas and mines, prompting the prebendary Domingo de Almeida to complain to both the audiencia and metropolitan see on the Indians' behalf: "All parents hide their sons and keep them from school, since even though they might learn to read well, and become a scribe or cantor, the outcome is no better than that of the most rustic laborer, for all must go to *tasa, tambo,* and *mita* (forced Indian labor draft)."[46] In the end, it may have suited native catechists that fewer children could read and write. As privileged intermediaries between native congregations and missionary clergy, they probably had little desire to propagate the Spanish skills that accounted for their position of authority.

In contrast to doctrina, royal boarding schools made it possible for native elites to obtain a *cacicazgo* (chieftainship) that would preserve the family's access to local resources and political power. One of El Colegio del Príncipe's main architects, the Jesuit Pablo José de Arriaga ([1621] 1999, 111), stated that caciques sent their sons to Lima for the social rewards of a Jesuit education. In the 1650s, the cacique and governor of Lampas, Don Juan de Mendoza, enrolled his son in the school with the hope that he would succeed him as governor. Mendoza reportedly sought help from the huaca priest Hernando Hacas Poma to ensure his son's success: "[Mendoza] ordered [Hacas Poma] to sacrifice llamas and offerings to the idol Yanaurau so that his son Don Alonso, who currently studies in the school of the Cercado, would learn to read and write and become a good 'letrado' and rise to the office of cacique and governor."[47] Knowledge of Spanish letters and culture created a reliable pathway to social advancement and material wealth for native society's traditional ruling class.

Knowledge of Spanish also had rewards for Indians without hereditary rank. For his work on the extirpation-of-idolatries campaigns in the region of Checras in the 1640s, the *fiscal de la visita* Thomas Guaman received eight heads of livestock from the property of a convicted dogmatist, apart from his tribute exemption. In authoring his *relación de servicios,* he underscored the contribution of his linguistic skills to the church inspectors. Ultimately, it was Guaman's status as a "ladino of good opinion and reputation" in the eyes of the church inspector, Tomás de Espinoza, that made his remuneration possible.[48] Like other commoners, Guaman may have learned Spanish in doctrina or through informal channels, such as domestic tutoring or contact with Spanish speakers in colonial mines or workshops. The Lima census of 1613 documents sons of caciques who learned how to read and write under the tutelage of Spanish maestros (Contreras [1613] 1968, 164, 328). By his own account, Guaman Poma ([c. 1615] 1980, 15) learned Castilian literacy at home from his half-brother, the hermit priest Martín de Ayala.

Assessing Native Literacy

A never-ending torrent of colonial legislation aiming to reinforce the Indians' training in Spanish provides indirect evidence of the Church's general failure to meet this goal. The Council of the Indies lobbied the Crown to ban Quechua for religious instruction and to strip ethnic lords of cacicazgos for not learning Castilian (Konetzke 1953, 2:38–40). Some proposals surfaced to eliminate native-language training for priests in order to pressure the Indians to acquire Spanish. Other proposals attempted to motivate Indians to learn the language with promises to reduce their tributary obligations.[49] Philip IV insisted that evangelization take place only in Castilian (*RLI* 1841, 1:65), and the licentiate Juan de Solórzano Pereira (1648, 220–22) recommended the prohibition of native languages, in keeping with the 1567 suppression of Arabic and forced acculturation of Moriscos in Iberia. As late as 1686, Charles II decreed Spanish-only instruction in schools throughout the Indies and five years later made the language a requirement for holders of colonial offices.[50] A sense of the Spanish authorities' deep frustration permeates the legislative record.

Yet direct and indirect evidence of lettered Andeans abounds. Many aided Jesuit priests in the creation of native-language catechisms, though their names remain anonymous. Diego González Holguín acknowledged the contributions of native associates in the prologue to his Spanish-Quechua *Vocabulario de la lengua general de todo el Perú* (1608): "I am not persuaded that this work belongs principally to me but to the many Indians of Cuzco I have questioned and with whom I have studied each word. . . . [T]hey are the principal authors of this work."[51] Ludovico Bertonio's Spanish-Aymara *Vocabulario de la lengua aymara* (1612) cited the translation skills of Indians trained at the Jesuits' school in Juli (Bertonio 1612c, s.f.). The Andean notable Don Martín de Sancta Cruz Hanansaya served Bertonio as the chief translator of *Libro de la vida y milagros de Nuestro Señor Jesucristo* (1612), an Aymara adaptation of Alonso de Villegas's sixteenth-century *Flos sanctorum* (Bertonio 1612b, 5). Bilingual Indians assisted Antonio Ruiz de Montoya in the elaboration of his *Catecismo de la lengua guaraní* (1640).

Native wills also document that Andean ethnic lords possessed books, writing instruments, inkpots, and, in exceptional cases, small libraries. In 1610, Don Gerónimo de Achacata, the cacique principal of San Pedro de Sipesipe in the district of los Charcas, bequeathed his assets, which included books, to a native school in the town of Oropesa. His donation included a Spanish war chronicle, fifty-six papal bulls on the military crusades, and a box of manuscripts of royal decrees and legal provisions.[52] The most extensive known library of the Lima archdiocese belonged to the cacique principal of Santo Domingo de Ocros in the province of Cajatambo, Don Juan Flores Guayna Malqui, which passed on to his first-born heir, Don Rodrigo Flores Caja Malqui, a graduate of El Colegio del Príncipe.[53] It consisted of one manuscript sheet and twelve bound volumes, half of which were devotional works and the rest covering topics such as Spanish military history, picaresque narrative and epic poetry (Mateo Alemán's *Guzmán de Alfarache* and Alonso de Ercilla's *La Araucana*), and legal culture (Nicolás de Yrolo Calar's *Politica de escripturas* and Archbishop Lobo Guerrero's ecclesiastical synod of 1613).

While Indians with extensive personal libraries were probably few, native intermediaries had access to the library of the parish priest and circulated books among themselves, which at times incited the alarm of Spanish authorities. Álvarez ([1588] 1998, 268) claimed that Indians shared copies of the *Siete partidas* (c. 1265), Alfonso X's legal code, and the *Practica civil y criminal e instruccion de escrivanos* (1566), Gabriel de Monterroso y Alvarado's popular manual for scribes, and he urged colonial authorities to watch out for Indians who studied Spanish procedural law. Viceroy Toledo also believed that book learning should preserve and not undermine the social order. "It is not advantageous that profane books be brought to this kingdom," he explained, "because the Indians will receive from them bad example and many now know how to read."[54] The Third Council, for its part, banned *libros profanos* (recreational literature), which it deemed inimical to good customs.[55] Caja Malqui's ownership of such works therefore signals a development in native literacy that Spanish colonial authorities were seeking to control.

The independent writings of indios ladinos provide the only direct source for examining native literacy in the Andes, but linguistic studies of native writings are surprisingly few. Jorge Urioste (1980, xxviii–xxxi) and José Cárdenas Bunsen (1998, 101–38) have examined the influence of Quechua on Guaman Poma's Spanish prose, and philological scrutiny of Pachacuti Yamqui's written Spanish has not been done. Rodolfo Cerrón-Palomino (2003, 148–70) and José Luis Rivarola (1985, 36–40) offer rare analyses of samples of Andean Spanish beyond the chronicles of Guaman Poma and Pachacuti Yamqui.[56] In the most systematic treatment to date, Rivarola (2000) has published a selection and linguistic analysis of texts that Indians produced through the civil and ecclesiastical courts. The archive of the Lima archbishopric houses a wealth of similar mundane writings that originated in church legal proceedings involving Indians and priests of the central highland region. Indian-authored documents are difficult to find; they often survive embedded deep within legal dossiers of dozens, if not hundreds of folios in length. Hardly a uniform corpus, the writings evidence varied patterns of Spanish competency among the native bilingual sector.

A 1631 denunciation of ancestral religious practices in the parish Santiago de Carhuamayo offers a case in point.[57] The *fiscal de la idolatría* Don Sebastián Carhuas and the municipal scribe Baltazar Quispi Vilca constitute the principal hands of the written denunciation against the alleged sorcerer Lorenzo Llacxa Guaroc, which includes at the base the signature of Amador Caro de Mazuelos, the prosecution's ecclesiastical sponsor. Carhuas's and Quispi Vilca's texts exhibit sophisticated script, faultless grammar, full mastery of notarial conventions, and stylish autographs and rubrics. The signature that Martín Caxa Poma affixed to his transcribed testimony of the record attests to a less practiced hand and probably lower degree of literacy. Indians often authored legal documents jointly, as did Carhuas and Quispi Vilca, or hired *protectores* (legal advocates), notaries, and other Spanish or native officials to draft documents in their name without attribution to the transcriber.[58] Literate agents at times copied papers and produced false signatures on behalf of native clients, making the authorship of many documents of the colonial archives difficult to know.

If we look closely at the body of materials for which Indian authorship can be established with certainty, a rough pattern emerges between the advanced written Spanish of native elites, on the one hand, and the functional literacy of native assistants without hereditary rank, on the other. In 1647, Don Alonso García González, the cacique principal and governor of Colcabamba, presented a written defense on behalf of himself and local parish officials in response to the charges of idolatry that his uncle and rival Don Gerónimo Auquiniven had brought against them.[59] The single-author document reveals an elegant hand, possibly acquired from training as a municipal scribe, as the legal formulae and notarial abbreviations of the document suggest. García González's prose reads fluidly, without syntactic or grammatical errors of any type, and exhibits a wide-ranging vocabulary, alternating verb tenses and moods, distinct linguistic registers, and Spanish rhetorical devices. Aside from the occasional alteration of consonants and vowels due to phonological influences of the cacique's maternal Quechua ("puplicar," "deferentes," "trebutos," "hechesero"), nothing would distinguish his language use from that of a well-educated Spaniard.

A personal letter by the fiscal Agustín Capcha to Governor Don Juan Rodríguez Pilco of the parish of Nuestra Señora de la Asunción de Ambar in the province of Cajatambo, presents a contrasting model of literacy.[60] Found among the idolatry proceedings that Capcha brought against the native governor, the 1663 missive urges the accused not to retaliate against a clergyman adversary. Despite a broad lexical range and verbal register, as well as stylistic subtleties such as indirect discourse and sermonic tropes, the language of the text manifests gender disagreement ("la que vmd. lo pasara por sus ojos"), confused spellings and vowels ("dios noestro s.r"), and unclear syntax ("no le quiro aguardar porque no mi en que tando") that possibly reflect underlying Quechua patterns. Capcha's fractured script discloses the lesser writing skills of Indians who did not attend the school for caciques but learned Castilian in parish schools or through private tutoring. He

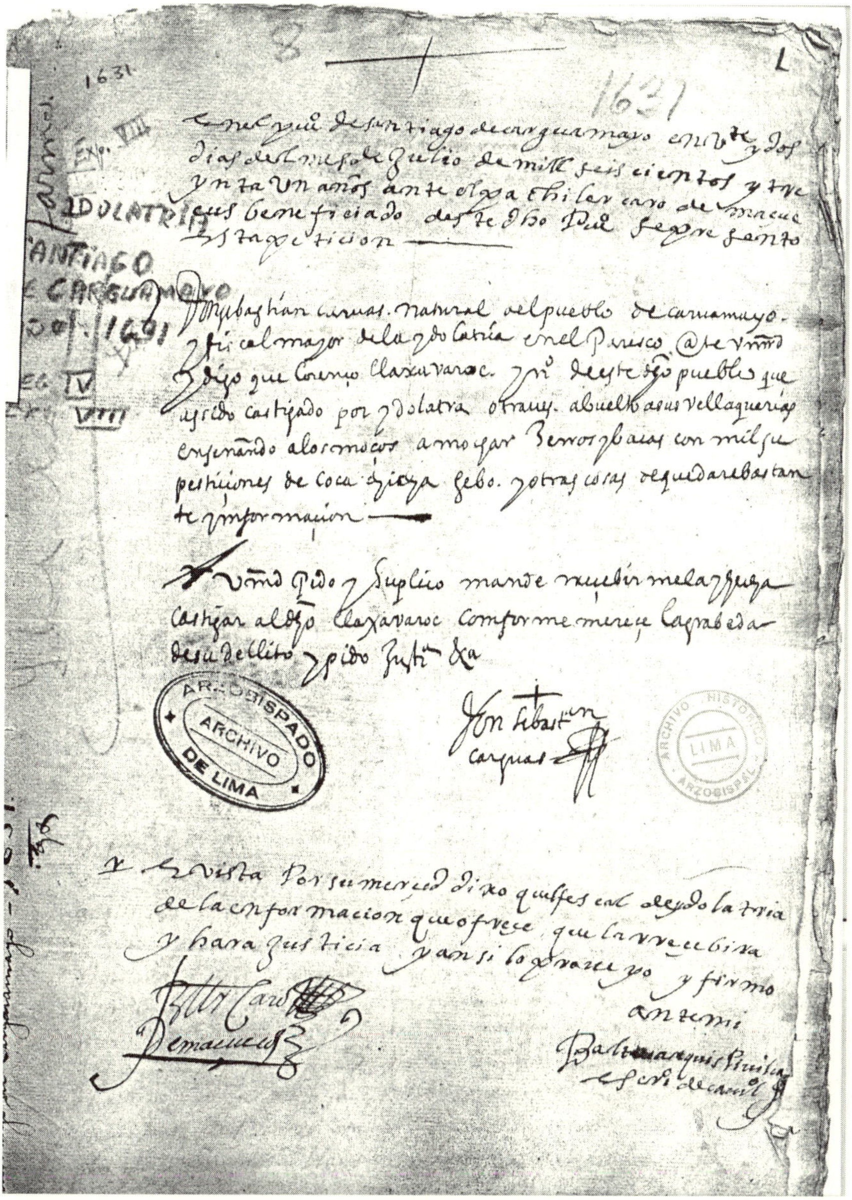

FIGURE 3.   Idolatry accusation. Don Sebastián Carhuas and Baltazar Quispi Vilca.
Courtesy of the Archivo Arzobispal de Lima.

En 27 de mayo de 1647 años

[handwritten manuscript text in 17th-century Spanish paleography]

FIGURE 4.   Petition of grievance. Don Alonso García González.
Courtesy of the Archivo Arzobispal de Lima.

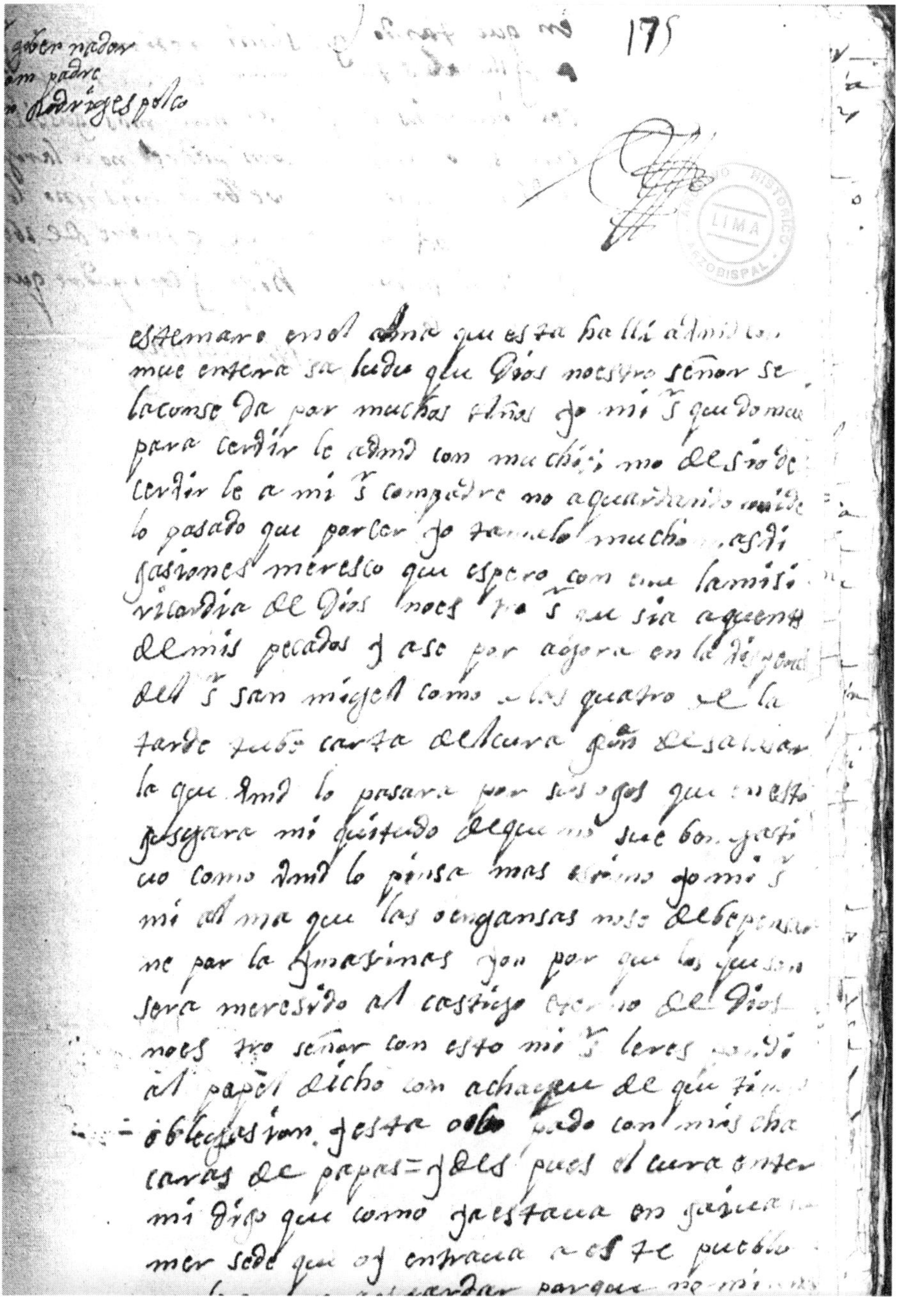

FIGURE 5. Letter to a native governor. Agustín Capcha.
Courtesy of the Archivo Arzobispal de Lima.

nevertheless achieved sufficient literacy to serve as a municipal scribe before joining the parish staff of Ambar.[61] The letter also confirms that written Spanish was a means of communication between Quechua speakers, whose own language had no parallel tradition of alphabetic writing.

Making Legal Records

Guaman Poma placed Spanish literacy at the center of his proposal for missionary reform. The native chronicler extolled the Christian benefits of reading and writing for native students (Guaman Poma [c. 1615] 1980, 685–86, 872) and criticized parish priests who failed to obey the Spanish laws on native schooling that would ensure the Indians' cultural improvement: "[T]hey do not want there to be schools or that Indians learn to read and write, preferring instead they be idolatrous infidels."[62] He described himself as an instructor of Spanish language and Christian doctrine (499), though it is unclear whether he did so in an official church capacity, and shared the Third Council's vision of a literate Andean society brought to Christian order through the disciplining power of the printed catechisms, which he knew well and mentioned by name (1089). Guaman Poma placed special blame for the Indians' cultural state on the priests who neglected their spiritual ministry, but all sectors of parish society, including native intermediaries, earned his reproach.

Guaman Poma's model for good doctrina and parish government points out the ways in which shifting relations of dominance and insubordination mediated the process of religious conversion through Castilian language and custom. Guaman Poma ([c. 1615] 1980, 684) depicted the abusive "maestro de coro y de escuela" of Huanca, Francisco de Palacios de Luna, who spared no punishment in teaching native students Spanish literacy and song. The illustration conveys the high risks for Andeans that the acquisition of Castilian literacy involved. Indian boys appear to read or sing aloud the religious lesson under the threat of severe lashings. Their books of Christian instruction communicated a new order of rules, practices, and social hierarchies that were not only spiritual, but also disciplinary.

However, one student—furtively, it appears, without the instructor Palacios de Luna's knowledge—writes a document that begins with the unmistakable notarial formula common to legal instruments that Spanish and indigenous notaries drafted for proceedings in the colonial courts: "Sepan

FIGURE 6.   The Choir Master. Guaman Poma,
El primer nueva corónica y buen gobierno, 684.
Courtesy of the Royal Library, Copenhagen, Denmark.

cuantos . . ." (Let it be known . . .).[63] Was this a legally binding testimony that denounced the maestrescuela's abuse or a lawsuit against a Spanish priest of the type that Bartolomé Álvarez abhorred? Perhaps the student practiced on the side a skill more practical than Christian recitation: the legalese that would guarantee his employment at a notary's workplace. In Guaman Poma's vision for Andean Catholic society, Spanish literacy took on uses beyond the teaching and learning of the catechism and became a tool for defending indigenous parishioners in courtrooms, notarial workshops, and other arenas of social conflict.

Though Guaman Poma promoted the edifying potential of books, he understood the dangers of written documents, particularly the kind that Spanish officials used to humiliate Indians and justify their subjugation. For that reason, native peoples must learn to read and write in Spanish, he claimed, not only to assimilate Christianity, but also to defend themselves against the invaders' deceitful stratagems (Adorno [1986] 2000; Burns 2005a). For him, evangelizing through literacy went hand in hand with the teaching of legal advocacy and ethical principles: "I had many disciples and they have turned out to be Christians and high-ranking ladinos, and friends in the defense of the poor."[64] The chronicler believed that Indians needed sources of moral instruction beyond the official publications of the Third Council, as his support for native juridical writing made clear.

Lawsuits filed with the magistrates of the Lima see and royal audiencia were often the Indians' only alternative for protecting themselves from abusive church authorities. The countless admonitions in missionary writings against native legal activism indicate that Andeans exercised openly the legal right, enjoyed by all subjects of the Crown, to file grievances. Priests thus faced the quandary of how to spread literacy for the purpose of indoctrination yet restrict its uses to the religious domain. Arriaga recalled the words of a parish priest, who when asked why there was no parish school, told him: "It wasn't worth having the Indians know how to read and write because knowledge of letters only served them for making lawsuits against their priests."[65] Guaman Poma ([c. 1615] 1980, 609) also confirmed, from an Andean perspective, the indios ladinos' well-earned reputation for denouncing priests.[66] What separated the clergy's view of native litigants from Guaman Poma's, however, was whether they filed lawsuits in pursuit of justice or subversive objectives.

Colonial authorities took measures to reduce the large number of written documents that overburdened the legal bureaucracy. The Second Lima Council of 1567 stated that when traveling to native parishes, ecclesiastical magistrates should hear native lawsuits "summarily and with paternal love,"[67] which meant receiving oral arguments rather than written actions and deciding cases swiftly, so as not to involve Indians in prolonged and financially taxing proceedings that sustained local frictions. Secular authorities, Viceroy Toledo among them, argued that Indian justice would be better served if judgments took effect in local Andean communities rather than in the distant courts of the archbishopric and royal audiencia (Levillier 1921–1925, 8:312).[68] Well into the seventeenth century, the Crown and Lima audiencia cited similar concerns in their aim to resolve indigenous cases promptly and thereby curb the proliferation of written petitions and grievances (Solórzano Pereira 1648, 233–34, 564–65), which suggests that the Indians' relentless petitioning went unchecked.

The abundance of native litigation in the documentary record indicates that Indians acquired literacy more for the practical purpose of contending with the colonial legal system than for the spiritual purpose of reinforcing the Christian lessons they received at doctrina. Indios ladinos learned Spanish writing in order to file lawsuits, record tribute quotas, communicate royal and church orders to native parishioners, and fulfill other duties required for the business of local governance and evangelization.[69] When Indians turned to writing on their own, it was usually outside the religious classroom, in the conflictive arena of the colonial tribunal. Andeans knew that written words had punitive effects and that writing was a form of social action tied to the goal of reforming and managing colonial society. Recently published materials have shown that Guaman Poma learned juridical writing long before taking up historical narrative. In all likelihood, it was the loss of family lands by order of the colonial courts that in part motivated him to compose his chronicle of more than one thousand folios to the Spanish king (Adorno 1993).

Because written documents held such authority, Indians approached writing not as a transparent medium, but critically. Religious education aimed to teach neophytes to speak, read, and write in Spanish. But native schooling was dangerous insofar as Spanish letters provided students "a weapon of the weak" (Scott 1985) with which to contest the forces of colonialism that regulated their lives. Guaman Poma's rendering of native scribal activity in the classroom evidences a tension inherent to the process of acculturation through literacy. Whereas books had the power to impose uniformity of thought and behavior, individuals could produce variable meanings outside the textual frameworks imposed upon them (see Chartier 1994, 36). Spanish literacy assisted Indians to meet the requirements of Christian practice and gave them a tool for responding to missionary methods. It encompassed "passive" and "active" uses of writing that could take opposing paths.[70] Though Spanish authority fostered the use of Castilian for the purposes of political and cultural unification, it cast a suspicious eye upon Indians whose linguistic practices surpassed the limits of social action established in religious books.[71]

Michael Clanchy's observations about writing practices after the Norman Conquest of England places Guaman Poma's drawing in broad historical context: "Making records is initially a product of distrust rather than social progress" (1993, 6). Andean writing emerged in a parish arena of mutual suspicion in which native parishioners saw writing's power to exact and control and used it to make records of their own. Guaman Poma explained that native literacy took root in doctrina but extended to the legal sphere. In his mind, all caciques should know Spanish letters in order to uphold Christian law and keep colonialist abuses in check: "[The cacique] should be raised as a ladino Christian, and if possible, know Latin and how to read, write, and count, and draft legal petitions and interrogations for the defense of his people and his Indians and subjects, vassals, the poor of Christ."[72] Nearly all mentions of indios ladinos in his work refer to their actions in denouncing priests and corregidores through the Spanish courts. In short, native literacy emerged as much from the bureaucratic and political needs of local parish communities as from the efforts of the Church and Crown to evangelize the indigenous populace.

Letrado, in Covarrubias's early modern formulation, designated a wide array of social types, ranging from learned humanists and theologians to everyday lawyers and notaries who excelled in legal matters (Covarrubias Orozco [1611] 1995, 712). Though it was rarely a category to designate American Indians who knew how to read and write, native petitioners and scribes performed functions in the Spanish legal system that overlapped with those of Spanish letrados. Whereas "letrado" was, from the perspective of Don Juan de Mendoza, a title of status befitting the noble lords who studied with

Jesuits and imposed Spanish law, for Álvarez and many clergy, the term applied to litigious Indians who usurped the authority of priests in the pursuit of self-interest. In contrast, Guaman Poma's high-minded letrado used writing to petition against the colonial establishment for the defense of native vassals. Such variable and opposing perceptions of native literary activity point to the fluid nature of the category "letrado" and the unstable roles that literate Indians took on. The spread of Spanish literacy was a slowly evolving historical process. That no single category or label can fully capture what it meant to be a lettered Indian bespeaks the complexity of that experience in Andean parish society.

Developments in native literacy reshaped colonial distributions of power and forced parish priests to rethink what constituted the legitimate exercise of writing. At the same time, Andeans who took up writing found that the roles to which they were assigned were far from clear and constantly in flux. Legal advocacy in the Church was not a straightforward question of enforcing canon law; it required native church officials to chart an uncertain path in a dynamic environment of changing social and political circumstances. The difficult task for these officials was to employ certain laws to uphold their mediating authority against rival Spanish and native groups and to impose other laws that contained the values of Indian society as a whole. To understand how the intermediaries went about this requires an assessment of the written testimonies they presented to church magistrates on the state of Indian ministry and the actions of parish priests. Theirs is an uncommonly vivid look at the day-to-day challenges and tensions of rural parish life.

Chapter 2

Catechesis in Quechua

Linguistic Ignorance in the Sierra

In 1634, the young nobleman Rodrigo de Guzmán Rupay Chagua left his home in Huamantanga and set off southwest to the Lima capital, where he spent the next six years learning the Spanish language and Christian doctrine under Jesuit supervision at El Colegio del Príncipe. Like other sons of ethnic lords throughout the archdiocese, Rupay Chagua trained to be an ecclesiastical assistant and civil government administrator, equipped to dissuade native parishioners from their attachment to the traditional divinities. By being removed in adolescence from the religious influences of his kin group and being educated in Christian values, the future cacique principal and governor of Huamantanga would become what the school's chief patron, Viceroy Francisco de Borja y Aragón, the prince of Esquilache, called "a living example of Christendom and virtue for his subjects and all Indians."[1]

However, in setting forth these goals, the viceroy did not anticipate that a future student such as Rupay Chagua would one day apply his Catholic schooling to police not only the idolaters of his parish, but also its Mercedarian authorities. In 1669, ostensibly frustrated by the survival of native ritual practices in Huamantanga, Rupay Chagua filed a grievance with Archbishop Villagómez against the recently appointed interim doctrinero, Fray Francisco Torrejón Velasco. The governor blamed the religious error under Torrejón's watch on the state of native-language religious instruction, arguing that the friar's inability to speak Quechua impeded the Indians' spiritual development: "From experience, he has shown that he does not know the general language of the Inca, or possess a title or royal license, for during the eight months of his ministry, he has not preached in the aforesaid language or in Spanish, to the grave detriment and harm of the impoverished Indians."[2] Rupay Chagua asked the archbishop to remove Torrejón from the post and replace him with a priest who could minister in Quechua, in keeping with the orders of the Third Council of Lima.

From the start of the Spanish invasion, missionary priests adopted Quechua, the administrative language of the Incas, as a tool for instructing native peoples in Christianity. Yet Rupay Chagua's petition hinted that language practice in Andean parishes impeded the work of evangelization. The conflict between imperial and aboriginal languages is a heated political issue with deep historical precedents and modern corollaries. Spain was not the only European colonial power to face the problem of how to employ its language together with an already dominant regional language as tools of administrative and religious conquest. Beyond South America, Spanish colonization resulted in the dissemination of Nahuatl in New Spain and Tagalog in the Philippines in ways that anticipated the British Empire's promotion of Bengali in India and Belgium's utilization of Swahili and Lingala in the Congo, to name a few examples (Mannheim 1992, 78). These historical processes transformed the linguistic and cultural landscape of the conquered territories as well as the social and political relationships between colonizers and colonized. Native church assistants, versed in both Quechua and Castilian, had a uniquely qualified perspective on the clergy's use of native languages. The record of their testimony reveals unforeseen details about the repercussions of imperial language policies for indigenous peoples and about the ways in which priests communicated Christian beliefs.

The petition of grievance against Torrejón was one of Rupay Chagua's many interventions in colonial tribunals as an advocate of the interests of his community. He filed numerous legal complaints in his at least thirty-year career as governor in Canta and consulted regularly with secular and church authorities. His noble forebears were powerful landholders, as the last will and testament of his grandfather Rodrigo, the one-time district governor, confirms.[3] As a native authority, the younger Rupay Chagua ruled the Indian tributaries of up to six parishes in the area of Huamantanga. He ensured that Indians met their parish obligations, oversaw native labor and payment of tribute, and updated Spanish authorities on the status of the district's human and natural resources. Given the influence of native governors over spiritual and economic affairs, conflicts often developed between them and local priests and corregidores, a surprising number of which centered

FIGURE 7. The pueblo of Huamantanga. Courtesy of the Emilio Harth-Terré Collection, Latin American Library, Tulane University.

on the interconnected problems of language and religious exchange. The ecclesiastical tribunal constituted a space of Spanish-Andean interaction from which emerged outlooks on language practice that called into question official church reports on the effectiveness of Quechua-language religious instruction in the central sierra. Its papers show that the views of native intermediaries on the state of intercultural communication stretched from the native parishes of the highlands to the inner chambers of Lima's viceregal authority. Indigenous litigants put forward ideas about evangelization in the Andes, and royal and ecclesiastical powers responded to their proposals.

Creating a Quechua Suitable for Doctrine

A central problem the colonizers faced was choosing the right language for teaching Christian doctrine. Secular and church authorities long debated whether to evangelize in Spanish or turn indigenous languages into written ones for the purpose of religious instruction.[4] Proponents of Castilian held that native languages were unreliable mediums for expressing Christian ideas and that the abolition of local languages offered the surest means

44   Chapter 2

of eliminating idolatrous beliefs and assimilating native peoples. Yet hard-line measures proved difficult in a linguistically diverse Andean region. Strictly maintained boundaries between local languages and the attachment of indigenous groups to their maternal tongues contributed to an abiding situation of multilingualism under Spanish colonial rule (Mannheim 1991, 45, 52; Cerrón-Palomino 1995, ix). Though educating Indians in Castilian was the colonizers' ultimate aim, the complexity of the linguistic landscape made the use of Andean languages unavoidable. The Crown and Church thus pursued a twofold agenda: to educate Indians in Spanish for political and administrative purposes, but to tolerate the use of native languages for evangelization.

Peru's first evangelizers believed that the vocalization of Spanish and Latin prayers could summon divine grace despite the Indians' ignorance of the languages.[5] But they soon came to recognize that teaching in native languages would push Indians beyond the unfamiliar litanies to a fuller understanding of doctrine. Taking this view, Acosta maintained that native peoples should learn Spanish, but urged Catholic ministers to meet them halfway: "If a few Spaniards in a foreign land cannot fully forget their language and learn a foreign one, . . . who could possibly think that countless peoples should forget the language of their parents while still in their own land and use only a foreign language they hear rarely and against their will?"[6] Furthermore, wary of undue reliance on local interpreters in foreign lands, the Jesuit advised the clergy that the salvation of indigenous peoples could no longer be entrusted to unprepared native lenguas (Acosta [1577] 1984, 1987, 1:95, 2:55).

The Church's first backing of Andean languages came on the occasion of the First Council (1551–1552). Evading Charles V's earlier injunctions against native-language instruction, the councilors authorized the creation of a manuscript catechism and religious dialogues in Quechua, ordered priests to instruct Andean adults in the local language prior to baptism, and established a course of study in Quechua at the Cathedral of Lima to train clergy for Indian ministry.[7] The Second Council (1567) also stated that evangelization should take place in the vernacular, if necessary, to ensure the Indians' understanding of doctrine, and approved the use of native-language catechisms.[8] Other decrees instructed clergymen to learn the language of their parishioners and to avoid excessive reliance on native interpreters or face economic sanctions.[9]

In 1582–1583, church leaders throughout South America convened at Lima's Third Council with the goal to improve native-language religious instruction through a qualified clergy. Conciliar decrees urged all ministers to teach Christian doctrine in their parishioners' language, thereby eliminating obligatory Latin prayer,[10] and hear confessions in the local language without the assistance of native lenguas, "since a good judge can only be he who gives sentence in a language he understands."[11] The council advised bishops to assign for indigenous ministry only candidates who could demonstrate working knowledge of "the language of this land."[12] Philip II's more liberal stance on native languages matched the Third Council's position. The Crown required Quechua training for all parish priests and created professorships in the language at Lima's University of San Marcos to support the chair in Quechua that Viceroy Toledo had founded in 1579.[13]

The next step was to equip the clergy with practical tools for carrying out its mission. By order of the council, Acosta recruited a team of translators responsible for the creation of the standardized books of religious instruction that would be used in native parishes throughout the viceroyalty.[14] Acosta and the team's efforts resulted in the *Doctrina christiana* (1584), *Confessionario* (1585), and *Tercero catecismo* (1585), all published in trilingual format, in Spanish and the widely disseminated *lenguas generales* Quechua and Aymara. Peru's high clergy trusted that the uniform diffusion of Quechua (still, in colonial times, the widespread language of the Incas) and Aymara (broadly spoken over certain southern areas) would respond to the region's linguistic diversity and improve the possibility of communication between missionaries and native audiences.

The books' authors insisted that fruitful indoctrination efforts rested on transparent language usage: "lenguaje comun, facil, y proprio" *(Doctrina christiana* [1584] 1985, 167). Leading historians of the time believed that indigenous languages had lost their ability over time to communicate knowledge of the divine and expressed only the errors of false religion.[15] Acosta, for one, viewed the inseparability of native languages and idolatrous beliefs in hereditary terms, stating that false religion passed from one generation to the next by way of language. Native superstition was, for him, "a hereditary idolatrous disease, . . . contracted in the very breast of the mother and fed by her milk."[16] The linguists of the council moved, therefore, to cleanse the languages of their alleged impurities in order to separate native

Andeans from the harmful traditions of an autochthonous past. This meant establishing the linguistic integrity of Quechua and Aymara—that is, their ability to signify "properly" *(con propiedad)* as legitimate mediums of religious discourse.

To standardize Quechua, the Third Council departed from the linguistic model that the Dominican grammarian and lexicographer Domingo de Santo Tomás was first to champion, which encompassed central and coastal dialects, in favor of what it termed the more dignified and authoritative speech of Cuzco, the former capital of the Incas.[17] The language reformers explained their position in the tract "Annotaciones, o scolios, sobre la traducción," which was appended to the *Doctrina christiana*. Citing linguistic diversity as the chief impediment to evangelization, they dismissed the "corrupt" variants spoken in the central mountain region, far from the southern imperial city. According to the authors, the deficient sonority and lexicon of the regional languages extending north of Huamanga, broadly defined as the language of Chinchaysuyu, rendered them illegitimate for teaching Christian doctrine:

> The imperfection or barbarity that exists in those who speak the Quechua language corruptly is less a matter of pronunciation than the variety of words, which are different from those used in Cuzco and somewhat coarse, taken from regional idioms or from the usage commonly learned by all the Chinchaysuyos.[18]

The linguists promoted a simplified version of Cuzco speech with the goal of eradicating vocabulary that sustained the memory of past superstitions: "words once used by the Incas and native lords, or borrowed from other nations with which they have dealings."[19] Moreover, because Quechua lacked the precise terminology for communicating Christian ideas, such as the holy sacraments or the existence of one God, Acosta and the translators introduced Spanish loan words into the Quechua text. Examples of these included: *Dios, cruz, rezar,* and *matrimonio*.

Missionary priests and native assistants would from this point forward teach indigenous students the published text of the *Doctrina christiana*. The catechism's authors took the diverse verbal register of Quechua speakers and submitted it to precise rules by means of the written word. In doing so, they distinguished the language that communicated "truth" (Cuzco-based Quechua) from the dialects that harbored "falsehood" (the tongues of the central Andes) and at the same time affirmed the precision and durability of the written catechism over the "illegibility" and "corruption" of native oral traditions.[20] With the catechism in hand, parish priests were, in theory, equipped to transcend the cacophony of regional vernaculars and to teach native students in a reasoned discourse appropriate for Christian ideas. This was the language of Cuzco, the new ecclesiastical Quechua, to which Rupay Chagua referred in making his complaint.

The "Linguistic Policy" of the Incas

Missionary linguists expressed support of the language of Cuzco in the decades after the Third Council. Adherents to the values of Renaissance humanism, they identified elegant and refined speech as that spoken in urban centers of cultural and religious life. Fray Luis Jerónimo de Oré expressed the idea that Cuzco speech exceeded all other Quechua forms: "The city of Cuzco is the Athens, where one speaks with all the rigor and elegance imaginable; like Ionic in Athens, Latin in Rome, the Castilian Romance of Toledo, thus is the Quechua language in Cuzco."[21] He extolled the Inca language and eschewed regional dialects, labeling them corrupt deviations from the aristocratic norm of the Inca's colonial descendants: "[T]he farther away from this city [such dialects are spoken], there is more corruption and less elegance."[22]

The Cuzco position found particular favor among members of the Jesuit order, especially Blas Valera. A translator of both the Quechua and Aymara texts of the *Doctrina christiana* (Bartra 1967, 365–66), Valera occupied a privileged position to sway the direction of Third Council language policy. Though the extent of his influence cannot be fully determined, the surviving pages of his history, as transcribed by El Inca Garcilaso, reveal the uncommon zeal of a language purist. For Valera, proper Quechua was "la lengua cortesana," the language of the Cuzco court, defined in opposition to the unsophisticated speech of provincial areas outside the Inca capital (Garcilaso [1609] 1960, 2:248). Drawing on principles of natural law, which equated linguistic union with political integration, Valera contended that just as Latin had enlightened the primitive peoples of Europe, the Inca language could inspire Andeans to trade their barbarism for proper customs:

When the Puquinas, Collas, Urus, Yuncas, and other simple and ignorant nations, who because of their ignorance speak even their own language poorly, manage to learn the language of Cuzco, they shed the simplicity and ignorance they once had for political and courtly affairs, and they strive for loftier pursuits of the intellect. As a result, they become more capable and suited for receiving the doctrine of the Catholic faith.[23]

According to the Jesuit, the edifying properties of Cuzco speech made it ideal for educating native peoples in the precepts of the Christian faith.

The fact that Valera, a mestizo from the northern Andean town of Chachapoyas (an area that resisted Inca rule), defended the Quechua spoken in the southern region of Cuzco underscores the currency of such thinking in the Society of Jesus. In their discussions of native linguistic activity, members of the order repeatedly associated the humanistic ideals of propriety and purity with the speech of Cuzco.[24] It was there, on the occasion of the order's Second Provincial Congregation of 1576, that the Jesuit Alonso de Barzana authored the Quechua-Aymara catechism that later served as the model for the Third Council's *Doctrina christiana*. The provincial authorities aimed to transcend the linguistic chaos of the Andes and reconcile native peoples with the "inviolate" Quechua of the Incas, which supposedly possessed the transparency required for speaking religious truths. When granted royal license in 1599 to conduct language exams for parish assignments in the Cuzco diocese,[25] the Jesuits undoubtedly applied the same linguistic standards.

What is more, proponents of this position argued for a return to the sound language policies of the Inca past. The Spanish military conquest of the sixteenth century had displaced the lingua franca from the political domain and had fortified regional languages and other forms of Quechua (Cerrón-Palomino 1992, 210). Valera complained that the Babel of languages had brought missionary efforts to a standstill: "That confusion and multitude of languages, which the Incas tried to eliminate with such care, have arisen once again; . . . for this reason . . . it is impossible that the Indians of Peru . . . can be well instructed in the faith and good customs."[26] In his view, the Inca sovereigns understood the relationship between language and good customs, and the practical advantages of imposing a single language. Obligating all conquered peoples to learn Quechua, the Incas had achieved social and linguistic harmony: "The Incas ruled and governed all their empire in peace and tranquility, and the vassals of many nations considered themselves brothers because they all spoke one language."[27]

Recent advancements in the field of linguistic anthropology have demonstrated that clerical misreadings of Andean history aided the effort to canonize the Quechua of Cuzco. Bruce Mannheim (1991, 64) has argued that the former lingua franca of the Incas remained inaccessible to administrators on the empire's periphery and failed to achieve hegemony even among Indians in the vicinity of Cuzco. Only native elites affiliated with the Inca state spoke the common language, which remained absent from the domestic sphere and unknown to the majority of the Inca's subjects. Rodolfo Cerrón-Palomino (1995, xi–xii) has speculated that the Incas originally spoke Puquina and Aymara before adopting Quechua in the last stages of their imperial expansion and that their administrative language was a Quechua amalgam similar to the variant of the south-central coast, not the language of Cuzco. Cerrón-Palomino's research has caused a fundamental reassessment of the pronouncements of Garcilaso and his contemporaries on the history of the Quechua language and its usage in the Peruvian viceroyalty (see Cerrón-Palomino 1991).

Despite the claims of Valera and others, the Incas did not share the Church's concern with taming the confusion of vernaculars. While the former rulers perceived the rewards of imposing a common language of political administration, they remained tolerant of regional languages and cultural practices. Missionary writers referred to the linguistic consolidation achieved by Huayna Capac, the last Inca to rule over a united empire, but such assertions were fueled by nostalgia for a lost harmony that never was. In contrast to early modern Europe, where political states standardized a national language in order to unite subjects, the Andes of pre-Hispanic times accommodated linguistic diversity and ethnic fragmentation. Language as a state-sponsored tool of national unification, in the sixteenth-century Spanish sense, had no point of comparison with the lingua franca of Tawantinsuyu. The Incas disseminated Quechua through the bilingualism of a select class of native administrators, and this spread had negligible impact on the language practice of the native peoples as a whole.

But what did the language of Cuzco, the newly codified missionary Quechua, mean to native parish assistants? Part of the answer surfaces in the papers of ecclesiastical lawsuits, church inspection reports, and idolatry trial testimonies. Yet because of the highly mediated nature of these documents, a full examination is needed of the legal procedures and ladino-priest interactions that gave shape to the linguistic realities they describe. Trial documents that resulted from the *visitas* (parish inspections) in Huamantanga at the time of Rupay Chagua's governorship, for example, show that missionary language practice was a chief concern of clergymen and indios ladinos, but also one in a large constellation of issues about local parish authority that lead to additional lines of inquiry about the unofficial ways in which evangelization in the Andes took shape.

Causas Against Priests
A Typology

In 1609, Archbishop Lobo Guerrero launched the first systematic campaigns to eradicate idolatries in the Lima archdiocese, which researchers have generally viewed as a course of action separate from the Church's move to enforce the doctrinal conformity of parish priests. However, ecclesiastical legislation reflects the church hierarchy's aim to correct not only native religious error, but also the clergy's pastoral neglect. Native parishioners dreaded the arrival of the visita and the interrogations and punishments it produced. Idolatry visitas disrupted the clergy as well, for they gave Indians the opportunity to voice misgivings about the state of pastoral affairs.[28] In this sense, the campaigns provided a fertile breeding ground for the exchange of reciprocal accusations between priests and native authorities who competed for political and spiritual authority in local communities. Indigenous lawsuits emerged from the same idolatry trial complex that persecuted traditional Andean beliefs and rituals; in many parishes, charges against priests for moral and material transgressions were preceded or followed by the Church's prosecution of the native worshippers' alleged crimes. What Kenneth Mills (1996, 185) has termed the "atmosphere of mutual scrutiny and sense-making" that characterized parish relations thus provides a necessary context for approaching legal cases, in which native litigants turned to the power of written documents to denounce the corruption of Catholic ministers.[29]

As with the laity in Spain, Indians had the right to file grievances before an ecclesiastical judge, in diocesan and archdiocesan tribunals or in the more improvised courts of the sierra. Catholic courts declared on matters of canon law, which encompassed civil and criminal charges against priests, with the ultimate rulings emanating from the local prelacy or, in the case of successful appeal, the royal audiencia.[30] To file a legal grievance, or *causa de capítulos,* native litigants could journey to Lima and submit complaints directly to the archbishop or *provisor* (chief ecclesiastical judge of the archdiocese), but usually they presented arguments to the *visitador de idolatrías* or other *juez ordinario* of the sierra. Some plaintiffs, such as Rupay Chagua, composed and filed legal grievances independently, but a greater number sought the representation of regional protectores or *procuradores de los naturales,* Crown-appointed defense attorneys responsible for overseeing the welfare of indigenous subjects in the district.

Rupay Chagua demanded Torrejón's removal based on his ignorance of Quechua. However, native lawsuits against the clergy usually entailed lengthy series of charges, or capítulos. Itemized complaints within a single legal action could range in number from a mere half-dozen to more than one hundred and fell into three general types of ministerial abuse: (1) fiscal exploitation; (2) immoral behavior; and (3) spiritual neglect. In terms of sheer numbers, the accusations of the first type far surpassed those of the latter two. By canon law, the padre doctrinero received a *sínodo* (stipend), which Indians paid in community goods or equivalent monies, as well as a small group of *mitayos* (native laborers assigned to the mita) to work in his personal service.[31] Some clergy supported themselves on this and voluntary offerings of parishioners, but others gained extra income through illegal business and forced donations.[32] Money-making operations, or *tratos y granjerías,* included the production and sale of woven fabrics and clothing; the breeding and trade of community livestock; the cultivation and vending of fruits, wines, and other agricultural products through unpaid labor; and the purchase of basic goods from Indians at low rates for resale at higher prices. Native litigants also accused priests of demanding fees for sacraments, burials, celebrations of the liturgy, and holy festivities.[33] The injunction against manipulating indigenous wills for personal gain and Guaman Poma's censure of the practice suggest that the clergy had a well-established reputation for doing this as well.[34]

The second type of charge cited the "bad example" of priests. To uphold the clergy's sacramental and social image, the Lima see censured habits such as gambling, smoking tobacco before Mass, and consorting with women.[35] Andean plaintiffs modeled allegations of this kind on the language of the conciliar decrees. In 1623, the caciques principales of Barranca denounced Cristóbal Quintero's carousing and womanizing: "[The priest's] bad way of living has reached such a degree that he provides a bad example for the Indians."[36] Other accusations charged priests for physical violence against native parishioners (including the pregnant, the elderly, and the infirm) and for sexual deviancies that reached antisocial extremes.[37]

Indian petitioners claimed spiritual neglect on two main grounds: the priest's refusal to administer the sacraments and teach Christian doctrine. Regarding the holy sacraments, the most frequent and serious charges involved the failure to baptize ailing infants before death and to confess the dying and give last rites. Native church officials submitted to ecclesiastical judges the *padrones* (sacramental registers) of baptisms, confessions, and last rites as proof that the cura had forsaken his sacral duties.[38] In addition, visita reports and native grievances stated that missionary priests either ignored the Indians' religious education or left incompetent native catechists to teach Christian doctrine in their place.[39]

Interparish Conflict in Huamantanga

While Indians seized the opportunity of the visita to bring charges against priests, it was also common for plaintiffs to find themselves in the aisle of the accused. Rupay Chagua was no exception. From 1656 to 1669, the cacique principal was repeatedly tried and jailed for his role in safeguarding the idol Guaracani, the principal divinity of Huamantanga and its surrounding area since pre-Hispanic times. In the course of the licentiate Pedro de Quijano Zevallos's discoveries throughout Canta Province in 1656, as well as those of Visitador Juan Sarmiento de Vivero before and during the decade of the 1660s, native witnesses reported that Rupay Chagua served as the chief patron of the community's ritual ceremonies and sacrifices in honor of the huaca-protector. The cacique principal sought prayers and sacrifices from native religious specialists for his own spiritual health and for legal victory in suits he had pending against rivals who questioned his claim of noble rank and colonial office.[40] At one point in Quijano's investigation, the huaca priest Hernando Caruachin protested Rupay Chagua's dogged appeals for spiritual assistance, stating that "he was tired of making so many sacrifices [for Don Rodrigo and his wife, Constanza] and wasting his message on them without having been given any money in return."[41] This and other testimonies of the governor's participation in such ritual acts suggest that Guaracani and other sacred objects were vital sources of spiritual devotion and political authority in the religious activities of Rupay Chagua and his followers.[42]

The trail of the cacique's battles with the ecclesiastical justice system also surfaces in records of Sarmiento's campaigns as general inspector of idolatries. A letter to Sarmiento from chief prosecutor Nicolás Rodríguez at the start of their 1659 inspection in Canta illustrates vividly the contentious interactions between Rupay Chagua and extirpation officials. Rodríguez wrote that, following the visitador's instruction to detain the governor for questioning, he proceeded to Rupay Chagua's house only to encounter a hostile witness who "with impudent words and gestures" threatened to denounce him before the *protector de los naturales* and viceroy for carrying out Sarmiento's "baseless" order of arrest. According to Rodríguez, a violent struggle ensued, but eventually a Spanish alguacil and two native deputies were able to restrain Rupay Chagua with rope. The extirpation team ushered the captive to the town jail adjoining Sarmiento's temporary residence and shackled him to the pillory, where he was ordered to remain, stripped of his belongings, for the rest of the visita.[43]

The next day, claiming to have suffered injuries from his confinement, Rupay Chagua petitioned for transfer to the archdiocesan prison in Lima, perhaps reasoning that the prospect of freedom would improve nearby the more sympathetic watch of his former Jesuit educators. Rodríguez cautioned the visitador against the move, labeling the governor a "crafty Indian" *(indio cauteloso)* who feigned his ailments only to plot escape while en route to the capital. To substantiate the cacique's duplicitous character, the prosecutor informed Sarmiento of Rupay Chagua's "commitment to the sin of idolatry" and impertinent use of the Quechua name "Apo" when filing petitions before the court. A reverential term of address in traditional Andean society, *Apo* designated the supreme creator as well as the idols of various mountain peaks in the Huamantanga region. It was, according to Rodríguez, a title unbefitting a graduate of the Jesuit school for noble lords:

> Be advised that the aforesaid Don Rodrigo signs the aforesaid petition "Don Rodrigo de Guzmán Apo Rupay Chagua," and this surname "Apo" means "Lord of All" in the native language of the Indians, and this surname "Apo" does not come from his ancestors,

rather, he gave it to himself, and he does not sign with it ordinarily, except when he writes to the Indians of his district, but not when he writes to the corregidores and other legal authorities, which indicates malice.[44]

In the prosecutor's judgment, Rupay Chagua was a Janus-faced calculator, serving his own interests by looking both ways at once. To his Spanish superiors he was "Don Rodrigo," the faithful Christian and colonial official, but to native constituents he was a divine "Lord" who claimed ancestral ties to regional deities in a false bid for local authority. Noting the cacique's guile and well-known legal acumen, Rodríguez insisted that Rupay Chagua, though "more ladino than necessary," could not be trusted to represent himself in court. Instead, he should be required to make future appeals by mediation of a Spanish defense attorney of the inspector's choosing. Sarmiento agreed to this and the governor's continued incarceration in Huamantanga, stipulating additional punishment of one hundred lashes for any further use of the traditional Quechua title.[45]

Rupay Chagua's imprisonment did not signal his defeat or soften his activist resolve. By 1665, his clash with the forces of extirpation had reached a fragile truce, as a personal letter of that year from Sarmiento to the native governor makes clear. In an about-face, the idolatry inspector reserved high praise for the cacique's renewed devotion to the Virgin Mary and assistance to the visita efforts in Canta, which had led to the destruction of more than nine hundred idols in the town of Ihuari alone. He also vowed to pray for the native lord's continued health and to help him secure the cancellation of unjust debts he had incurred with the local *corregimiento.* However, documents of the same file show that the visitador accused him soon after of religious crimes, jailing him this time in Lima's house of reclusion, yet not before the governor charged Sarmiento, now his "chief enemy," with exploiting the district's workforce through unauthorized labor and forced payments totaling one thousand pesos.[46] The governor's dealings with various groups, including the local Mercedarians, the traveling extirpators, and local native adversaries, belie the straightforward versions of strict accommodation that customarily have been used to describe the experience of the graduates of El Colegio del Príncipe.[47]

Rupay Chagua may have filed the countersuit in an attempt to neutralize the legal proceedings against him or to defend a constituency from the

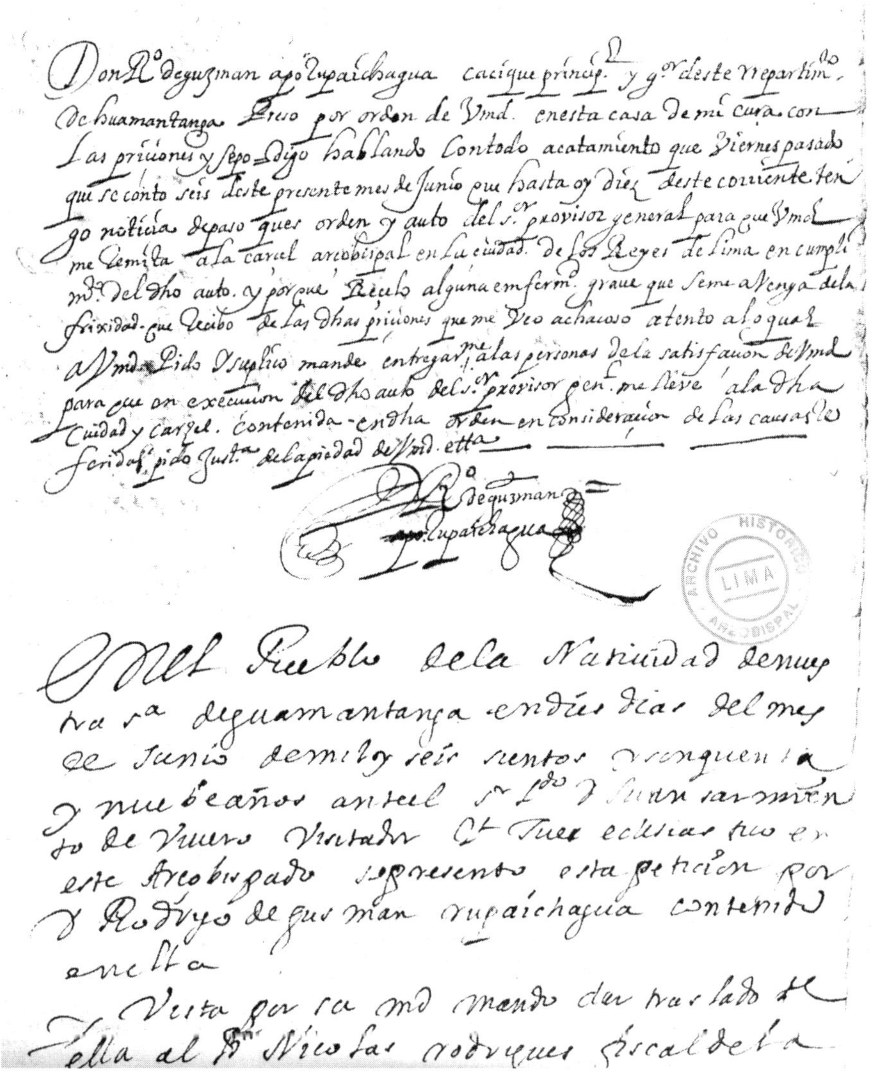

Don Rº de guzman apo rupaichagua cacique princip.l y g.or deste repartim.to
de huamantanga preso por orden de Vmd. en esta casa de mi cura con
las prisiones y sepo = digo hablando con todo acatamiento que viernes pasado
que se conto seis deste presente mes de Junio que hasta oy diez deste corriente ten
go noticia de paso que es orden y auto del s.or provisor general para que Vmd
me remita a la carcel arçobispal en la ciudad de los Reyes de Lima en cumpli
m.to del dho auto. y porque recelo alguna emferm.d graue que se me a venga de la
frixidad que recibo de las dhas prisiones que me veo achacoso atento a lo qual
a Vmd. pido y suplico mande entregar me a las personas de la satisfacion de Vmd
para que en execucion del dho auto del s.or provisor gen.l me lleve a la dha
ciudad y carcel. contenida en dha orden en consideracion de las causas re
feridas pido just.a de la piedad de Vmd. etta

Don Rº de guzman
rupaichagua

ARCHIVO HISTORICO ARZOBISPAL LIMA

En el Pueblo de la Natividad de nues
tra s.ra de guamantanga en diez dias del mes
de Junio de mil y seis sientos y cinquenta
y nueve años ante el s.r l.do d. Juan sarmien
to de Vivero visitador g.l juez eclesias.co en
este Arçobispado se presento esta peticion por
d. Rodrygo de guzman rupaichagua contenido
en ella
Vista por su md mando dar traslado d
ella al br. Nicolas rodriguez fiscal de la

FIGURE 8. Signature of Don Rodrigo de Guzmán "Apo" Rupay Chagua. Courtesy of the Archivo Arzobispal de Lima.

extirpator's abuse. Whether he sought to serve the interests of his own welfare or the native peoples' or both is not clear. It is certain, however, that in early 1669 Rupay Chagua won release from prison and brought charges of linguistic ignorance against the Mercedarian friar Torrejón.[48] While parish records show that Andean-priest relations were nothing if not ambiguous in the litigious climate of Huamantanga, the quantity of legal actions does not invalidate Rupay Chagua's case or the many others in which a complaint of substandard Quechua offered native officials a means to defend the community's professed Catholic integrity against a priest they deemed unqualified for ministry.

Doubts about Ecclesiastical Quechua

Indios ladinos of the central highlands raised questions about the Third Council's language policy. They inhabited the provinces of Chinchaysuyu, which church authorities associated with corrupt uses of Quechua. Throughout the seventeenth century, the clergy censured native church assistants of the region for incorporating lexical borrowings into their speech in violation of conciliar norms. In 1649, the Franciscan friar Diego de Molina, doctrinero of Santa María del Valle near the town of Huánuco, expressed the unease he shared with many clerics: "Erroneous concepts are so naturalized, particularly in the Chinchaysuyos, that they ignore the Cuzco terms in which Christian doctrine was translated."[49] Chinchaysuyu speakers violated the supposed purity of the ecclesiastical language and, by extension, its authority to express Christian ideas. It was there, according to the *Doctrina christiana*, that Andeans changed the letters of Quechua words and created different meanings: "some pronouncing the language more gutturally than others . . . or removing or adding or changing letters, . . . [and] failing at times to maintain proper sentence structure, instead committing solecisms."[50]

Testimony from the extirpation campaigns provides clues regarding the types of linguistic errors that concerned ecclesiastical officials. The Jesuit Arriaga argued that errors in the teaching of Christian doctrine were rampant due to reliance on untrustworthy native fiscales, who misrepresented the text of the official Quechua catechism: "They teach with many errors, alternating or changing certain words or letters, by which they create different meanings."[51] As an example of the "distortions and errors" that Andean instructors made, Arriaga cited how they taught the Apostles' Creed: "[I]n the Creed, instead of saying 'Hucllachacuininta,' which is the communion or meeting of the saints, they say 'Pucllachacuininta,' which means the deceit or trickery of the saints."[52] He contended that native catechists of the central sierra departed from the Quechua script of the *Doctrina christiana* in a willful attempt to teach heterodox ideas. In the practice of doctrina, a gap had emerged between the text of the catechism and the teachings of native fiscales.

Thierry Saignes (1999, 114) has speculated that the native fiscales of Arriaga's complaint substituted the composite Quechua word for "communion of the saints" (based on the root *huc,* the Cuzco form of the number one, as in "to unite in one"), which would have been unintelligible to native speakers, for the more comprehensible term for "pastime of the saints" (based on the root *puklla,* meaning "to play" or "to amuse"). Because the catechism's literal translations could render Christian doctrine meaningless to local audiences, native assistants put forward alternatives, even at the risk of provoking the censure of church inspectors.[53] The printed catechism was not a fixed instrument for shaping religious beliefs and practices, but varied in signification according to the expectations and interests of native communities. Though the dearth of testimony makes the local indigenous modifications of the *Doctrina christiana* impossible to determine with certainty, dimensions of native oral traditions and interpretations of Christianity inevitably came to the surface despite the corrective intentions of religious books.

If native assistants of the central highlands deviated from the language of the basic catechism, what values did they attribute to the Quechua in which it was published? Current understanding of the linguistic situation of the midcolonial Andes relies on valuable clues from the work of Quechua linguists César Itier (1992) and Gerald Taylor (2000), whose investigations have shown that the usage of southern Quechua in the central provinces was conditioned by underlying patterns of local speech. Generally speaking, they contend that language practice in the region was characterized by a double diglossia: the polarization of Spanish and standardized Quechua, on the one hand, and that of standardized Quechua and local languages (including regional forms of Quechua), on the other. For native parishioners living outside the immediate environs of Cuzco, ecclesiastical Quechua was often a second or even third language.

Guaman Poma and Pachacuti Yamqui celebrated this linguistic plurality while downplaying the authoritativeness of missionary Quechua. Guaman Poma emphasized the language diversity of the Andes and the difficulty he faced as a historian in uniting the region's diverse ethnic and oral traditions in a single account:

To make sense of these aforesaid histories I had so much work since being without writings or letters of any kind but only *khipu* (knotted cords) and accounts of many languages, bringing together the Castilian language with Inca Quechua, Aymara, Puquina, Colla, Canche, Cana, Charca, Chinchaysuyo, Andesuyo, Collasuyo, Condesuyo, all the words of the Indians.[54]

While Guaman Poma ([c. 1615] 1980, 483, 624, 1089) mentioned in his work the languages widely used for evangelization—"la lengua ynga," "la lengua del Cuzco," "quichiua," "chinchaysuyo," and "aymara"—he did not draw hierarchical distinctions between them and regional languages. He resisted the category "lengua general" (a term that for him designated not a language, but Pizarro's interpreter Felipillo) and noted its limited application in an Andean setting marked by linguistic pluralism (45). The fact that he referred to "la lengua ynga" (presumably synonymous with "la lengua del Cuzco"), "quichiua," and "chinchaysuyo" as distinct idioms points to the complex internal diversity of the Quechua linguistic family and casts doubt on the claims of Garcilaso and others that Cuzco speech predominated in the Andes under Inca rule.

Though Pachacuti Yamqui ([c. 1613] 1993, 183, 198) employed "lengua general" twice as a linguistic descriptor, he also accentuated the linguistic mixture that defined the Andean world since ancient times. He explained that Andean peoples identified themselves by their *paqariku* (the geographical origin of their ancestors, to where they would return after death), the first Inca having granted each ethnic group distinct languages and dress corresponding to their place of origin: "[Manco Capac] mandated that the vestments and clothing of each people be different, likewise their speech, so that they be known, for in that time it was not possible to recognize the Indians and to know to which nation and people they belonged."[55] Linguistic variation—"la lengua de aquella tierra," "la lengua de cssa provincia," "Mayta Capac Ynga [les inventó] los mas retóricos lenguajes"—was a central motif in Pachacuti Yamqui's history ([c. 1613] 1993, 193, 211). His attention to linguistic differentiation contested the ecclesiastical notion that the Incas aimed to unify native subjects politically through a shared language.

Parish inspection records of the Lima archdiocese show that in the mid–seventeenth century the reach of standardized Quechua in central mountain areas was still partial. Andean witnesses testified that the Quechua of their priests did not match the form spoken in native parishes. Though accredited to evangelize in the normative lengua general, missionary priests could not readily communicate with the Quechua-speaking peoples of the region. Two compelling testimonies from the central sierra, which present views of language practice different from those of Governor Rupay Chagua's, provide a sharper portrait of this landscape. Garcilaso and Guaman Poma were not the only voices of protest against the linguistic shortcomings of priests. Inspection reports also reveal that there was nothing transparent about the language that priests and native assistants used to communicate Christian doctrine.

In 1656, during an idolatry prosecution in the town of San Pedro de Acas, in the province of Cajatambo, the native parish official Andrés Chaupis Yauri offered ecclesiastical interrogators the following declaration, previously identified by César Itier, which reveals that the local villagers used two types of Quechua simultaneously:

> In the aforesaid town [the witness] heard night-time proclamations to abstain from salt and *ají* pepper before the feast of San Juan and Corpus, and though the criers did not speak his general language of the Inca, but used their maternal language instead, the Indian men and women told this witness in the general language of the Inca that the elders and leaders of the kin groups said to abstain from salt and pepper, and that it was time to pray to their ancestors.[56]

It appears that the native residents of San Pedro de Acas were familiar enough with the standardized Quechua spoken by Chaupis Yauri to inform him of the nocturnal proclamations of local religious specialists. However, the parish assistant did not understand the maternal Quechua of his informants. The speech he used to carry out his religious tasks approximated the southern form instituted for evangelization.

Two years earlier, in 1654, the ethnic lords of Chavín de Pariarca, in the district of Huánuco, filed legal charges against the priest Francisco de Guevara, citing among his many pastoral failings the problem of linguistic incompetence. To support their complaint of spiritual neglect, the litigants called the parish cantor Juan Malqui to testify before the ecclesiastical judge. According to Malqui, Guevara could not confess the parishioners even though he knew ecclesiastical Quechua:

The aforesaid priest does not know the general language [of the village] well, and for this reason many Indians do not receive confession. Since he does not know the language, he cannot hear confessions properly, and the Indians do not have anyone else to confess them. The priest does not know this language, the general language of the newly converted Indians, but he knows the other general language of the Inca quite well, and here one understands only the language of the newly converted Indians.[57]

Malqui identified two forms of language coexisting in Chavín de Pariarca: on the one hand "la lengua general" (the language of the community) and on the other "la lengua general del ynga" (the language known to the parish priest). It was common for missionary clergy such as Guevara, though trained for pastoral ministry in the ecclesiastical language, to encounter difficulties in the field, even in townships where Quechua was the maternal tongue. One year earlier, the church inspector Pablo de Paredes had described Guevara as a "gran lenguaraz" (great linguist) who preached with skill in the language of his parishioners.[58] Despite his apparent command of Cuzco-based Quechua, which earned the visitador's praise, native parishioners stated that Guevara could not carry out his basic sacramental duties.[59]

Malqui's statement did not result in reprimands or sanctions for his priest, but it offers unique insight into what Andean officials of the central provinces understood the category "lengua general" to mean. Malqui departed from the Third Council's definition of lengua general, which identified the language of Cuzco as the one and only lingua franca disseminated since Inca times, and instead granted the Quechua of his pueblo the favored status of general language. His classification of the linguistic variant of Huánuco as lengua general may reflect knowledge of what the administrative language of Tawantinsuyu actually was, thereby raising new questions regarding the true language of Inca administration. Equally significant, Malqui's appropriation of the term conferred status to a linguistic form of the central region that church authorities had censured for its corrupt sonority and lexicon: the language of Chinchaysuyu. In this sense, the codified language of the clergy made little impression upon native parishioners living far from the former Inca capital. Central Quechua was, for them, the language of prestige.

The codification of Quechua for purposes of evangelization produced a degree of linguistic homogenization. Quechua devotional literature published after the provincial council reflected the new orthographic and lexical norms (Cerrón-Palomino 1992, 211, 218), as did Quechua writing produced outside the ecclesiastical establishment, such as the 1616 correspondence of the Andean ethnic lord of Cotahuasi and the anonymous manuscript of Huarochirí (Itier 1991, 70; Taylor [1987] 1999, xv).[60] Idolatry trial documentation shows that missionary activity brought southern Peruvian Quechua to central mountain regions and generated native speech practices with features of the Cuzco dialect (Itier 1992, 1011–12). Beyond religious communication, the church-sponsored southern variant became a medium for commercial interaction between ethnic lords and Spaniards in northern and southern provinces (Peña Montenegro [1668] 1985, 464; Cerrón-Palomino 2003, 146 n. 14).

However, native intermediaries testified to Quechua-language practices that clashed with missionary norms. Andean church officials questioned ecclesiastical definitions of native linguistic activity and the authoritativeness of the "lengua general del ynga," which was for them a term imposed from without upon the heterogeneous linguistic landscape of the Andes. Instead, they affirmed the values of linguistic diversity that defined Tawantinsuyu and exposed the Church's imperfect control over the models of communication it sought to introduce. According to native assistants, the region's multiple languages manifested—far from linguistic corruption—an ancient history of linguistic pluralism that continued to prosper in colonial times.

The Chinchaysuyu Alternative

Despite the linguistic situation in the central highlands, Lima church authorities aimed to impose the Quechua of Cuzco in all aspects of missionary activity: in the classroom, from the pulpit, and through the printing press. After the publications of the Third Council (1584, 1585), the anonymous lexicographer (1586), and Diego González Holguín (1607, 1608), the missionary linguists Diego de Torres Rubio (1619), Juan Pérez Bocanegra (1631), Juan Roxo Mexía y Ocón (1648), Francisco de Ávila (1648), and Fernando de Avendaño (1649) authored bilingual pastoral complements. The second wave of catechetical literature not only adhered to, but also sought to improve upon the lexical and orthographic recommendations of the Third Council (Cerrón-Palomino 1987, 88–89; 1992, 221–23). Ecclesiastical synods also moved to fortify the southern variant. In 1613 and 1636, respectively, Archbishops Lobo Guerrero and Arias de Ugarte ordered priests of the Lima archdiocese to administer sacraments only in ecclesiastical Quechua.[61]

Francisco de Ávila was a leading champion of the language of Cuzco. Born and raised in the former Inca capital and educated in Quechua at Lima's University of San Marcos, Ávila possessed a native command of the southern dialect. At the close of his missionary career, Ávila authored *Tratado de los evangelios* (1648), a Spanish-Quechua sermonario based on the liturgical calendar, which he intended for wide use in Indian parishes. Ávila (1648, 80, 96) stated that, aside from minor orthographic modifications, the sermonic texts represented the "proper" speech of Cuzco and that the further dissemination of books composed in official missionary Quechua would eradicate regional dialects and create linguistic order and orthodoxy throughout the archdiocese. But even Ávila, who had considerable missionary experience in Huarochirí, recognized the practical difficulties of such a proposal in the central highlands: "I have seen in many areas very good linguists (and I am one of them) who cannot identify the errors of their parishioners or understand the words they use."[62]

Regional diocesan authorities also found that southern Quechua alone was not sufficient. The Cuzco synod of 1591 ordered missionary priests of the diocese to know both Quechua and the maternal language of their parishioners.[63] In 1599, the royal audiencia gave the Jesuits of Cuzco authority to examine candidates for parish appointments in Quechua, Aymara, and Puquina.[64] In Arequipa, then-bishop Pedro de Villagómez commissioned books of religious instruction in Puquina.[65] The bishops of Quito ordered the production of catechisms in six regional languages.[66] Luis Jerónimo de Oré authored the *Rituale seu Manuale Peruanum* (1607), which included catechisms in Puquina, Mochica (or Yunga), and Guaraní, and a few decades later Fernando de la Carrera composed a grammar of the Yunga language (1644) for priests of the Trujillo diocese.[67]

The testimony of native leaders of Quechua-speaking areas stirred tensions between Third Council policies and new models of evangelization that developed in the seventeenth century. Andean church officials alerted ecclesiastical inspectors to the fact that the native parishioners could not understand the language of the basic catechism. Their declarations show that the artificiality of standardized Quechua limited its practicality, especially in the central provinces. Acknowledging the gap between the ecclesiastical language and the speech of local communities, a group of clerics, many of them Peruvian born and native speakers of Quechua, began to question the policies of the metropolitan see. Following the attitude of Fray Diego de Molina, who questioned the effectiveness of Cuzco speech in the Lima archdiocese, Creole linguists—such as the native *huanuqueño* and distinguished chair of Quechua at the University of San Marcos, Alonso de Huerta; the parish priest of Huancabamba in the province of Tarma, Juan de Castromonte, also from Huánuco; and the seasoned preacher and extirpator of idolatries, Fernando de Avendaño, among others—vindicated the central Quechua long discredited by the church hierarchy and urged linguistic reforms toward creating a new standard that might integrate the dialectical diversity of the sierra (Torero 1995, 17–19).

Alan Durston (2002, 2007) has documented the varying degrees of central lexicon and morphology in the Quechua writings of these authors, focusing primarily on Castromonte's unpublished "Ritual Romano en la lengua general Quichua" (c. 1650), a pastoral guide for administering the sacraments in the language of the central sierra.[68] In the absence of a lexicon or grammar of the Chinchaysuyu language, the reformist texts adhered mainly to the terminology and syntax of the Third Council variant, but incorporated new vocabulary and orthographical changes to create a southern-central amalgam more attuned to the speech of their target audience. As chief linguist at San Marcos, Huerta published *Arte de la lengua quechua general* (1616), which included a lesson in basic Chinchaysuyu to compensate for the lack of teaching materials in the central dialect.[69] Most striking is Durston's discovery of certificates in Quechua proficiency that reflect the grammarian's broad-minded interpretation of the conciliar language requirement. In 1616, for example, Huerta approved three priests for Andean ministry, not according to the candidates' knowledge of the Cuzco standard, but for having demonstrated, as in the case of candidate Luis Mejía de Estela, the "custom and practice of speaking with the Chinchaysuyu Indians."[70] Similar backing for central Quechua appeared in works published outside the university. In the prologue of his Spanish-Quechua *Sermones de los misterios de nuestra santa fe católica* (1649), Avendaño summed up the position of Huerta and others of this Quechua-speaking clerical faction: "It is my position . . . that in this archbishopric, preaching should be done principally in what the people speak, the Chinchaysuyu language. This is the most genuine and up-to-date translation, not the [language of Cuzco] that the learned have introduced with the result that the people do not understand them."[71]

Such views confirmed the testimonies of indigenous officials, in opposition to the statements of the "learned" lawmakers of the viceregal capital. In similar fashion, the heated debate over the rights of European descendants to occupy benefices, prelacies, and other dignitarial offices of the Church hinged upon the divisive issue of language practice in the Lima archdiocese. According to Bernard Lavallé (1993, 48–50, 65), the Andean parish was a principal site of Spanish-Creole conflict, key factors of this discord being the affinity of Quechua-speaking Creoles with the indigenous peoples and the discrimination that Peruvian-born clerics experienced from Spanish *peninsulares,* who often blocked their appointments to diocesan posts despite notable linguistic expertise.

Statements of Creole letrados of Lima's secular government administration add weight to Lavallé's contention. Throughout the seventeenth century, lawyers of the royal audiencia and *chancillería*—Juan Ortiz de Cervantes (1620), Gutierre Velázquez de Ovando y Zárate (c. 1658), Diego de León Pinelo (1661), and Pedro de Bolívar y de la Redonda (1667), to name a few—directed memoriales to the Spanish Crown that affirmed the superiority of Quechua-speaking priests for Andean ministry. In 1620, as *procurador general* of Peru at the court of Philip III, the Lima native Ortiz de Cervantes argued in favor of Creole parish appointments, attributing the survival of native idolatries in his home district to the problem of linguistic ignorance:

No one can compete with [the American-born clergy] because the ones [native to the Lima region] know the languages and customs of the Indians, their rites, and their competence and leadership, and therefore cannot be misled. The ancient idolatries, which had been concealed from the bishops and priests in the province of Lima, have now been discovered by the ecclesiastics who were born there and the visitadores who go there regularly to preach.[72]

The letrado's call for an improved clergy invoked the dangers of traditional native religiosity, but for reasons different from those the Third Council articulated. A stunning implication of Ortiz de Cervantes's argument was that now, at the start of the metropolitan see's anti-idolatry crusade, the breakdown of evangelization could be traced to the Spanish priests' lack of schooling in the language and customs of the central highlands.[73] To rephrase this argument in linguistic terms, the Chinchaysuyu alternative did not fuel the practice of ancient superstitions but instead offered a potential solution to the threats they posed.

Advocacy of central Quechua, whether explicit or implicit, did not lead to the creation of a solely Chinchaysuyu catechism or raise the variant's status to the category of lingua franca, as the publication history of contemporary native-language literature evidences. Books of religious instruction in Cuzco-based Quechua proliferated at the start of Villagómez's tenure as the archbishop of Lima (1641–1671), and the trilingual catechisms of the Third Council remained the authorized books of indoctrination in the Peruvian viceroyalty through the eighteenth century.[74] However, the emergence of church and viceregal authorities whose reformist ideas on language dovetailed with the testimonies of native officials tempers a lasting image of colonial religious history: one of European priests forever joined in hostile conflict with headstrong native communities (see Mills 1997, 3). Spanish and indigenous views on language were neither harmonious nor absolute, but the exchange among clergymen, secular authorities, and native assistants signals a mutual dependency that furthered the reevaluation of existing language policies. Indigenous witness statements confirm the profound resonance of specific clerical and royal concerns about the conduct of missionary activity and help to expose the fissure within the church establishment on the central issue of language practice in the central highland region.

Language in Native Lawsuits

Doctrinal teaching fell short in the view of native parishioners because of the clergy's incompetence in the regional forms of Quechua. Consider, for example, Guaman Poma's mocking diatribes against the ruinous state of native-language religious instruction. In one satirical rendering of a priest's Quechua homily, the Andean chronicler alleged: "He knows only four words: 'Bring the horse! Don't eat! Go see the priest! Where are the single women? Where are the girls? Bring them to church!' and nothing more."[75] His portrait communicates that the problem of linguistic deficiency was tied into a much broader critique of ministerial comportment that ranged from excessive demands of indigenous goods and labor to the sexual debasement of female villagers. But on the topic of language, indios ladinos presented a resolute condemnation of the missionary rank and file: parish priests without proper Quechua training used their authority for personal gain.

Royal and church laws mandating proselytization in Quechua provided the juridical foundation of the complaint that Rupay Chagua filed against the friar of Huamantanga. In petitioning to have Fray Francisco Torrejón removed from the parish, the native leader cited the clergyman's failure to preach on Sundays and religious feasts, his ignorance of the "lengua gen.l del ynga," and his lacking the title ("colasion") and royal license ("presentasion R.l"), the credentials bestowed upon the graduates in Quechua at San Marcos, that were required for parish appointment. Language ability was, in fact, a decisive factor in the clergy's pursuit and maintenance of a native benefice. Aspiring candidates who entered *oposiciones* (competitive examinations) for parish posts began their written appeals to the archbishop by certifying their Quechua studies and proven native-language skills.[76] Like other plaintiffs, Rupay Chagua understood the weight that the charge of linguistic insufficiency carried: visitadores could suspend doctrineros who failed to present authorizing papers and demonstrate their knowledge of Quechua (Solórzano Pereira 1648, 630; Torres 1970, 51).[77]

Yet why would Rupay Chagua, an ethnic lord without claim to Inca ancestry, uphold the laws supporting a southern form of the language that had limited application in the central province of Canta? In effect, the native governor denounced Torrejón for his ignorance of a Quechua variant that was foreign to the parishioners. The answer to this question begins with an acknowledgment of the rules according to which ideas about language practice could be debated and exchanged. Formulating persuasive arguments to church authorities required petitioners to adopt the conventions and ideologies of normative legal discourse, which meant endorsing the supposed authority of the Cuzco Quechua demanded of priests.

Rupay Chagua was not the only Andean litigant to denounce clergy on what appear to be arbitrary linguistic grounds. In 1617, the cacique principal of Santo Domingo de Tauca, Hernando de la Cruz, brought charges against his priest for not knowing the "lengua general del ynga."[78] Similar examples occurred throughout the seventeenth century, including a second case in Huamantanga, where in 1674 the Andean lord Don Miguel Menacho attempted to discredit the Mercedarian friar Luis de Aguilar y Alarcón in the same terms that Rupay Chagua had previously accused Francisco

Torrejón: "[H]e claims to be the priest of the parish without understanding the general language of the Inca or having a title, canonical appointment, or royal license."[79] In the 1630s and 1640s, Indians of the highly ladino coastal villages of Ica and Cañete denounced their priests for not knowing the "lengua general," applying what was by all accounts an impractical law so as to remove two unpopular clergymen.[80] Evidence also points to doctrineros of the coast who tried to sidestep the Quechua-language requirement. In 1634, the friar Juan de Merlo of the parish of Lurin faced charges of hiring a fellow Dominican to take his place for the duration of a church inspection: "[B]ecause [the defendant] was ignorant in the language, he fraudulently presented to [the inspection team] another friar who knew [the language], and after [the inspection team] left, [the defendant] stayed in the parish."[81]

Aware that magistrates looked unfavorably upon petitions that questioned the fitness of the juridical order, native plaintiffs vindicated the "lengua general del ynga" in order to show familiarity with royal and church law and, by extension, their adherence to the goals of evangelization. Surely Rupay Chagua was mindful of how the linguistic category endorsed the value of Quechua while communicating biases against the vernacular languages of his home terrain. The governor's presumed awareness of the conventionality and arbitrariness of the Spanish legal code was beside the point; the institutional conditions of the ecclesiastical tribunal regulated proper knowledge and deliberation about the conduct of evangelization. In 1655, the visitador Diego de Sarzosa praised Luis Mejía de Estela of Santa Olaya for his knowledge of the "general language of the Inca," perhaps unaware, or unwilling to validate in writing, that the priest spoke a fluent Chinchaysuyu Quechua for which Alonso de Huerta had commended him thirty years before.[82] Rather than question the prevailing linguistic ideologies, Spaniards and Andeans utilized them in order to bolster the juridical authority of their claims. Such expressed support of language policy formed an integral part of their self-representation as law-abiding, Christian subjects.

Rupay Chagua's petition was not a blanket condemnation of the Mercedarians in Huamantanga or of pastoral methods as a whole. His views on the religious order were far from monolithic, as indicated by his praise to Archbishop Villagómez of Torrejón's predecessor, Fray Jacinto de Esquivel, who exhibited "virtue and competence in the language, devoting himself to preaching to the Indians and teaching them Christian doctrine with great results" before his sudden transfer to the parish of San Buenaventura.[83] After Rupay Chagua's plea for a capable replacement, Torrejón received orders from Villagómez to appear without delay in Lima for examination in Quechua or risk formal censure, though he was later granted fifteen days to present his authorizing papers. The friar claimed to know the general language but could produce only a provisional license to minister in Huamantanga that the visitador Juan de Blanco had given to him five months earlier. According to reports, upon discovering the parish without a priest in residence, the church inspector had summoned Torrejón from neighboring San Juan de Lampián and appointed him *cura interino* without formal assessment in the language.[84] Indians occasionally won the reassignment of clergy and compensation for lost goods and revenue, and it is possible that without the proper credentials, Torrejón was suspended from the parish.

At the very least, the judicial process vindicated Rupay Chagua's role as monitor of church policy and provided him a means of communication with the Lima see and royal audiencia.[85] The language question served as a mechanism by which he and other native litigants applied their training in law and literacy to insert themselves in church affairs. Their focus on the pedagogical priority of improved dialogue between missionary clergy and native parishioners also implied an alternative to repressive approaches to indoctrination. Such concern for the performance of verbal communication in the conduct of evangelization gives meaning to Antonio Cornejo Polar's observation of the "recurrent and almost obsessive evocations of orality" at the sites of colonial misapprehension in the chronicles of Guaman Poma and Garcilaso (1994, 42). Cornejo Polar has contended that focus on the linguistic problems that obscured Spanish-Andean interactions was a prominent characteristic in the writings of lettered Andeans who traversed the cultural divide.[86]

Rupay Chagua's petition represents the ambiguous positions that literate Andeans adopted as mediators of colonial law and shows that colonialist ideas about native languages had legal applications and corollaries that missionary theorists did not expect. When considered within a broader purview of indigenous voices, the cacique's appeal is by no means a neutral record of the linguistic situation in Huamantanga. Rather, it contains multiple layers of interpretation that point toward a more critical awareness of the juridical conventions employed in church tribunals and the conflictive relationships that shaped the Indians' literary activity. Above all, the native governor's assimilation of imperial linguistic models reveals the understanding he shared with indios ladinos in general of the fundamental paradox of their confrontation with the law: the most consequential response to Spanish authority came not from championing the incorruptibility of Andean traditions in a postconquest world, but from learning and putting into force the very laws that sought their erasure.

Chapter 3

Mediating with Cords

Tangled Confessions

Traditional scholarship has understandably viewed written words as instruments of colonialism that supplanted native American ways of record keeping and communication. Accounts of the Europeans' destruction of native holy objects and media reveal the indisputable role of books in the Spanish colonization of indigenous memory and symbolizing practices.[1] The Archive, in this sense, notably undermined native sources of expression and forced Indians to play by new rules. But colonial-era writings that testify to the resiliency of native technologies pose new questions about the process by which this colonization took place and the true impact of alphabetic literacy in local native communities. In fact, archival documents show that native intermediaries drew on various media traditions when negotiating between the colonizers and indigenous peoples. One such tradition were Andean *khipus:* the knotted cords that the Inca used for accounting and historical record keeping, which indigenous assistants employed in colonial times to teach Christian doctrine and monitor sacred ritual. Native church personnel kept records of parish activities on paper as well as cords, yet little is known about these "indigenous archives" or how they functioned in Andean social contexts.[2]

The khipu is one of the most enigmatic historical objects of pre-Columbian origin. Early Spanish chroniclers of South America marveled at the complex variety of information that the Incas stored on knotted cords and the reliability of string devices for carrying out the business of imperial administration. But how the Incas were able to govern the vast empire of Tawantinsuyu without a European-style system of writing or accounting is a question that confounded Spanish observers of the colonial period and still

FIGURE 9. Inca khipu of the Early Nasca Period.
Courtesy of the President and Fellows of Harvard College,
Peabody Museum of Archaeology and Ethnology, 32-30-30/55.

confounds students of Andean history today.[3] Since the pioneering studies of L. Leland Locke (1923) and Marcia Ascher and Robert Ascher (1981),
which first explicated the material structure and computational function
of string records, uncovering the types of information encoded in khipus
has become a quest of vital interest to ethnographically minded scholars
of Andean studies. In the past decade, historians and anthropologists have
tried to advance previous theories of Inca practices of accounting and to
determine whether the khipu contained more than statistical records. Some
research in this vein posits that string registries also may have been capable of representing discursive modes or units of speech that could be "read"
for meanings in ways similar to alphabetic writing systems (Urton 1998).[4]
Without prejudgment against such a possibility, the discussion that follows
draws from approaches that investigate the conditions and practices of colonial Andean media traditions and the khipus' capacity for recording social
action in native parish settings.[5]

A privileged source in this regard is Guaman Poma's chronicle, which
includes several drawings that illustrate the "semiotic pluralism" (Salomon 2004, 8) of Andean cultural life. The work portrays native officials of

various types who fulfilled duties in the Spanish colonial administration. Two examples, the *sayapayaq* (messenger) and the *regidor* (chief accountant), hold aloft the tools of their trade: European books and Andean khipus (Guaman Poma [c. 1615] 1980, 204, 814). It appears from these drawings that written culture did not immediately displace native forms, but was imposed gradually in a negotiated process undertaken by Spanish and Andean authorities alike. Less clear, however, are the relative meanings and power that native intermediaries assigned to these instruments of colonial rule and the diverse goals to which they were directed. What special powers did the keepers of indigenous archives hold?

A first answer to this question begins with striking testimony on khipu specialists in the parish of Andahuaylillas, in the diocese of Cuzco, taken from a bilingual Spanish-Quechua book of rites, the *Ritual formulario e institución de curas,* published in Lima in 1631. The ritual's author, the priest Juan Pérez Bocanegra, included in the work a caution to readers about the dangers of allowing parishioners to confess using strings. He explained that with these cords—or "tangles for their souls" *(enredos para sus almas)*—the parishioners of Andahuaylillas had turned confession into a collective, disorderly affair. They falsified khipu, exchanged them freely among themselves, confessed to sins they did not commit, and failed to declare others they did:

> As a result, they do not know what they are confessing or saying,
> and they confuse the confessor, in judging and absolving, and I
> have found they keep such knots for future confessions, though they
> confess shortly thereafter or another year. They also lend them out
> to those who need to repeat their confession, . . . [thus] entangling
> themselves, with these khipus and memory aids, in countless errors.[6]

What concerned him, aside from the breakdown in communication that khipus caused between confessors and penitents, was the fact that cord keeping was practiced outside the clergy's surveillance, allowing the specialists who prepared the registries with which Andean neophytes confessed to advance teachings incompatible with Catholic orthodoxy.

Pérez Bocanegra focused his criticisms on the suspect credibility of khipus and those who fashioned them, but he did not mention the Church's position on the role of knotted strings in parish life, the signifying properties

FIGURE 10. The Regidor/Surquyuq, or Chief Accountant.
Guaman Poma, *El primer nueva corónica y buen gobierno*, 814.
Courtesy of the Royal Library, Copenhagen, Denmark.

that made them amenable or hostile to clerical efforts, or the social con-texts that gave shape to the contentious Andean-priest interactions his work described. In their respective investigations of the *Ritual formulario,* Juan Carlos Estenssoro Fuchs (2003, 223–27) and Regina Harrison (2002) have identified the cloud of heterodoxy that enveloped khipus and their handlers at the time of the book's publication, which helps to explain the priest's hos-tile reaction to their use in Catholic ritual (see also Durston 2007, 284–85, 287). However, an added source for assessing the clergy's attitudes toward khipus is the ecclesiastical court proceedings in which khipu registries served another record-keeping role: the accounting of crimes. In the colo-nial context, cord records acquired confessional as well as legal applications, and their function in these roles met, initially, with approval of Spanish authorities. To appreciate the full context of Pérez Bocanegra's remarks, then, an assessment of the close association between the two uses is needed.

Spanish Assessments of Cord Records

In contrast to Pérez Bocanegra's criticism, early European accounts gener-ally described khipus favorably, as tools that might assist in making Catho-lic teachings meaningful from an indigenous cultural perspective. Acosta asked himself how native Andean peoples, who had no knowledge of writ-ing until the arrival of the Spanish, had managed to preserve their ancient traditions faithfully without the aid of alphabetic script. He claimed that the Andeans' system of registering history matched the effectiveness of writ-ten words: "For all that books can tell us about histories, laws, ceremonies, and administrative accounts, khipus compensate so well that it provokes wonder."[7] This method of recollection, he continued, was exemplified in the *khipukamayuq,* the native American precursor of the Spanish Empire's *escribano público* (public scribe), who shared his official record with the Inca and to whom all faith in state affairs was given. They were, for many of Acosta's contemporaries, the indispensable keepers of regional accounts as well as the Inca's imperial "archive," maintaining for posterity vital infor-mation on matters ranging from population figures and livestock records to local sacred laws and the royal chronicles of war and peace (Guaman Poma [c. 1615] 1980, 361; Murúa [1590] 2004, 77v).

Peru's sixteenth century, especially the years of Viceroy Toledo's gov-ernment (1569–1581), witnessed Spanish efforts to transfer into writing the vast amounts of historical and statistical data from pre-Hispanic times that khipukamayuqs held on cords (Urton 2002, 6–10). The cord keepers of this period occupied a central place in the Crown's general inspections, which gathered information about the institutional frameworks, powers of dominion, and tribute-making capabilities of native groups so as to govern them more effectively. Early chroniclers also narrated Andean sacred histories and the political and cultural achievements of Inca rulers with the help of khipukamayuq informants. While the reports of these native archivists were shaped by the objectives of the Europeans who transcribed them, the use of khipu sources was the means by which European writers certified their historical accounts (Duviols 1979, 589).

But colonial authorities took more than an antiquarian interest in the Andeans' knotted cord records and the stories their handlers told. With regard to evangelization, missionary priests tried to identify benign aspects of native custom that could assist in making doctrine comprehensible to indigenous neophytes. Descendants of Inca rulers, ethnic authorities of all ranks *(apus*, curacas, *kamachikuqs)*, provincial functionaries *(mitmaqs)*, and successors of the Inca's retainers (yanacunas) played central roles in evangelization, and Spanish authorities encouraged the use of khipus among them. In 1567, the jurist Matienzo put forth a broad plan for imposing Christian order upon the indigenous peoples who had been relocated into parish settlements. As part of his founding vision, he urged the Crown to bring back the *t'uqrikyuq*, or provincial overseer of pre-Hispanic times, and to adapt the office to the needs of Spanish colonial rule. To reinforce ecclesiastical and secular authority in each district, this intermediary would judge legal disputes between parishioners, maintain public order, punish absenteeism from Mass and catechesis, and keep count of the taxable subjects and baptized Christians by means of written records or khipus in the event he did not know how to read and write (Matienzo [1567] 1967, 51–56). Guaman Poma ([c. 1615] 1980, 806) identified this figure with the *alcalde mayor* of the viceregal era, though it remains unknown whether indigenous subjects actually served in the colonial post of t'uqrikyuq that he and Matienzo envisioned. The Andean chronicler also likened other native officers of Spanish administration to the officials of Inca times. Among them were the regidor/*surquyuq* (chief accountant), the *mayordomo/suyuyuq* (administrator of community property), and the *correón/chaski* (royal messenger); the drawing of the accountant given earlier shows that this officer was familiar with books as well as with knotted cords (814, 820, 825).

Toledo's thorough overhaul of Spanish colonial administration upheld the central place of khipu specialists that Matienzo had recommended for the workings of royal and church governance. The primary vehicle for carrying out Toledo's reform of Andean society was the establishment of Iberian-style municipal councils, or *cabildos de indios,* in the seats of each administrative district. In 1575, he established a group of local officials— among them, the alcalde, the regidor, and the notary-khipukamayuq—to exercise civil authority over the community and monitor religious activities, including the parishioners' absences from Mass and the comings and goings of priests (Levillier 1921–1925, 8:305–12; Burns 2005a, 10).[8] Six years later, Toledo's successor, Martín Enríquez de Almanza, made knowledge of Spanish letters and khipu a requirement for alcaldes mayores throughout the viceroyalty, charging them with the maintenance of census figures for native settlements, inventories of local goods and assets, and annual tributary contributions of native communities to royal and church agents (Espinoza Soriano 1960, 223). Viceregal provisions thus authorized khipu accounting practices for the fiscal and religious administration of native communities.

Khipus for Doctrina

Because the Church lacked sufficient numbers of ordained personnel, above all during the first period of evangelization, the lion's share of day-to-day parish administration and community policing fell to native authorities, including those educated in khipu accounting. Fray Diego de Porres's instruction for parish governance, likely authored at least one decade following the deliberations of the First Council, offers a unique look at how cord records became a vital resource of native church assistants once directed to the goals of ecclesiastical law.[9] With this directive, the future provincial of the Mercedarian order intended to offer a guide for implementing the decrees of the First Council of Lima concerning religious instruction and parish administration. First priority of newly appointed priests, he declared, was to announce the synod's laws before the congregated village and have the local cacique record them in writing and khipu, "so that the Indians not feign ignorance of their spiritual obligations."[10] These registries were also to maintain crucial statistics required by visitas, such as the community's assets and tributary contributions, absences for Mass or catechism, baptismal and other sacramental records, and celebration of liturgical feasts.[11] Martín de Murúa's codex of 1590 confirms that khipus were used in this way, much like the strings that recorded the religious laws and statutes of the Inca before the Spanish conquest. Murúa recalled encountering an ethnic lord in the parish of Capachica who at the behest of a Mercedarian friar had retained on his cords the rules of the Church and the saints' days of the holy calendar, understanding them so effectively "as if by paper and ink."[12] Murúa's chronicle endorsed a dual recordation method involving khipus and written documents for ordering Andean spiritual life.

In a departure from Inca practices, the missionary clergy saw the potential value of cords for teaching the catechism. The first known advocate of this approach, Porres instructed priests to have parishioners make khipus for learning the basic prayers (Our Father, Hail Mary, Apostles' Creed, and Salve Regina) and the Ten Commandments, the presumption being that khipus could store meanings of religious concepts and assist in the oral recitation of prayers:

> Give them the four prayers and commandments they are obliged to know by khipu, just as they pray them with their pauses and syllables, and give orders that no Indian old or young be without the said khipu in order to know the said prayers and they should carry it at all times wherever they go, even when traveling outside their district, so that they have Christian rule and give account of the said prayers and the meaning of each whenever asked.[13]

By fostering the khipu as a tool of catechesis, missionaries aimed to popularize a native cultural practice that had previously been of elite domain. Jesuit testimonies of the period following the First and Second Councils document this colonial development. In 1578, a Jesuit priest of the doctrina of Juli reported that knotted cords helped native villagers commit their religious lessons to memory and inspired them to embrace Christian doctrine with fervor: "Many men and women and boys and girls carry their khipus throughout the day, like students repeating their lesson, [even though] when we first arrived here the Spaniards told us that the only way to bring the

Indians to catechism was by force."[14] Many clergy of the period expressed favorable views of this recordation technique.

Missionary accounts of the Andean catechisms are opaque, but they suggest where priests thought string objects coincided with European ideas of legibility. In describing the ways in which the knotted cords should be used for teaching doctrine, Porres suggested they could store meanings of religious concepts and assist in the oral recitation of prayers by indicating pauses and the syllables of words. As his and Murúa's testimonies show, missionary writers drew analogies between alphabetic writing and string registries, especially when relating indigenous performances of historical narration and catechesis. It is often held that the Andeans' initial rejection of books—Atahualpa's alleged dismissal of the "talking Bible" at Cajamarca being the most called upon instance—revealed the strangeness of European written culture from a native perspective.[15] Whatever the historical accuracy of the colonial remembrances of that event might be, khipus do not appear to represent for the Spanish commentators of the postconquest era an irreconcilable division that separated the two sides.

"Writing," in this context, follows the Aristotelian definition of a graphic device for representing phonological elements, which has endured in modern times, most famously in the work of Ferdinand de Saussure (Olsen 1994, 65–66; Salomon 2004, 25). In 1492, the Spanish grammarian Antonio de Nebrija ([1492] 1992) penned his influential argument of the superiority of this type of writing, or alphabetic script, as an instrument for exercising imperial power and controlling oral expression. Given the acclaim of the idea in early modern times, missionary clergy may have steered khipu technology in the direction of a code for transcribing spoken language since evidence of the Andeans' religious conversion depended on the word-for-word recitation of the catechism. Unfortunately, colonial sources do not provide sufficient detail to understand the signifying principles that may have linked, in theory, the mnemonic units of cords to Castilian speech or the more widely used Quechua.

Did khipus record sounds or function in other ways akin to phonetic script, as Porres's instruction seems to imply? Could the woven knots and colors stand for phonemes and morphemes, which many Spaniards perceived, or were they nonverbal signs that the cord keepers rendered into spoken words? Acosta ([1590] 2002, 386) was clear that the groupings of threads denoted "countless meanings of things," in ways similar to but in no part the same as the Roman letters that combine to form "words." As Frank Salomon (2004, 30) argues on the basis of this passage, philologically grounded studies of the era such as Acosta's point to the fact that the markers on khipus did not necessarily stand for the sounds of words or their component parts; rather, they more likely indicated "semasiographs" (Sampson 1985, 26–45), or abstract referents unconnected to any particular spoken language that the holder of the strings verbalized. Interpretative referents combined with mnemonic cues may provide a more accurate description of their symbolizing function. While the possibility remains that some knotted cords represented speech, as Gary Urton (1998) maintains in his research on Spanish transcriptions of the Andeans' "narrative record keeping," no reliable case yet exists to confirm that khipus worked in phonetic or syntactic ways (Salomon 2004, 6, 28).

In this sense, Porres's attribution of legibility to khipu catechisms may signal for the colonial Andes what James Lockhart (1999) has termed the "double mistaken identity" of Spanish-Nahua interactions in postconquest Mexico. According to Lockhart's theory, each side of the colonial encounter grasped a particular concept or mechanism of intercultural communication in terms of its own tradition while failing to understand the other side's perception of that mechanism's use or meaning. The Indians interpreted Spanish-imposed forms and ideas as similar to their customs and beliefs, whereas the clergy viewed the Indians' adoption of the new media for catechesis as a triumph of evangelization, not recognizing the continuation of indigenous cultural concepts. Each group's capacity to understand the other's practices in familiar ways raises the possibility that European priests and Andean parishioners worked at times in isolation from one another, without viewing the functioning of knotted strings and the meanings they conveyed in ways that were mutually intelligible. Did khipus represent statistical data or religious ideas presumed to be held in common, yet encode them for each camp in different terms? Cord signs had their verbal counterparts, but the khipukamayuq's voicing of the Our Father did not prove the strings' phonological features, his understanding or acceptance of the words he prayed, or the connection of khipus to them. Further understanding of the symbolic coding of strings and how Spaniards and Andeans interpreted them can be achieved by turning to the place of cord registries in a tradition that had deep roots in both cultures: the ritual practice of penitence.

Ritual Uses of Cords

In the decades leading up to and following the Jesuit-influenced Third Council of Lima, khipus reached broad acceptance as a mnemonic aid for learning prayers and recalling sins prior to confession. Jesuit priests displayed a notable respect for cord records when documenting their use in the regions of Cuzco, Lake Titicaca, and the central highlands. Juan Sebastián de la Parra testified to early-seventeenth-century devotional practices in the parish of San Damián, in the province of Huarochirí: "All was about making khipus for confessing and learning what they didn't know about the catechism, and [with them] everyone confessed, fasted, disciplined themselves, and generally attended to the salvation of their souls."[16] In letters and published writings, Acosta commended the integrity of confessions he witnessed on tours of Jesuit missions and the effectiveness of threads to inventory sins and the rules of Christian doctrine (Acosta [1590] 2002, 386; see also Egaña 1954–1986, 2:280, 622–23). Even Murúa, for whom the Andeans' untruthfulness was a constant obsession, acknowledged that confessional khipus were a "marvelous medium" that inspired neophytes to produce a "complete and credible" account of their transgressions ([c. 1611] 2001, 362).

As Estenssoro Fuchs (2003, 206–8) has documented, the close attention that Jesuit writers paid to the Andeans' performance in confession evidences an overriding belief in the Society of Jesus that observance of the sacrament was critical to the Indians' salvation. Ritual confession and penitential discipline marked Jesuit charism in opposition to alternative missionary approaches, such as that of the Dominicans, for whom confession was indispensable only in the case of mortal sin. Guaman Poma, Murúa's one-time associate and an outspoken enthusiast of Jesuit pedagogy, held that it was the duty of native church personnel to teach penitents how to confess with cords: "Each Indian should make a khipu of his or her sins, and the Indian man and the Indian woman should be taught how one ought to confess each sin."[17] The chronicler testified that confessional khipus created a new pathway of authority for native assistants, in particular those, adept in the art of knotted-string making, who presided over local religious instruction and elucidated for neophytes the distinctions between mortal and venial sins. To demonstrate one's atonement, Guaman Poma ([c. 1615] 1980, 652) advocated the fabrication of khipus for recording the charitable offerings he believed Andean Christians should make to the crippled and infirm and the elderly and orphaned.

But the chronicler also denounced khipu practices that strayed from the methods of penitence he endorsed. For Guaman Poma, knotted cords rightfully played a central role in the Lenten rites of Andean parishes. What troubled him, however, were local *camachicos* (leaders of *ayllus,* or kin groups) working outside direct clerical supervision, who used khipus to undermine Catholic authority and spread false teachings about fasting and atonement:

> The Indians say that one should not receive ash but eat meat during
> Lent, and they enter [the parish] to discipline themselves with their
> khipus. The camachicos and those who discipline themselves say
> that one should eat meat on Holy Thursday and that one should get
> very drunk before flagellating oneself and that everyone should go to
> Mass by khipu and account. What terrible lessons they are teaching![18]

Guaman Poma's concern was not directed at a resurgence of ancient customs in Christian ritual, but rather at the actions of native officials who misconstrued the place of discipline in spiritual reconciliation and the function of khipus in achieving that end. In the hands of some Andean assistants, khipus lost their utility as a mnemonic tool for ordering proper devotion and became instead a scourge of debased spectacles of mortification.[19]

But how was doctrina and confession with khipus supposed to have taken place? The Third Council advocated the spread of literacy via written and oral channels but was hesitant about how written culture should fit in relation to the realm of the unlettered, particularly when it came to the issue of knotted cords. Estenssoro Fuchs (2003, 221) and Harrison (2002, 268) have located partial illustration of the Third Council's khipu methodologies in the *Tercero catecismo* (1585). Sermon 12, devoted to the reconciliation sacrament, proposed the language with which priests should instruct the Andean penitent on how to prepare for confession:

> First, my son, you must reflect earnestly upon your sins, and make a
> khipu of them, just as when you are *tambocamayo* (storekeeper) you
> make a khipu of what you give and what you are owed. Make thus
> a khipu of what you have done against God and your neighbor, and
> how many times, if many or few. . . . After having examined yourself

and made a khipu of your sins by way of the Ten Commandments, or as best you know, you must ask God's pardon with great sorrow for having offended Him.[20]

In ways that paralleled Andean methods of storehouse inventory, confessional khipus recorded the quantity and value of the sinner's credits and debts. The arithmetic function of knotted strings proved especially valuable for a sacramental rite whose integrity rested upon the accurate recall of transgressions and their frequency. Penitents were instructed to examine their conscience following the sequence of the Ten Commandments, maintaining the procedure for confessing neophytes outlined in printed confession manuals of the period, including the *Confessionario para los curas de indios* (1585). A decimal-based accounting system, as modern specialists have described complex khipu numerology (Locke 1923; Ascher and Ascher 1981), would thus appear to have been ideally suited for the effective recollection of God's precepts and one's violations of them.

Pérez Bocanegra's hazy description of confessional khipus confirmed they held quantitative as well as typological data: knots to tally the number of sins and colors to catalog them by kind.[21] Harrison (2002, 280–81) puts forward the theory that colored threads had iconic value for encoding different types of sins, though the size of knots or diverse weaving patterns may also have represented tokens of this sort. Colonial observers entertained similar ideas, most notably the Augustinian friar Antonio de la Calancha ([1638] 1974, 1:206–7), who maintained that the colors of knots could symbolize nonnumerical meanings such as war and death, the Inca, and geographical places (Sempat Assadourian 2002, 129–30; Salomon 2004, 17). The indexical possibilities of confessional strings has also been raised by a 1602 *carta annua* of the Jesuit provincial Rodrigo de Cabredo, which narrates the four-day confession of a blind man who had prepared for the purpose a massive khipu "out of six lengths [*varas*] of twisted cord, which had a thread that crossed through it at certain intervals as well as some signs that were made of rocks or eggs or feathers conforming to the material [*materia*] of the sin he had to confess."[22] In this interpretation, signs and referents united to communicate the nature of the infractions and perhaps the circumstances or persons involved. Khipus, more accessible to the largely illiterate Andean audiences than the printed catechism, gave the abstract concept of sin tangible meaning in the hands of new converts.

The Interface of Khipus and Books

Conciliar law stated that evangelization consistent with the official catechisms and confession manual was crucial for establishing uniform Christian belief. These books contained the religious tenets that Andeans required for salvation and the words with which they should address God for spiritual guidance. Compulsory recitation of the catechism gave priests an explicit standard by which to chart the progress of native parishioners in Catholic doctrine, but to memorize the text of the catechism was hardly an easy task for Indians, particularly in light of widespread illiteracy, not to mention the artificial, compound nature of the ecclesiastical Quechua in which it was published. In this sense, khipus played a compensatory role in helping unlettered neophytes recall points of the catechism, though one can imagine how a cord-based verbal performance guided by nonalphabetic units of meaning might have easily deviated from the script that Andean students had been ordered to follow.

A passage from the Jesuit history of 1600 signals the simultaneous use of khipus and books that developed in the confessional rites mediated by native church assistants. The order's anonymous chronicler described the enthusiasm with which parishioners of the Jesuits' southern highland missions approached the sacrament: "[T]hey hastened to the confessions with many tears and repentance and truth, bringing their memory aids they call khipus, some in thread, others in writing, and others in ledger books, as best they could, encouraging one another."[23] This rare passage documents an analogy between cord keeping and alphabetic script that operated in the parish without reference to European hierarchies and that reflected the clergy's endorsement of recording sins by native methods. Here the Quechua category "khipu" encompassed for Andean parishioners a set of recordation technologies of comparable standing, which responded to individual preferences, capabilities, and necessities. Two further details stand out: the elastic boundary separating knot registries and writing in a native society that was new to Spanish literacy and the overriding dependency that the parishioners had on either or both forms of communication to meet the challenges of Catholic ritual observance.

European writers attempted by means of analogy to trace signs of legibility in what was a nonalphabetic medium. However, the reason why the coexistence of the two forms was appealing to priests and native students was that, from a pragmatic standpoint, they functioned in ways that were not mutually interchangeable. As Salomon has argued, following Émile Benveniste's assertions on the relationship between concurrent systems of signs, "The point of having coexisting semiotic systems is that they are non-redundant" (2004, 35). In other words, khipus thrived, but not because they duplicated the functions of phonetic script, as Braille might substitute for Roman letters in adherence to a shared alphabetic principle. Rather, cord records had their own specific powers to produce variable meanings and compensate for writing's deficiencies in local Andean communities.

Presumably, knotted strings offered Quechua-speaking Andeans, untrained in alphabetic literacy, a visual and tactile mode of accounting and expression that was more easily comprehensible and adaptable to traditional signifying practices, as was the case of native Mexican penitents who used handmade drawings to communicate with their confessors (Estenssoro Fuchs 2003, 221; Pardo 2004, 106). From a clerical perspective, khipus solved many of the problems of evangelizing in a landscape marked by linguistic variation, where the spread of Castilian remained negligible and problems of communication persisted. Without discounting the idiosyncratic features of certain khipus, Urton (1998, 412; 2002, 16–17) has maintained that traditional cord accounting represented a universal system of communication that linked culturally and linguistically diverse peoples under the administrative rule of the Inca. Murúa, for one, applauded pre-Hispanic techniques of communication and perceived the advantages of strings records for disseminating Christian tenets and practices: "for throughout this kingdom there is a great multitude of towns and peoples, and they placed everything on their khipus and cords with profound order and agreement by which they understood each other with the same ease that we do in our language through writing."[24]

Church Law Reverses Course

Shortcomings in the Church's instructional methodologies came to the fore when missionary priests began to suspect that khipus did not always reinforce orthodoxy or sound communication, but instead created alternative meanings and patterns of social action in spheres independent of Spanish religious authority. The Third Council's official legislation shows that, despite the sermonario's ostensible backing of confessional string records, the bishops set out to suppress khipus due to the acclaim they had achieved at the expense of books. Citing the idolatrous cultural memory that cord records sustained, chapter 37 of the council's third session ordered them to be confiscated in dioceses throughout the viceroyalty lest their use would undermine further the goals of conversion:

> Because in place of the books, the Indians have used and continue
> to use ones like registers made of different threads, which they call
> khipus, and with them they preserve the memory of their ancient
> superstition and rites and ceremonies and perverse customs, let
> the bishops act with diligence so that all the memory aids or khipus
> that nourish their superstition be taken away completely from
> the Indians.[25]

The simultaneous advocacy of khipus, on the one hand, and call for their confiscation, on the other, suggests that there may have been disagreement among the authors of the Third Council's decrees and its pastoral complements with regard to the place of traditional Andean cult objects in the evangelization program. Viable channels for inculcating Christian devotions were desired, but for some ecclesiastics this came at the risk of perpetuating native ideas and practices antithetical to church teachings.

As the decree's language suggests, khipus and writing competed in overlapping "domains of validity," Benveniste's term for the area where a sign system imposes itself and is recognized or obeyed ([1969] 1985, 234; see Salomon 2004, 35). In this sense, the dual employment of knotted strings and books in catechesis produced a situation in which the former had begun to relativize the latter. Cord records had attained considerable power in the production of religious authority, and from an ecclesiastical point of view or that of a strict convert such as Guaman Poma, this authority was increasingly non-Catholic. European writers alleged that khipu specialists covertly directed practices of atonement that patterned orthodox ritual forms (Estenssoro Fuchs 2003, 210). The licentiate Juan Polo de Ondegardo, whose 1559 treatise on Andean idolatries was published together with the Lima synod's *confesionario,* denounced the activities of traditional Andean confessors, or *ichuris,* from whom native villagers sought absolution behind the backs of parish priests. Because of the power that these ministers had over local communities, many parishioners held that "there was just as much reason to believe their ancestors, and their khipus and memory aids, as there was to believe the elders and ancestors of the Christians, and their *qillqas* (graphic records) and writings."[26] The worrisome implication, for Polo de Ondegardo, was that native assistants acted within parish communities in the role of traditional confessors.[27] Spanish authorities attempted to delineate the boundary that separated the so-called idolatrous customs of the ichuris from the Catholic practices of native intermediaries, and denouncing cords and their keepers was one way for them to do that.

However, official directives that sought to marginalize indigenous offenders from the supposedly more compliant native populace obscure what Kenneth Mills (2007, 508–39) has identified as the widespread and continually evolving religious and cultural reformulations that characterized Andean parish life. Native parishioners exercised considerable independence from ecclesiastical authority and cultivated ritual practices and relationships with holy objects that the church hierarchy deemed suspect. It was not uncommon for baptized Andeans to "self-Christianize"—to recast the codes of conduct imposed upon them and redefine the standards of proper religious belief and custom according to their own terms and expectations. With regard to the ritual of confession, the distance that emerged between authorized Catholic teachings and local practices indicates a dynamic pastoral environment of cultural selections and substitutions, and forms of religious worship that could be at times both analogous and conflicting.

Even still, the high clergy continued to find ambiguous value in string registries long after the Third Council deliberations. Arriaga considered knotted records central to the Lima see's extirpation-of-idolatries campaigns. In his guidelines for extirpation, the Jesuit urged visitadores to have Andean parishioners prepare cords of their sins prior to confession, in keeping with sanctioned missionary practice (Arriaga [1621] 1999, 123). At the same time, he mandated that accused dogmatizers provide testimony of their activities by means of khipus because, in his view, these memory aids held the most reliable data on regional huacas and their devotions (131, 133).[28] Thus, well into the seventeenth century, khipus had an uncertain role to play in evangelization insofar as they recalled points of Christianity as well as native Andean tradition. The same cords that helped new converts examine their conscience provided church inspectors with data on forbidden cults. Idolatry inspection records for that period in the province of Cajatambo, for example, include the story of the khipukamayuq Domingo

Nuna Callam, who served as chief sorcerer of the parish of San Francisco de Mangas.[29]

The leaders of the Third Council admonished the ritual khipu practices conducted outside clerical supervision. But the autonomy of cord specialists, like those Guaman Poma condemned, who mediated penitential rites within the Church, also motivated the push for sacramental reform. Given the widespread linguistic deficiency among the clergy, native church assistants had considerable authority in local parishes as language interpreters and even celebrants of sacramental rites, as when called upon to baptize ailing infants in the absence of priests.[30] Parish priests also said Mass and heard confessions and marriage vows with the assistance of native interpreters.[31] Though the Second Council (1567) and Arequipa synod (1638) banned third parties from the confessional,[32] this rule was largely disregarded in practice, as Pérez Bocanegra's testimony makes plain. Church legislation subsequent to the ban frequently mentioned, albeit with reservations, the important service of native assistants in the confessional, particularly in the diocese of Cuzco, under whose jurisdiction Andahuaylillas fell.[33] In the diocese of Quito, the clergy was encouraged to seek the help of bilingual Indians when necessary for hearing confessions (Peña Montenegro [1668] 1985, 319–20). While the *Tercero catecismo* advocated khipu-based confessions, the work made no explicit provision for the involvement of native intermediaries in the sacramental rite. Third Council legislation stressed, however, that not all priests were suitable for confessing new converts, which suggests there existed an averse but ongoing demand for native interpreters.[34] Acosta ([1577] 1987, 2:52–59, 430–33) reluctantly acknowledged that interpreters could be recruited for the confessional, but he insisted this take place only in extreme cases in which the priest lacked sufficient language skills to understand the gravest of sins.

What preoccupied the clergy, beyond the obstacles that accompanied linguistic translation, was the interpreters' alleged treachery and the claims they made about khipus. Pérez Bocanegra's manual included questions that priests should ask when interrogating Andeans who assisted the sacrament. Did the interpreters violate the confidentiality and sanctity of the confessional by divulging to third parties what was said? Was this done to harm the penitent's reputation or his or her estate? How many people were told and how many times? (Pérez Bocanegra 1631, 340–41). A final query points to his suspicions that native intermediaries falsified the knotted cord accounts of the neophytes under their charge: "When finding khipus, on which an Indian man or woman of your acquaintance had knotted their sins in order to recall their confession, did you look at them or make up the sins they committed by manipulating the colors of the knots? Did you then divulge or tell them to someone, causing the Indian man or woman notable dishonor for having told?"[35] Such a line of questioning suggests the power these individuals had to manipulate assets, defame characters, and disrupt the already tenuous grip that priests had on local affairs. To understand how they accomplished this requires a consideration of the topic of indigenous legal activism.

Khipus in the Courtroom

In 1649, at the end of a decades-long career as extirpator in the Lima archbishopric, Fernando de Avendaño (1649, 8r) warned of the power that khipu specialists continued to have on the beliefs and actions of Andean peoples. The situation he described confirms the findings of Antonio Acosta Rodríguez (1979, 1987) and, more recently, Frank Salomon and Karen Spalding (2002), who have painted for the first colonial period a compelling picture of the formidable power base that activist cord masters created for themselves in Huarochirí to ward off Spanish colonialism's advance. At first, the precise data that khipukamayuqs maintained on the political and economic resources of local native communities made them coveted allies of invading Europeans who sought to gauge and appropriate indigenous assets and labor potential. As the accountants of seized or forfeited possessions, cord specialists also played a central role in later Andean attempts to regain lost property through the Spanish legal system, and they submitted to the courts khipu records as evidence to substantiate these claims.

A well-documented flashpoint of Spanish-Andean tensions for that region occurred in 1607 in the parish of San Damián, where the native leaders accused Francisco de Ávila of fiscally exploiting the indigenous workforce (Acosta Rodríguez 1979, 3–10; 1987, 571–75; Salomon 2004, 118–20). Don Martín Puiporosi, the ethnic lord of the nearby village of Santiago de Tuna, filed the charges on behalf of the parishioners, and to substantiate them before the visitador Baltazar de Padilla, he recruited the services of a regional khipukamayuq to corroborate the prosecution's case. Puiporosi claimed that Ávila's theft of goods and services from the local church, including foodstuffs, livestock, and the outstanding wages of tributary Indians, could be verified on the strings of the indigenous accountant's khipu registry.[36] The legal clout of Huarochirí's cord masters resurfaced in the trial's later stages, when Ávila enlisted a group of indigenous supporters, the khipukamayuq Miguel Jilca Yauri among them, to refute the prosecution's charges. As representative of an ayllu loyal to Ávila, Jilca Yauri presumably held exculpatory records of the priest's transactions, though the fact that the petition bearing his name made no specific mention of khipu data suggests that his contribution to the case was largely symbolic.[37] The identification of conflicts between rival khipukamayuqs in San Damián is nonetheless crucial, for it shows that cord keepers within native parishes did not necessarily maintain the same records for the community or speak on its behalf with one voice.

After a protracted litigation of two years, Ávila was exonerated, which prompted his renowned career on the trail of extirpation and the filing of accusations against his courtroom adversaries (Acosta Rodríguez 1979, 5–10; 1987, 593–606). But despite the plaintiffs' legal defeat, Andean string registries continued to play a key evidentiary role in the making of indigenous complaints against the missionary clergy of Huarochirí. In 1622, Don Francisco Muchay and Don Juan Vilca, the Andean notables of San Francisco de Chaclla, filed a legal claim for restitution against Luis Mejía de Estela, who they alleged had participated in a series of economic abuses and moral scandals in his first twelve months as parish priest. They stated that the priest had stolen animals and provisions from the community without authorization, failed to pay native laborers for services rendered to the maintenance of the church, consorted with women, and generally neglected his sacramental responsibility to baptize infants and confess the infirm. Vilca included himself among the victims, which indicates the personal animosities that likely motivated the complaint: when a mule belonging to the parish died under Vilca's watch, Mejía forced him to reimburse the church in the unfair sum of eighteen goats from his own private stock. As before, the local administrators who suffered the abuse claimed to possess knotted string accounts that proved Mejía's graft:

The said priest forces the said Indians of this parish and its administrators to give him hens, chickens, potatoes, *cocopa*, and corn, claiming that is what the tribute quota list orders them to give, and he imposes this upon the administrators of the settlements, and if they do not comply, he orders them to be punished severely, and for this, the said priest must pay them a large amount of silver in restitution, as their khipus will prove.[38]

It appears that the cords registered mostly statistical information such as the types of products and the quantities exchanged, and the sums of restitution and to whom it was owed. The litigants' statements about the priest's moral and sacramental failings, however, made no reference to khipus. This suggests that cord records of baptisms, confessions, saints' days, or other data on ritual activities, which Porres had recommended for an earlier time, no longer monitored and memorialized the parish life of seventeenth-century Huarochirí.

Such examples notwithstanding, the extent of the admissibility of khipus in the seventeenth-century courtroom is difficult to assess. Spanish colonial law referred only indirectly to their validity as evidence, and the final resolution of most legal proceedings of this type, including the causa de capítulos against Mejía, remain lost from the archival record.[39] It is certain that in the earliest colonial era, royal authorities demanded that Andean cord masters keep specific types of cord information for purposes of verification. Khipu tallies were needed not only to inform Spanish officials of available tributary goods and labor, but also to ensure for the Andeans' protection that their forced payments and services did not exceed the Crown's expectations. Carmen Beatriz Loza (1998) has documented that cord specialists complied with this mandate. As early as 1554, Huanca ethnic lords cited string records as evidence when petitioning the Council of the Indies for reimbursement of properties surrendered to the Spanish invaders, and Andean notables of that time commonly offered khipu data as proof of allegiance to the Crown in the *relaciones de méritos y servicios* (reports of merit and service) they presented to the monarch (Loza 1998, 144; Salomon 2004, 110). Tristan Platt (2002) has examined tribute-restitution charges that ethnic lords brought in the southern district of La Plata against the estate of the encomendero Alonso de Montemayor, which mention khipu records of the Indians' tribute payments from 1548 to 1551. Mónica Medelius and José Carlos de la Puente Luna (2004) have analyzed similar trial uses of khipus in the valley of Jauja in the 1570s. In the narration of his childhood in Cuzco, El Inca Garcilaso ([1609] 1960, 2:206) recalled the assistance he gave to the curacas and Indians of his Spanish father when they came from the countryside to pay tribute on Christmas and the feast of St. John. Wary of written accounts, the Andeans sought out Garcilaso to verify the Europeans' tribute records against the information they held on their cords. The historian learned at a young age that khipus could frustrate Spanish attempts to deceive by means of writing.

This legal practice was endorsed by Viceroy Toledo, who in his juridical reforms of the 1570s sought to utilize string registries in the service of Spanish juridical administration within and beyond the sphere of the cabildo's notary-khipukamayuq. His ordinances to regulate the authority of the corregimiento implied approval of the admission of cord evidence in Spanish tribunals. Andean laborers, he decreed, should carry khipus as testimony to defend themselves against the exploitative schemes of tribute collectors: "[T]he said corregidor must give orders that each Indian of those who are subject to tribute carry his khipu of what he ought to pay so that [the corregidores] understand they are not to take more tribute [than is required]."[40] Toledo's reforms also ordered khipu specialists to help Spanish judges receive Andean complaints of lost wealth (Salomon 2004, 111), which probably entailed substantiating property inventories before the court. In this way, the viceroy slightly adapted Matienzo's proposal for the adjudication of indigenous disputes by the cord-keeping t'uqrikyuq. In Matienzo's vision, this official would record by khipu the data related to "any civil and criminal grievances that occur between Indians, together with the lawsuits that the Indians might bring through their caciques or notables, be they civil or criminal," in addition to details of the sentence rendered.[41]

The most direct legal precedent for the actions of cord keepers against the clergy can be found among the duties that Toledo set down for the notary-khipukamayuq. A more literate embodiment of Matienzo's t'uqrikyuq, this individual was expected to transfer into the "more certain and durable" medium of written documents all witness testimony that came before the municipal council on matters of wills, property inventories, or legal complaints, plus relevant khipu data on the activities of corregidores, Andean parishioners, and priests:

[A]ll the remaining information that the Indians customarily record
on khipus must be reduced to writing by the hand of said notary
so that it be more certain and durable, especially with regard to the

[parishioners'] absences from doctrina and the comings and goings of priests and their absences [from the parish], and the same applies to the corregidores and their lieutenants, and other particular matters that they tend to record on the said khipus.[42]

As Kathryn Burns (2005a, 11) interprets this ordinance, Toledo transformed the cord keeper into a "kind of moral policeman," much as we saw in Diego de Porres's early projection of native parish governance. Not only the Andeans but also the Spanish priests and corregidores fell under the watchful eye of the khipukamayuq. Even though Spanish authorities imposed greater reliance on written forms of record keeping with hopes of spreading Castilian literacy, they still recognized the enduring value of Andean khipus for weeding out corruption in their own ranks.

Scholars have generally asserted that by the last decade of the sixteenth century, written documents in Spanish had effectively replaced Peruvian cord registries as the only legally recognized means of record keeping (Urton 1998, 410). According to Salomon and Spalding (2002, 2:861), the khipu registry continued informally subsequent to the ascendancy of paper accounts, but surfaced mostly in "folk-legal proceedings," such as the trial of Francisco de Ávila, and reflected more the indigenous peoples' support for their validity than any official Spanish endorsement (see also Salomon 2004, 118). The jurist Solórzano Pereira questioned the character of native record keepers and the veracity of the string registries they presented before Spanish magistrates: "I will not venture to give any or such great faith or authority to these khipus, because I have heard from those who know about them that the form of making and interpreting them is very uncertain, deceitful, and obscure. . . . The [khipukamayuqs] are Indians whose faith wavers, just as they will waver in the explication they attribute to their khipus."[43]

Despite such attitudes, parish inspection reports of the Lima archbishopric produced some fifty years after Toledo's ordinances confirm that some ecclesiastical magistrates solicited legally binding cord accounts well into first half of the seventeenth century. When, in 1619, the ethnic lords of the parish of Andajes in the central highland province of Cajatambo filed capítulos against the Mercedarian friar Miguel Márquez, the high clergy of Lima dispatched the visitador Cristóbal Loarte Dávila to investigate. The inspector posed a set of twenty-six questions to the native witnesses concerning

Márquez's alleged mistreatment of laborers, illicit money making, and inattention to the sacraments and religious instruction of the parishioners. One of these questions touched upon the priest's illegal use of khipus: "if [the Indians] know the said priest has forced his parishioners to make offerings either by his own hand or that of his fiscales or sacristans or other persons, charging them by khipus."[44] Whether the implication was true or not, the inquiry demonstrates that the high clergy had reason to believe that priests employed string registries to categorize and sum what should have been each churchgoer's voluntary contributions at Mass and on feast days. One year following the start of Loarte Dávila's inspection, the *cura doctrinero* received the legal order from Archbishop Lobo Guerrero that his right to minister in the parish was revoked due to "the abuses and the bad example that he has given."[45] Did the same khipus that Márquez used to register the illegal donations serve as evidence of Márquez's crime?

In 1623, the inspector Baltazar de Padilla returned to the topic of forced contributions by khipus when investigating Andrés de Mujica's conduct in San Juan de Huanchor, in Huarochirí province. After reviewing charges that the parish's Andean notables had filed against the priest, Padilla wanted to know: Had Mujica, in fact, coerced the parishioners to make church offerings on All Saints' Day and other solemn feasts by means of "tribute quotas, khipus, and written parish registries"?[46] The second mention of this concern within the sphere of the ecclesiastical tribunal hints at the Church's continued recognition of the evidentiary value of khipus; in the seventeenth century, a priest's tolerance or exploitation of cord accounting would not necessarily conceal his abuses from Lima's church authorities. These accounts raise another intriguing possibility: that the native method of recordation appealed to the traveling magistrates not only as a record of ancient superstition or personal sin, as Arriaga had proposed, but also as potential evidence of the transgressions of fellow Catholic ministers or exploitative Spanish corregidores.

An improbable work, surfacing outside the legal docket, brings to light a related but clandestine use for khipus in that period. In 1602, the Lima printer Antonio Ricardo published Diego Dávalos y Figueroa's *Miscelanea austral,* a wide-ranging treatise in prose and verse on such diverse subjects as love and dreams, the music of Tuscany, and indigenous America's propensity for Christianity. Drawing on several decades as a soldier and miner in the southern Peruvian highlands, the Spanish-born author included the following account, as told from one *limeño* to another, which was meant to illustrate the native Andeans' belief in the afterlife:

> Passing down the streets of a town called Atunjauja in company of the corregidor, we saw an old Indian with a large bunch of cords in his hand that were made of firmly twisted wool and diverse colors, which they call khipus. When this Indian realized that the corregidor and I had seen him, he tried to hide what he was carrying, but before he could do that the corregidor summoned him and asked what the long accounts contained. Flustered, the Indian began to vacillate, which made the corregidor want to know even more, so he threaten to thrash him and cut his hair (the greatest injury one can do to them). Eventually the Indian confessed, explaining that the khipu, together with other very large ones he owned, were the account he had to give to the Inca upon his return from the other world of all that had happened in that valley during his absence. The account included all the Spaniards who had passed down the royal road, what they had asked for and bought, and what they had done both for good and for bad. The corregidor seized and burned his accounts and punished the Indian.[47]

The story of the Inca's return was compatible with Catholic teachings on the resurrection of the dead and the immortality of the soul, and one that Andeans and missionary clergy of the period commonly embraced, though sometimes with competing interpretations (Estenssoro Fuchs 2003, 353–54). What makes Dávalos y Figueroa's narration valuable for the present discussion, however, is that it points to the existence of informal cord-based surveillance practices similar to the "moral policing" technique that Toledo had demanded of the cabildo's notary-khipukamayuq. The Spanish corregidores, it is clear, did not welcome the viceroy's position on these types of accounts and had good reason to suppress them, given the cords' well-known capacity to record colonialist abuses. Here the elderly man's strings not only registered the commercial transactions of the Europeans, but also the good and evil deeds they had done.

The origin of such practices of denunciation can also be linked to the Third Council's confessionary model. Returning to the *Tercero catecismo*'s instruction to penitents underscores the imprecise boundaries that separated the private custom of the sacrament from the public act of denunciation. To establish for Andean converts the meaning of confession, the sermon manual's authors employed the metaphor of storehouse exchange as a way to capture the economy of sin and its countable aspect: "you make a khipu of what you give *and what you are owed*" (emphasis added).[48] The priests' official homily thus accentuated the social obligations of Christian practice and the vital place of accounting one's debts and those of others in upholding the civil order. One can imagine how for Andean neophytes the conceptual domain of individual wrongdoing and absolution would overlap with that of public crime and reparation. As the sermon's language suggests, the same cords that penitents used to catalog sins could also record the transgressions that fellow Andeans, Spanish corregidores, or parish priests committed against them. It is worth asking, then, whether the ambiguities inherent to the Church's goal of making the sacrament more intelligible to native audiences partly inspired the activism of cord holders. Khipu specialists may have perceived a link between the confessional and the ecclesiastical court—that is, as complementary fora designed for the accounting of transgressions.[49]

Andean tradition validated the use of khipus for recording and denouncing the misdeeds of others more explicitly. Garcilaso explained the similarity between pre-Hispanic khipu conventions and postconquest Christian customs. In ancient times, he recounted, the Inca's strings archived the laws of the state religion, the record of violators and their transgressions, and the penalties each was obliged to receive: "In this way, each thread and knot recalled for them the information that it contained, similar to the Ten Commandments or the articles of our Holy Catholic Faith and the works of mercy, for which we understand from the number what each one requires of us."[50] Garcilaso's testimony highlights the continuity between the numbers that registered the dictates of Christian doctrine and Inca strings that inventoried religious crimes and penalties of restitution. This functional ambiguity that derived from both Inca and Catholic teachings shows that for Andeans, the distance separating the private realm of the confessional and the public realm of the courtroom may not have been as great as previously thought.

Cord Keepers as Rival Authorities

Pérez Bocanegra's account conveys that confessional practices responded more to local needs and circumstances than to the expectations and goals of the church hierarchy. Some of these expectations and goals were strictly doctrinal. The clergyman reproved the collective, localized nature of confessions at a time when canon law ordered confession to be a private face-to-face dialogue, excepting cases that required linguistic interpretation. Native assistants taught penitents to make khipus of their own sins and those of others, and told them what to reveal and what not to reveal to the priest. Pérez Bocanegra also condemned the parishioners' habit of reusing the same knots for repeated confessions, in apparent ignorance of the sacrament's power of absolution. Under the leadership of Andean catechists, to whom he applied the charged epithet *alumbrados*, the Indians had adopted an independent approach to the sacrament outside proper ecclesiastical channels, thus evoking what Estenssoro Fuchs (2003, 227) has described as "the Protestant phantom" that afflicted missionary clergy throughout Peru: the fear of individualized interpretations of Christianity that would supplant the authority of the Church and its ministers. Pérez Bocanegra's ultimate concern was not the survival of pre-Hispanic confessional practices, but rather the heterodoxy of native intermediaries whose activities escaped his control.

A brief review of the parish's litigious history indicates that Jesuit confessionary methodologies may have formed the basis of the presbítero's complaint. According to the biographical summaries by Harrison (2002, 270) and Bruce Mannheim (1991, 48, 146), Pérez Bocanegra assumed posts in the cathedral of Cuzco and that city's parish of Belén before his appointment as *cura propietario* of nearby Andahuaylillas, where he also acted as examiner general of Quechua and Aymara for aspiring curas de indios of the diocese. A more than twenty-year labor, his *Ritual formulario* (1631) was composed and published during a lengthy period of litigation between the diocese and the Society of Jesus, which sought to annex the parish as a Quechua-language training ground for members of the order. Granted royal approval for the takeover, the Jesuits sought to replace Pérez Bocanegra in 1628, but were forced to cede the parish to him eight years later due to the relentless protestations of the ecclesiastical cabildo.[51]

FIGURE 11. The church of Andahuaylillas. Courtesy of the Emilio Harth-Terré Collection, Latin American Library, Tulane University.

In this context, the author's conceivable hostility toward the Jesuits surfaces in his proposals for sacramental administration. He denounced the cataloging of sins by khipus, a Jesuit-endorsed practice, and their utilization to reiterate prior confessions. Regarding the latter practice, Peru's Jesuits were known for their advocacy of "general confessions," which encompassed the recurring enactment of the penitent's entire biography, to attain a deeper knowledge of the penitent's life, instead of the more conventional recounting of only those sins committed since the previous sacrament (Estenssoro Fuchs 2003, 206–7 n. 160). In a thinly veiled critique of the parish's earlier stewardship, Pérez Bocanegra asked the Andeans about the bad ways of their devotion, and he was eager to publish in his manual their reply: "[T]he Father or Fathers they knew growing up had taught them these things."[52]

His recommendations for how to confess Indians rounds out this fragmentary portrait of a cleric besieged by Jesuits and parishioners alike. He devoted an astonishing seventy questions of his confession manual to finding out whether Andean penitents had violated the eighth commandment's prohibition on dishonest testimony. Questions touched all indigenous social groups and forms of bearing false witness, but litigious community leaders stood out as his foremost concern. Curacas should be asked if they had falsely accused the clergy, and the notary-khipukamayuq if he had falsified indigenous wills to the detriment of the church's estate (Pérez Bocanegra 1631, 271, 278). The most direct reference to the priest's familiarity with native litigation came in a question posed to the parishioners in general: "Have you denounced another's sin before any judge, out of the hatred you had for that person, or to take revenge on him because you were not able to prove the crime of which you accused him?"[53] Though this line of inquiry was characteristic of the confession manuals of that time, it places Pérez Bocanegra's concerns about native moral conduct in the sphere of an indigenous activism that threatened clerical authority in parishes throughout the viceroyalty, in all probability including his own. In his mind, Andean penitents had identified a correlation between confessing the sins of third persons and denouncing them in the ecclesiastical courts, which further indicates the porous boundary that divided sacramental practices from legal action. It is not established that the priest himself had been singled out for crimes, but his criticisms of both khipu handlers and native litigants implies that these intersecting social groups undermined his goal to impose religious orthodoxy.

Estenssoro Fuchs (2003, 224) has observed that the true scandal underlying Pérez Bocanegra's complaint against khipus was that the "elder brothers and sisters" (hermanos y hermanas mayores), as the native assistants were known by the villagers, had usurped the sacramental authority that belonged to the clergy. In the words of the priest, "Before the Indian penitent goes to the feet of the confessor and priest, he or she has already confessed all the sins to these Indian women and men."[54] Pérez Bocanegra also charged that the native intermediaries ridiculed the linguistic skills and ritual methods of Catholic ministers, who remained isolated culturally without viable means of communication with the parishioners: "After having confessed with the priest, they go to consult these Indians about what Father told them and the penance he gave. [The cord keepers] make fun of him, saying he does not know how to examine the penitent or he does not understand their language, and they mock the way he absolves them."[55] To curb their influence, he called for uprooting the "juntas y ruedas" (secret meetings) in which they prepared knotted strings and spread falsehoods about priests and Catholic teachings (Pérez Bocanegra 1631, 134).

The containment of cords and their keepers should also come, Pérez Bocanegra argued, through the triumph of the printed word. In lock step with the Third Council's more aggressive recommendations, he advised priests to seize and destroy the Andeans' knotted strings and to use in their place the directives of his published manual: "[T]each them to confess by the rules of this confesionario and take from them those accounts and knots, and burn them in their presence, and deny them the sacrament of the Eucharist until all have been brought to the proper method of confession."[56] The book promised to stabilize the form of missionary ritual, which the khipu "palimpsests" of the cord masters' spiritual repertoire had misdirected. At issue for the priest was not merely the danger of heterodox confession, but more important the question of who controlled the mechanisms of religious exchange and therefore power over the community.

Still, that Pérez Bocanegra threatened to withhold communion from the parishioners represents an implicit acknowledgment of their fervent approach to the Catholic devotions. To highlight their alleged ignorance, he explained that Andean penitents mistakenly believed they were sanctified after confessing with strings. Yet his remarks underscore the Catholic intentions with which the Indians attempted the sacrament and the parishioners' conviction that they did so within the bounds of Christian orthodoxy (Estenssoro Fuchs 2003, 225). Pérez Bocanegra's depiction of the challenges he faced leads to a fundamental question that Peru's clergy struggled to answer: how to categorize as "Catholic" Andeans who employed traditional media in their quest to fulfill the sacraments and pursue claims before Spanish authorities. Cord keepers occupied positions that overlapped in unexpected ways the various social groups that made up colonial parish society. The fact that they belied the patterns of acculturation or resistance that European sources ascribed to them invites reconsideration of the notion that priests and Andeans took up one side or another of a cultural divide or that books were the only means of imposing Spanish rule on native communities. Both colonizers and colonized engaged in a continual process of reformulating their messages and media in response to new colonial realities.

While scholars are still far from knowing how native intermediaries communicated with strings, a group of rare but significant documents highlights the places where Andean representational practices intersected with those that governed the Archive. On an obvious level, these sources cast doubts on writing's smooth triumph over native peoples. But the shortage of existing data may point further: that well into the seventeenth century indigenous archives continued to prosper outside the law's surveillance, taking on functions in native communities that alphabetic literacy could not perform. It is hardly difficult to imagine, given the facts of Andahuay-lillas, that native intermediaries carried on making records, on both paper and string, according to local needs and following their own set of rules. The cord specialists, it appears, constituted a robust parish network, which, taken as a focus of analysis, may still provide answers to the many questions about the extent of that authority and the semiotic pluralism it embraced.

Chapter 4

Writing about Clerical Violence

Testimonies of Violence

"Reading must be taught together with writing to all children," insisted Covarrubias in his *Tesoro de la lengua castellana* (1611), "so as men of reason they are able not only to work the fields but also to keep accounts in order to know what they pay and what they receive, rather than do it mentally, or making signs on a wall, because that way they can make mistakes and be cheated."[1] The lexicographer defined *escribir* (to write) in practical terms, as a useful instrument that laborers should acquire to regulate social and commercial interactions and protect their assets from the deceits of others. Property inventories, last wills and testaments, and trial and notarial records of Spain's imperial archives show that the practice of accounting in script permeated all sectors of early modern Spanish society (Castillo Gómez 2001). One of the era's most widely disseminated imprints, the Jesuit priest Jerónimo Martínez de Ripalda's 1591 *Doctrina christiana con una exposicion breue,* featured a multiplication table and lessons on fractions and division, which indicates that the teaching of religious dogma was also frequently combined with the teaching of numbers.[2]

In colonial Peru, references to the use of ledger books of credits and debts, both in urban areas and remote villages, shows that understanding of the importance of writing for meeting economic and spiritual demands was pervasive. Covarrubias and Ripalda's emphasis on keeping accounts in writing recalls the instructions that Guaman Poma ([c. 1615] 1980, 814–15) set down for native Andean leaders: the regidor, or municipal officer, wrote the chronicler, should maintain books, khipus, and other accounts for the accurate reckoning and collection of duties owed to the Crown and Church. Yet while Guaman Poma promoted literacy and record keeping among Andeans to respond to the colonizers, and counter their schemes, he also noted the extreme punishments that the powerful imposed on subordinates when settling accounts. For instance, regidores and other native intermediaries were subject to harsh penalties when they failed to meet the Spaniards' tribute quotas: fifty public lashes, hair cropping, and a ten-peso fine payable to the district administrator.[3] Nowhere was literacy more tied to the punitive aspects of native officialdom than in the realm of fiscal management.

To underscore this point, Guaman Poma ([c. 1615] 1980, 503) illustrated the scene of a corregidor who commands an African to flog a native alcalde for collecting a tribute that falls two eggs short. Drawings of this kind throughout his work suggest that intimidation by force was a significant dimension of the lives of Andeans who enforced colonial rule through the collection of fees. As economic middlemen, native officials worked an uncertain ground marked by the threat of violence; they were required to collect tribute from native villagers, on the one hand, and to protect against Spanish abuses, on the other. But lacking proper context, the illustration raises many questions about the coercive methods of the colonizers, the fiscal activities of native intermediaries, and the relationship between the two. Did the alcalde of Guaman Poma's drawing record and collect fees willingly or always under the threat of severe punishment? Did he fail to keep accurate tribute records or make records that contradicted the accounts of the corregidor? What other types of inventories did he keep and for whom?

Testimonies from Lima's ecclesiastical archives document that high stakes were also involved for the native intermediaries who kept the accounts of parish priests. Indigenous authorities had responsibilities beyond teaching Christian doctrine and assembling parishioners for Mass; they also assisted the clergy with tribute collection and law enforcement, maintaining the padrones, or church books, that registered the names of all parishioners in order to chart their fulfillment of Christian obligations and eligibility to provide tributary labor, community payments, and parish fees. The fiscal duties of native intermediaries therefore placed them in between and at times in direct competition with the parish priests and secular authorities who vied for control over native assets. Punishments that derived from the workings of the colonial fiscal system triggered an especially strong response from indigenous officials. In fact, the frequency of Andean litigants' objections to the colonizers' excessive discipline, which tied directly to this economic function, suggests that the abuse of native church assistants over record keeping was generalized and routine.[4]

Typical is the report of plaintiff Domingo Llasta, which lends a name and a story to the anonymous victim of Guaman Poma's portrait. In 1636, Llasta, the native alcalde of the cabildo of San Bernardo de Yamor in the province of Cajatambo, filed a petition of grievance with Archbishop Arias de Ugarte against Juan Celis de Padilla, the cura of the parish of San Agustín de Cajacay. The first-person account, in a fractured Spanish of the alcalde's own hand, denounced the beating that the priest had given Llasta on account of faulty bookkeeping:

> I, Domingo Llasta, *alcalde ordinario* of the pueblo of Yamor, appear before Your Excellency to testify that the said Don Juan Celis has committed a very grave offense against me, first giving me twenty lashes in the chapel of Cotopara, and then he tied me to a tree where he whipped me again. . . . Then [he brought me to] the village of Cajacay, [where he gave me] thirty more lashes while tied to the pillory, and the day of Palm Sunday he examined the Indian men and women using the padrón, and because the infirm and crippled and maimed were missing [from the padrón], he gave me thirty lashes, and then he beat me with the staff that the bailiff carries and broke it over my body without cause, and then [I endured] more kicks and beatings inside the church by his consecrated hand.[5]

According to Llasta's testimony, Celis beat him over the head with the *vara de la real justicia* (staff of royal justice), then left him in the hands of "the negro Simón" for more punishments. Hours later, Simón paraded the alcalde through the public square of Cajacay, where he left him near death in a pool of his own blood. Miraculously recovered from this "notable offense," Llasta now beseeched the archbishop: "I beg Your Excellency to prosecute the said priest in order to restore my honor and to serve justice."[6]

The numerous lawsuits of this type point out not only the underlying violence that accompanied day-to-day fiscal administration, but also the continual disagreements among Lima church authorities, parish priests, and Andean officials about what the Indians' tribute obligations should be and what role clerical violence should play in their enforcement. Scholars of colonial history have gainfully explored the relationship between coercion

FIGURE 12.   Punishment of an alcalde. Guaman Poma,
El primer nueva corónica y buen gobierno, 503.
Courtesy of the Royal Library, Copenhagen, Denmark.

and religious change among the indigenous peoples, focusing primarily on the area of confession and penitential practices, on the one hand, and the area of forceful conversion and extirpation, on the other.[7] But mostly unknown are the ways in which clerical violence intersected with the fiscal exploitation of the Indians. Native protests against the coercive methods of priests contain insights into the nature of local ecclesiastical authority, the ties between clerical violence and the everyday maintenance of the parish fiscal system, and the views of priests and native assistants about the proper meaning and function of church law with regard to ministerial violence.

Contemporary thinking about the jurisdictional limits of ecclesiastical authority did, in fact, inform the claims that native intermediaries put forward about clerical violence. Andean litigants knew the colonial debates over whether parish priests could lawfully resort to force, and these debates entered into the conflicts between Indians and the clergy, as both groups jostled for local power. Llasta, for one, maintained that Celis acted in ways that defied the rule of law. Written from the perspective of a cabildo officer, the grievance also indicates that in Yamor there occurred a blurring of secular and ecclesiastical jurisdictions. How a parish priest such as Celis came to exercise "royal justice" over a native officer of the local municipal council is a question worth examining, as are the views of native assistants with regard to the comparative reach of ecclesiastical and secular authority in local parishes, and how they envisioned their place in the enforcement of the two.[8] Corporal punishment relating to parish record keeping and fiscal activity was a central topic in the litigation and jurisdictional maneuverings between priests, corregidores, and native church personnel. Seen within broader social and political dynamics that characterized native parish life, the complaints of Llasta and other litigants reveal new facts about the fiscal role of native officials, the history of clerical violence in parish management, and the mechanisms by which Andean intermediaries utilized the law to confront the coercive methods of the colonizers.

Keeping the Parish Books

According to royal law and the Tridentine decrees, one of Llasta's duties as church assistant was to maintain the padrón, or sacramental register and census book, which visitadores from Lima would check periodically to see it was kept "with the order and decency that the Holy Council and synodal constitutions of this archbishopric stipulate."[9] The padrón recorded the names of all parishioners so that they could receive the sacraments and be corrected when absent from Mass or classes of religious instruction. Canons laid out instructions for how parish officials should maintain the books and set monetary fines for noncompliance (Franciscans 1619, 31v; Torres 1970, 25–26). Pérez Bocanegra's *Ritual formulario* included "formulae for how to write the books that parish priests should keep" (1631, 632–43), which signals the precision expected of those who kept the church's padrón. Ideally, parishes had five books: separate annual records of baptisms, confirmations, marriages, deaths, and a general census of the parishioners. Names appeared in lists according to gender, age, physical condition, legitimate or illegitimate birth, pueblo and kin group of origin, and other traits that indicated sacramental needs and tributary status.[10] Native church personnel showed the books to visiting priests and church inspectors; the books recorded any sacramental misconduct or fiscal irregularities that might have occurred since the previous inspection.

Because the padrón listed Indians eligible for tributary labor and taxation, native assistants were, in effect, economic functionaries of the padre doctrinero. Fiscal and sacramental aspects of Catholicism were intertwined and played a key role in what Kathryn Burns (1999, 3) has called the "spiritual economy" of Andean evangelization: the complex web of material and sacred interests and investments that made convents, parishes, and other religious institutions strong actors in colonial society. The padrón documented the parishioners' comings and goings from church as well as their payments and debts to the Crown and the Church. Around 1560, Fray Diego de Porres instructed the caciques of each settlement to record tribute payments "in accordance with the padrón," meaning on the same register that memorialized the parish's ritual activities.[11]

Native church assistants had the power to collect tribute for the maintenance of the church and its estate, and for the priest's salary or sínodo, provided such collections did not prejudice the well-being of the parishioners.[12] Competition for benefices in the Lima archdiocese often derived from economic necessity, given the modest backgrounds of the majority of priests (Tibesar and López 1971, 43–44). Though curas de indios could depend on community and church resources to sustain themselves minimally and call on the services of two native mitayos, most contended with corregidores and caciques for access to indigenous labor and goods so as to enrich themselves

FIGURE 13. *Padrón de los indios que se hallaren*
en la ciudad de los Reyes del Pirú of 1613.
Courtesy of the Biblioteca Nacional de España, Madrid, Spain.

and gain local influence (Acosta Rodríguez 1982, 12; Cahill 1984, 243).[13] Some clergy ran profitable businesses by claiming the Indians' harvests and livestock, or obliging them to produce textiles and other goods, which they sold for profit in urban centers. Forced donations, nominal tithes, and illegal fees for weddings, baptisms, funerals, and feasts could also augment the clergy's income.

The Crown assigned the corregimiento to manage the native workforce and collect tribute. Andean officials of local cabildos nominally supervised indigenous labor and fiscal contributions, receiving labor and tribute exemptions, *derechos* (service royalties), and in some cases salaries in return (Spalding 1984, 218).[14] However, priests and native church assistants fulfilled tasks for the royal fiscal system as well; they provided census information for tax purposes and for collecting state tribute and other levies (Cahill 1984, 262). Church assistants presented the padrón to the arriving corregidor or, in his absence, to clergymen with fiscal responsibilities. Records of baptisms, confessions, marriages, and burials furnished corregidores and visitadores with the numbers of Indian tributaries of each ayllu who were eligible for labor services and taxation.[15] In 1575, Viceroy Toledo extended labor and tax exemptions to native intermediaries of the Church and ordered that maestrescuelas and other parish assistants receive a yearly salary of crops, livestock, and clothing taken from the local communities.[16]

At times, Andean advocates praised clergy who forgave the debts of the indigent or allowed partial and late payments of derechos and tribute.[17] However, they alleged mostly that priests and native assistants used the parish books to track the illegal forced offerings of monies and goods. In 1631, native litigants in the parish of Santa Ana de Tusi stated that Father Pedro del Campo misused the padrón on All Saints' Day and Easter, charging married Indians one real and the unmarried one-half real, claiming these were the contributions they owed to the Church, and ordered Don Gregorio Armico, the parish cantor, to punish those who refused.[18] Twenty years later, in 1651, Don Gabriel Guzmán Camacguacho, the cacique principal and governor of the district of Mangos, accused Fray Nicolás de Ávila Pizarro of using the parish registry to charge offerings of corn and other goods: "[Ávila's] fiscales look after only this, without seeing to that [the Indians] attend doctrina."[19]

The padrón registered the sacred and material activities of the parish, but for Indian claimants it signified the gross forms of economic exploitation that Catholic ministers carried out under the guise of spiritual interests.

A census account, log of tributary contributions, and record of participation in the Church, the parish book represented Spanish colonial authority and added weight to the demands that the colonizers and their indigenous agents imposed upon native parishioners.[20] Yet native litigants disputed the legitimacy of that authority, given the ways in which priests and fiscales used the padrón to justify earnings at the Indians' expense. The registry of ritual and taxation brought Andean subjects into a system of interdictions established by Spanish colonial law (see González Echevarría [1990] 1998, 49–50). A written record of native transgressions and financial obligations, the book mediated a relationship between parishioners and church officials that was not just economic and spiritual, but also punitive.

The Role of Violence in Parish Life

Henry Kamen (1993, 201) has observed that in early modern times, clerical violence was an everyday part of the Church's social function to supervise the behavior of its members. Invoking the rhetoric of paternal authority, the clergymen of the Indies asserted their obligation to protect and teach the "children in the faith," as indigenous neophytes were called, and, when necessary, to punish them for the purpose of moral edification. Even the Franciscan Bernardino de Sahagún, a friar known for his devotion to the study of the language and culture of the Nahua Indians, remarked that because the Indians were prone to error, they should be "lovingly propelled toward heaven by blows" (Kamen 1993, 209; see also Hanke 1959, 86). Though evangelizers struggled with the idea that only force could induce the Indians to respect them, corporal punishment was common for subjects who transgressed the norms of the Church, especially the native peoples, who occupied an inferior social position. Priests established their local authority through the exercise of force within and without the limits of royal and church law.

Indians recognized the pedagogical value of just and proper punishments as well. Guaman Poma ([c. 1615] 1980, 282, 285, 689–90) admired the extirpator Cristóbal de Albornoz for his zeal in chastising presumed idolaters in his campaigns of the late 1560s against the nativist movement Taki Unquy (see Adorno 1991, 255). The chronicler also praised the Inca justice system and its tradition of corporal punishment as a mechanism for upholding social harmony. In the "Chapter of the Inca's Justice," Guaman Poma ([c. 1615] 1980,

303–16) included a lengthy catalog of what he considered the just disciplinary measures of the pre-Hispanic period: death by stoning for adulterers; hangings for rapists; life imprisonment for traitors; and whippings, exile, and forced labor for drunkards, thieves, and lesser offenders. Harsh punishment was, in this description of Inca times, an effective tool for the regulation of political and social order, producing "a very just land, with fear of the law and penalty, and good examples."[21] The colonizers' use of corporal punishments, though modeled on already existing practices in the Iberian Peninsula, appears to have been consistent with traditional Andean forms of punishment.

While violence played a critical role in sustaining colonial authority, Lima's high clergy nevertheless debated the limits of the curas' disciplinary function and the distinction between legitimate force and cruel mistreatment. Drawing from the teachings of Solomon and Paul, Acosta ([1577] 1987, 2:145) acknowledged, like Sahagún, that the "servile condition" and "puerile customs" of many Indians required compulsory approaches to evangelization (Pagden ([1982] 1986, 158–60). The secular arm should impose corporal punishments, he argued, but given the lack of corregidores in rural settlements, the meting out of discipline inevitably fell to priests. Acosta declared whippings, hair cropping, and monetary penalties to be immoral and, for the most part, counterproductive, for they often inspired native resentment. When punishments were administered, the framework of religious instruction was crucial. Acosta reasoned that because Indians were susceptible to disobedience and evil, sensible discipline, aimed to hurt but not cause lasting injury, could teach the wayward to respect God's laws.

Legal procedure obliged church magistrates to require a high standard of proof before sentencing the laity to corporal punishments (Hevia Bolaños 1619, 213r, 218v–219r). Extrajudicially, public lashes, presumably ones less severe than those applied to Domingo Llasta, were considered the best medicine for smaller infractions. Diocesan synods recommended whippings for public sins, such as drunkenness, adultery, concubinage, blasphemy, and usury (Torres 1970, 27). The Quito diocese ordered punishments for native assistants who failed to report ritual drinking and other sins: twenty-four lashes for first offenses and fifty for subsequent infractions.[22] In general, legislation gave priests substantial leeway in deciding when everyday punishment was appropriate for the correction of wrongdoers. In the words of Juan de Hevia Bolaños, Castile's expert in procedural law, "Ecclesiastics may discipline laypersons for any sin in order to push them toward penitence and liberate their soul from eternal death."[23] Interrogations and punishments, within and without the ecclesiastical courts, also functioned as an extension of sacramental confession and penitence. Thus, what separated moral instruction, criminal punishment, and heavy-handed coercion was largely left to priests, even though such distinctions were nothing if not ambiguous to their native charges.

In general, church authorities believed that evangelization would improve if parish priests distanced themselves from lay society and exchanged worldly pursuits for spiritual ones. The Third Council ordered the curas de indios to abandon their "tratos y granjerías," including forced offerings for sacraments, as well as improper pastimes such as gambling, smoking tobacco before Mass, and consorting with women.[24] Clerical violence was also a top concern. Emphasizing the clergy's sacramental character, the councilors hoped that parish priests would stand apart as spiritual guides rather than as repressive enforcers of a dubious justice. To promote the image of a responsive clergy, the Third Council decreed that only native parish assistants should administer corporal punishments for public sins and other forms of disobedience.[25]

Theoretically, Andean officials administered floggings for public crimes and religious violations, such as ritual drinking or absenteeism from Mass,[26] but parish priests disregarded royal and church directives, as Celis's beating of Llasta suggests. In 1661, Protector General of the Indians Diego de León Pinelo (1661, 9v) remarked that the method of instruction by humiliation was a factor in evangelization's failures. He based this claim on the lawsuits against priests that had reached his office in the Lima audiencia. In one case, a native parishioner in Chancay protested the twenty lashes that his priest had given him for baptizing a son without permission. Other litigants reported a general practice that took place after church on Sundays: "[O]nce Mass is over the priest stands in liturgical dress to one side of the door of the church, with the maniple in his hand, and the fiscal on the other side with a whip, and as the Indians go out one by one, he forces them to kiss the maniple and give alms."[27]

Native assistants thus developed reputations as the enforcers of a capricious Spanish authority. In 1606, the native parishioner Martín Malqui of San Pedro de Mama in the province of Huarochirí reported that the alcaldes of nearby Santa Olaya, without provocation and at the directive of the parish priest, bound him to the public pillar, stripped him of his clothing, and gave him a whipping of fifty lashes, "with so much cruelty that they left his back scarred and covered in blood."[28] Indigenous litigants cast themselves as victims of suffering and public humiliation at the hands of the clergy's assistants, and royal authorities worried that priests as well as local native administrators had overstepped the limits of their authority to punish (Solórzano Pereira 1648, 224). In addition, the motive of avarice was the Spanish authorities' perpetual concern. The Third Council's *Confessionario para los curas de indios* ([1585] 1985, 226–27, 230, 231–32) included questions that priests should ask curacas, alcaldes, and alguaciles to probe whether they engaged in illicit commerce or exploited Indians for financial gain.[29] In 1619, the bishops of La Plata forbade native fiscales and notaries from purchasing the right to the titles from priests, which indicates, beyond the corrupt ecclesiastical practice of selling colonial offices, that Andean assistants had established a reputation for economic opportunism.[30]

Native parishioners mistrusted church officials because of their power to defend or undermine communal interests and assets. The "fiscalillos," as Indians derisively called the priest's economic functionaries, kept the books that symbolized the injustice of the colonial order and allowed priests to access native resources. Parishioners accused these officials of crimes ranging from extortion and malfeasance to physical assault and sexual pandering with the consent of priests. Francisco de Ávila purportedly used the native assistants of San Damián as tribute collectors; the Indians stated it was difficult for them, living at a subsistence level, to pay the severe quotas of tribute and goods.[31] When in 1623 the Andean nobles of San Mateo de Huánchor, also in the province of Huarochirí, accused Father Andrés de Mujica of charging forced offerings by khipu and padrón, they too condemned the native fiscal for a series of violations, including arresting suspects without jurisdiction, taking bribes from Indians accused of concubinage and other public crimes, and demanding goods from parents when their children were absent from doctrina.[32] According to indigenous victims, the native officials' generalized money-making activities were plainly illegal, "as if this were the tribute they had to pay." Guaman Poma denounced native intermediaries who exploited Indians for material gain: "For what reason do they want to be the lengua of the corregidor or the magistrate of the visita of the Holy Church or the inspection tours or the encomenderos of the said provinces? To rob the poor Indians of their haciendas. And for that there is no remedy."[33]

Serving Against Their Will

Keeping written tabs on parishioners triggered dilemmas and frictions for native assistants. For one, parish priests mistreated native church personnel, imposing upon them fees and excessive work obligations, as they did upon Indians in general. A 1651 lawsuit against the cura of San Cristóbal de Huánuco stated that he employed a native fiscal as a domestic servant without pay.[34] The conflict in San Bernardo de Yamor highlights another predicament that native intermediaries faced. Domingo Llasta claimed Celis whipped him for failing to record in the registry the sick and disabled ("los enfermos y cojos y mancos"), who because of their condition were unable to attend Mass and receive the sacraments in church. A closer look at the complaint suggests that the alcalde may have left disadvantaged Indians off the books intentionally so as to protect them from the forced offerings that Celis demanded at Mass by roll call. Llasta's colitigants alleged that on previous occasions the priest had obliged contributions using the padrón, as he did on the feast of San Bernardo, in violation of the synodal constitutions.[35]

Some parish officials abandoned their posts rather than do the bidding of corrupt priests. León Pinelo (1661, 27r) reported that Don Blas Ignacio Catacora, the cacique and governor of Acora in the province of Chucuito, renounced his office, citing undue pressures of having to enforce the mita of Indian tributaries. Though he was, in León Pinelo's estimation, "one of the most praiseworthy Indians of the upper provinces," Catacora had relocated to Lima, where he became a donado of the Franciscan order, living with the friars in the convent and serving them in monastic life. When clerical violence was extreme, church assistants attempted to protect Indians from abuse, as Llasta did when leaving indigents off the padrón. In 1623, the cacique principal Don Carlos Llagua Caja of the district of Huamalíes filed suit against the beneficiary Antonio Luis López for economic exploitation and unjust punishments. "As a result [of the abuse]," he claimed, "the fiscales do not dare send for [the priest] so as not to see him in their district, and because of that, the said Indians have died without confession."[36]

In 1630, Don Fernando Anicama complained to the archbishop about the difficult compromises he faced as Francisco Pacho de Herrera's assistant in the parish of Ica. Once a respected leader of the community, Anicama recounted the humiliation he experienced as an economic functionary reduced to collecting forced offerings at Mass:

> I am the governor and am seated in my rightful place beside the caciques and indios principales of the said pueblo, and [the priest] orders me to guard the door of the church so as not to allow any Indian men or women to leave, only those who have made offerings, and with this he has caused enormous dread and fear, frightening them with the great wrath and words with which he warns them, and as a result, no one dares to come [to Mass] without the said offering. And with this motive, he makes me get up from my seat, being the governor, so that the Indians see me positioned as a doorman in the entrance of the said church, and they do not have the respect for me that is required, and though I tell them that I am there to defend them, I also help the said Father Francisco Pacho de Herrera do things that should not be done, especially to people so poor and wretched as the said Indians are, for they can hardly pay the tasa and tribute to their encomendero and other persons.[37]

In Andean custom, the ethnic nobility defended the norms that regulated interactions within the community and enforced the claims of poor Indians to goods and resources entitled to them (Spalding 1973, 584). As dependants of the clergy, however, native church officials imposed the unwelcome demands of the colonizers, which jeopardized the Indians' well-being and discredited the officials in the eyes of native subjects.[38] To participate in the "tratos" of the priest undermined Anicama's traditional authority and social status. For the governor, the benefits that accompanied parish service did not compensate for the loss of respect it entailed.

A Conflict of Jurisdictions

There is reason to argue that clerical violence of this type was a natural outgrowth of the Church's colonial function. In Spain and the Indies, the Crown controlled ecclesiastical administration, which meant that the clergy entered into the service of secular authority, often directing local finances with access to the coercive apparatus of the state (Kamen 1993, 206–8). Given the lack of political organization at the start of colonization, European churchmen were often the only mediators between the native peoples and royal authority, and in the absence of secular authorities the padres doctrineros imposed the rule of law in Andean settlements. Fiscales, alcaldes, and alguaciles of native parishes assumed civil functions as representatives of the king.[39] Armed with the staff of royal justice, native assistants collected tribute, assisted in the distribution of lands, patrolled the streets after curfew, and made arrests for criminal infractions. Control over the lives of Indians rested on a complex blend of competing civil and religious authority, leading to a near integration of the secular and ecclesiastical domains at the local level. The regulation of jurisdictional separations was, in this sense, more a theoretical goal than a practical one.

The overlap of royal and ecclesiastical government, which characterized the Hapsburg conception of the state, had a long medieval history, originating in the *Reformatio* of Pope Gregory VII (1075–1122), when the papacy developed its own court hierarchy and legislative bodies to assert power over secular rulers (Berman 1983, 19–23).[40] From its inception, canon law functioned as an autonomous legal system with broad judicial scope. The Church declared its jurisdiction over clerics and virtually all social groups that required its punishment or protection, as well as over a wide range of beliefs and behaviors, from spiritual concerns involving family relations and sexual practices to financial activities relating to tithes, benefices, and the management of the Church's estate. Ecclesiastical courts not only claimed full authority to intervene where they deemed secular administration insufficient, but also insisted that litigants had the right to avail themselves of the Church's jurisdiction if they felt justice would be difficult to obtain through secular channels (Berman 1983, 223; Benton 2002, 37).

In 1560, Viceroy Andrés Hurtado de Mendoza challenged the Lima Church's autonomy in native governance: he ordered the election of just one native alcalde in each pueblo, under the supervision of the corregidor instead of the parish priest (Montesinos [1642] 1906, 1:258–59). Five years later, Governor Lope García de Castro supported this effort by prohibiting curas from appointing their own alguaciles (Levillier 1921–1925, 3:128–29, 130). Archbishop Loayza wrote to Philip II in protest of the corregidores' new mandate. The prelate argued for the founding of doctrinas in which priests and native alcaldes would alone oversee secular and religious affairs. "Spanish corregidores would not be needed," he explained, "because they are very injurious and costly [for the Indians]."[41] Against secular provisions, Loayza's Second Council ordered parish priests to appoint their own native officials.[42] Though the see objected to the corregimientos' enlistment of church officials for tributary service (Lisson Cháves 1943–1948, 3:99–100), the first period of evangelization shows that priests were nevertheless able to assemble large teams for parish administration. In 1566, one corregidor stated that the clergy of his district had appointed sixty-three alguaciles to gather Indians for Sunday Mass (Levillier 1921–1925, 3:137; Spalding 1984, 218), and seven years later the Crown attorney of the Lima audiencia declared the vast numbers of native church assistants to be unwarranted (Lohmann Villena 1957, 401).

The Church's ideal of an autonomous parish system collided with the ambitions of Viceroy Toledo, who foresaw a greater role for royal administrators in the religious and fiscal supervision of the Indians. In his administrative overhaul of the 1570s, Toledo imposed the power of the cabildo de indios over the secular and religious affairs of native parishes.[43] The cabildo's maximum authority, the alcalde mayor, together with the curacas of the district, collected tribute, oversaw the distribution of lands, and safeguarded the *policía cristiana* of the Indians. As a judicial officer, the alcalde represented Indians in trials and mediated native contacts with the corregidor. Toledo established the annual election of regidores, mayordomos, and alguaciles, who assisted the alcalde in enforcing secular law and rooting out public sins, such as concubinage, ritual drinking, and absenteeism from Mass. Corregidores and outgoing cabildos were to select new officials for one-year terms out of a pool of candidates nominated by the local community. The notary-khipukamayuq was a lifelong appointee who recorded all legal actions and municipal dealings with provincial authorities.[44]

Toledo placed the enforcement of religious obligations and moral behavior under the council's domain and restricted the number of noncabildo officials who could work exclusively for priests and thus avoid taxation and tributary service. His ordinances authorized one fiscal, four cantors, one maestrescuela, and one sacristan per parish, apart from the cabildo officials, who also assisted priests.[45] In 1581, Toledo's successor, Viceroy Martín Enríquez de Almanza, expanded the council's pastoral role by establishing the new cabildo position of *alguacil de la doctrina,* responsible for teaching

FIGURE 14. The *cabildo de indios* of Chincheros.
Courtesy of the Emilio Harth-Terré Collection,
Latin American Library, Tulane University.

Christian doctrine to Indian boys and girls.[46] Viceregal provisions and royal decrees sought to limit the clergy's authority and transform the council into the central governing institution in native parishes.[47] Guaman Poma underscored the cabildo's prominent role in evangelization through his illustrations of municipal council officers.[48] A staff of justice and rosary in the hands of the alcalde represented the combination of secular and ecclesiastical duties that cabildo officials fulfilled (Guaman Poma [c. 1615] 1980, 808).

Viceroy Toledo also wished to curtail the clergy's involvement in the prosecution and adjudication of public crimes. Priests claimed the right to judge and castigate Indians rather than remit offenders to the corregimiento or audiencia, as ordered by royal law. To counteract the clergy's influence, cabildo officials were instructed to monitor their activities in fiscal and disciplinary matters. For example, native alcaldes should record the number of days priests spent away from the parish so as to discount that time from the amount of the sínodo the community owed him (Frasso 1684, s.f.). The archival record of the cabildo of León de Huánuco includes a manuscript transcription of two chapters of the Third Council that prohibited curas from money-making businesses and the collection of offerings by force.

FIGURE 15.   The Alcalde Ordinario. Guaman Poma,
El primer nueva corónica y buen gobierno, 808.
Courtesy of the Royal Library, Copenhagen, Denmark.

Did Huánuco's municipal scribe document the conciliar decrees in order to report more accurately to royal and church authorities on the local priests' transgressions?[49]

Acosta ([1577] 1984, 1:591) felt that evangelization called for the collective effort of all authorities, civil and religious, not only to improve native religious instruction, but also to correct insufficient clergy. Visitadores heeded Acosta's recommendation, calling on cabildo officials to report on matters of spiritual interest, such as the survival of idolatrous customs and the performance of parish clergy. Yet by and large the Lima see resisted the encroachments of civil authority. Church synods forbade corregidores to impede the labors of parish assistants, particularly through forced labor service.[50] Nor could they appoint or remove native fiscales, a practice Toledo had attempted to institute (Lisson Cháves 1943–1948, 2:711–12).[51] Fiscales continued to enjoy high standing and bear the staffs that identified them to local communities, as Guaman Poma's drawing of the native church officer indicates (Guaman Poma [c. 1615] 1980, 675). Moreover, Peru's churchmen ignored Toledo's limits on the numbers of parish assistants, especially in rural areas removed from the diocesan sees. In 1570, approximately one fiscal served between eight hundred and one thousand Indians. By 1618, the number of fiscales had increased to one for every one hundred (Duviols [1971] 1977, 282).[52]

Despite religious chapters and synods that instructed ministers not to interfere in matters of royal governance,[53] the clergy continued to exercise an expansive jurisdictional role in areas where the corregimiento remained weak. This explains the power that Juan Celis de Padilla had over the officers of the native cabildo, Domingo Llasta among them. Guaman Poma had curas like Celis in mind when he stated: "The parish priests lose authority by meddling too much in the administration of justice. . . . Only a beneficiary, [the priest] wants to be the corregidor."[54] Priests blurred the separation between royal and church authority in order to control local communities more effectively. Osvaldo Pardo (2006, 85) has speculated that Franciscan friars in colonial Mexico provided native parish assistants with staffs of office so as to keep Nahua peoples from understanding the distinctions between civil and ecclesiastical jurisdictions. Though the vara symbolizing royal authority belonged only to cabildo officials, the Spanish Church authorized fiscales, alcaldes, and alguaciles to carry an "ecclesiastical staff."[55] The fact that the royal audiencia of Quito prohibited priests and friars from bestowing varas on native assistants suggests that similar practices took place in South American territories as well.[56]

Native petitioners charged that priests manipulated cabildo elections in the corregidores' absence. Guaman Poma, for example, denounced the curas' practice of hand-picking municipal officers: "The said priests of the doctrinas interfere in the election of the alcaldes and then take away from them the staff of royal justice and give it to whomever they please."[57] The complaint of Domingo Llasta and other leaders of Cajacay alleged that Celis usurped the corregidor's jurisdiction in cabildo elections as well: "The said Don Juan Celis, our priest, controls the election of alcaldes ordinarios for seats in the cabildo as if he were the corregidor, saying 'I want that one, or I don't want this one,' without there being any vote of the will of the Indians, simply because he doesn't want there to be."[58] Priests and corregidores competed for control over the town council, removing officials they considered disloyal and assigning others who would act in their interests. Holding sway over the cabildo allowed priests to manage native parishioners more closely, though the conflictive relationship between Celis and Llasta shows this could be hard to accomplish.[59] Like other indigenous officials, Llasta mediated two sets of judicial tension that intersected in Andean parishes: the tension between royal and ecclesiastical authority, on the one hand, and the tension between centralized Lima church authority and local clerical authority, on the other. Andean assistants vied for authority with royal and church officials, and adjusted their allegiances in keeping with the parish's shifting dynamics of power.

Rival Factions in Cajatambo Province

Llasta's first-person appeal to Archbishop Arias de Ugarte was unique. Typically, statements of grievance resulted not from independently authored writings, but from oral declarations of the victims, made in Quechua though the mediation of Spanish-speaking interpreters and in response to the thematic prompting of the fiscal or judge. A notary then recorded the statements in Spanish, in third-person narrative, according to scribal conventions and formulae.[60] In this sense, the "authorial voice" of the petitioner, once transferred to legal script, was intersubjective insofar as it derived from the convergence of the discourses of the witness, interpreters, and interrogators, and relied on set notarial operations. The "testimonial situation," as Andrea

Frisch (2004, 12) describes this, involved not a transparent declaration of an individual's speech act, but an intricate web of social relationships, ethical standards, and rhetorical constraints. Coming to terms with the events that Indian witnesses described thus requires an assessment of the mechanisms and invisible hands that shaped the declarations as well as the institutional, social, and historical contexts in which they were produced.

Trial documents reveal the protocols that church authorities established for the visitadores and jueces ordinarios who received complaints in the course of parish inspections or through direct appeal to Lima's church authorities. For lawsuits against the clergy, protectores de los naturales or Andean advocates first presented a notarized list of accusations in their own name and those of the aggrieved. The Church's legal team then substantiated the accusations through examination of the litigants and witnesses in private interviews. Before providing an account of events, witnesses voiced an oath to God, with a hand on the Cross, to ensure the magistrate or fiscal that the statement was true.[61] To avoid linguistic distortions and curb false claims, canon law insisted that Indians testify in their native language through the mediation of two interpreters (Hevia Bolaños 1619, 80r).[62] Declarations took place before an interrogator and notary, who directed the testimony according to predetermined topics of interest and interrupted to ask for reiterations or clarifications. The notary "gave faith" to the oral declaration in the presence of at least two observers and with his signature provided material support to the witness statement and judged it to be efficacious (Hevia Bolaños 1619, 83v). Because disputes between Indians were often decided in Lima, written instruments allowed litigants to represent cases to the archdiocesan court in stages or in absentia, in contrast to folklaw tradition, which required the face-to-face meeting of opponents (Clanchy 1993, 273).

The highly mediated process by which Indians testified was not a strategy for suppressing the agency of witnesses. More accurately, it responded to the interrogators' need to evaluate and verify statements for the judicial system, for the benefit of the plaintiffs and the accused, and to establish reliability in the face of linguistic and cultural constraints. Visita records show that the recruitment of witnesses was often based less on the Indians' knowledge of events than on their social and ethical standing within the Church. Jurists examined vulnerable witnesses to find the alleged perpetrators of crimes, but, generally speaking, they relied on caciques principales, parish officials, and other indios ladinos of *buena fama* (good reputation) to verify claims against the clergy. False testimony was not to be tolerated, especially when it was intended to damage the honor and integrity of parish priests. The Third Council ordered magistrates to remind witnesses that lying under oath was a sacrilege and to subject perjurers to public whippings and hair cutting so as to set an example for others.[63] The Lima see demanded summary judgments, but distrust of indigenous plaintiffs made justice uncertain, despite the careful procedures for making statements legal.[64]

Llasta may have calculated that his claim against Celis would have greater force if presented in less negotiated terms than those of the formulaic deposition that passed through the hands of the ecclesiastical notary (even though as an independent first-person accusation, his statement cannot be regarded as "witness testimony" in the strict legal sense). Free from the constraints of the question-and-answer witness deposition, Llasta's plea highlights the affective field of his experience of bodily punishments, which lends credence to the account. Yet the testimony's emotive quality does not mean it should be understood as separate from the legal and social transactions that provided the conditions for its production. The authority of courtroom documents, including independent writings such as Llasta's, rested on a complex blend of social interactions, judicial procedures, and prescribed notions of legal proof.[65] What were the contextual factors that came to bear on the alcalde's petition of grievance?

Llasta produced his complaint as part of extensive litigations between the Indians of Cajacay and Celis that point to a history of contentious rivalries in the province of Cajatambo. The alcalde's denunciation came with an empowerment for another to represent his grievance, whose signature belonged to the native governor and cacique principal Don Rodrigo Flores Caja Malqui of the parish of Santo Domingo de Ocros.[66] Caja Malqui's hand in the accusation shows that clerical violence was just one of an assortment of troubles with church authority that concerned the Indians of the region. Other infringements of canon law that Caja Malqui and his colitigants had compiled against Celis included sacramental neglect, moral impropriety, linguistic ignorance, and the usurpation of secular jurisdiction in the adjudication of criminal disputes and in the monitoring of cabildo elections. The principal litigants began their accusations with Llasta's tale of abuse together with a series of independent victim accounts, which added verisimilitude and moral unity to the accusation: Don Gonzalo Fernández, the cacique of Yamor, claimed Celis had stolen one of his native tributaries; Diego Guaranga stated the priest had accosted him physically; Doña Francisca Carhua Hutui, the *cacica* and widow of Don Juan Flores Guayna Malqui, Caja Malqui's father, alleged that Celis had caused the loss of three hundred sheep from the family estate after forcing native pastors to work for his benefice; Juana Yaro complained that the minister underpaid the women he had hired to weave; and Diego Rimay sought money the priest owed him for watching over the church's livestock.[67] The succession of first-person accusations set a persuasive frame for the witness statements to follow.

Extant records of Celis's native ministry both support and undercut Llasta's claim of abuse. Peruvian-born and of illegitimate birth, Celis received holy orders in 1628, having passed studies in Quechua and sacred theology at Lima's University of San Marcos.[68] Visitations of the benefice of San Agustín de Cajacay in 1646 and 1654 concluded that he conducted himself with moral virtue, taught Christian doctrine in the Quechua language, and kept an orderly church and sacristy.[69] On both occasions, however, Lima's visitadores admonished Celis for heavy-handedness in punishing native misconduct. The indio ladino Juan Agustín, sacristan of Yamor, testified in 1646 that the minister publicly disciplined Indians who "do not live as they should."[70] In 1654, Judge Pablo de Paredes reprimanded Celis for cutting off the hair of Indians who filed complaints against him. "Indians should only be chastised for reasons and crimes that deserve punishment," Paredes advised him, "and [with punishment] appropriate to the said crimes and with the form of correction that the priestly vocation requires."[71]

As Carhua Hutui's complaint suggests, animosities between Celis and Caja Malqui had begun long before, when the benefice threatened assets of the cacique's family. In 1635, Lima's protector general of the Indians Juan del Campo Godoy petitioned Archbishop Arias de Ugarte on Caja Malqui's behalf, stating that Celis had imprisoned the cacique in Santo Domingo de Ocros and confiscated his sword and dagger. Though the cura alleged that Caja Malqui was actively encouraging the native parishioners of Ocros to file grievances against him, the protector maintained that the detention was part of the priest's scheme to assume the role of executor of Don Juan Flores Guayna Malqui's bountiful will.[72]

Celis responded aggressively to Caja Malqui's initial salvo. In 1642, the cura's allies—Felipe de Medina, the priest of Concepción de Gorgor, and

Francisco de Herrera, the fiscal of the metropolitan see—assembled evidence and witnesses, including a powerful rival cacique of the pueblo of Cochas, Don Cristóbal Yaco Poma, who alleged that Caja Malqui had committed religious crimes. Caja Malqui, they claimed, was an idolater devoted to the regional cults of Cajatambo, including the *malqui* (mummified body) of one of his ancestors, and maintained incestuous relations with his uncle's daughters. With the defendant imprisoned and protesting his innocence, Martín Jurado, one of the prosecution's native witnesses in the parish of Ocros, accused Caja Malqui of sponsoring traditional rituals for the ayllus of his district as well as idolatrous sacrifices that his mother Inés Yaro Tanta performed:

> [The witness] said it is true that he knows the said Don Rodrigo
> since he was little, and he knows that about four or five years
> ago the said [cacique] took the occasion to make a famous sac-
> rifice to the lightning bolt commonly known as Libiac, . . . [and]
> that to carry out the said sacrifice and feast that was arranged,
> Don Rodrigo Caja Malqui dressed and adorned the indios princi-
> pales . . . in traditional fashion with blankets and shirts of *cumbe*
> he had inherited from his ancestors, and once dressed, he ordered
> them to a mountain top called Racian, where the principales and
> the other men and women who had followed them killed a gua-
> naco and shared the meat among themselves, performing Gentile
> rites and ceremonies, offering it first to the said lightening bolt in
> order to placate the anger and wrath that they believed Libiac held
> against them.[73]

Jurado contended that the governor used Libiac and other sacred resources to fortify his political authority. After more than three years of charges and countercharges between the rival cacical factions, the provisor and vicar general of Lima, Martín de Velasco y Molina, absolved Caja Malqui of religious crimes and freed him from jail, with the admonishment to cease relations with his concubines. He declared Yaco Poma, on the other hand, a "false and calumnious litigant" who encouraged dishonest testimony, exiled him from his parish for six months, and ordered him to pay the legal fees of the accused in accordance with the Second Council's proscriptions against frivolous lawsuits.[74]

Defense testimony revealed the legitimacy of Caja Malqui's hereditary rank as well as his elite academic background. Caja Malqui was a graduate of El Colegio del Príncipe, where he studied in the 1620s ("Libro de la fundación" 1923, 801). The Jesuit priest Luis de Teruel, his former teacher, came to his defense at trial, verifying on record the cacique's studies in adolescence and his fulfillment of Christian obligations into adulthood as governor of the pueblos surrounding Santo Domingo de Ocros. Teruel also recalled that during Fernando de Avendaño's 1618 visita de idolatrías in Cajatambo, Caja Malqui's parents assisted the extirpation team in uncovering the malquis of their ancestors and gathering the townspeople for doctrina and Mass.[75] It is reasonable to assume that Caja Malqui's ties to the Jesuit order bolstered the litigants' defense and counterclaims against Celis.

Jurisdictional tensions also informed the Andean governor's legal strategy. It was common for native litigants to place secular and church authorities in opposition and to convince one side to support their version of events.[76] Caja Malqui's case had the support of the corregidor and justicia mayor of Cajatambo, Francisco del Doz. With Doz's backing, the accused governor argued in ecclesiastical court that the corregidor had declared the case *mixti fori* and therefore within the purview of secular jurisdiction. Indeed, the corregidor later cleared the cacique of Yaco Poma's "malicious" charges, stripped Yaco Poma of his office for six years, and sentenced him to four years of penitential service in Lima's Hospital de Santa Ana.[77]

Native litigants readily exploited the conflict between civil and ecclesiastical authority. Solórzano Pereira viewed the clergy's jurisdictional intrusions as a matter of great consequence. Civil and criminal lawsuits pertained to royal justice, he insisted, and should not appear before the bishops or ecclesiastical magistrates. In his view, the Lima see's judges erred in matters of civil and criminal law, entered into cases to expand their jurisdiction, ordered unjust imprisonments, and extorted money and goods from litigants in exchange for favorable rulings. Apart from clerics, only groups requiring the Church's protection, such as widows, the needy, and other *miserables* (defenseless persons), should be heard in its tribunals (Solórzano Pereira 1648, 547–48). Ecclesiastical jurists agreed in theory with the distinction between canon and civil law (Hevia Bolaños 1619, 18r), yet both legal systems shared judicial practices and principles, making the separation of the two difficult to establish, particularly given the diminished presence of secular authority in rural areas. Though the church tribunal rejected Doz and Caja Malqui's assertion, the cacique revealed his willingness to seize all procedural resources available to him. The litigation in Cajatambo shows that royal and church legislation was not merely an abstraction, but rather an integral part of the regulation of the social and fiscal interaction between Indians and Spaniards alike.[78]

Targeting "Bad Priests"

Litigation against Celis, which lasted for more than fifteen years, came to a conclusion in the early 1650s during the tenure of Archbishop Villagómez, when Caja Malqui turned to civil law, this time through the jurisdiction of the archdiocesan court and agency of the protector de indios. As governor of Santo Domingo de Ocros, Caja Malqui cared for the church's livestock. Though he was responsible for the maintenance of only six hundred animals belonging to the benefice, Celis had purportedly overburdened native tributaries with the custody of 1,300 animals without just compensation, and for this he owed them restitution.[79] The governor stated that the parish's ledger accounts, which he had kept, confirmed the numbers of livestock and unpaid monies. In this way, Caja Malqui's accounts monitored the parishioners' sacramental activities and material debts as well as the priest's. Such use of parish accounts was not unique. In earlier trials of curas in the provinces of Huaylas and Cajatambo, native litigants submitted padrones to church magistrates as evidence that priests had not fulfilled their obligation to confess the infirm and baptize infants.[80] For native assistants, then, padrones were not merely static instruments that repressive colonial authorities imposed upon them. More accurately, they were written records used to protect the community's needs and punish parish priests, in ways similar to the ones Covarrubias had envisioned for Castile's laborers.

Like activist cord keepers, Caja Malqui knew the obligations of Christian practice and the place of accounting debts in upholding the social order. His civil suit affirmed that dishonest exchange was a sin and that strict moral codes governed the exchange of goods and offerings. Early modern handbooks of commerce, the most notable being Thomas de Mercado's *Tratos y contratos de mercaderes y tratantes* (1569), emphasized the financial restitution of debts: "Our way of doing business is so avaricious, rare is the man who does not owe something to someone else. God loves us so much, and considers our debts His own, that He does not wish to befriend he who is our bad enemy, nor does He wish to reconcile with he who does not want to honor his debts to us."[81] The padrón was a tool of accounting that gave Indians a way to describe clerical misconduct in accordance with the same moral codes.

Despite the evidentiary record, Celis won his day in court, claiming that Caja Malqui violated the Third Council's prohibition against false and malicious accusations. Caja Malqui, he claimed, was a mere "indio"—a parvenu cacique who passed himself off as Christian yet used his knowledge of Spanish to manipulate the legal system and conceal his devotion to the ancestral divinities of Cajatambo.[82] Celis also stated that the punishments he had administered were in keeping with the mandates of Villagómez's *Carta pastoral de exortación e instrucción contra las idolatrías* of 1649:

> The said Don Rodrigo Flores has filed this petition out of the hatred and enmity he has always had for me, only because I did not allow him in my parish given the scandal he has caused there with his superstitions and idolatries, about which I have made complaints . . . and carried out general punishments and demonstrations of understanding in conformity with what so sacredly Your Excellency has ordered in your *Carta pastoral.*[83]

In 1652, the apostolic judge of appeals concurred, ruling that the protector de indios had no authority over the fiscal affairs of the benefice, whose parish accounts Archbishop Arias de Ugarte had commended in the decade of the 1630s.[84]

The priest's adversaries remained undeterred. That same year Domingo Llasta and two curacas of the parish of Yamor denounced Celis for repeatedly obliging them to perform mita service in Cajacay. They explained to Villagómez that caring for the cura's personal livestock was not a duty of native officers and that the work obligations came at the expense of their families and haciendas.[85] Celis claimed to have provisions authorizing three native mitayos for his personal service, but denied that the plaintiffs worked for him in Cajacay. Again, he alleged that Llasta and others had been induced to fabricate their "sinister account" at the behest of Caja Malqui.[86] Suspecting the native governor had falsified the complaint, and doubting the supplicants had even signed the grievance themselves, Celis asked the archbishop to demand they appear in Lima to verify the document that bore their signatures: "because if not, it will lead to new petitions being filed again and again, as you well know, especially when [the petitions] come without the signature of the protector or one of his attorneys."[87] Legal agents, both Spanish and Andean, often signed documents for others, which made the authenticity of certain testimony hard to determine. Whether Caja Malqui had actually done so or not, Celis appealed to the metropolitan see's doubts about grievances like Llasta's, that Indians penned independently, without the mediation of Spanish attorneys.

Accusations of false witnessing were constant in native lawsuits. Proving the fraud of adversaries could result not only in their legal defeat, but also in their banishment and loss of colonial title and office, as Martín de Velasco y Molina's sentence against the curaca Cristóbal Yaco Poma demonstrated. Alfonso X's *Siete partidas* called false testimony "one of the greatest evils man can commit" and declared exile or death to be fitting punishments for lying before a judge (Alfonso X [c. 1265] 1587, 27, cited in Adorno [1986] 2000, xxxvii). A claim of suborning or inducing testimony, as Celis made, offered litigants an effective strategy to invalidate an accusation against them. Keen to issues of legal procedure, Andean leaders accused padres doctrineros of compelling witnesses to testify falsely as well. The ubiquity of the charge of *jurar falso,* which each side would employ against its adversary, also suggests that witnesses conducted themselves in ethical solidarity with specific communities or actors, be they priests, corregidores, or native litigants, regardless of the empirical merits of the case. Frisch (2004, 24–25) provides a valuable clarification on this point that has implications for the study of legal trials in the colonial Andes: in the courtrooms of early modern times, "ethical witnesses" did not so much declare their observed knowledge of events as affirm publicly their support of the moral character of the person implicated in a dispute.

The trial record does not show whether Caja Malqui received punishments, but other documentation indicates that Celis overcame the charges and ascended to a high post in the extirpation-of-idolatries campaigns. In 1653, Celis acted as visitador and *juez de comisión* (Crown-appointed judge) in the inspection of the parish of Recuay in the province of Huaylas.[88] Five years later, he deposed Quechua-speaking witnesses as part of an ecclesiastical team investigating the activities of Visitador Bernardo de Novoa in San Pedro de Acas, which confirms his advanced standing among Lima's high clergy (Duviols 2003, 530). In all likelihood, Celis's continual appeals for justice as the embattled cura of Cajacay had earned the sympathy of Villagómez, whose policies showed little tolerance for traditional Andean religious practices or the native litigants who challenged the authority of priests.

The type of discipline that Celis meted out in the management of his benefice was a normal facet of Andean parish life. Lawful public beatings connected to the maintenance of political and religious boundaries and the configuration of alliances within the community. Still, Acosta's attempt to set priests on a higher moral plane did not stop ministerial excess, for priests operated within a colonial system that depended on native labor and resources, however equal under God the Church professed Indians to be. Violence was also a consequence of royal patronage over the Church, by which the clergy attended to the secular duties of tribute collection and law enforcement. Recourse to coercion did not always follow the ideals of reform put forth by provisions and canons, nor did it always guarantee a clergyman's hold on power, as the record of indigenous uses of the law attests. Ultimately, native advocates objected less to the Church's privilege to regulate commerce and protect Indians from sin than to the arbitrary violence that accompanied the exercise of corrupt ministerial authority. Litigants insisted that reprimands should occur within a juridical context, not extraofficially at the whim of priests.

Trial records evidence an intricate mosaic of social affiliations. Celis allied himself with native factions that supported and advanced his personal ambitions, and he attacked others that contested his control. At the same time, Andean communities were connected, for better or worse, to the priests who managed their secular and ritual lives.[89] Because priests had a central function in native society, one can assume that rival groups pursued the clergy to snare the attention of Lima authorities and advance their interests or concerns about economic and social affairs. In the accusatory papers of the Archive, priests and their adversaries stood for the extremes of human conduct, each side presenting the other as the foil against which their own Christian integrity could be portrayed. For native advocates, the strategy of targeting "bad priests" or, conversely, defending "good ones" lent authority to the values and concerns of the Lima Church and served as a conduit to achieving political outcomes at the local level.

In other words, alarm over clerical violence within the republic of Spaniards and that of Indians confirms the reality of abuse; however, the integral role that priests and native assistants had in fiscal governance placed them at the center of interparish conflicts, making them ready targets of Andean litigants who sought power or redress. Like the other complaints against the clergy, Domingo Llasta's appeal for justice presents, on the surface, a straightforward narrative of cruelty. But it also fits into a larger, interlocking set of issues about the secular and religious functions of parish priests and the jurisdictional complexities that accompanied Catholic rule. The history of clerical violence in native parishes is thus far more than a simple narrative about bad priests and indigenous victims. Locating the accusers and the accused in the Archive, side by side, produces a less univocal story line, where the inconsistencies within and between the testimonies are hard to resolve and Indian demands for justice become woven into a broader canvas, of which Guaman Poma's illustration forms one small part.

Chapter 5

Idolatry Through Andean Eyes

Untold Alliances

Studies of the Lima see's campaigns to extirpate idolatries often begin with Francisco de Ávila's well-known achievement of 1609: the capture, punishment, and forced atonement of Hernando Pauccar, the curaca and chief huaca minister in the parish of San Pedro de Mama. Ávila, the cura de indios of nearby San Damián, departed from the central highlands to Lima ten days following the investiture of Archbishop Bartolomé Lobo Guerrero, bringing with him a sizeable collection of the Checa people's ritual objects and mummified ancestors, as well as the imprisoned Pauccar, minister of the huaca Chaupi Ñamca. Within weeks of the display, the archbishop orchestrated an auto-da-fé outside the Lima cathedral in which Ávila, before the viceroy, high officials of the Church and royal audiencia, and hundreds of the city's Spanish and Indian residents, denounced from the pulpit the crimes of idolatry and superstition that still endured eighty years after the Europeans' initial invasion. Ávila drew a portrait of a war between Christianity and the devil's false religion, in which God's ministers, through divine grace and personal sacrifice, would eventually triumph. Following the sermon, the cathedral's attendants bound Pauccar to a pole, sheared his hair, and flogged him two hundred times, then set the sacred objects and the bodies of his ancestors ablaze. An ecclesiastical notary recorded his confession of idolatry for preservation in the archives and read aloud the sentence: perpetual banishment to a Jesuit house of penitential reform in Santiago de Chile (Ávila [1648] 1918, 67–69).[1]

The extirpator and the idolater constitute the rival pillars upon which the traditional historiography of extirpation in the Andes has rested. Ávila described a religious landscape in which the enemy huaca minister had revitalized pre-Columbian beliefs and practices in defiance of the Church. Repeating the views of Ávila and other colonial missionaries, pioneering studies of the extirpation campaigns have attributed the survival of autochthonous beliefs and models of identity to native resilience in the face of Spanish colonial authority. According to this view, evangelization in the Andes was marked by the capacity of native religious specialists to undermine the work of the clergy.[2] Yet while it is true that many Andeans such as Pauccar opposed extirpation's advance, hardened resolve does not account for the whole of indigenous experience under Catholic rule. Consideration of the native officials who assisted Ávila and other priests in uprooting the Indians' sacred objects and sites of worship illuminates a history in which the effort to contain traditional Andean religiosity owed as much to the indigenous forces within native parishes as to the European forces without.

Few accounts of extirpation mention the central part that Indian officials had in carrying out its mandate. In his classic history of Peru's so-called Inquisition for the Indians, Pierre Duviols ([1971] 1977, 283–85) was first to observe that bilingual Andean mediators collaborated with church magistrates in the extirpation of idolatries and were often the source of the inspectors' most important discoveries.[3] More recently, Rolena Adorno (1991) has examined how Guaman Poma and Pachacuti Yamqui perceived their role in similar campaigns in the regions of Huamanga and Cuzco, respectively. Still, the native assistants of extirpation in the central sierra remain anonymous masses whose individual contributions to anti-idolatry efforts are mostly unknown. Duviols' landmark 1986 publication of idolatry trial manuscripts, produced in the province of Cajatambo between 1565 and 1664, privileges the unmistakably heterodox testimonies of Indian ministers who upheld ancestral cults. Ethnographically oriented scholars have profitably examined this vast record for narratives of cultural revitalization, subaltern resistance to Catholicism, and inventive adaptation. Yet the published corpus supplies limited data on the activities of the native fiscales de la idolatría: extirpating Indian prosecutors, highly literate in Castilian, who directed judicial investigations of huaca priests, elicited confessions of sorcery, and recommended punishments.[4] Additional trial documents of the Archive contain the stories of the native officials who joined the Spanish side and became practitioners of its cultural and political forms. These documents present an alternative model for understanding indigenous social action and cultural practices in the process of coercive evangelization.

Indians throughout the Americas recognized the power of writing as an instrument of colonization, and many used it to challenge Christianity. But not all native literary activity was anticolonialist in nature. Two native fiscales surface repeatedly in the archival record as illustration of this fact: Don Juan Tocas and Agustín Capcha, who prosecuted religious crimes in the parishes of San Pedro de Acas and Nuestra Señora de la Asunción de Ambar, respectively. Aware of the power of language to effect social action, Tocas and Capcha utilized writing to mediate disputes between visitadores and native ministers and influenced the direction of the extirpation inquiries, sometimes over the will of local priests, sometimes against the interests of native communities. Their experience offers an instructive vantage point by which to evaluate the consequences of Andean literacy for the evangelization process. The first task is to learn what "idolatry" meant to Tocas and Capcha and what their views were compared to the views of parish priests and those of accused Indians. A complementary goal is to understand the competing pressures that visitadores and native idolatry ministers enacted upon them and how these pressures influenced the role they performed within the idolatry trial complex. In short, how did extirpation not only constrain the behavior of Indians, but also function as a site for the emergence of new forms of social engagement, cultural meaning, and perspective?

The Idolatry Inspection Team

Ávila's portrayal of Pauccar as symptomatic of a widespread evil in native parishes spurred Archbishop Lobo Guerrero's advocacy of forced conversion as a means of eliminating the Indians' fidelity to the traditional divinities. In 1609, drawing from Ávila's rallying cry and the support of the Society of Jesus, the archbishop instituted formal procedures for the judicial investigation and prosecution of Andean ministers in order to combat the Indians' backsliding and rejections of Christian teachings. Thus began the extirpation-of-idolatries campaigns that assailed native parishes of the archbishopric intermittently for more than a century.[5] Whatever the personal motivations of the first idolatry campaigns might have been or the so-called novelty of Ávila's discovery, the Lima Church took seriously the possibility of anti-Catholic heresy and other threats to Spain's political and religious dominion.[6]

The inspection teams that scoured Andean parishes for native dogmatists normally consisted of three Spanish or Creole officials. An ecclesiastical
judge, or visitador, of the archbishop's choosing directed the investigations
and trials of suspected idolaters and sentenced the guilty; the fiscal was a
bilingual Spaniard in charge of mediating interactions between the visitador and local authorities and arresting the accused; and a notary maintained
a written record of all evidence and witness testimony acquired during the
course of the visita. In some cases, a small group of churchmen (typically, in
the early years of extirpation, two or three Jesuit priests) assisted the inspector with the inquiries and trials of native religious specialists (Duviols [1971]
1977, 249–51). In his manual for visitadores de idolatrías of 1621, the Jesuit
Pablo José de Arriaga advised church inspectors to travel with as small an
entourage as possible, made up solely of the visitador's handpicked notary
and fiscal. For the latter post, he warned against recruiting Indians, whom
he considered unreliable: "It is best not [to employ] an Indian, for they have
caused many difficulties, and I have witnessed serious ones, but rather [to
employ] a person who is diligent and trustworthy."[7]

Most visitadores ignored Arriaga's counsel on native appointments. In
fact, they prized the assistance of the "indios de razón y confianza" who
interpreted languages, denounced native ministers, and evangelized Andeans under the scrutiny of the inspection teams. Idolatry trial records also
document the participation of indigenous notaries,[8] as well as several native
fiscales who brought formal complaints against Andean religious specialists. Fiscales mayores de la visita figure prominently in the archival record:
Don Felipe Condor Chagua, Don Sebastián Carhuas, Don Antonio Chupica, Don Tomás de Acosta, as well as Don Juan Tocas and Agustín Capcha,
both of whom carried out investigations and prosecutions in the service
of Archbishop Villagómez.[9] The penmanship and rhetorical command of
Carhuas's writings shows that the office of fiscal mayor belonged to indios
ladinos with advanced degrees of Spanish literacy. Capcha presumably
learned notarial writing and legal procedures in the late 1650s as the scribe
of Ambar's cabildo de indios. First as a native scribe and later as fiscal de la
visita, he wielded substantial influence over rival Indians as well as priests.[10]

Indian prosecutors of idolatries exercised special powers before ecclesiastical magistrates.[11] They identified offenders, initiated legal proceedings,
appointed native officers to capture suspects and assist in interrogations, and
recommended sentencing for the convicted. In 1644, Don Antonio Chupica,

FIGURE 16. The Visitador, the Native Fiscal, and the Idolater.
Guaman Poma, *El primer nueva corónica y buen gobierno*, 689.
Courtesy of the Royal Library, Copenhagen, Denmark.

a graduate of Lima's El Colegio del Príncipe and governor in the region of Checras, accused a group of Indian tributaries in the pueblo of Paccho of venerating a local huaca.[12] Chupica recruited an indigenous notary and language interpreters for the examination of witnesses, ordered native subordinates to arrest and confiscate the properties of the indicted, and stripped the defendants of their sacramental rights for the duration of the trial.[13] One of the governor's interpreters was a Quechua-speaking African, which was a post that other African assistants of visita tours held.[14]

On the opposite side of the tribunal were the legal defenders of the accused. Spanish lawyers usually played this role, but church magistrates also appointed bicultural Indians of the local community to call witnesses and argue for the defendants. As in the idolatry trials conducted by Spanish agents, the legal proceedings of native fiscales often culminated in a public confession under torment, the flogging of the accused, a procession of penance and shame, and the crier's proclamation of the crime (Mills 1994, 92). Ecclesiastical magistrates banished the most threatening ministers to Lima's Casa de Santa Cruz for convicted sorcerers, the Hospital de Santa Ana, also in the capital, and other houses of penitential reform.[15]

The Catholic Church had long advocated the practice of denunciation within parish communities as a way to cast out disruptive influences and preserve the uniformity of values (Lease 1996, 819–20). Edicts of the visita de idolatrías taught Indians that it was the obligation of Christians to identify prohibited rituals and idol keepers (Arriaga [1621] 1999, 169–72), and many obeyed, if not always of their free will. All sectors of Andean society aided the church inspection teams, in particular Indian youth, who were more inclined than native elders to cooperate with the visitadores. In a letter of 1648 to Archbishop Villagómez, the Jesuit Francisco Patiño praised the contribution of the "muchachos indiecitos" recruited by force in the region of Huamanga: "The visitador examined with great [care] four or six boys, and with a few threats of the whip, they revealed some sixteen shrines and twelve dogmatists."[16] Trial records from Cajatambo indicate that Indian boys and girls maintained cult objects and knew the location of huacas and the names of their custodians.[17] Also, indigenous parish officials gathered villagers to welcome the extirpation team, brought accused idolaters to the judge, and translated witness testimony.[18] According to Guaman Poma, native religious specialists feared the ladino informants who allied themselves with the extirpators: "To keep their idols and huacas, and pray to demons, they do not want the said priest, or corregidor, or any indio ladino Christian to know."[19]

Extirpators cultivated local native elites who knew the locations of forbidden shrines and the names of native ministers. Following Acosta's recommendation to "remove idolatries first from the hearts of curacas and principales" (Acosta [1577] 1987, 2:263–65), Arriaga counseled visita teams to secure the assistance of caciques and parish officials as its chief order of business:

> The first [task] is to win over an "indio de razón," and to do this with total discretion, offering him great awards and assuring him that no living person will know, and persuade him to reveal the principal huaca of the pueblo and the sorcerer who maintains it, and as much as he might know about this, and the first time, put him at ease and thank him and even pay him for whatever little he might say.[20]

Francisco de Ávila owed much of the success of his campaign in Huarochirí to the Andean lord Don Cristóbal Choque Casa. By the priest's account, his 1608 encounter with Choque Casa outside San Damián led to the discovery that the Indians secretly celebrated the pagan festival of Paria Caca in conjunction with the feast of the Assumption (Ávila [1648] 1918, 63). Other leaders of Huarochirí, including Choque Casa's father Don Gerónimo Cancho Huaman, aided Father Cristóbal de Castilla's earlier crusade against huaca worship, though Cancho Huaman was less decisive in Christian devotions in his final years and confessed to reverting to idolatry before his death (Salomon and Urioste [c. 1608] 1991, 103–4). Native elites of north-central provinces assisted the clergy as well. Fernando de la Carrera of San Martín de Reque described his recruitment of Andean ethnic lords in the uncompromising rhetoric of military conquest: "Once the cacique was vanquished, it was easy to vanquish the rest."[21]

A common technique of the extirpators was to oblige the caciques and other local religious authorities to renounce publicly their allegiance to the huacas and to persuade their subjects to do the same. Indigenous conversion narratives were demanded of Andean leaders as a means of persuading common Indians to embrace Christianity (Duviols [1971] 1977, 286–89). During his inspection tour of 1577 in the province of Huarochirí, Acosta obliged a cacique and confessed sorcerer to tell his story of Christian conversion to the native peoples they encountered on the road to Lima (Egaña 1954–1986, 2:232). Thirty years later, the crowning achievement of Ávila's investigations was Pauccar's coerced public declaration of guilt. A living symbol of "atonement" and "conversion," Pauccar was a powerful rhetorical ally of the extirpator on his proselytizing march from Huarochirí to the capital (Ávila [1648] 1918, 67–70). In 1617, Archbishop Lobo Guerrero ordered that Indians who reported idolatries be exempted from tribute for two years (Gareis 1999, 236, 248 n. 25), the cost paid from the coffers of convicted idolaters, though no evidence exists to prove that native informants received such privileges.

Defining Idolatry

Specific charges of idolatry varied; extirpation officials accused Indians of crimes ranging from malqui worship to diabolic healing. Yet the discursive continuity between Spanish- and Indian-authored prosecutions shows that visita teams presented a united front against idolaters no matter what the charge. The writings of the cacique principal and fiscal mayor of San Pedro de Ticllos, Don Juan Tocas, who assisted Visitador Bernardo de Novoa in the province of Cajatambo, illustrate the lines of argument that Indian fiscales employed. In March 1656, Tocas joined the extirpator on a visita de idolatrías in San Francisco de Cajamarquilla and served as Novoa's fiscal in at least six inquiries in parishes annexed to San Pedro de Acas over a two-year period.[22] Tocas composed his denunciations in keeping with topics and juridical formulae that extirpators used, which suggests he did so in partnership with Novoa and his Spanish officials.

The allegations of native prosecutors disclose the rhetorical mechanisms by which church officials aimed to replace pre-Hispanic values with Christian ones as well as the impact that the ideas of the Third Council, and of Acosta in particular, had on missionary approaches to local customs. Acosta's notions about religious customs in the Andes resonated not only in the literature of extirpation, such as printed sermonarios, but also in the legal discourse of Andean fiscales. In *Historia natural y moral de las Indias* (1590), Acosta classified the native peoples' diverse forms of religious expression into two basic types of "idolatry." He stated that Indians adored "natural things," such as celestial bodies and occurrences or elements of nature, as well as "things of human invention," such as man-made idols and mummified ancestors ([1590] 2002, 301–2; see also MacCormack 1991, 265). His definition of idolatry also extended to an analysis of its underlying motivation. While he assailed the clergy for its deficient methods of religious instruction, Acosta traced the fundamental cause of the Indians' mistaken belief in natural phenomena and inanimate objects to the work of the devil ([1590] 2002, 299).[23] Drawing from the writings of his Jesuit predecessor, Arriaga ([1621] 1999, 84) alerted Peru's extirpators that Satan and his ministers conspired to keep idolatry present in native hearts and minds.

Literate Andeans learned the Church's views on idolatry from the publications of the Third Council, through access to the books of the parish priest, and in their work alongside the clergy as catechists in parish and visita settings. The extirpation campaigns included a daily schedule of religious instruction following methods that Arriaga ([1621] 1999, 118–23) prescribed in his manual for church inspectors, which Archbishop Villagómez (1649, 52r–54r) repeated in his Carta pastoral. Kenneth Mills (1997, 181) calls attention to this "lesser-known instructive side" of the visita: mandatory catechesis and confession in the mornings and afternoons, daily Mass with anti-idolatry sermonizing, religious processions and devotional song, and nighttime readings of biblical parables followed by sessions of penitential discipline. The "reprehensions," or reproofs of native practices, that Pérez Bocanegra (1631, 381–450) included in his Ritual formulario, on topics such as sorcery, huaca devotions, and dream keeping, suggest that the confessional also functioned as a principal site of instruction on religious error. Such books detailed the forbidden religious customs that all converts were to report to the clergy.

Still, in Acosta's pedagogical vision, native-language preaching was the surest and most lasting remedy for indigenous superstition and huaca worship (Acosta [1577] 1987, 2:51). The Third Council's Tercero catecismo (1585), whose principal author was Acosta (Vargas Ugarte 1951–1954, 3:88, 95), and other sermon collections for Indian ministry, such as the works of Ávila (1648) and Fernando de Avendaño (1649), whose publication coincided with Villagómez's renewal of the extirpation campaigns, combined instruction on Christian morality with refutations of traditional Andean beliefs and devotions. The Tercero catecismo in particular was an essential tool in the curas de indios' ministerial repertoire.[24] Extirpators and parish priests used the sermon collection to address native audiences in the course of idolatry visitations. In fact, Arriaga ([1621] 1999, 105) ordered church inspectors to fine parish priests if they failed to preach in Quechua or to read the *Tercero catecismo* from the pulpit on Sundays and feasts.[25]

The thematic and rhetorical similarities between the published tracts and idolatry prosecutions suggest that the exhortations of the extirpation manuals (and of other sermons that priests delivered in the process of the campaigns) provided models of argumentation that Andean fiscales used to refute traditional Andean religious beliefs and practices in *causas de idolatrías*. Unlike the sermons that attempted to persuade native audiences of the vanity of huaca worship and the truth of Christianity, however, the legal denunciations of idolatries aimed to convince ecclesiastical jurists of the defendants' guilt. Indian prosecutors repeated the destructive arguments that missionary priests employed against Andean religion, but eschewed the use of cultural analogies and the affective tone that Acosta recommended for preachers. As a general rule, the allegations of Indian fiscales de la idolatría underscored three basic points about suspect Andean religiosity: the native ministers' rejection of God and the Church, the arrogance and vanity of believing in false gods, and the devil's role in traditional cult practices.

In 1656, Tocas brought charges against the native religious specialists of Acas and its environs for various crimes, including the adoration of malquis, ritual drinking and confession, magical healing ceremonies, clandestine burials, and the sacrifice of livestock to regional gods. Tocas's wording of the charges reflects the mechanisms by which Novoa's team aimed to impose its symbolic authority over native rivals. At the start of the one-folio complaint, Tocas named the principal offender, Don Hernando Hacas Poma, and alleged that he, together with the curaca Cristóbal Poma Libiac and other ayllu leaders in the area of Acas, practiced huaca rites in defiance of the authority of God, the Church, and the Spanish Crown:

> I state that it has come to my notice that all the aforementioned
> [Indians], with great disobedience, scandal, and little fear of
> God Our Lord, have neglected in every way our Holy Catholic
> Faith and distanced themselves from it without any fear of
> royal justice.[26]

In the native prosecutor's view, idolatry was first and foremost a crime against God's supremacy and the jurisdictional authority of the Spanish, not merely a sin of nature. Hacas Poma's idolatry network threatened the political legitimacy of the Church and Crown.

Tocas's representation of the devotions of Hacas Poma and his followers fit hand in glove with Acosta's two-part typology of idolatries, which encompassed "natural things" as well as "human inventions." The *Tercero catecismo* held that the veneration of natural phenomena and objects of human inspiration contradicted the notion of one Supreme Being, in violation of God's first commandment. Sermon 6 of the collection decried the "great lunacy" of the Indians' ancestors, who believed that celestial bodies (the sun, moon, Pleiades) or natural wonders and occurrences (mountains, thunder, streams) could "respond, hear, and take heed of their words and sacrifices" *(Tercero catecismo* [1585] 1985, 420–21). Sermon 19 ridiculed Indians who considered huacas and idols as gods (579).

In language that patterned the sermon manual's, Tocas stated that the native ministers' beliefs and ritual practices included ceremonies for the veneration of the dead, trust in false divinities of the physical world, such as celestial bodies (the sun and moon) and natural phenomena (whirlwinds and rainbows), and veneration of objects of human creation (idols):

> They remain in a heathen age, maintaining the rites, ceremonies, and superstitions [of that time], worshipping and giving cult to the malquis, or bodies of the deceased heathens, and other idols, household gods, and rocks called *conopas,* the sun, the morning star, two small stars they call Chuchu Coyllor, the seven stars called Pleiades, the sea, rivers, great whirlwinds, the rainbow, the bird they call Yuyoc, and especially the idol Yanac Tarqui Urao.[27]

Like the sermonario, Tocas stated that the accused failed to recognize that the inanimate world was subordinate to God as part of His creation. Furthermore, by defining Acas's religious practices as remnants of an earlier pagan age, he established a temporal division between the pre-Hispanic past and the colonial present in order to discredit forms of worship that originated in Peru before the arrival of Christianity. In Tocas's view, the

Indians of Acas lingered at a stage of cultural evolution behind that of Christians.[28]

To conclude his complaint, the fiscal repeated the *Tercero catecismo*'s claim that Indian sorcerers were "Satan's ministers" who imitated Christian rites, such as the confession sacrament, to enrich themselves with offerings and lure native parishioners away from the Catholic faith *(Tercero catecismo* [1585] 1985, 397, 565–66).[29] Tocas described the devotions of Acas as "simulacros del demonio." He claimed that Hacas Poma and his acolytes had established a counterministry and served the devil in ways that missionary priests served God:

> [The ministers safeguard] the malquis and make sacrifices to
> them with llama blood and tallow, coca, chicha, and guinea pigs
> on two different occasions of the year, forcing the Indians to
> confess with them over the course of five days in order to wor-
> ship their said idols, asking them for life and health, taking away
> the worship and cult that is owed to God Our Lord and giving it
> to simulacra of the devil and other creatures, dogmatizing and
> teaching the rest of the common Indian men and women that
> they are not to worship God Our Lord but rather their idols and
> malquis.[30]

Assertions of Satan's power surface in the writings of native fiscales as well as in the trial testimonies of Indian witnesses, who attributed their participation in forbidden rituals to the native ministers' staging of diabolic cults. During the idolatry investigation in Paccho in 1644, the native fiscal Don Antonio Chupica asked Angelina Chumbe why she had remained silent about the huaca devotions of the native ministers. She responded "that the devil had deceived her to keep her quiet."[31]

Anti-idolatry tracts, such as that of Arriaga ([1621] 1999, 41–49), described huaca devotion as a religious system that fulfilled a social and spiritual role parallel to that of the Church. Drawing on familiar Catholic terms, Tocas portrayed his adversaries as "ministros" heading formidable networks of "confesores," "predicadores," and "sacristanes," whose ritual duties mimicked those of church officials.[32] His writings show that in 1661, when Agustín Capcha denounced the alguacil Francisco Martín for a simulacrum of baptism and Mass in Ambar, legal precedents existed for accusing Andeans of usurping the role of missionary priests.

Predicaments of Collaboration

In 1617, Archbishop Lobo Guerrero decreed that church assistants who consorted with sorcerers were to be whipped and shorn, stripped of their exemption from tribute and service, and banned forever from holding the office of fiscal, alcalde, or alguacil.[33] But in pueblos where devotions to huacas were strong, Indians faced social ostracism for their collaboration with extirpating authorities. Don Cristóbal Choque Casa, for instance, told Ávila that the Checas would kill him if they were to find out that he had revealed the festivities of the god Paria Caca and his sister Chaupi Ñamca (Ávila [1648] 1918, 63–64). Areas of Cajatambo were especially unwelcoming for visita assistants due to the influence of native religious specialists, such as Hacas Poma, who attained considerable status for his professed ability to communicate with sacred ancestors, ward off epidemics, and predict harvests. Native witnesses stated that the huaca priest opposed all forms of Catholic observance and admonished Indians for venerating the "Spanish God" and his "mute" saints. Hacas Poma claimed that unlike the huacas, the Catholic saints could not speak or respond to the Indians' prayers.[34]

The parish fiscal of Acas, Francisco Poma, told Tocas that Hacas Poma cast spells on native officials who enforced the will of priests (Griffiths 1996, 202). According to Poma, the huaca minister forbade him to summon Indians to Mass and doctrina, especially at times of the year that the rules of ancient tradition had reserved for ritual fasting and confession to the malquis. Poma said that when he resisted Hacas Poma's order and forced the huaca priest to attend church, he suffered a mysterious illness that lasted six months, which the fiscal attributed to the minister's curse.[35] On the verge of death, having requested the final sacraments, Poma sought remedy in the source of his affliction by asking Hacas Poma's wife to have the minister sacrifice a llama in his name to appease the malquis and the divinity Yanaurau. The fiscal's deposition to Tocas stated:

> From that day and hour, [the witness] began to recover from his illness, and as soon as he was well, this witness went to see the said Hernando Hacas Poma to thank him because he was now healthy,

and he said: "Yayamic [father] and my lord, you are a great wise man and doctor, tell me who did this harm to me." And the said Hernando responded to him saying: "I am the one who made you sick because you took me and all the Indians to the church by force and blows at the time when we were fasting for our idols and huacas, and be sure not to do it again because I will have to do the same harm to you again."[36]

Hacas Poma's threat was not isolated. Poma testified that Pedro Capcha Yauri, the camachico of Santiago de Chilcas, had warned that anyone who assisted Novoa's investigation would be whipped and punished following the departure of the inspection team.[37] By Poma's account, such threats neutralized his loyalty to extirpation and convinced him of Hacas Poma's authority. His experience shows that there existed native parish officials who continued to maintain associations with huacas and the spiritual adversaries of the Church.

In 1657, Tocas expanded the pursuit of Hacas Poma's network to the pueblo of San Juan de Machaca and collected information on local practices from the parish official Pedro García. The *maestro de capilla* divulged the names of huaca leaders and led the visita team to *machays* (ancestral burial sites) where native ministers honored divine forebears and performed rituals of fasting and confession during the festivals of Pocoimita and Caruamita, which Indians celebrated in conjunction with the agricultural cycle. However, the informant's betrayal of the group came with social penalties. García informed Tocas that Machaca's leaders instructed villagers to avoid contact with Catholic priests and their Indian assistants:

Since this witness was and remains maestro de capilla and always walks with the priests, and when he was returning to his pueblo at the time of the said fasting and confessions, the said sorcerers sent an Indian to tell him not to enter the pueblo or join them in the said fasting and sacrifices because he came dirty, or "raccha," for having been with the said priest, singing and officiating the Masses, and for this reason, he was not to join them because the said malquis and idols would be angry and the said sacrifices would be for naught, and because of this, he did not enter [the pueblo] out of fear they would kill him.[38]

Fearful of retribution and the stigma of cultural "uncleanliness," García elected not to confront the religious specialists, as the research of Nicholas Griffiths (1996, 203) has previously noted.[39] Novoa commended García's honest testimony and help in locating malquis, but concluded that the chapel master had not done enough to impede the forbidden practices. He sentenced García to six months of personal service in the local church and threatened him with harsher punishments in Lima's Casa de Santa Cruz for any future lack of resolve.[40]

Despite warnings of severe penalties, native intermediaries continued to abet traditional beliefs and ritual activities in the parish communities they served. The 1656 idolatry trial of Governor Don Rodrigo de Guzmán Rupay Chagua disclosed the huaca minister Hernando Caruachin's knowledge of Spanish missionary culture and ties to native church personnel. Caruachin, minister of Guaracani, the mountain peak that overlooked the parish of Huamantanga, heard confessions and performed sacrifices to secure protection from natural misfortunes such as crop failures and human injuries.[41] To the alarm of extirpators, he confessed his allegiance to a holy stone (huanca) that the native parishioners revered inside the church in ways similar to their Catholic devotions. Concealed in the altar beside the crucifix, the sacred object allowed them to hear Mass without abandoning the traditional source of favor.

Extirpators suspected that even rituals conducted in the clergy's presence disguised what Estanislao de Vega Bazán (1656, s.f.) called "a very subtle idolatry" from view. Caruachin's testimony corroborates the allegation that Indians used traditional sacred objects in Catholic rituals. Caruachin recounted the time when he brought the ailing wife of the parish cantor to request the huanca's cure. Inside the church, they approached the altar, where Caruachin raised his hands aloft and addressed the stone in a way that evoked the Christian notion of the Supreme Being: "Father and our God, You who took the health from this poor woman, grant her life and take away her affliction."[42] He then cast holy water and coca leaves upon the altar, set down the offering of a dead baby llama, and burned the sacrifice in tallow until it became ash. Following the ceremony, they returned to the woman's home for a final remedy of condor's blood, after which her health, according to the minister, was restored.[43]

The observance of traditional devotions within the church shows that despite the isolation and anti-Christian posture of some huaca ministers, many practiced their craft in ways that intertwined with parish life (Mills 1997, 246). Andean parishioners, including officials of the Church, absorbed and refashioned Christian lessons and observances within a blended religious framework that included adaptations of ancestral devotions and sacred topographies. Native church officials adhered to Carhuachin's spiritual authority, which touched all sectors of Huamantanga, including the cantor's family and Rupay Chagua's. His ritual activities also met with the public approval, if not the direct participation, of the alcalde of the native cabildo.[44] The actions of Rupay Chagua, who repeatedly sought the assistance of the huaca minister to bolster his authority and punish political rivals, offers one example of the native church officials' pragmatic approaches to religious devotion.

The divide between loyal Christians and subversive idolaters in the daily practice of church life was hard to discern. Even Hacas Poma's power structure consisted of indios ladinos who held parish and civil government posts. Tocas's prosecutions in Acas and San Francisco de Otuco reveal that cabildo scribes, alcaldes, and alguaciles safeguarded Hacas Poma's cult objects and disciplined parishioners who did not attend his ritual ceremonies.[45] Two of the colonial officers assisting Hacas Poma—the alcalde Domingo Rimachin of Acas and the fiscal Andrés Chaupis Yauri of Otuco—guarded the mythic traditions of their respective parishes.[46] Rimachin's and Chaupis Yauri's accounts of the ethnic origins and religious beliefs of their forebears provided extirpators with valuable information on the regional devotions. Considering Guaman Poma's and Pachacuti Yamqui's oral histories of pre-Hispanic times, one can appreciate the thin line that separated the roles of two kinds of native intermediaries in Andean parishes: the accused idolaters who preserved the stories of regional gods and the lettered authors who expressed Christian values with reference to ancestral native traditions.

Though Hacas Poma and his assistants taught Indians to reject Spanish authority, they practiced sacred rites, made spiritual claims, and adopted institutional structures similar to those of the Church. Salomon has argued that the huaca devotions of Huarochirí survived alongside Christianity because native ministers posited traditional Andean beliefs as a "faith" that compared favorably to Catholicism's system of laws, rituals, and deities: "If huaca priests had retained the loyalty of people officially bound to Christianity, it was in all likelihood because they had succeeded, under the adverse conditions of clandestinity and church hegemony, in presenting huaca religion as comparable in cogency with the church's teachings" (1991, 3). The Christian concepts of moral obligation, ritual sacrifice, and prophetic action, to name a few, likely interacted with Hacas Poma's message and methods in Cajatambo as well.

Denouncing Native Ritual

Agustín Capcha's pursuit of religious crimes in the doctrina of Ambar began on 21 December 1661, when, while serving as sacristan of the parish, he denounced the cacique principal and native governor Don Juan Rodríguez Pilco before the visitador Juan Sarmiento de Vivero. According to the accusation, in June of that year, on the Sunday of the octave of Corpus Christi, the native parishioners had gathered to celebrate the body of Christ with the formality that typified celebrations of the holy feast throughout the Andes. As in other pueblos, the Indians dressed in the finery of their ayllus and assembled before decorative altars erected along the periphery of the square. They adorned the procession route with flowers and plumes, sang hymns to God and the saints, and kneeled as the host passed before them in its solemn march to the doors of the church. The cura of Ambar, Juan de Salazar Montesinos, together with his native acolytes, greeted the Holy Sacrament at the church with music and incense, and the assembly proceeded inside for Mass.[47] After the service, Governor Rodríguez Pilco and the leaders of the native cabildo organized a public banquet in the town square that included the performance of *takis* (traditional Andean dance and song) and abundant food and drink for the native parishioners, in keeping with the time-honored custom of reciprocity.[48] Salazar attended the afternoon's festivities, but quickly excused himself in order to oversee personal business at a nearby *chacra* (agricultural plot).

At around five o'clock, at the height of the celebration, the alguacil of the native cabildo, Francisco Martín, emerged from the back door of the church wearing a bearded mask and the priest's multihued stole, white surplice, and black biretta. Assisted by his brother Alonso, Martín circled the plaza, aspergillum in hand, "blessing" onlookers with sprinklings of water and incense, including those who performed the ritual dance. Next, the brothers approached two men, costumed as husband and wife, who presented the alguacil with a baby doll, which he anointed in the name of the Holy Trinity. Martín then advanced to an altar and received from his assistant a book, a loaf of bread, and a wooden chalice. In view of Rodríguez Pilco, the governor's brother Don Juan de Alvarado, also cacique principal of Ambar, and the cabildo officers, Martín genuflected and pronounced: "Dominus vobiscum." He stood up, removed from his vestments a piece of paper cut in the shape of the Host, and raised it aloft, thus completing a ritual that the tribunal would classify as "the crime of derision of the Holy Sacrament and Holy Sacrifice of the Mass."[49]

The scene moved all present to laughter, with the notable exception of Capcha. When Martín displayed the false Eucharist, the sacristan stormed the altar, tore the alguacil's costume, and called for an end to the "simulacrum of Mass" that debased the sacrament that Corpus was meant to honor. Capcha's tirade on the dais was brief. The cabildo's alcalde quickly seized the sacristan and brought him to Rodríguez Pilco, who called Capcha a "drunken dog" and thrashed him repeatedly over the head. According to Capcha, if not for the intervention of unnamed Spanish bystanders, who ushered him to the church for refuge, he would have died at the hands of the Indian governor.[50] Nevertheless, he survived to report the events to Sarmiento, who initiated legal proceedings, which lasted nearly four years, against Martín, the native governor who backed his performance, and Salazar, whose absence from Ambar had allowed the feast to transgress the standards of Catholic propriety.

Capcha's disclosure of the false Mass no doubt touched on many fears that Lima's high clergy had concerning ritual conduct in Andean parishes. Holding aloft a representation of the host, Martín feigned a sacramental function that no Indian could perform, no matter how loyal to the Church or versant in Catholic theology. However, native intermediaries frequently sought to occupy the role of priests and to participate in the administration of the holy office, as suggested by the Second Council's ban on the Indians' wearing of "priestly ornaments" other than a stole when assisting services in the church. In fact, church legislation reflects the continual worries of the ecclesiastical command about the high degree of autonomy that native assistants exercised in the pastoral supervision of indigenous parishioners.[51]

The sacristan would also have been aware of the extirpators' hostility toward Indian "error" and "excess" during the celebration of Corpus. Viceregal authorities endorsed the Indians' celebration of the feast, noting its value as both a weapon against heresy and an instrument of social cohesion. Yet they also recognized its potential as a platform for the undermining of colonialist agendas, especially when native parishioners invoked ancestral beliefs and customs in their adoration. The missionary guidelines of Acosta ([1577] 1984, 1:151, 591) and the Third Council allowed for ceremonial dances and banquets of Inca tradition on holy feasts, provided they took place in the public square, where parish priests could watch closely and, if necessary, castigate drunkenness and other improprieties, such as the worship of idols in Catholic guise.[52] There is reason to believe that indigenous groups of the central highlands associated local religious traditions with the feast of Corpus. In the province of Cajatambo, the Eucharistic celebration coincided with the festival of Carhuamita, the time of confession and sacrifice to the huacas in return for protection of the maize crops (MacCormack 1991, 418, 420–21). The Huarochirí manuscript indicates that on the eve of Corpus, the Mama people made sacrifices of guinea pigs and performed ritual dances for the huaca Chaupi Ñamca to show their appreciation for the harvest (Salomon and Urioste [c. 1608] 1991, 84).

Perhaps the most damning aspect of the report was its confirmation of the Indians' so-called penchant for derisively imitating the holy office. Capcha underscored the irreverent nature of Martín's performance: "[P]utting his head down, pretending to be an old man, with his hands trembling and preparing the ceremony of sanctification, he raised the paper, displaying it before the crowd."[53] Even through the highly mediated lens of a witness deposition, Martín's actions—the "blessing" of a baby doll, the trembling hands, the host made of paper, a garbled Latin prayer—appear to be more a caricature of Catholic ritual conduct than a sincere effort to approximate the celebration of the sacrament.[54] Did the feast's sponsors intend to parody the clergy's conduct in ritual? Were ecclesiastical ideas about the Indians' "mimetic desire" to undermine the sacraments, which native communities heard repeatedly in the course of visitas, the real target of ridicule?

Whatever the Indians' intentions actually were, Capcha's testimony more than satisfied the requirements for judicial inquiry. Sarmiento deposed Capcha's supporting witnesses, who reported that in addition to the governor's sponsorship of the impious ritual, Rodríguez Pilco generally failed to bring the parishioners to Mass and doctrina, and kept them occupied instead in the maintenance of his fields and livestock. By January, Sarmiento had ordered the detention of Francisco Martín, Rodríguez Pilco, and Don Juan de Alvarado, confiscated their possessions for the duration of the investigation and trial, and named the *alférez* Pedro de Salazar Negrete as defense attorney.[55] The visitador believed that the Indians' public piety was at minimum a sham, if not a cover for idolatry, and deserving of prosecution.

Tocas and Capcha's accusations suggest that extirpating Indians conveyed stock ecclesiastical views of Andean religious error. James Lockhart (1999, 271, cited in Burns 2005b, 375 n. 102) has located similar discursive uniformity—what he terms a "frozen zone of orthodox expression"—in the Nahuatl-language wills that indigenous notaries composed in colonial Mexico in accordance with juridical requirements. Setting Capcha's denunciations within the broader purview of internal parish conflict in Ambar, however, points to disparities between the unvarying prose of the idolatry complaints and other records of his social action, which allow for consideration of the conflictive local relationships and interests that informed his literary activity.[56] What can the statements of the accused and other witnesses reveal beyond Capcha's tidy expressions of Catholic piety? Historicizing additional documentation that revolved around the customs and social frictions in the parish shows that the sacristan's decision to testify against his adversaries was not wholly attributable to religious motivations.

Capcha's account of what happened the day after the violence highlights his estrangement from Salazar and Ambar's native leadership. On Monday morning, Salazar returned to town and entered the church, where he found the sacristan agonizing from his injuries. After hearing the sacristan recount the previous day's trouble, the priest began to scold him, asking why he had dared to call Rodríguez Pilco's authority into question. Capcha's second deposition in the case, given before Sarmiento on 20 January 1662, describes the conversation:

> There the said priest pointed to the Holy Sacrament and said "that
> Lord who is there and judging us has allowed for this to happen
> and will make sure this bad Indian [Don Juan Rodríguez Pilco] is
> punished," and when this witness [Capcha] began to cry, the said
> priest told him to be quiet and stop crying, for he knew well that
> Don Juan was at fault from what the others had said the night before,
> and to go with the said priest to the [priest's] house, and if there [the
> priest] should give him lashes, [Capcha] should bear them for the
> love of God.[57]

The priest then escorted Capcha to the rectory, where they encountered the native governor, a Spanish resident of the town named Juan Martín, and the native fiscal Alonso Malqui. Salazar ordered the sacristan to remove his clothes, kneel before the cacique, and confess to those present that "his governor was the maximum authority of this pueblo." Over the protests of Juan Martín, the priest thrashed Capcha several times with the help of his fiscal, then commanded him to get up and kiss Rodríguez Pilco's feet.[58]

Salazar's actions indicate that curas and native leaders persecuted Indians who threatened to disrupt local power-sharing arrangements. Despite Salazar's promise to Capcha that God would punish Rodríguez Pilco's bad deeds, the priest saw deference to the governor in the public sphere as a way to minimize conflict within the parish. Salazar was not the only parish priest to find personal advantages in ceding ground to traditional Andean authorities and their señorial power. Many priests believed that accommodating ethnic hierarchies and the local customs they supported was the best way to achieve gradual indoctrination or financial profit or simply to keep the parish free from strife. Typically, according to such agreements, the Indians' cultural and political autonomy was paid for through concessions to the economic interests of the clergy.[59]

The campaigns of extirpation disrupted such mutually beneficial alliances. Sarmiento jailed the priest for failing to supervise the banquet and for disciplining Capcha to appease the native governor and stripped him of his rights to minister in Ambar for the duration of the trial.[60] Likewise, the *promotor fiscal* of the Lima see cited Salazar's pastoral neglect as the reason for his punishment: "[The imprisonment] was for the said priest having abandoned the pueblo, leaving on a trip that day when he should have been attending to the problems and dangers that occur on such days of celebration in Indian pueblos."[61] From the visita's standpoint, the power sharing between the priest and the native leadership had more to do with advancing both groups' personal interests than with addressing the Indians' spiritual needs.

Karen Spalding's (2002, 67) research on idolatry trials in the Lima archbishopric poses a vital question relevant to the present case: Why did Indians accused of religious crimes frequently commit them openly, knowing full well that their actions could be taken as a violation of church law? Rodríguez Pilco and the cabildo officers directed the ritual in plain sight of the pueblo and, apparently, with Salazar's consent. After a half-century of extirpation campaigns throughout the central sierra, there can be little doubt that the native authorities understood the potential legal ramifications of their conduct. The trial dossier reveals Rodríguez Pilco and his allies to be well versed in Castilian letters and in the laws of the Church and secular administration. Capcha testified that after his beating, the governor warned him of the consequences should he or the priest complain to the Lima church authorities. "The Inquisition's ministers ... had no jurisdiction over the Indians' lawsuits," Rodríguez Pilco told him, "and if the priest were to take any action in defense of this witness [Capcha], everyone would bring capítulos against the said priest."[62]

The trial in Ambar resembles the legal cases studied by Spalding in which native authorities made sacrifices to the huacas publicly so as either to affront the parish priest or draw him into a lawsuit they considered winnable. Communal festivities, such as the celebration of Corpus Christi, therefore contained political implications insofar as they provided Andean ethnic lords an opportunity to demonstrate before the pueblo their power to control the ecclesiastical authorities who threatened native autonomy. Whether the supposed risks to Rodríguez Pilco were of an economic or a spiritual nature is difficult to know. Perhaps the irreverent feast was simply a form of ritual humiliation designed to affirm the governor's symbolic power over the parish. In any case, the priest's submissive conduct suggests that Rodríguez Pilco initially had reason to trust in his power to defend himself legally against possible accusations of religious crimes.

Within Extirpation's Mandate and Beyond

Capcha received handsome rewards for his allegiance to church authority. Because of his actions and testimony, Archbishop Villagómez named him to the post of fiscal de la visita, a position Capcha fulfilled with zeal throughout the 1660s as assistant to Sarmiento in Cajatambo. Sarmiento's repeated visitations throughout the Lima archdiocese are the most extensively documented extirpation campaigns of the Villagómez era. Named in 1660 to the prestigious office of visitador general de idolatría, the Lima-born, Jesuit-educated cleric responded to his commission with fervor, conducting in a ten-year period more than fifty visitas in the provinces of Huarochirí, Yauyos, Checras, and Cajatambo (Mills 1997, 272–73 n. 13). As Sarmiento's chief native aide, Capcha exercised his powers both within and without the legal parameters of extirpation in ways that many of Ambar's parishioners deemed excessive.

On 12 April 1662, not yet four months after denouncing the events on Corpus, the fiscal seized upon his new mandate by initiating four idolatry prosecutions. The first charges of "sorcery and superstition" targeted four Indian women of Ambar—Juana de los Reyes, Juana Mayguay, María Juliana, and María Canchan—who worked as specialists in matters of love and physical healing.[63] Capcha began his letter of denunciation to the archbishop by stating his credentials as fiscal mayor and the oath he took before Villagómez to denounce public sins. He then described the offense: Juana Mayguay orchestrated the group, which traveled throughout the region, using herbs, flowers, colored dirt, guinea pigs, and special ointments to cure ailments, resolve marital disputes, and fix unrequited affections. Capcha informed the interim cura, Fray Bernabé López de Burgos, of the crimes, arrested the offenders, confiscated their possessions, and ordered the cabildo scribe to record all trial actions and testimony in writing. The conclusion of Capcha's letter discloses material objectives as well: "I ask and beseech Your Mercy [to order] they be condemned with punishments for the crime they have committed . . . and that I be paid the royalties that are my due in accordance with the law, for which I ask justice and payments."[64] His explicit appeal for remuneration suggests that the boundary separating moral principle and economic interest in the conduct of extirpation was porous.

Capcha brought three more actions in November. First, he alleged that Domingo Guaman Iauri, the widower of Isabel, a well-known sorceress of Ambar, practiced witchcraft in a chacra in the pueblo of Ayllon.[65] Capcha then charged a group of Indians with performing a forbidden song and dance (guacón) to preserve the memory of ancient superstitions: "They dance with the women, who sing in their native language, praising the men for their ancestors or mountains peaks or punas, and claiming they descend from these mountain peaks and punas."[66] (With the assistance of the Spanish fiscal Juan Sánchez de la Cruz and unnamed officials of the native cabildo, Capcha raided the homes of the dancers and confiscated drums, "ugly masks," and traditional vestments.) Last, Capcha imprisoned Francisca Leonor, the ritual healer of nearby Hayba Valley, for killing her husband's lover and an ailing Spaniard with a magical concoction of poisoned herbs.[67]

Not all of Capcha's prosecutions went according to plan. At Guaman Iauri's trial, for example, witnesses confirmed the sorcery of his deceased wife, but refused to substantiate the allegations of witchcraft against the widower. Undeterred, Capcha accused Guaman Iauri's court-appointed defense attorney, Don Luis Gerónimo Rodríguez Pilco, of inducing false testimony in order to protect the idolatry network of his brother, the governor Don Juan.[68] The Lima see's response to Capcha's allegations is not known, but the native fiscal's involvement in the ongoing trial of Francisco Martín and the governor indicates that he had not yet spoken his last word against the powerful Rodríguez Pilco family. The records of Capcha's prosecutions against Ambar's ritual dancers and Francisca Leonor are also inconclusive. However, Sarmiento's achievement in convicting idolaters makes it likely that these cases also resulted in the confessions of the accused.

With the idolatry prosecutions in Ambar under way, Agustín Capcha extended the scope of his jurisdiction, initiating no fewer than ten prosecutions of community members for illicit cohabitation, adultery, and incest.[69] His accusations of "public scandal" touched all sectors of Ambar society—common Indians, aboriginal nobility, and mestizos—and expressed the moral imperative for exemplary punishments. "It is just that [the crime] be punished as a warning for many," stated Capcha in one of his many denunciations of sexual offenders.[70] When denouncing adultery and relations between family members, Capcha availed himself of the church's padrones of baptisms and marriages to substantiate the lawbreakers' kinship.[71]

Beyond the avowed desire to prosecute immoral behavior, Capcha's actions suggest his effort to cleanse a key vehicle of Ambar's corporate identity, the native cabildo, of its corrupt officials and allied nobility. Capcha decried the fact that when Santiago Guaranga brought a woman into the home he shared with his wife, the alcaldes of the municipal council refused to punish him because of his purported noble status. Elsewhere, the native fiscal asserted that Juan de Espinoza thought he could skirt ecclesiastical justice because he was the son of the alcalde Don Antonio de Heredia, as did Martín de Todos Santos, whose ties to the cacique Domingo Rodríguez Pilco allegedly shielded him and María Magdalena from the town council's vigilance.[72] According to Capcha, the cabildo's regidor Alonso de Todos Santos sired a daughter outside of marriage and used his office "not for the service of God, but to offend Him as a very bad Christian without any fear of God Our Lord."[73] Along the same lines, the fiscal declared that the alcalde Don Luis Gonzaga misused the authority of his position and friendship with Governor Rodríguez Pilco to seduce and rape women with impunity and baptized an illegitimate son in a church celebration with wine and dance, to the shock of native bystanders "who do not commit such sins of the lustful."[74]

The litigation thus extended well beyond the limits of the typical idolatry inquiry. Gonzaga came under fire for misuse of funds belonging to Ambar's confraternity of the Holy Sacrament. Capcha charged that in his two years as the cofradía's mayordomo, Gonzaga collected offerings of silver, corn, potatoes, and eggs, and bequests from the deceased, without keeping proper accounts.[75] Other parishioners had to answer for similar crimes. Capcha claimed that Juan Guaman withheld proceeds from an apple orchard owed to the confraternity of San Pedro, as stipulated in the last will of Barbola Quillay, which Capcha himself had drawn up in 1659 as Ambar's cabildo scribe. After reviewing the will and payment receipts that Capcha had drafted and submitted as evidence, Sarmiento authorized him to seize the property of the offender, who had fled the parish to avoid the visitador's justice.[76] For his part, Don Juan Rodríguez Pilco was also ordered to repay three bushels of wheat he was said to owe the confraternity of the Holy Sacrament.[77]

In addition, Capcha used extirpation's authority to pursue the clergy. First, his censure of Martín and Rodríguez Pilco for the celebration on Corpus resulted in Salazar's imprisonment for pastoral neglect.[78] Second, the fiscal targeted the presbítero Fernando de Paz Melgorejo, another interim cura in Ambar, for the ways in which he administered the sacraments. On 2 December 1662, Capcha filed two separate complaints against the priest for marrying Indians without researching possible impediments to their union. Before officiating the Mass of Juan Pérez and María Cristina, Paz allegedly declared the marriage banns in Spanish, for he could not speak the parishioners' Quechua, and officiated the sacrament without verifying the couple's origin or legitimate birth.[79] Capcha also claimed that only a cursory notice of intended marriage preceded the union of María de la Cruz and an unnamed Indian outsider. In the fiscal's view, Paz took more interest in collecting royalties than instructing the parishioners in the holiness of the sacrament.[80]

Capcha stated further that the clergyman exhibited a violent temper, as when Paz thrashed the Indian woman named María Magdalena for having cast a spell upon him: "He said she had placed a hex on him, making him ill with a stomachache, and he grabbed the said Indian by the hair, saying to her 'Indian dog, you have cursed me.'"[81] The accusation suggests not only that the priest believed in the sorceress's magical power to inflict harm, but also that Capcha was willing to cast Andean healers in the role of victim if it served to strengthen his prosecution against a rival priest. Capcha's fourth letter to Sarmiento in protest of Paz's ministry confirms that tensions between them ran deep. According to the fiscal, the embattled priest had insulted him publicly, calling him a "tattletale" and "thief," and had convinced the other clergy of the district to spurn his authority:

> As a priest and minister of God, the said licentiate could assist me, but has not done so, preferring to encourage the other priests to lose respect for me, and since the same ecclesiastics treat me badly, they also want to lose respect for me in order to pursue their vices and sins, without receiving punishment for their bad custom of paying little attention to the justice of the Crown and the visitadores who represent the figure of the archbishop, my lord.[82]

Capcha alleged that Paz acted without any deference to his title of fiscal mayor and mandate to castigate sins for the good Christian example of others.[83]

After reading Capcha's news of turmoil in Ambar, Sarmiento returned from his visitation in a neighboring parish. The visitador was angered to learn that an Indian had died without last rites due to Paz's oversight and that Paz had entrusted Don Luis Gerónimo Rodríguez Pilco with the keys to the sacristy in disregard of Lobo Guerrero's synodal constitutions. He ordered Paz to pay fines of twelve pesos and eight reales, and recommended the suspension of his appointment, pending Archbishop Villagómez's final judgment.[84] Fray López de Burgos, who served as the notary of Sarmiento's visita, entered his account of the conflict into the written report for Villagómez, which highlighted the intraparish conflicts that Capcha's policing activities had caused. López de Burgos informed Villagómez that from the hallway of Sarmiento's Ambar residence, he had overheard a conversation between the visitador and Paz in which Sarmiento told the priest to leave town immediately "because he had caused havoc and verbally abused Agustín Capcha, his ecclesiastical minister."[85] The friar-notary implied that the visitador acted to protect the authority of his native officials more than that of the parish priest, and gently called into question Sarmiento's claims about the purely religious motivations of his conduct. Burgos's testimony shows that the authority that native church personnel exercised in the conduct of idolatry visitations was an issue on which the opinions of Spanish extirpation officials diverged.

Capcha's legal activity provides a clear picture of the role of native intermediaries in the frictions that developed between extirpation officials, on one side, and curas de indios and native parishioners, on the other. Neither priests nor Indians wished to see visitadores and extirpation assistants interrupt the productivity of the benefice and avail themselves of community goods during the course of prolonged stays. Without official funding since the days of Lobo Guerrero, many idolatry inspectors felt they had a right to finance investigations and increase their stipend through voluntary and forced contributions of products from the Indians and payments for religious services (Mills 1997, 157–58). Guaman Poma ([c. 1615] 1980, 1121) repeated the well-known accusation that Ávila had confiscated the goods of Huarochirí's Indians "so color de idolatrías"—that is, under the pretext they provided for idolatrous cults.

In 1658 and 1660, with the assistance of the procurador de los naturales, Thomas Hurtado, Indian leaders of Acas, Machaca, Chilcas, and Cochillas brought litigation against Bernardo de Novoa for excesses in the conduct of the investigations of Hacas Poma and his associates. They alleged that Novoa had induced false confessions through extreme torments and imprisonments, which resulted in the deaths of Hacas Poma and Don Cristóbal Aca Malqui, and that with Tocas's assistance, he had confiscated livestock, corn, and silver, alleging these resources supported the worship of huacas.[86] Yet Novoa received no sanctions for the purported abuses and conducted idolatry trials throughout the 1660s. A key witness, Francisco de la Llana, interim cura of San Juan de Cochas, rejected the Indians' claims of Novoa's cruelties and financial extortion. The priest attributed the litigants' claims to fear of being sent to Lima's Casa de Santa Cruz and asserted that Hacas Poma and other convicted idolaters had died of natural causes.[87]

Before and after Sarmiento's time in Cajatambo, Indians in the provinces of Huarochirí and Canta brought charges against him for cruelty in the conduct of his inquiries (Mills 1997, 158–59). Having worked for many years as chaplain of the Convento de la Encarnación in Lima before his commission as an idolatry inspector, Sarmiento was rare among extirpators for not having served as a cura de indios, many of whom maintained affective bonds to the communities they once ministered. Bartolomé Jurado Palomino, visitador of the archbishopric, Quechua linguist, and beneficiary of San Francisco de Ihuari, aided Sarmiento in the arrest of Indians for cohabitation during Sarmiento's 1662 inspection in Sayán, in the province of Chancay.[88] But four years later, Jurado had grown disillusioned with the extirpator's methods and complained about the local unrest his idolatry visitations had caused. According to the inquiry of Juan Cabello, the promotor fiscal of the Lima archbishopric, Jurado had instructed the villagers of Ihuari to flee the area in advance of Sarmiento's arrival so as to protect them from the visitador's extortions and harsh punishments.[89]

Similar grievances in Ambar confirm Sarmiento's pattern of overburdening native parishes. In December 1662, the alcaldes of the native cabildo, Don Luis Gonzaga among them, traveled to Lima to denounce the visitador for exploiting the Indians and their assets for the three months of his still-ongoing visitation. They claimed that Sarmiento confiscated the parishioners' animals and produce, forcing them to sign papers legalizing the "sales," and fabricated charges of idolatry and cohabitation to punish those who did not support the criminal allegations against Governor Rodríguez Pilco.[90] The indictment also mentioned the imprisonment, torture, and hair-cutting of several native authorities, including Domingo Guaman Iauri, Martín de Todos Santos, and Alonso de Todos Santos, some of whom the inspector released from jail, but only after seizing their houses or demanding monetary bribes. Unable to tolerate the abuses, many Indian families had fled the parish, leaving their homes and plots behind. On 8 January of the following year, Archbishop Villagómez dispatched the beneficiary and vicar of Huaura, Pedro Ruiz de Garfias, to Ambar in order to investigate. Native witnesses in the parish confirmed the alcaldes' story of abuse, which Villagómez then sent to the protector de los naturales and the promotor fiscal of the Lima archbishopric for further review.[91] Though records of Villagómez final judgment are missing, the fact that Sarmiento faced accusations of corruption and cruelty in the region of Canta in 1665 indicates that his abusive conduct went unabated.[92]

Behind the Official Story

By 1663, toward the end of the trial of Martín and Rodríguez Pilco, Capcha's leading role in the policing of Andean parish life was clear. Initially,

Rodríguez Pilco denied involvement in the false Mass and refused the terms in which it was expressed. The only "crime," he stated in an elegant written Spanish of his own hand, was "allowing the Indians of his district to use ecclesiastical vestments to celebrate their dances and feasts,"[93] and not derision of the Holy Sacrament, as Capcha had alleged. But after three years of litigation in which Rodríguez Pilco made repeated but unsuccessful appeals to the Lima see to release him from confinement, the governor changed the tone of his defense, stating that Capcha's legal motivations were personal. Capcha was an "easy Indian" given to drink and fabrication, and the governor's "capital enemy" because the native lord had mistreated an Indian woman named Clara, the church assistant's friend. Moreover, the governor claimed that not he, but Capcha had participated in the mock ritual.[94] Though Rodríguez Pilco cried malice, at no time did he call into question the prerogatives of extirpation or the gravity of the charges, which in this case, points to the campaigns' success in eroding the traditional power and ideologies of the Andean nobility.

A remarkable epistolary exchange located among the papers of the trial casts light on a private record of personal attitudes and shifting relationships that took place outside the official courtroom proceedings and that rarely surfaced in juridical testimonies. In September 1663, after winning provisional release from jail, Father Salazar wrote a confidential missive to his "compadre" Agustín Capcha in an attempt to make amends with his former sacristan and secure his help in controlling the imprisoned governor, whom he now considered a nemesis. The priest reiterated his support of Capcha and his distrust of the native governor, who according to him, abused the poor, lived with women outside marriage, and mocked God's sacred rituals. Salazar stated his hope that Rodríguez Pilco, in his words a "pícaro" and "vengeful plaintiff," would lose his cacicazgo and receive many years of exile for his mistreatment of the visita assistant.[95]

Salazar also warned that Rodríguez Pilco had induced witnesses to report to the protector de los naturales Juan de Padilla that it was Capcha who had lied about what happened during the Corpus festivities. At the governor's behest, they informed Padilla that Capcha had given Francisco Martín the ecclesiastical vestments, ordered him to say the false Mass, and chastised those who interfered in the ritual. For that reason, the witnesses explained, the governor stripped Capcha of the office of sacristan, which supposedly clarified why the sacristan made the scurrilous charges against the governor. Given these trial developments, Salazar pleaded for Capcha to make haste to the parish of Huaura so that the two could return together to Ambar and mount a joint legal effort to keep the cacique principal behind bars.[96]

By that stage of the trial, however, the tables had turned, and the now-powerful Capcha saw little benefit in aligning himself with the now-disgraced priest. Going against Salazar's request for secrecy, Capcha wrote a letter to Rodríguez Pilco in which he enclosed the priest's missive. Weary after years of mounting litigation, he told the governor that he had no intention of aiding Salazar: "I responded to the [priest's] said letter with the excuse that I had obligations and was busy with my potato field."[97] At the same time, Capcha advised the governor not to seek revenge against his enemies, which included the priest, and to cease making false claims through the ecclesiastical court: "Vengeance should not be considered or even imagined because it will be deserving of God's eternal punishment."[98] The reproachful language of his letter shows that the institution of extirpation gave aspiring Indian commoners such as Capcha a weapon with which to contest the power of the traditional native hierarchy, not to mention priests, in ways that did not respect previous norms of deference.

Rodríguez Pilco submitted the letters to the court as evidence of Salazar's duplicity and Capcha's support. He petitioned Archbishop Villagómez to uphold Salazar's removal from Ambar so as to prevent the priest's manipulation of witnesses and issuing of false charges against him.[99] The request was denied. In 1665, Sarmiento declared Rodríguez Pilco guilty of deriding the Eucharistic sacrament and ordered his banishment from Ambar for six years; he would serve the first three years of his sentence in Lima's Hospital de Santa Ana.[100] The "false priest" Francisco Martín confirmed Capcha's account of the events, and at the conclusion of the trial's surviving documents, remained under arrest until final sentencing. In the final analysis, Rodríguez Pilco had misjudged the strong response that his actions would provoke from the extirpating authorities, who this time demonstrated their ability to punish heterodox practices.

Inconsistent testimonies make it difficult to know what motivated Martín and his sponsors to celebrate Corpus in such a way. Did the ritual convey the Indians' attempt to transcend their subordinate status and communicate with the Christian God on their own terms, without ecclesiastical guidance or supervision? Was the intention to ridicule Christian priests and the Eucharistic sacrament, as the extirpators held, in keeping with an anti-Catholic philosophy? Did the extirpators uncover a habitual Andean form of religious expression that took place according to collective arrangements, with the full consent of the parish priest? The juridical text narrates a ritual act that in all likelihood served a variety of functions simultaneously, given the many viewpoints and objectives of its diverse participants.

Idolatry trial records provide glimpses of Andean ritual life but not the code for deciphering its multiple and contradictory meanings. Plainer to see are the antagonisms that the Lima see's campaigns of extirpation provoked in native parishes among the various overlapping Spanish and Indian groups that made up colonial society. Internal parish confrontations and shifting alliances signal the political and social interests that motivated and sustained the accusations of religious crimes. But the idolatry campaigns represented more than the legal expression of political divisions; they reveal how native Andean communities tested and defined the limits of Christian teachings on morality and ritual in local settings.[101]

The writings of Indian prosecutors reveal unexpected ties and discontinuities between visitadores, parish priests, and native leaders, and temper the idea that Andean idolatry was simply a collective indigenous rejection of Christianity based on religious outlook. Indian prosecutors denounced idolatries, despite Arriaga's call to conduct extirpation through the clergy, and they enforced Catholic rule in native parishes. Unfortunately, the records of their legal activity exist only in archival fragments, but the stories they contain suggest that the cultural perspectives of some Spaniards and some Andeans were not always at odds, and that the words of an ecclesiastical lawsuit were not always words that were written by a priest. Monolithic perceptions of the extirpator and the idolater obscure the dynamics of religious change and social activism that the institution of the visita made possible. The indigenous writings of the colonial tribunal show that Europeans offered competing examples of what it meant to be Christian and that Indians did as well.

Chapter 6

The Polemics of Practical Literacy

Accessing the Lettered City

When in 1658 Archbishop Villagómez reported to Philip IV on the state of evangelization in the central highlands, the campaign to extirpate native idolatries was embroiled in controversy.[1] Four years earlier, Juan de Padilla, the top criminal attorney of the Lima audiencia, had written the first of several missives to the Crown in which he denounced the Andeans' ignorance of Christian doctrine and sounded the need for a more practiced and attentive missionary clergy. A 1657 memorial offered an especially damning portrait of the Indians' treatment under Villagómez: incompetent bishops and visitadores neglected their duty to supervise the conduct of parish priests and take seriously indigenous complaints of mistreatment (Padilla [1657] 1966, 391–96). Given the mounting evidence of the extirpators' abuses and the lack of pastoral achievement, it was clear that Padilla's attack targeted indirectly the policies of extirpation that defined the archbishop's tenure. Villagómez and his opponents agreed that native distortions of Catholicism required urgent attention. But Padilla and reformers within the audiencia saw better religious instruction as a more sensible remedy than harsher punishments of alleged idolaters.

Padilla's memorial stoked already bad relations between the audiencia and the archbishop, who complained to the king about the waning support for extirpation among secular authorities and certain missionary groups, namely the Jesuit order, which played an instrumental role in the early campaigns but had grown disillusioned with the extirpators' punitive methods.[2] In 1660, eager to resolve the conflict and gain a tighter hold on native religious error, Philip IV ordered the viceroy, Villagómez, and officials of the audiencia to convene and produce a unified strategy. Diego de León Pinelo, brother of the royal chronicler Antonio and Peru's venerated protector general of the Indians, penned the commission's response to Padilla's allegations. Laws for the protection of Indians abounded, he wrote, and stricter enforcement of them should curtail the excesses of visitadores and parish priests, and lead to the improvement of temporal and spiritual affairs in native parishes (León Pinelo 1661, 1r).

Reports of the clergy's bad conduct and the Indians' religious deviations were routine. However, the protector included a fact that was missing from Villagómez's letters to the king. León Pinelo stated that numerous and protracted native lawsuits against priests and extirpators overwhelmed his office; what is more, the litigation constituted his primary source of knowledge about the conditions in native parishes. The legal cases that had passed before him in the five years of his mandate were myriad: the Andean governor Don Juan Piric of Huánuco charged Fray Juan de Vara of mistreating laborers in his textile workshop; Indians of Cajatambo filed capítulos against their priest, Fernando de Avendaño; native parishioners denounced Father Juan Gutiérrez Censio; others in Canta claimed mistreatment from the visitador Pedro de Quijano Zevallos, leading to the suspension of his office; the cacique Don Antonio Chaibac of Huanchaco incriminated two Franciscan friars; Don Pedro Angas Lingón sued the priest of Cajamarca, and Don Baltazar Ticsi Canguala, the priest of Concepción in the valley of Jauja; in Chancay, an Indian complained that his priest had whipped him twenty times for baptizing his already-christened son; native grievances from as far as La Plata had reached León Pinelo's desk as well (León Pinelo 1661, 7v, 9v). Atop the protector's list was one of the Lima archdiocese's most trying conflicts: the ongoing dispute in Huamantanga between the Mercedarian friars and Don Rodrigo de Guzmán Rupay Chagua.

Colonial-era imprints rarely mentioned Indians by name, which points out the general exclusion of native Andeans from participation in the "lettered city." Even more infrequent is to find in print the names of individuals whose activities fill the manuscript proceedings of church archives. León Pinelo's report once again shows that there existed legal avenues that connected Andeans of the sierra with the viceregal authorities of Lima and calls into question the idea that a republic of Indians lived divided, physically and administratively, from a republic of Spaniards. The writings of Rupay Chagua and the native governing class had reached the desk of the protector general in great numbers, indicating to him that native resistance to the demands of priests and visitadores was endemic. Also striking is how closely the Indians' petitions of grievance coincided with the Spaniards' reformist discourses on evangelization. León Pinelo perceived his own views and interests as directly tied to native literary practices, which brings to light the unexpected connections between the writings of Lima's elites and the mundane literature of rural native society.

Spanish observers universally acknowledged the native peoples' extensive use of the legal system, the litigious Indian being a recurring trope in colonial writings ranging from juridical treatises to the chronicles of the Indies. Colonialist images of native litigation clustered around one of two contradictory poles. On the one hand was the poor and defenseless Indian who sought a justice that was far from certain. The plaintiffs of León Pinelo's account had to come to terms with the fact that even though their complaints had reached the highest Lima authorities, favorable rulings were unlikely. In the words of the protector, "Experience shows that such lawsuits always turn out to be hard to prove."[3] On the other hand was the calculating type who acted out of self-interest, not in the service of Spanish authority. To the critics of native legal activity, Villagómez among them, allowing Indians access to colonial tribunals was one thing; allowing them to clog the ecclesiastical bureaucracy with lawsuits was another. What divided the two camps was the question of why the Indians were so assertive in pursuing claims. Did the causas de capítulos respond to the Indians' lack of justice, or did Indians have subversive aims in mind? More perplexing, why did they continue to file lawsuit after lawsuit when, as León Pinelo suggested, the possibilities of redress or retribution were slim?

Colonial historiography has dwelled on the crisis between native subjects and imperial law, with special attention to Spanish debates on the legality of New World conquest and the place that native custom should have in the colonial legal order (Hanke 1949; Pagden [1982] 1986). Scholars have also studied indigenous lawsuits as sources of social history, focusing on the Indians' entry into the Spanish courts over land claims and labor disputes in order to assess the ways in which law shaped native social initiative.[4] Yet, for the most part, knowledge of the role and outcomes of native litigation about missionary affairs is modest.[5] Data on the collaboration between Andean parish leaders and Spanish legal agents such as León Pinelo are even more sparse, making it difficult to pinpoint where Spanish protectionism ended and native agency began. Working through the official stereotypes of the indigenous plaintiff requires historicizing the process and effects of native litigation within this key and largely neglected arena of Spanish-Andean encounter.

To make claims of clerical abuse or neglect, Andean plaintiffs acted independently or sought assistance from a wide variety of legal specialists, from native governors and cabildo officers to ecclesiastical magistrates to Spanish judges of the countryside, even the protector general of Lima's audiencia. Lengthy appeals obliged them to navigate the long distance from the highlands to the coast and included a paper trail involving Spaniards and Indians that moved from one jurisdiction to the next. What was the fraught legal process by which Andean leaders of the central sierra gained access to Lima's inner circle? By what discursive strategies did they merge their literary personae and interests with the moral economy and literary models of the lettered city? Answers to these questions detail the unforeseen ways in which native litigation collided with Villagómez's extirpating designs and the places where it left an enduring mark. The archive of the Lima archdiocese provides case studies for necessary insight.

The Office of the Protector

Padilla's and León Pinelo's memoriales form part of a long history of Spanish opposition to the Indians' persecution. A paternalistic impulse toward native subjects began early in the Spanish conquest, when in 1516 King Ferdinand bestowed upon Las Casas the title of "universal protector of all the Indians of the Indies" in an attempt to curb the destructive effects of the *encomienda* (grant by the Crown of native labor and land to a Spanish trustee) (Cutter 1986, 10). The bishops were the first but not the only group to assume this role. Alfonso X's *Siete partidas* (c. 1265) documents the Crown of Castile's medieval custom, based on Roman precedents, of providing assistance in legal matters to "miserables en derecho," meaning poor or otherwise defenseless subjects in need of special protection (Benton 2002, 44). In the sixteenth century, the monarchy granted Indians similar legal status, which came with various assurances of justice, such as access to the administrative support of royal audiencias, reduction in the costs of bringing suits, and Spanish legal representation in urban and remote areas through Crown-appointed protectores de los naturales, who facilitated and presided over native lawsuits, and procuradores, the Indians' courtroom advocates (Solórzano Pereira 1648, 230–38).[6] Lima's Third Council upheld the bishops' obligation to ensure the legal protection of native peoples.[7] Yet Philip II had already transferred the office of protector to the Lima audiencia in 1554, believing that royal justice would better serve Andean peoples than the overtaxed bishops, and one decade later, royal attorneys represented Indians in civil and criminal lawsuits (Bonnett 1992, 19). Most suits involved property claims and tribute complaints against secular authorities, but a large segment alleged the corrupt activities of priests.[8]

A principal motivation of Viceroy Toledo's support for the office of the protector was to take writing out of the Indians' hands and prevent their bothersome meddling in Lima's institutions of justice. He named a protector de indios and *juez de naturales* together with minor officials for each province, preferring that Spanish agents work together with the corregimientos to settle native disputes at the local level (Ruigómez Gómez 1988, 123). However, the legal support teams of rural areas proved unreliable, making the job of Lima's protector general of the Indians larger than Toledo had anticipated. Royal decrees of the sixteenth and seventeenth centuries routinely denounced the lack of qualified attorneys; in some cases, protectors failed to shield Indians from the clergy's abuses, and, in others, freelance lawyers acted outside the authority of the audiencia only to profit at the expense of native clients.[9] Guaman Poma ([c. 1615] 1980, 411, 918) stated that filing petitions was a sure way for Indians to lose money and called Spanish attorneys "lesenciasnos" (licentiate-asses) and "proculadrones" (procurer-thieves) (cited in Adorno 1991, 233; 2007, 31). The judge of the royal audiencia Juan de la Reinaga Salazar knew procuradores de los naturales who could neither read nor write.[10] Even León Pinelo endured the harsh criticisms of Visitador Juan Cornejo for allegedly neglecting his office and charging Indians markedly high fees.[11]

Despite alarming reports, Spanish agents played a strong part in expanding native participation in colonial tribunals. Protectors and Andeans developed mutually beneficial alliances, however ethical or self-serving their activity in the courts might have been. But native litigation was not solely the outcome of royal paternalism. Literate Andeans composed and filed grievances without legal representation; caciques hired and fired lawyers according to changing legal needs and fortunes; plaintiffs gathered witnesses and journeyed far distances to present documentation to the seats of courts (Mumford 2008, 12). The archival record verifies the existence of indigenous procuradores de los naturales whom local native cabildos appointed to represent the interests of the community. Don Sebastián Álvaro, who in the 1660s served as cacique principal and procurador in the district of Nasca, constitutes one such example.[12] The reality of indigenous advocates who acted in an official capacity makes it difficult to underestimate the agency that Indians exercised in making and carrying out the lawsuits that confronted Spanish authority.

When parish priests and corregidores of a district worked together, they could prevent native accusations against either party from reaching Lima. However, royal protectionism was a powerful tool that Indians used against the clergy for activities outside church jurisdiction or when ecclesiastical judges ignored clerical abuses. The causas against priests that fill the "Derecho Indígena" section of Peru's Archivo General de la Nación corroborate the Lima audiencia's steady intervention in matters of the clergy. Secular judges could not sentence priests or friars; they referred judgments to the archbishop or the provincial in cases involving members of religious orders (Borah 1983, 162). While it is true that church magistrates invoked ecclesiastical privilege to impose penalties on the clergy, this did not keep native litigants from exploiting jurisdictional ambiguities so as to gain leverage in their lawsuits. The structural and rhetorical features of the legal writings they produced with and without the protectores de indios' collaboration tell one part of the story of how they accomplished this. Native litigation records include characteristics that also indicate the areas where indigenous voices coincided with the discursive norms of Spanish agents and the areas where the voices diverged.

Causas de Capítulos as Legal Genre

Native intermediaries authored a wide variety of legal documents for the ecclesiastical tribunal. Indian agents of the Church composed denunciations, petitions, records of witness testimony, empowerments, census rolls, and sacramental registries, to name a few. Notarial records of indigenous cabildo scribes, such as wills, bills of sale, and titles of office, also found their way into lawsuits against priests.[13] In keeping with notarial prescriptions, most native writings included the date and place of their drafting; the names, social ranks, and signatures of the author, testifying witnesses, and other persons at hand for the documents' composition, such as prosecutors or interpreters; and a formulaic opening and closing to the archbishop, juez ordinario, or other addressee. The causa de capítulos is the genre of native writing that appears most frequently in the trial dossiers of the archive of the Lima archbishopric. As accusations of wrongdoing and appeals for the punishment of priests, causas were a mixed genre that united the formal and thematic characteristics of the legal complaint with those of the legal petition.

Petitions of grievance consisted of a beginning statement, a litany of the accused's transgressions, and a request for the priest's removal or payment of restitution. The opening salvo of the cacique principal Don Hernando de la Cruz's 1617 grievance illustrates a line of argumentation reminiscent of Rupay Chagua's complaint against Fray Francisco Torrejón. Writing "on his own behalf and in the name of the pueblo," the protector and procurador de los naturales having refused his pleas for assistance,[14] the cacique addressed Archbishop Lobo Guerrero directly:

> Don Hernando de la Cruz, principal and natural of the pueblo of Santo Domingo de Tauca in the province of Los Conchucos, I appear before Your Excellency to criminally accuse the licentiate Fray Lucas Mudarra, cura and beneficiary of the said my pueblo, and presenting the case of my accusation with the precedents and formalities of the law, I state that the aforementioned, with little fear of God Our Lord and in great disservice to Him, and with disregard of ecclesiastical justice and injury to his conscience, in the period of more or less six months that he has been cura of the said my pueblo, and though having the said father the obligation by order of the Holy Provincial Council and synodal constitutions of Your Excellency to ensure and take great care for our protection and defense and seek our growth and salvation with the care and diligence that is required, he has not done so.[15]

De la Cruz peppered his reverential address to the archbishop with the Spanish juridical phrasings and terminology common to legal petitions: "with little fear of God" (con poco temor de Dios), "in disregard of ecclesiastical justice" (en menosprecio de la justicia eclesiástica), "to ensure our protection" (mirar por nuestro amparo) underscored Fray Lucas Mudarra's alleged contempt for God's authority and the legal obligations of parish stewardship.

The cacique listed seventy-two criminal charges over twelve folios that detailed the Indians' nightmarish reality under Mudarra: merciless overworking and beatings of notables and commoners who worked the friar's textile trade; lack of doctrina and sacraments due to the padre's ignorance of the "lengua general del ynga"; extortions of goods and monies for baptisms, burials, and other sacral rites; the friar's payment of gambling debts on the backs of Indian laborers; Mudarra's disrespect toward the Eucharist in religious processions; his total reliance on the native sacristan when reciting the divine office. Argument by means of accumulation reinforced the extent of the friar's damage and the truth-claims of the petitioner. De la Cruz declared all crimes to be "público y notorio," meaning crimes that took place openly before the entire pueblo and therefore actionable on the basis of two witness statements, without the accused's confession or formal allegations of individual victims.[16]

Concluding the grievance, De la Cruz reiterated his statement of the pueblo's suffering and overburden, and the archbishop's moral and legal obligation to provide "remedy" and "amparo," the Indians' right of protection and assistance. Returning to the deferential formula of address, he requested a new priest who could provide the Indians a model of social morality and, most important, teach Christian doctrine in the parishioners' native Quechua:

> I humbly ask and beseech Your Excellency be served by ordering these charges to be held as certain and true, and by ordering the remedy of so many abuses against me, the other caciques and principales, and Indian men and women of the said my pueblo, thereby satisfying the conscience of Your Excellency and granting us an upright priest who will treat us well, provide good example, and preach in the general language of the Inca.[17]

The charge of linguistic ignorance with which native advocates repeatedly began and ended their accusations indicates the resonance of the Church's Quechua-language policy in their writings. And though absent from De la Cruz's appeal, "This complaint is not out of malice but rather to achieve justice" was the refrain that typically concluded petitions of grievance.[18]

Itemized litanies of clerical abuse usually contained scattered and imprecise references to canon law.[19] James Brundage (2008, 440) has indicated that lawyers of medieval times kept allusions to legal sources vague in order to prevent opponents from attempting to contest the interpretations they applied to them. Whether Peru's indigenous advocates employed this tactic or simply had a more abstract grasp of colonial law is difficult to know. Blanket reference to ecclesiastical law, if not the specific decrees, was a defining feature of native juridical writing. Andean plaintiffs identified the power of law as a symbolic language and used it to make the arguments against priests more compelling. De la Cruz invoked the Third Council decrees and the constitutions of Lobo Guerrero's synod of 1613, alluding in a general sense to the rulings of the "Holy Council" and "synod": "going against what is decreed by the Holy Council," "it being ordered by the Holy Council and constitutions by Your Excellency," "the said father does this against what is decreed by the constitutions and synods," "it being ordered by the synodal constitutions of Your Excellency."[20]

At the same time, De la Cruz recognized the jurisdictional conflicts within the Church and seized upon them when composing his grievance. The Lima see's push to secularize native parishes at the expense of the religious orders provided native litigants an extra weapon with which to bolster legal complaints.[21] "I ask and beseech you to order that we be given a priest-cleric and not a friar," he wrote, "for Padre Mudarra says that he is not a priest-cleric but a friar and that he lives in a convent and answers to his own bishop, and here there is no one to whom I can turn."[22] Complicating matters further, Mudarra served as Viceroy Francisco de Borja's personal chaplain, having journeyed to South America just two years earlier in company of the new viceroy.[23] However, the cacique missed no opportunity to test the archbishop's confidence in his own authority to govern native parishes: "It is not right that the padre says, as he always does, that he can get away with anything because he is the chaplain of the viceroy and that Your Excellency will not hear our pleas."[24] De la Cruz asked Lobo Guerrero to take the parish of Tauca back from the newly arrived Dominican and return it to the secular clergy who had ministered there previously.

Native litigants grappled with law at the local level, where the jurisdictional boundaries separating the secular Church, civil authority, and the religious orders were hotly contested and far from clear. Plaintiffs often used royal law to accuse priests of interfering in matters of secular jurisdiction, such as cabildo elections or municipal law enforcement. The 1623 report of the caciques principales of San Juan de Huanchor to Visitador

Baltazar de Padilla cited Andrés de Mujica's actions beyond a strictly ecclesiastical function: "[Mujica] does not consent to the meddling of officers of royal law, for he alone administers justice with his native fiscal."[25] Guaman Poma claimed that the ideal native litigant possessed a working knowledge of both canon law and Toledo's ordinances for civil governance: "[The advocate] was ladino, knew how to read and write, knew Toledo's ordinances and the Holy Council, and always responded to the padre doctrinero, the encomendero, the corregidor, the lieutenant, and the encomendero's overseers."[26] In church tribunals, citing knowledge of secular law was a way for Indian plaintiffs to communicate that grievances of clerical misconduct would find a welcome hearing in secular tribunals. De la Cruz stated his intention to seek royal justice if the archbishop failed to act: "If justice is not granted, I ask that you provide me with an affidavit in order to seek out the King Our Lord and his royal audiencia so that they grant justice to us."[27]

Mastering Legal Formulae

Causas de capítulos introduced statements and formulae that native litigants reproduced time and again. Indigenous legal narrative followed distinctly Castilian forms, while concealing private aspects of litigation that lay beneath courtroom papers, such as traditional Andean notions of justice, native styles of address, and collective disputations that informed written repertories of clerical abuse. The formal similarity of native grievances, when taken as a whole, suggests that Andean litigants had access to common discursive models and legal guidance.

Formulary collections with templates for producing written documents in colonial tribunals circulated widely throughout Spanish America (Luján Muñoz 1981; Burns 2005b). Bartolomé Álvarez ([1588] 1998, 268) observed that native litigants possessed Gabriel de Monterroso y Alvarado's *Practica civil y criminal e instruccion de escrivanos* (1566), the notarial manual for officials of lower courts, which Guaman Poma ([c. 1615] 1980, 361) mentioned by name in his chronicle. Don Rodrigo Flores Caja Malqui owned New Spain's first guide for notaries, the *Politica de escripturas* (1605) of Nicolás de Yrolo Calar. The *Curia filipica* of the jurist Juan de Hevia Bolaños was the definitive formulary of Castilian procedural law in the Indies as well as Spain. Originally published in Lima in 1603, encompassing rules and written formulae of both the ecclesiastical and secular courts, the *Curia filipica* underwent several reprintings throughout the colonial period and into the nineteenth century, becoming as valuable a reference tool for lawyers as Antonio de Nebrija's *Gramática de la lengua castellana* (1492) was for Spanish grammarians (Lohmann Villena 1961, 161; Kagan 1981, 149). Other widely known formularies included Francisco Ortiz de Salcedo's *Curia eclesiástica* (1615) for legal specialists of church tribunals and, in the late-colonial period, Manuel Silvestre Martínez's ten-volume *Librería de jueces* (1763–1768), for secular judges, corregidores, and municipal council officers.

Book inventories of Peru's curas de indios demonstrate that legal agents utilized Hevia Bolaños's manual in Andean parishes; Juan Ordóñez, beneficiary and ecclesiastical judge in the northern province of Chachapoyas, declared ownership of the handbook and various legal papers in his will of 1637.[28] The *Curia filipica* and similar resources instructed plaintiffs in the Spanish forms and legalese that characterized the prose of De la Cruz, Rupay Chagua, and others. Consider Hevia Bolaños's step-by-step instructions for writing a "libelo," or petition of criminal or civil grievance that legal agents directed to the magistrates of ecclesiastical and secular tribunals:

> After the name of the accuser, the accusation will state "as best suits the law." . . . Then one puts another clause, stating "I accuse and demand, or I place a demand on so-and-so." . . . After this, one puts a brief and clear narration of the facts. . . . Then one puts another clause that states "I ask Your Mercy to accept my account as true." . . . Then another clause that states "May you condemn," which serves as conclusion. . . . Then another clause follows that states "And I implore the order of Your Mercy." . . . Then one stating "And I ask for justice." . . . After this clause one puts another that states "And I protest the payment of costs." . . . The final clause is "And I swear [my demand] is not out of malice." . . . And this should be included in all demands, accusations, denunciations, exceptions, oppositions, and other like petitions that require it, before and after the demurrer, and in all lawsuits, be they secular or ecclesiastic.[29]

Even more explicit, Ortiz de Salcedo's *Curia eclesiástica* provided a uniform statement for grievances with stock legal terms and phrases and blank spaces for inserting the names of relevant actors.[30] Legal handbooks and formularies addressed readers who were mostly self-taught in matters of law. Much like the "prácticos" of early modern Spain (Kagan 1981, 148), Peru's native petitioners acquired legal know-how through Spanish handbooks and courtroom experience. In contrast, high-ranking notaries and learned jurisconsults of the viceregal capital wrote in Latin and had extensive university training.

Collaboration in the trials of extirpation, inspections of local secular government *(residencias),* and parish inspection tours also exposed Indians to the Lima authorities' legal expectations for civil officers and parish priests. Monitoring the clergy's compliance with the dictates of canon law fell chiefly to the indios ladinos of native parishes, who testified to the visitadores on the clergy's missionary conduct. The Council of Trent's obsession with the pastoral commitment and good character of priests, which José de Acosta and Peru's ecclesiastical councils shared, was not lost on native plaintiffs, who tapped into the Lima see's insecurities about priests of questionable ability or moral virtue.[31]

Indians learned the Lima see's concerns about parish administration through the questions that church inspectors posed to them about the activities of priests. Visiting magistrates ordered parish priests to exhibit their titles of benefice and royal license for Indian ministry, the mandatory books of religious instruction, and the condition of the church and its sacred objects. Secret interviews of native parishioners took place as well. The report of Visitador Loarte Dávila's 1619 investigation of Fray Miguel Márquez's care of the parish of Andajes included a transcript of twenty-six questions. A sampling of Loarte Dávila's interrogation of the parishioners reveals the line of questioning typical of visita inquiries:

1. First, if they know the said cura and for how long up to the present, and if he knows the general language of the Inca.
2. If they know that the said cura has been negligent in the administration of the holy sacraments and if by his fault any Indians of his curate or any infants have died without baptism.
3. item, if they know that the said cura taught Christian doctrine as was his obligation on Sundays, feasts, Wednesdays, and Fridays, personally and while wearing a surplice. . . .
12. item, if they know that the said cura proceeded with the good example he should. . . .

17. item, if the said cura committed any abuses or mistreatments against his parishioners, taking from them their haciendas or forcing them to work for him without compensation. . . .

26. item, if the said cura had ever left the benefice without leaving an authorized priest in his place.[32]

Inspection teams also read an "edict of public sins" that invited members of local communities to come forward with information not only about the offenses of laypersons, but also about the clergy's sacral activity, social conduct, and business affairs (Ortiz de Salcedo 1691, 150v–152r).

In effect, the visitas were public assemblies by which Indians learned the rules of Christian practice that applied to parishioners as well as to priests. Parish inspections imparted to native peoples critical understanding on issues of canon law and parish governance, and deepened the Indians' sense of their legal prerogative to voice critiques of the clergy. Causas de capítulos developed the standard themes and language of visita reports, documenting clerical infractions of canon law in itemized fashion, which points to the impact of church inspections on native literary activity. Indians knew the Lima see's procedures for evaluating priests and borrowed from this model when writing up evaluations of their own.[33]

Rhetorical Self-Fashioning

Causas de capítulos adhered to the formulae of legal supplication but also reserved space for expressing judgments, characterizing the actors and witnesses of crimes, and narrating stories about previous events. In this sense, rhetoric connected directly to the practice of law. Hevia Bolaños and Ortiz de Salcedo's manuals instructed advocates on forensic discourse, or the art of persuasion toward the judgment of people and past actions.[34] The language of petition traversed several verbal registers, from the reverential and supplicatory to the reproving and exhortative. Natalie Zemon Davis (1987, 3–4) has argued that by Renaissance standards, the rhetorical artifice of legal documents did not mean that an account was false, for the telling of a story to a judge conveyed more than just documentary value; it brought verisimilitude or moral implications. The forms of address in native grievances also reveal the various ways in which native writers situated themselves discursively in relation to the Lima high clergy, Spanish agents, Andean parishioners, and parish priests. Amid the legalese of native petitions, highly personalized dimensions of indigenous advocacy come to the fore.

How did De la Cruz construct his literary persona in the public forum of the ecclesiastical tribunal? The Andean noble's grievance of 1617 contained a number of standard rhetorical tactics that appeared in the writings of native petitioners. De la Cruz explained that the action against Mudarra stemmed from his witnessing of the friar's "abuses and injustices" and his gathering of similar reports from the caciques principales and native villagers. As lord and warden of the Indians, he claimed to write "for myself and in the name of the entire pueblo of Santo Domingo de Tauca"; lawsuits against priests tended to be collective, though petitions for individual redress also occurred. Moreover, his avowal to protect the Indians undercut the local clergyman's claims to authority. By emphasizing Mudarra's linguistic ignorance and violent example, De la Cruz portrayed himself as a pious leader more committed than the friar to the parishioners' well-being. The declaration of his Christian credentials and concern for the Indians' mistreatment and deficient schooling provided rhetorical grounding for the demand that the villagers receive the protection and doctrina that canon law prescribed.

Church legislation also guaranteed the Indians prompt justice. "May [the abuses] be remedied shortly," the cacique stated, "by what pertains to the satisfaction of the conscience of Your Excellency."[35] Spanish legal philosophy held that judges, be they secular or ecclesiastic, had the duty to reconcile earthly justice with the principles of God's law. Invoking a recurrent theme in native petitions, De la Cruz stressed the archbishop's moral obligation to watch over the "miserables en derecho," which implied that the cacique principal shared the high clergy's compassion for the poor. Applying the status of "miserables" to his vassals, but not himself, however, the cacique asserted his distance from the native impoverishment that he condemned. As did Guaman Poma in his petition to King Philip III (Adorno [1986] 2000), De la Cruz equated his moral principles with the archbishop's so as to empower himself as an authority on the missionary practices that affected his people.

Matthew Restall (1997, 57, 243) has noted the "communal nature" of the writings that indigenous cabildo notaries produced on behalf of native clients in colonial Yucatán. Collaboration between Maya writers and the community was both literal, insofar as plaintiffs had a say in the petition's contents, and symbolic, insofar as the cabildo officer claimed to represent corporate interests. For the Andes, there existed laws that directed legal agents to represent the concerns of the entire pueblo. Toledo set down rules for protectores de indios to follow when authoring native grievances to secular authorities, which applied to ecclesiastical tribunals as well: to reduce paperwork, litigants were to organize the petitions by sets of "relaciones por capítulos" to ensure that the complaints affected the Indians as a group and not represent merely offenses against particular individuals (Ruigómez Gómez 1988, 123).[36] However, the clergy's abuses were rarely as universal as litigants claimed; indigenous plaintiffs always invoked the collective, but they normally wrote on behalf of certain Indians or native factions. Advocates protected above all the concerns of their own welfare, which often ran counter to the will of rival Indians or the native majority.[37]

Facts of the dispute in Tauca rest on a one-sided grievance that did not accommodate competing versions of Mudarra's administration. After legal agents in the province of Conchucos refused De la Cruz's request for assistance, the cacique made the long trek to Lima in order to present his grievance to the archbishop along with the statements of victims and witnesses. In the capital, he secured the help of Alonso de Torres Romero, the procurador general de los naturales of the audiencia, who represented the charges to the see. Finding ample cause for inquiry, the canon Feliciano de Vega ordered the immediate dispatch of a visitador to the parish, where he would conduct a full investigation of Mudarra's activities and, if necessary, proceed to local trial.[38] Perhaps the unnamed visitador who traveled to Tauca judged the case summarily, without undue paperwork, in keeping with the wishes of Lobo Guerrero. Absence of additional legal filings, such as an appeal on behalf of the friar or accusation of idolatry against the cacique, leaves a portrait of Mudarra's behavior that is unequivocally negative. Whatever the case, the lack of written records on the parish's administration leading up to and following the filing of the cacique's grievance does not exclude the possibility that De la Cruz's interests were more personal than communal. Lawsuits that produced a more sizeable corpus of papers demonstrate the multiple issues of political authority, social frictions, and cultural understandings that gave rise to local parish conflicts. The dizzying stream of colliding viewpoints that emerged from the protracted litigations of Rupay Chagua and Caja Malqui are exceptional in this regard.

De la Cruz's aims were to make known the clergyman's despotic character and methods, and to persuade the archbishop to take remedial action. Demonstration of Mudarra's abuses thus rested on the stark opposition, which surfaced repeatedly in petitions of grievance, between the innocence of the victims and the cruelty of the friar. Charge 10, though particular in its details, typifies De la Cruz's polarizing characterization of the actors from beginning to end:

> Item, the said father, being priest, cruelly punished Domingo
> Poma Mango, principal, Don Alonso Cargua Rupai, Rodrigo Car-
> gua Yaure, Pedro Guanca Poma, Martín Jurado, Don Pablo Cargua
> Yaure, Agustín Cargua Namba, and Juan Gua[nca?] Yanai, whipping
> them by his own hand, because the said father is a tyrant, it being his
> natural condition to be cruel to all the said principales without any
> cause whatsoever, just because they did not send him their horses
> quickly enough to the ranches called Quichis and Quillca, thirty
> horses for thirty lots of wheat, all to his profit, which is public and
> well known.[39]

De la Cruz's account included no signs of direct native resistance or allowance for good deeds on the friar's part. He stated that as a last measure, the most vulnerable of the community had begun to flee, implying that the depopulation of native parishes was counterproductive to the benefice's need for revenue.[40] The temperance and fortitude with which the Indians purportedly bore Mudarra's abuses elevated the virtue of their suffering and the worthiness of their redress.

Rhetorical self-fashioning was a multidimensional process; native litigants saw advantages in portraying themselves as both poor and empowered. At certain moments, De la Cruz identified with the suffering that he described, introducing facts that made himself appear pitiful. The cacique detailed his own victimization in graphic detail: routine beatings for not collecting the friar's cotton and wool quickly enough; fifty lashes with a leather strap for attending Mass in another pueblo without permission; hair cropping and sixty lashes for punishing an Indian woman for missing church, not knowing she was allied with the friar; public garrotings to humiliate him before the town's native subjects.[41] De la Cruz stated that he had vacated his parish post on account of Mudarra's abuses: "I renounced the office of fiscal mayor, because he is so cruel and of such bad character that I could not bear it anymore, for he took vengeance on any pretext and has given me thousands of punishments, as is well known."[42] Petitions of grievance called attention to the contradictions of the native intermediaries' legal status: Spanish colonial law constituted them as defenders of native subjects, and at the same time it deemed all Indians "miserables en derecho." Making convincing arguments required De la Cruz to embrace the paradox of the Indians' position of inferiority. The cacique's subjugation was the basis of his appeal for justice.

Poverty was a supreme value in the moral economy that native petitioners described. The Andeans' books of religious instruction praised humility and denounced earthly desire for goods and power; native-language sermons, for example, routinely admonished the selfish pursuit of wealth and political influence that indigenous ministers supposedly enacted through the worship of false gods. However, Andean litigants reversed the situation, taking the criticisms that the clergy unleashed against native parishioners and directing the same criticisms against Catholic priests.[43] They equated exploitation and pastoral negligence with all seven of the capital sins, though the sins of wrath, greed, and pride figured most prominently. Criminal and civil lawsuits argued that the clergy's behavior had political as well as theological implications.

In two lawsuits of 1630 against Martín de Mena Godoy, which the protector Torres Romero also represented, the native leaders of Ambar brought into play the gospel metaphor of the Christian shepherd to underscore the injustice of their victimization: "[W]e, the young sheep of this pueblo, are scattered all over out of fear, because the person who was supposed to watch over us has terrified us with his mistreatment and bad example."[44] Mena's purported crimes were "scandalous" even by the standards of native litigation: divulging secrets of the confessional, nightly card games in the rectory, living in sin with a mulatto woman, siring four children, making death threats against Indians from the pulpit. When confronted about not confessing a dying parishioner, Mena allegedly responded: "Let the devil take him and the rest of the Indians because they are all *capitulantes*."[45] To other complaints, he answered "that he could do it because he was the pope and king of this pueblo and that the provisor of Lima was nothing to him and that not even the archbishop could take away his *doctrina*."[46] According to the plaintiffs, Mena had claimed the prerogatives of the pope, the Spanish monarch, and the authorities of the Lima see. When De la Cruz accused Mudarra of having "little fear of God" and "disregarding ecclesiastical justice," he too implied that the friar's crimes amounted to a treason that warranted divine punishment and temporal justice. Litigants reminded the high clergy that priests were subject to the laws of Rome, Castile, and the ecclesiastical court.

At the foundation of colonial law and juridical language were the basic concepts, values, and rituals of Catholicism (see Berman 1983, 165). Metaphors of the Last Judgment and Purgatory, God as the source and final arbiter of civil power, and the magistrate as pardoner of sins underscored the religious dimension of legal discourse. Guaman Poma repeatedly decried the sinful pride ("soberbiosos, cin temor de Dios y de la justicia") of Peru's clergy and, in keeping with the lessons of the Last Judgment in the *Tercero catecismo* ([1585] 1985, 732–77), warned of the eternal perdition that awaited them after death (Adorno [1986] 2000, 72–73).[47] The Christian message that all were equal under God, that hell was a place for Europeans as well as Indians, appealed to native litigants as well. As they put it, God would take up the defense of the lowly, whether the Crown and the Church that represented His law did so or not.

A Shared Textual Network

The interplay between native petitions of grievance and the rhetorical formulae and stratagems of Spanish legal specialists raises the thorny issue of authorship. Most capitulantes asserted the collective production of lawsuits through their representative function as governors, caciques principales, or parish or cabildo officers. Generally speaking, the Indians' shared experience of hardship and neglect validated the legitimacy of the claims, whereas the experiences of the author-petitioners and specific individuals took on a secondary role. Though internal parish factionalism surfaced, a united front against clerical misconduct was the strategic norm. Moreover, legal documents involved additional hands beyond those of the plaintiffs and witnesses. Solicitors or notaries put the charges into writing, usually by name but sometimes anonymously, and the plaintiffs affixed their autograph or the mark of a cross, if unable to write.

Less common in this regard, De la Cruz's written complaint bore only his signature; ostensibly, he filed the document independently on behalf of

Tauca's parishioners. After reaching Lima, however, the cacique needed the protector Torres Romero to provide counsel and represent the causa before the archdiocesan tribunal. From rural parishes to urban courts, native plaintiffs consulted Spanish agents on points of legal procedure and forensic argument. Excepting rare cases, protectors and procuradores had an advisory, if not leading part in the drafting and filing of native petitions, empowerments, and other legal instruments. It is rarely easy to determine where the hand of Spanish agents ended and that of Andean plaintiffs began.

The question of multiple authors is central to the examination of the causas de capítulos. Michel Foucault's classic essay "What Is an Author?" (1977, 113–38) established the inutility of romantic conceptions of the authorial function when approaching most writings of early modern times. According to this view, positing an individual as the exclusive producer or proprietor of a written document obscures the complex textual dynamics and mechanisms of production that inform its meaning. This is especially true for the multilayered juridical petitions of colonial tribunals. Attributing the source of a legal grievance to a particular author sets up the limits of its interpretation, for to place trust in authorial integrity grants the presumed writer undue credibility with regard to the text's referential value. Rolena Adorno (1999) makes this point, arguing that colonial writings were by nature polemical, not faithful renderings of experience. In this sense, it is more instructive to analyze the positions that a text articulates than to rely exclusively on anachronistic notions of self-determination and individual agency.[48]

Equally reductive is to define texts based on assumptions of the author's ethnicity. Discursive alliances cut across the cultural divide between Spaniards and Indians, and sustained themselves based on social and political relationships that were mutually favorable. The papers of church magistrates, protectors of Indians, and Andean advocates were not the discrete writings of individual authors, but rather documents that formed part of an interconnected dialogue on the state of missionary affairs. Legal dossiers contain intricate textual networks, conflicting viewpoints, and collective efforts involving Europeans and native subjects. In this regard, lawsuits against priests reveal less the separation of Spanish and Indian voices than a complex blending of the two. Positing legal manuscript culture in terms of collective authorship and shared discursive networks highlights points of Spanish-Indian contact as opposed to apprehending native writing as assimilationist and derivative of European styles and formats.

Added to the assortment of papers that originated in lawsuits against priests, Spanish lawyers of the Lima audiencia composed lengthy memoriales to the Crown on the state of affairs in the Indies. Covarrubias defined a "memorial" as a legal genre or "petition that is submitted to the judge or lord as a reminder or notification of some affair."[49] The memoriales of the protectors of Indians and high officials of the audiencia featured language that paralleled the language of native causas de capítulos, which suggests overlap or modeling of one type of writing on the other. While Juan de Padilla's and Diego de León Pinelo's memoriales constitute the most well-known criticisms of the Lima see's pastoral mission, other reports of audiencia officials that discussed the Indians' mistreatment included those by Juan de la Reinaga Salazar (1626), Gutierre Velázquez de Ovando y Zárate (c. 1658), Nicolás Matías del Campo y de la Reinaga (1673), and Pedro Frasso (1684). In terms of form and theme, little separated the memoriales of Spanish attorneys from the causas of Andean plaintiffs.

Padilla's 1657 report brings into view the similarities. In line with the format of petitions of grievance, the memorial consisted of the criminal attorney's reverential salutation, itemized lists of the "abuses" and "injustices" that the Indians endured, enumerations of the "causes" of native hardship, and detailed petitions for "remedy" of each abuse and injustice. Padilla divided his catalog of abuses into two sections; the first treated the trials of native peoples in the spiritual realm ("trabajos en lo espiritual"), which focused on pastoral abuses, and the second referred to the Indians' trials in the temporal realm ("trabajos en lo temporal"), principally the horrid conditions and suffering of native laborers in the royal mines. The numbered list of spiritual charges reads very much like a causa de capítulos: untold parishioners expired without the sacrament of confession and other rites; padres doctrineros enriched themselves by forcing Indians to make offerings for Mass, burials, and holy feasts; native children worked at the command of parish priests in fields and textile workshops when they should have been learning Christian doctrine. A proponent of centralized administration of native parishes through secular church authority, Padilla contended that friars were especially prone to laxity or excess. In his view, the Lima archdiocese desperately required an able missionary clergy who could speak the Quechua language and devote themselves to spiritual concerns rather than earthly ones (Padilla [1657] 1966, 391–93).

FIGURE 17.   Frontispiece. Juan de la Reinaga Salazar, *Memorial discursivo sobre el oficio de protector general de los indios del Pirú* (Madrid: Imprenta Real, 1626). Courtesy of the John Carter Brown Library at Brown University.

Though more temperate than Padilla in rhetorical style, León Pinelo agreed with the criminal attorney's condemnation of Villagómez's lack of pastoral oversight. A key part of the solution, the reformers concluded, entailed more consistent and rigorous visitations of parish clergy, including the archbishop's resumption of personal inspections of the parishes in his jurisdiction and the removal of doctrineros who lacked certification or failed to teach doctrine (Padilla [1657] 1966, 394–96). Padilla charged that nepotism led to the appointment of unqualified visitadores, ignorant of Quechua, who ignored native complaints and took bribes from priests in exchange for positive evaluations. The attorney cited the example of a visitador he encountered in the province of Conchucos: "When on commission [to investigate the conduct of a priest, the visitador] took the petitions of grievance that the Indians presented him and turned them over to the doctrinero."[50] While numerous inspection reports of the period attest to clerical negligence, the fulsome accounts of certain visitadores suggest that Padilla's accusation was credible. Visitador Antonio Garavito de León, who conducted parish inspections in the 1640s under Villagómez, was the type of inspector that Padilla likely had in mind. Garavito produced glowing reports on the controversial ministries of Juan Celis de Padilla and Pedro de Quijano Zeballos, despite well-known native allegations of physical and economic abuses against both.[51]

Spanish and Andean writings on the need for pastoral improvement abounded. In fact, there was nothing remarkable about the commonality between the reports of Padilla and León Pinelo and those of native capitulantes. Indigenous lawsuits constituted the *materia prima* of a larger corpus of reformist writings on the problem of the Indians' exploitation, making it difficult to separate Padilla's appeal to Philip IV from the words of a native authority such as De la Cruz. Consider the plea for remedy with which Padilla concluded his memorial to the king:

Take pity, Your Majesty, as no doubt you will, on these, your poor and miserable vassals, giving remedy to their misfortunes, in a way that has results beyond the words of your mandate, so that it not be true that which a few days ago, the cacique of Tarama said to his doctrinero: 'Oh Father, how expensive this Gospel of ours is costing us!' It would be less harmful if we endeavored, as justice demands, that [the Indians] take you [as their protector], and then God Our

Lord, who sees and does not forget their persecutions, will be served by removing the scourge of calamities from Your Majesty's monarchy, restoring [the monarchy] to its former peace and grandeur, and granting Your Majesty the life and succession that Christendom so requires.[52]

Padilla used the testimony of the aggrieved cacique to enhance the credibility of his appeal and inspire the king's compassion. Moreover, the attorney reminded the monarch that God was the source of his power and advised him to uphold his divine obligation to protect the "miserables yndios" of Spain's overseas possessions. The metaphorical "scourge of calamities" meant, for Spanish reformers, the ongoing difficulties of the Crown in providing justice, whereas for native capitulantes, the scourge was, no doubt, a literal figure of the costs and persecutions that characterized indigenous experience under the domination of corrupt parish priests.

Clerical Backlash

Native advocates paid a high price for making complaints. Priests attempted to silence Indian plaintiffs outside the courts, through physical violence and economic coercion, and within the legal system through allegations of religious crimes.[53] Guaman Poma stated that legal retaliation against capitulantes was common: "When the caciques principales and Indians ask for justice against the padre, he raises accusations against them and says they are sorcerers and adulterers and other great insults."[54] As Indian plaintiffs came to occupy positions of authority, distrust and attacks against them increased. Accused priests blamed native litigation on multiple causes, from anti-Catholic sentiment and political treachery to the Indians' innate greed and proclivity for conflict.

Spanish legal theorists also expressed displeasure about indigenous uses of law. Authorities of the Lima see and royal audiencia believed that native litigation harmed all parties involved. Church legislation referred to litigious troublemakers whose allegations placed the "honor" and "security" of parish priests in jeopardy, and stated that native clients would receive better justice via summary trials.[55] Acosta ([1577] 1987, 2:323–25) claimed that the Indians' fondness for causas derived from the bad example of Spaniards who sought profits through litigation; for him, curbing the influence of corrupt agents was one way to reduce parishioners' worldly impulses. Jurists held that lawsuits occupied Indians in costly and drawn-out conflicts that profited Spanish and Andean agents at the expense of native communities. The problem of a growing legal class was not only Peru's. Solórzano Pereira summed up in an ironic proverb the harm that the "schemes of litigants" caused in his native Spain: "He who seeks immortality ought to file an ecclesiastical lawsuit."[56]

How could the Church and Crown at once protect the clergy's authority, curtail the influence of the lawyerly class, and ensure the Indians' access to justice? High authorities concurred that lawsuits depleted native resources and overburdened the legal system, but they differed on the causes of native litigation and its appropriate remedy. Archbishop Lobo Guerrero spared no measures in his attempt to destroy Andean religious error and to discipline its purveyors. But he also charged the jueces ordinarios with correcting bad priests and providing justice to native parishioners. The constitutions of Lobo Guerrero's 1613 synod ordered inspecting magistrates to adjudicate the Indians' complaints and protect them from reprisals by the clergy.[57] Complaints about the "excesses and disorders" of the padres doctrineros, especially religious clergy, were constant in the archbishop's reports to Philip III as well. In his vision, more rigorous visitas, increased oversight of friars, and punishment of rogue priests would end the bad state of religious instruction and abuse of native laborers (Vargas Ugarte 1953–1962, 2:242–44, 301). When De la Cruz brought charges against Mudarra, the Lima see believed that native complaints had a basis in fact.

After Lobo Guerrero's tenure, however, the prelacy showed a less protective strain. Whereas midcentury audiencia officials such as Padilla and León Pinelo prized the testimony of native litigants and urged for better regulation of the clergy, diocesan synods of the period attempted to protect the clergy from litigation, imposing criminal punishments on false accusers and payment of the defendant's trial costs for "malicious" allegations.[58] No group within the audiencia or Lima see questioned the reality of dishonest priests. What they debated was the suitability of placing trust in Spanish and Andean advocates as a solution. Licentiate Cristóbal Martínez de Ureta's controversial tenure in the parish of San Juan de Huariaca in the 1640s and 1650s placed the disagreement between Archbishop Villagómez, the protector general, and Andean litigants on the subject of native litigation into sharp relief.

FIGURE 18. A chapel in Huariaca.
Courtesy of the Emilio Harth-Terré Collection, Latin American Library,
Tulane University.

Trouble in Huariaca began in 1548, when the procurador Alonso de
Castro represented the lawsuit of the Andean lord Don Francisco Huaro
Poma, who accused Martínez de Ureta of usurping his lands to graze cattle
with unpaid Indian laborers.[59] On the surface, the allegation caused no great
alarm; Martínez de Ureta stated the claim was frivolous, and the provisor of
Lima called for a routine investigation. With the inquiry under way, however, the cacique of the pueblo of Yacan and graduate of Lima's El Colegio
del Príncipe, Don Francisco Chavín Palpa, seized the opportunity to represent charges of his own. Emboldened by Huaro Poma's lawsuit and the
procurador's support, Chavín Palpa and allied witnesses described a parish in turmoil. He alleged that Martínez de Ureta operated a brutal regime
of forced workshop labor together with the encomendero and partnered
clergy.[60] Two years later, Chavín Palpa filed a second petition of grievance
that detailed the priest's arbitrary exactions of monies from Yacan's confra-
ternities, married and unmarried parishioners, and families of the deceased

at times of burials. In terms of pastoral care, Martínez de Ureta made the sick and disabled travel to Huariaca to receive the sacraments, and many died without them as a result. The cacique alleged that Indians who could make the journey refused to confess with the priest; a hearing impediment forced the padre to shout, making the confessional too much for them to bear. Chavín Palpa asked the archbishop to confiscate the priest's goods and use them to pay restitution to the victims. In response, Martínez de Ureta denied the charges and called the cacique a "falso delator."[61]

After a decade at the helm of the archdiocese, Villagómez had grown tired of the litigation that distracted from a key objective: the extirpation of native idolatries. In a rare intervention for cases of this type, the archbishop responded directly to Chavín Palpa's petition and made his disdain for native lawsuits quite clear. After reviewing the accusations and counteraccusations, Villagómez penned an extended letter of reprimand against the cacique and his cocapitulantes. Trial statements of archbishops consisted of titles of appointment, requests for information, enforcement orders, occasionally a legal decision; they were invariably terse and formulaic in nature. But here Villagómez's unvarnished anger was on full display:

> [The Indians] who tend to [file grievances] are not the good Christians (in truth, there are few good ones among these people) but the bad ones, and not just any bad ones, but the worst kind, and being one and all so easily inclined to bringing false allegations and repeating them under oath, the danger to the honor of the priests is evidently much greater.[62]

The archbishop found good reason to anger. Visita reports in the years leading up to the causa de capítulos documented Martínez de Ureta's exemplary ministry, from his custody of church property to his administration of the sacraments. Native informants had told church inspectors that the padre was "one of the greatest Quechua speakers they knew" and tended the Indians' spiritual and temporal well-being with great care.[63] To Villagómez, it was outrageous for Chavín Palpa to claim an unrecorded history of abuses in a parish stewardship that extended back to 1625. As for the charge that Martínez de Ureta was deaf, the prelate had sent an examiner to Huariaca who found him to have perfect hearing.[64] In the archbishop's view, the capitulantes showed no respect for church authority or the procedure of law, wishing instead to pick and choose the priests and judges whom they considered amenable to their interests. "Many Indians (I am inclined to say almost all) will keep filing suits until they find a priest to their liking," Villagómez concluded, "and no priest who performs his office dutifully will be left standing."[65]

In 1656, the office of the protector general attempted to end more than five years of litigation. Álvaro de Ibarra, León Pinelo's predecessor, wrote to the Lima see on behalf of the Indians of Huariaca with his judicial recommendation. He concluded that Martínez de Ureta should pay the Indians for all wages he owed them for labor in his textile workshops.[66] León Pinelo (1661, 49v) remarked in his report to the king that he oversaw the restitution of monies to Don Antonio Guayna Llanqui, one of Chavín Palpa's coplaintiffs in Tarma province. Lost from the documentary record is Villagómez's judgment, though his distaste for the priest's accusers makes it unlikely he followed the protectors' counsel. Trial sources that mention Lima's protector general are rare, but they do not portray the archbishop and the defender of the Indians as opponents every time. When in 1660 Francisca Melchor traveled from Huarochirí to Lima in order to secure León Pinelo's help against the abuses of Visitador Sarmiento, the protector de indios sent her back home with orders to cooperate with the extirpator's investigation.[67] Whether the protector acted based on economic or political self-interest is not known.[68] In general, attorneys of the audiencia expressed dissatisfaction with the Lima see's oversight of the curas de indios. But this dissatisfaction was not always uniform, nor did it always imply a categorical indictment of extirpation.

Manuel Marzal (1983, 222) and Nicholas Griffiths (1996, 195) have argued that the Indians' use of the courts dealt a major setback to the war against idolatry. Had Villagómez been allowed to choose, the campaigns of extirpation would have been more intense and recurrent than they came to be. But protracted legal actions tempered the ability of curas de indios and visitadores to bring native communities under control. By the archbishop's account, native litigation against the clergy produced chaos in highland parishes and prevented visitadores from punishing Andeans for religious crimes. In 1663, in the aftermath of Padilla's and León Pinelo's reports, Villagómez informed Philip IV that legal power struggles between priests and Indians all but crippled his extirpating designs:

I have continually sent visitadores, those best suited, to extirpate idolatries, and they have done as much as possible, but even still, some Indians are so wicked (especially some of the caciques) that . . . they file lawsuits against the visitadores, three of whom now face malicious charges, based on my understanding of the evidence, and [the native litigants] reveal their malice and insolence now more than ever, claiming the legal favors that Don Juan de Padilla, chief attorney of the royal audiencia, concedes to them without just reason.[69]

If Villagómez saw Lima as an alternative venue for trials, away from the contentious atmosphere of native parishes, the Indians' persistence and Padilla's activism complicated this plan. While lawsuits did not end the clergy's repressive methods, they limited the autonomy of parish priests and the effectiveness of the visitadores' investigations and trials. Scholars agree that following Villagómez's death in 1671, extirpation carried on, but at a quieter pace (Mills 1997, 164).

Royal and church law upheld the Indians' access to legal representation. But the excess of litigation forced the Lima see to harden its boundaries and mark native capitulantes as dangerous. From a colonialist perspective, the ecclesiastical visitas of the 1650s and 1660s produced mixed results. On the one hand, Villagómez rejuvenated the fight against traditional Andean forms of worship, yet, on the other hand, the inspection campaigns gave native peoples the opportunity to restrain the powers of the clergy through litigation. Ironically, the repressive visitas and extirpation trials contributed to native litigiousness. Encouraging Indians to challenge the authority of huaca ministers introduced them to the same legal channels by which they were able to challenge the authority of Catholic priests. In this way, native lawsuits highlight what Walter Mignolo has called the paradox of literacy in colonial situations: "While literacy is conveyed, initially, in order to govern and control the native population, it is prevented, ultimately, in order to have the same results" (1989, 72).

Pleading before the Archive

How successful were the native advocates' pleas for justice? Indian plaintiffs at times achieved the reassignment of priests and compensation for lost goods and revenue, but the documentary record usually excludes the final resolution of native appeals. The huaca priest Hernando Hacas Poma of Acas bragged that his sacrifices to the divine ancestor Guaman Camac had led to success in the pueblo's legal petition to remove four local priests.[70] Lobo Guerrero ordered the dismissal of Fray Miguel Márquez from Indian ministry for his misconduct in Andajes.[71] The outcome of Hernando de la Cruz's lawsuit of 1617 against the Dominican Lucas Mudarra is less clear. Records of 1636 show a secular priest in charge of the benefice of Tauca, and Mudarra appears as a defendant in a series of litigations of the 1640s and early 1650s as the cura of the parish of San Martín de Chacas, also in the province of Conchucos.[72] With the help of the procurador Torres Romero, De la Cruz likely convinced Lobo Guerrero to force Mudarra'a reassignment upon the Dominican's provincial. The cacique's victory was strictly local, then, for it did not prevent the friar from reestablishing his textile business in neighboring Chacas two decades later.[73]

Canon law gave Indians the right to demand restitution of lost income and goods.[74] Restitution was a Christian obligation that native peoples learned time and again in the confessional, from the pulpit, and when putting last wills into writing. The protectores de indios, Las Casas being the most prominent example, saw the return of lands and goods to the Indians as the most clear-cut political solution for the thievery and exploitation of the colonizers (Adorno [1986] 2000, 61). Extant records of such judgments are sporadic. When in 1605 the Indians of San Pedro de Mama brought nine charges of economic abuse against Alonso Pérez de Vivero, the ecclesiastical magistrate absolved him of six charges and ordered payment of restitution for three: two reales per day of journey to each native tributary whom he sent to Lima to conduct business, two reales per day to the Indian who provided him twelve months of domestic service, and two reales per day to each worker who cut timber and sold it in Lima on the priest's behalf.[75] Still, convicted priests could file appeal or simply refuse to comply, making justice uncertain.

Guaman Poma expressed repeatedly the disappointment that many native litigants experienced in prolonged and fruitless requests for justice.[76] In his view, bribery, coercion, and forgery tainted the legal process and kept it from addressing the Indians' needs. The protector de los naturales Juan de la Reinaga Salazar (1626, 8r–v) stated that Andean plaintiffs traveled from the highlands to Lima to the detriment of health and hacienda: jurists heard native complaints only on Saturdays, if at all, and financial burdens were real. Furthermore, to discourage baseless claims, legal procedure demanded losing parties of suits that magistrates declared "unjust" to pay the victorious group's litigation expenses (Hevia Bolaños 1619, 86r–v). Reinaga Salazar's concern that expenses limited native possibilities for justice matched worries of legal reformers in Spain. As Diego de Saavedra Fajardo put it, "It's better for the litigants to receive a conviction right away than a favorable sentence after many years of litigation. . . . What type of restitution can the dispossessed hope for, if first so many are to fleece them [along the way]?"[77]

That few legal dossiers include a decision suggests that the litigants either abandoned the proceedings or reached out-of-court settlements. Causas de capítulos were not always end-all contests that carried on until a final verdict. Plaintiffs and curas pursued actions and counteractions to harass and pressure one another toward surrender or a mediated resolution. Indians and priests hardly welcomed the official reprimands and public humiliation that came from mutual allegations of economic abuse and immoral behavior. In the parish of Tauca, the restoration of De la Cruz's local authority and the relocation of Mudarra's workshops to Chacas probably created a result that was agreeable to both parties. William Bouwsma (1990, 139–40) has observed that in the early modern period, European jurists expressed the ideal of "pure justice" but in practice obeyed the sensible goal of managing conflict. Judges encouraged legal foes to compromise and avoided rulings that might aggravate tensions further and place the local social order in jeopardy. Yet no matter the outcome of particular cases, Peru's native litigants succeeded in creating social havoc and legal stalemates throughout the central highlands and placed limits on the types of missionary practices they would abide.

Whatever the veracity of specific allegations against priests, the causas de capítulos as a whole seem to express the native intermediaries' dissatisfaction with the sacramental and fiscal management of Andean parish life. Indigenous plaintiffs condemned the agents of the Church but never the institution itself.[78] They affirmed devotion to the same colonial system whose corrupt authorities overburdened the Indians and endangered their well-being. Around 1658, the Crown attorney Gutierre Velázquez de Ovando y Zárate summed up for the king the "perplexity" and "immense confusion" of Spain's overseas enterprise: "To execute all the royal decrees for the protection of the Indians, it would follow that there would be a total lack of workers in the mines, and the extraction of metals would come to a halt as would the organization of deliveries and annual shipments to Your Majesty, upon which the public good depends."[79] In other words, how could the Crown reconcile a matter of conscience, the protection of the Indians, with the empire's need for native tributary labor?

Despite the many obstacles to justice, suing the clergy was not a fatalistic gesture, but one that brought Andean officials both material and symbolic rewards. After all, for the Indians to maintain trust in the colonial system, as Jacques Poloni-Simard (2005, 181–82) has explained, they had to see the prospect of obtaining some justice in return. Native advocates had a stake in parish management, and from time to time they won judgments, however sizeable or limited, that advanced personal or community interests. Political agendas were not always clear, but the steady flow of native lawsuits pointed as much to the Indians' sense of empowerment as to their sense of desperation. If Villagómez's scorn was any sign, native litigation posed a threat to clerical authority and the goals of extirpation. Indeed, working with native Catholic authorities, such as Agustín Capcha, could be trickier for missionary priests than confronting huaca ministers, such as Hernando Hacas Poma. Extirpators identified enemies of the Church in order to dominate them more easily, but how were they to manage the Andean parish officials who had variable agendas and muddled neat distinctions between the colonizers and the colonized? The intricate social milieus and political instability of local native communities make it impossible to think about colonial relations simply in terms of dominant Spaniards and disempowered Indians.

Andeans who advocated for better missionary practices secured a position within the Catholic institution they contested. Lauren Benton's remarks on the ambiguous status of intermediaries in colonial regimes throughout history apply to the native advocates of Peru's ecclesiastical tribunals: "[I]t is tempting but wrong to view any participation in an imposed legal system as collaboration, on the one hand, and to represent any form of rejection of the law's authority as resistance" (2002, 17). To be more accurate, Indian officials simultaneously cooperated with the clergy and opposed evangelization's negative effects, as the cases of Capcha, De la Cruz, and many others make clear. The Lima Church and audiencia provided legal channels for promoting individual and group interests, and native intermediaries acted to uphold the laws that accounted for their status as colonial authorities and for the subjugation of Indians in general. Advocacy in the ecclesiastical courts fortified social bonds and legal obligations between Spaniards and Indians, albeit in accordance with the Church's hierarchical power structure. Freely or reluctantly, native litigants accepted the central place of Spanish colonial law in the regulation of social conflict and, in the process, granted legitimacy to the system of justice that was the source of their rights and also their oppression.

It is a commonplace in colonial historiography to describe native intermediaries as cultural hybrids "between two worlds," perpetually at odds with European clergy, on the one hand, and local native communities, on the other. As power brokers, Andean officials surely made enemies of all stripes. But they did not abandon traditional Andean forms of social and cultural interaction. Nor did they consider themselves isolated from the values and interests of Spanish groups that formed part of parish society. Dichotomous perceptions of the native intermediaries' social action overlook, in this sense, the dense web of alliances and models of identity with which they engaged.[80] Trials demonstrate the elastic ties and discontinuities between all colonial participants, not merely the separation of Europeans and Andeans into opposing groups. Overlapping coalitions emerged based on shared religious interests and political commitments.

Plaintiffs eschewed ancient rights and genealogies when making legal arguments. More pragmatically, they appealed for justice in the terms that Spanish agents taught them. The implausible alternative was persecution or exclusion from the colonial establishment. Roberto González Echevarría has posited historical writing in the colonial period as an activity that issued from "within a grid of strict rules and [legal] formulae" whereby "the individual manifested his or her belonging to a body politic" ([1990] 1998, 44). According to this view, the argumentative force behind the truth-claims expressed in the *Comentarios reales* (and in other chronicles of early America) derived from Garcilaso's grounding in the legal codes of Spain's colonial administration. Much like the Peruvian historian, Andean advocates sought legitimacy as petitioners by "pleading before the Archive, before knowledge classified and stored by the State" (83). Knowing royal and church laws, especially those governing missionary practice, was necessary for indigenous officials who produced documents for the ecclesiastical courts. The source of the litigants' authority was ultimately colonial, and if they embraced Spanish cultural forms and values, it was in order to assert their right to make themselves heard.

In short, it is impossible to grasp native literacy as separate from European concerns, for it was colonialism that produced the conditions for its development. Researchers of indigenous literatures have a great deal more to learn about the perspectives of Indian advocates of colonial tribunals who wrote in Spanish and expressed Catholic concerns. Lasting contributions on Peru's Andean chroniclers have provided theoretical and methodological frameworks for capturing the ambivalent moral and political outlook that pervades the writings of native intermediaries. Guaman Poma and Pachacuti Yamqui trained under Spanish Catholic influence and used the colonizers' language to affirm the place of indigenous peoples in biblical history. Yet they composed their vast histories at the margins of colonial institutions, drawing openly from native languages, technologies of memory, and concepts of space and time in order to establish their legitimacy as authors. The clear attraction of these writings, from an ethnographic and literary standpoint, in no sense discounts, however, the testimonies of countless Indians who authored petitions in ways less expressive of indigenous cultural traditions, within the more rigid codes of communication that prevailed in juridical settings. An expanded history of the colonial literature requires, in this view, a fuller examination of Andean legal genres as well as a greater acknowledgment of the Spanish cultural values that shaped the writings of literate Andeans and that literate Andeans, in turn, had a part in shaping.

Indigenous writings of the ecclesiastical tribunal reveal only one chapter in the history of lettered Indians. Native writers also negotiated political treaties of conquest, petitioned the Spanish Crown for privileges and compensation, translated the inquests of civil government officials, and authored empowerments and last wills. Study of other forms of native literary activity will provide a broader and alternative portrait of the experience of indios ladinos, beyond the ecclesiastical relationships and institutions on which this investigation has centered. Today, in the pueblos of the Peruvian highlands, bilingual Andeans continue to ply the writing trade in regional courts and notarial offices, and walk the missionary trail in the company of European priests. Though a select few don the stole and bless the sacraments, a greater number still watch over the sacristy, teach Quechua hymns to young villagers, and translate Sunday homilies into a language that the native congregants can understand. As before, life in the Andean parish remains a complex blend of fervent celebration, personal rivalry, joyous renewal, and doctrinal error. These are the challenges, the rewards, and the enduring legacies of conquest and evangelization. They are also the stories of the Archive that have not yet been fully told.

Notes

Introduction

1. AAL, Papeles Importantes, Leg. 23, Exp. 9, s.f.

2. Armas Medina (1953, 273–77) devotes four pages of his history of early Andean evangelization to the activities of native parish employees. In his five-volume work, Vargas Ugarte (1953–1962) comments on Andean assistants only sporadically. Taylor (1996, 324–42) discusses the contributions of indigenous officials to evangelization in colonial Mexico, and Yannakakis (2008, 66–69, 82–84), the mediating role of Indian notables and native church personnel in the Church's battle against idolatry in late-seventeenth-century Oaxaca.

3. Adorno (1994, 379–81; 2007, 24–25) examines the Iberian origin of the term *ladino* as traditionally applied to nonnative speakers of Latin and vernacular Romance and its use in colonial Spanish America to designate indigenous subjects who acquired Spanish customs and language. While *ladino* referred principally to subjects of the Crown who learned the language and the culture of the Spanish, it also extended to Andeans of the colonial period who became proficient in Quechua in addition to their native maternal tongue (Cerrón-Palomino 2003, 145 n. 13).

4. "¿No aueys visto a los Víracochas [los españoles] buenos como lo hazen? Y muchos indios ladinos que son buenos hijos y se confiessan entre año muchas vezes y rezan, y se disciplinan: estos son benditos de Dios: y los padres les quieren mucho. Porque no hareys vosotros lo mismo?" *(Tercero catecismo* [1585] 1985, 477). Translations of Spanish quotations are by the author unless otherwise noted.

5. "[L]os [indios ladinos] enseñan [a los feligreses] á idolatrar y los llevan á los sacrificios, como los cristianos los suyos á las iglesias" (Ávila [1608] 1904, 1:389).

6. Though examples are many, Spalding 1984 and Mills 1997 are two studies that emphasize the interconnectedness of European and Andean societies and the variegated patterns of indigenous adaptation to religion and social change under Spanish colonial rule.

7. Three broad geographical areas compose the Andes region, which roughly correspond to the ecclesiastical jurisdictions of early colonial times: the northern

Andes (the dioceses of Quito and Trujillo), the central Andes (the Archdiocese of Lima), and the southern Andes (the dioceses of Cuzco, Huamanga, Arequipa, and La Plata).

8. Colonial law aimed to limit the powers of the native governing class, but without fully eliminating its control over the Indians and access to regional assets. For assisting the Church and managing the native workforce, caciques were exempt from tribute and personal service (AGI, Patronato, 189, R. 21), and many embraced the opportunities for enrichment that their positions afforded them. As victims and beneficiaries of Spanish rule, the aboriginal nobility occupied an ambivalent position in relation to European superiors and a subjugated indigenous population. The bibliography on the strategic intermediary role of Andean ethnic lords in the colonial economy and political culture is extensive. Díaz Rementería 1977, Spalding 1984, and Stern [1982] 1993 are landmark studies in this area.

9. By his own account, Guaman Poma ([c. 1615] 1980, 282, 285, 715) assisted the ecclesiastical inspector Cristóbal de Albornoz in the campaigns to root out idolatry in the region of Lucanas Andamarca in 1566 and 1570. Pachacuti Yamqui's familiarity with the regions of Cuzco and Lima suggests that he also worked as an interpreter for church inspectors (Szemiński 1987, 2–3).

10. Less visible in the archive are testimonies of uneducated Indians, especially women, who were isolated from formal education and excluded from institutional posts, and whose perspectives are still left mainly to speculation. Indian priestesses did exist, as Silverblatt (1987) shows, and they played an integral part in social and religious change. Though outside the scope of this study, cofradías (lay religious fellowships governed by Indian men and women) also constitute a key site for examining indigenous agency within the Church in colonial Peru. For orientation on the topic, see Celestino and Meyers 1981, Garland Ponce 1994, and Varón Gabai 1982.

11. Lockhart (1972, 447–55) discusses the brief careers and untimely deaths of Francisco Pizarro's most well-known interpreters, Felipillo and Martinillo. Other studies of the interpreters of the first encounters between Europeans and Amerindians include, for Mexico, Karttunen 1994, 1–23, and Townsend 2006, 55–108, and for Brazil, Metcalf 2005, 17–53.

12. Wood (2003, 18) cites Guaman Poma's lament of a "world turned upside down" in a criticism of modern assessments of indigenous responses to the Spanish invasion of Mexico. Scarcity of records makes it hard to know how native lenguas actually carried out their mediating functions, though Lockhart (1972, 1993) contends that Nahua and Inca actors of the first encounters were probably less bewildered and powerless than colonial-era histories imply.

13. MacCormack 1991, Mills 1997, and Estenssoro Fuchs 2003, to cite the most notable studies, establish new models of interpretation for understanding European and indigenous contributions to Andean Christianity. Decoster 2002

contains essays of multiple disciplinary perspectives that study the ways in which native Peru's indigenous nobility interacted with Catholic ideas and institutions.

14. An early contribution in this area, Adorno 1982 brings together essays by Rolena Adorno, Frank Salomon, Regina Harrison, and Raquel Chang-Rodríguez, though influential studies are many.

15. Taking a similar approach, from the perspective of cultural history, Yannakakis (2008) examines indigenous appropriations of Spanish legal culture in negotiating conflicts between local autonomy and state rule in late colonial Oaxaca. Another model study of early modern literacy and social practice with corollaries for colonial Spanish America, Castiglione (2005) examines the ways in which literate villagers of early modern Italy employed papal laws and "adversarial literacy" to defend communal rights against the aristocracy.

16. The "lettered city" refers to Ángel Rama's description of the elite urban intellectuals who utilized writing at the service of Spanish colonialism with an aim "to advance the systematic ordering project of the absolute monarchies, to facilitate the concentration and hierarchical differentiation of power, and to carry out the civilizing mission assigned to them" (Rama [1984] 1996, 16). Rama restricts his attention to European and Creole intellectuals who consolidated power at the expense of marginal social groups. Indigenous writers who voiced opinions about issues that were debated within the Spanish community do not figure into his discussion, though they remain implicit.

17. Lima II, indios 74, Vargas Ugarte 1951–1954, 1:192–93.

18. "[F]uessen admitidos en las Religiones, educados en los colegios, y promovidos segun su merito, y capacidad a las dignidades eclesiasticas, y oficios publicos" (ASFL, Reg. I-2, Núm. 1, Exp. 41, 212r). Quito's Bishop Alonso de la Peña Montenegro ([1668] 1985, 356–57) argued that indigenous acolytes of legitimate birth should not only be considered for holy orders but even preferred for benefices and prebendaries due to their native-language ability and ethnic ties to the dioceses they served. In 1697 and 1725, Charles II and Philip V issued decrees in support of indigenous ordination (ASFL, Reg. I-2, Núm. 1, Exp. 41, 212r).

19. Higgins (2000) has utilized the concept of the "criollo archive" as a tool for studying the connection between knowledge and power in the writings of Creole intellectuals (American-born descendants of Europeans) in eighteenth-century Mexico. His analysis focuses on the ways in which these writers acquired textual erudition and scientific knowledge in order to legitimate themselves as learned subjects in the face of Spanish absolutism.

Chapter 1

1. "Para conocer su indignado intento no es menester mirar más que al indio—que quiere ser letrado para poner pleitos, sin haber estudiado—qué pretende. Y que, si lo examinasen, no sabría la ley de Dios; y si sabe la doctrina, no la

sabe entender ni declarar. . . . [L]os ladinos no han aprovechado en la lengua española, ni en la doctrina que han aprendido en casa de los sacerdotes, más que para ser peores que los otros y ser intérpretes de sus fines y nuestro daño" (Álvarez [1588] 1998, 268–69, 272).

2. "[N]o hay a quien no cause admiración y espanto el ver cuán boto y escurecido le tiene esta gente [la facultad del entendimiento], . . . a causa de faltarles las letras, ciencias y buenas artes que la suelen cultivar, perficionar y hacer más prompta y despierta en sus operaciones y discursos" (Cobo [1653] 1964b, 2:17).

3. See Mignolo 1989, 1995. Goody (1977) stresses alphabetic literacy's rapid and overwhelming impact on indigenous modes of thinking, social relations, and political organization. It is worth noting that the ascent of writing was uneven and took time, even in Europe. From the 1300s, individuals slowly developed the need to document topics and affairs through their interactions with the emerging bureaucracies of the Church and state (Clanchy 1993, 185–87; Burns 2005a, 2). In a mostly illiterate European society, Christian doctrine was still heard, recited, and sung far more often than it was transcribed or read.

4. Burns (2005a), Cerrón-Palomino (2003), and Rappaport (1994) offer exceptional models for the historical study of alphabetic literacy among indigenous peoples in the colonial Andes. In a similar vein, Jouve Martín (2005) examines the interactions of Lima's peoples of African origin with the literate practices of the Spanish between 1650 and 1700.

5. Spanish intellectuals of early modern times declared the authority of lettered culture to mold individual character, in contrast to traditional aristocratic ideals that saw letters as accessory to inborn civility and virtue (Bouza Álvarez [1999] 2004, 64). Acosta shared the view that people were more cultured and politic in places where there were books: "In no land are books or literary monuments found if the people lack culture and above all, political organization" (Pues en ninguna parte se encuentran monumentos literarios ni libros, si sus gentes no son cultas ni tienen, sobre todo, una organización política) ([1577] 1984, 1:63).

6. Mannheim (1991, 143–44) speculates that colonial law forbade the production of Quechua-language legal documents, though no royal decree to substantiate this possibility is known. Durston (2008) examines the limited corpus of Quechua writings of the colonial period and argues that notarial uses of Quechua were common among native elites but took place outside institutional channels. Lockhart (1992) offers the most systematic investigation of native scribal culture in colonial Mexico, for which there exists a considerable body of Nahuatl writings. For a survey of current ethnohistorical research on Mesoamerican-language texts, see Restall 2003.

7. Rivarola (1985, 2000) and Rappaport (1994) study the impact of Spanish literacy on native Andean groups based on analysis of Indian-authored legal documents. In Joanne Rappaport's view, "It is more properly within the legal document, accessible to native authorities and carefully guarded for posterity by

them, that the impact of literacy among Andean native peoples is most clearly evident, for it is with this type of writing that aboriginal communities came most frequently into contact. In other words, from the colonial period to the present, the legal document has constituted the major genre of written expression and of communication across the two cultures and of codification and transmission across time of indigenous oral and spatial memory" (1994, 272).

8. "[L]os demonios y diablos, como a gente sin letras y simples, ignorantes, ydiotas, con poca façilidad, se apoderaron haziéndose señor absoluto siendo tiranos antiguos" (Pachacuti Yamqui [c. 1613] 1993, 211).

9. "[A]utoridad no tendrá lo que declarase el ynterprete natural, aunque tenga agua de baptismo, por que no tiene asy la fee ni el temor de Dios con el gusto e sabor del español" (transcribed in Lisson Cháves 1943–1948, 1:112).

10. Charles V also mandated the establishment of schools in each conquered settlement that would prepare indigenous interpreters, in particular the sons of ethnic nobility (*RLI* 1841, Lib. I, tit. xxiii, ley 11, 1:141; *RLI* 1841, Lib. VI, tit. i, ley 18, 2:219–20; Eguiguren 1940–1951, 1:36–37; Lisson Cháves 1943–1948, 1:235). Before the conquest of Peru, the Laws of Burgos of 1512 had mandated that Indian notables entrust their children to mendicant friars for the purpose of religious instruction (AGI, Indiferente, 419, L.4, 124v, 127r–v). This order was reiterated in 1516, 1540, and 1541 (AGI, Patronato, 172, R.7; AGI, Lima 566, L.4, 118v, 258).

11. The Franciscan, Augustinian, and Mercedarian orders also trained Indians for missionary service (ASFL, Reg. I-9, Núm. 2, Exp. 1, 285r; ASFL, Reg. I-14, Núm. 5, 255v; Lisson Cháves 1943–1948, 2:551; Vargas Ugarte 1953–1962, 1:328–29).

12. In addition, the Crown advocated the employment of Spanish-born lay catechists, commonly referred to as *calpizques* (Acosta [1577] 1984, 1:173; Meléndez 1681, 1:237), under the assumption that they were better qualified than Indians to teach Spanish and Christian doctrine. Spanish encomenderos hired calpizques to oversee catechesis in accordance with the royal mandates *(RLI* 1841, Lib. VI, tit. iii, leyes 27–28, 2:231).

13. For council decrees and synodal constitutions on the responsibilities of lay assistants, see Lima I, naturales 12, Vargas Ugarte 1951–1954, 1:13–14; Lima II, indios 118, Vargas Ugarte 1951–1954, 1:219–20; Lima 1585, cap. 26, ACE, "Originales del Concilio Limense," 131v–132r; Lima 1586, cap. 4, ACE, "Originales del Concilio Limense," 150v–151r; Cuzco 1591, cap. 18, BNP, A 568, 9r; Cuzco 1591, cap. 37, BNP, A 568, 15r; Quito 1594, cap. 20, Campo del Pozo and Carmona Moreno 1996, 80; Quito 1594, cap. 93, Campo del Pozo and Carmona Moreno 1996, 121–24; La Plata 1619, tit. 1, cap. 6, BNP, B 1673, s.f.; La Paz 1638, Lib. I, tit. 1, cap. 3, Vega 1639, 4–5. In certain ecclesiastical districts, visitadores could also bestow titles on native fiscales and cantors (see Torres 1970, 16; *Constituciones synodales establecidas* 1739, 34).

14. Spanish officials often used the Taíno term *caciques principales* rather than the Quechua term curaca to designate ethnic lords of highest colonial rank.

Segundas personas was a term that designated Andean nobles of secondary rank. Most lay assistants were *naturales,* or native-born members of the communities they served, but the clergy would sometimes appoint outsiders. This was the case of Agustín de Gamarra, the indigenous alcalde of Santiago de Surco in the early 1620s (AAL, Hechicerías e Idolatrías, Leg. 1, Exp. 7, 1v). A native of the northern pueblo of Cajamarca, Gamarra likely came to the Lima region with Franciscan friars who had established missionary centers in both localities. Similarly, in 1655, Felipe Lupari, a Lima native, served as the alcalde of the highland parish of San Francisco de Ihuari in the region of Checras (AAL, Criminales, Leg. 19, Exp. 8, 4r). The appointment of native assistants sometimes followed a circuitous bureaucratic route that required collaboration between secular and religious authorities, as occurred in the 1627 appointment of four cantors in the Franciscan parish of Eten (ASFL, Reg. I-9, Núm. 2, Exp. 25, 434r). First, the friars notified the archbishop of the need for the cantors and secured from him the titles authorizing their service. With the titles in hand, the friars then obtained a provision from the viceroy, which ordered the corregidor of the district to entrust the requested Indians to the religious order and release them from tributary obligations.

15. For the provisions of Viceroys Martín Enríquez de Almanza and Pedro de Toledo y Leiva on the appointment of native maestros, see ASFL, Reg. I-13, Núm. 3, 226v; ASFL, Reg. I-14, Núm. 5, 256v–257r.

16. Lima III, actio 2, cap. 43, Vargas Ugarte 1951–1954, 1:340–41; see also Lima III, actio 3, cap. 29, Vargas Ugarte 1951–1954, 1:356; ACE, "Originales del Concilio Limense," 79r. Later synods mandated the appointment of maestrescuelas (Lima 1613, Lib. I, tit. 1, cap. 5, Lobo Guerrero and Arias de Ugarte [1613, 1636] 1987, 37–38; La Plata 1619, tit. 1, cap. 4, BNP, B 1673, s.f.; Arequipa 1638, Lib. I, tit. 1, cap. 8, BNP, B 1742, 73v–74r; Arequipa 1638, Lib. II, tit. 10, cap. 10, BNP, B 1742, 171v–172r).

17. Lima III, actio 5, cap. 4, Vargas Ugarte 1951–1954, 1:373–74. Diocesan synods reiterated the Third Council's Castilianization policies (Lima 1585, cap. 25, ACE, "Originales del Concilio Limense," 131v; Cuzco 1591, cap. 17, BNP, A 568, 8v–9r; Lima 1594, cap. 6, ACE, "Originales del Concilio Limense," 186v; Quito 1594, cap. 18, Campo del Pozo and Carmona Moreno 1996, 79; La Plata 1619, tit. 4, cap. 16, BNP, B 1673, s.f.; Lima 1636, Título de Constitutionibus, cap. 3, Lobo Guerrero and Arias de Ugarte [1613, 1636] 1987, 262; Arequipa 1638, Lib. I, tit. 1, cap. 8, BNP, B 1742, 73v–74r).

18. "[Q]uitarla, primero, de los corazones; sobre todo de los de los reyes, curacas y principales, a cuya autoridad ceden los demás prontamente y con gusto" (Acosta [1577] 1987, 2:263–65).

19. Alaperrine-Bouyer 2007 is a comprehensive institutional history of the two royal schools for the sons of Andean notables. The education of native elites had precedents in other parts of America, the most famous example being the Franciscans' Colegio de Santa Cruz de Tlatelolco, founded in 1536 in Mexico under the direction of Fray Bernardino de Sahagún. Olaechea Labayen (1962, 110–11;

1973, 405–6, 423–24) discusses Jesuit schools for Indians in Cuba, Mexico, and other regions of Spanish America.

20. Bernabé Cobo stated that the *colegio*'s curriculum focused on basic education: "At the school, the caciques learn how to live with policía, read and write in our Castilian language, assist Mass, and some, who are so inclined, are taught music and how to play instruments" ([E]n el colegio aprenden los caciques a vivir con policía, nuestra lengua castellana, leer y escribir y ayudar a misa, y a algunos que se inclinan a ello se les enseña música y tocar algunos instrumentos) ([1639] 1964a, 355).

21. The Protestant Reform and its focus on the book and reading practices altered Catholic methods of religious education. A new faith in education had emerged from the religious wars taking place in Europe, and teaching Spanish primary letters alongside the catechism touched all segments of Catholic society (see O'Malley 1993, 117–18).

22. Bartolomé Martínez (1995), Infantes (1998), and Viñao Frago (1999) describe the books and methods of primary education in early modern Spain. Valtón (1947) studies the first Mexican cartilla, printed in 1569. Cuzco's bishop, Sebastián de Lartaún, instructed priests to evangelize with the Latin catechism (Lisson Cháves 1943–1948, 3:61), despite the call of the Council of Trent (1545–1563) for religious instruction in vernacular languages.

23. As in Europe, the authority of print in South America took hold over time. Hand-written catechisms, sermons, sacramental manuals, edicts, and canon decrees circulated due to the lack of imprints. The Archivo General de la Nación of Peru holds manuscripts of colonial sermons, and visita records of the Lima archbishopric verify that parish priests maintained copies of their weekly homilies and *libros de mano*, such as ritual manuals, catechisms, and native-language dictionaries. Written copies of the decrees of the Second and Third Councils appear in the holdings of the Archivo del Cabildo Eclesiástico and Archivo Arzobispal de Lima.

24. Lima III, actio 2, cap. 3, Vargas Ugarte 1951–1954, 1:323.

25. "P. Que entendeys por la sancta Yglesia? / R. La congregacion de todos los fieles Christianos, cuya cabeça es Iesu Christo, y su Vicario en la tierra el Papa sancto de Roma. / P. Y si son baptizados, y han tornado a peccar, que han de hazer para no ser condenados? / R. Confessar sus culpas al Sacerdote, arrepintiendose dellas. / P. Y haziendo esso seran saluos? / R. Si seran, si permanescen en cumplir los mandamientos de Dios y de la sancta Yglesia, que son amar a Dios sobre todas las cosas, y a su proximo como assi mismo" (*Doctrina christiana* [1584] 1985, 53–55).

26. "[E]s pronunciar con palabras lo que por letras está escrito. . . . Leer, enseñar alguna disciplina públicamente. Leer a uno la cartilla" (Covarrubias Orozco [1611] 1995, 706, cited in Cummins and Rappaport 1998, 175). Scholars of "New Literacy Studies" have called into question the literacy/orality dichotomy as a

framework for understanding communication practices by considering written documents and speech as interdependent parts of a mixed literary culture (Stock 1983; Street 1984). This research has focused on the ways in which peoples of various social categories adapted to a world in which written documents, discourses, and practices took on an increasing role.

27. Burke (1987) and Nussdorfer (1993) make similar observations about the influence of writing on the illiterate population in early modern Italy.

28. Lima II, españoles 48, Vargas Ugarte 1951–1954, 1:123; Lima II, indios 32, Vargas Ugarte 1951–1954, 1:175–6; Lima III, actio 2, cap. 6, Vargas Ugarte 1951–1954, 1:325.

29. Toledo reproved the incompetence of native assistants in terms similar to Martel de Santoyo's of thirty years before: "The Indians are poorly taught, and most clerics employ the yanacunas as lenguas, on whom they depend out of necessity, and [the clerics] do not know whether they faithfully declare what they tell them. [The Indians] learn the prayers in Spanish, but they do not appear to turn out with more intelligence than birds demonstrate when speaking" ([E]stán los naturales mal enseñados, y que todos los más tienen por lenguas á los anaconas, en quien se fian los clérigos que han menester contralenguas, y no saben si guardan fidelidad en declarar lo que les dicen; muéstranles las oraciones en nuestro vulgar, pero no se entiende que queden con más inteligencia que los pájaros que muestran á hablar) (transcribed in Pidal and Salvá [1842–1895] 1964–1975, 94:257–58).

30. During Inquisition trials in Spain, interrogators asked defendants to recite the catechism from memory to determine if they took the Catholic faith seriously (Nalle 1992, 118).

31. "[E]ncontro con el diablo en figura de venado y que le vio echar ffuego por la boca y le causo espanto y este que declara resso el Credo con lo qual se fue el diablo y le dejo" (AAL, Hechicerías e Idolatrías, Leg. 1, Exp. 12, 6r).

32. A document from Lima's Archivo de San Francisco reveals that the first native governor and cacique principal of Lima could not sign his name (ASFL, Reg. I-14, Núm. 3, 96r).

33. "[H]abía tan poca curiosidad en aprender la lengua española, y en los españoles tanto descuido en enseñarla, que nunca jamás se pensó enseñarla ni aprenderla" (Garcilaso [1617] 1960, 3:49).

34. AGN, Tribunal Eclesiástico, Leg. 43, Cuad. 1, 92v.

35. "[E]n estos llanos se debe enseñar a los yndios la doctrina christiana en Romance porque casi todos son ladinos, y no entienden la lengua quichua" (AAL, Curatos, Leg. 20, Exp. 6, 8v).

36. "[D]ixo que en este pueblo se usa muy poco de instrumentos para bayles por ser los indios casi todos ladinos y criados entre españoles" (AAL, Hechicerías e Idolatrías, Leg. 1, Exp. 9, 6r). For similar testimony, see AAL, Hechicerías e Idolatrías, Leg. 2, Exp. 6, 18v.

37. "[E]stán tan bien instruídos en policía y cristiandad [y] . . . tan españolados que todos generalmente, hombres y mujeres, hablan nuestra lengua y en el tratamiento de sus personas y aderezo de sus casas parecen españoles" (Cobo [1639] 1964a, 3:353).

38. AAL, Capítulos, Leg. 21, Exp. 1, 10v, 13r; AAL, Hechicerías e Idolatrías, Leg. 3, Exp. 10, 17r; Duviols 2003, 194; AAL, Hechicerías e Idolatrías, Leg. 1, Exp. 8, s.f.; AAL, Hechicerías e Idolatrías, Leg. 2, Exp. 7, 4v–5r. In some highland regions, however, in particular Jauja and the Mantaro Valley, Castilian made significant inroads, owing, according to church inspection reports, to the diligence of Dominican and Franciscan friars (Arriaga [1621] 1999, 85; Lisson Cháves 1943–1948, 5:143).

39. See AAC, Colonial, LXXV, 4, 72, 6v; AAC, Colonial, LXXV, 79, 1r.

40. "[Q]ue su p.e ni su m.e no sabian rezar y que le decian que no rezase que p.a que era rezar" (AAL, Hechicerías e Idolatrías, Leg. 3, Exp. 1, 16v).

41. Studies of catechization in sixteenth-century Spain indicate that educated parishioners could recite prayers more accurately than the illiterate but that literacy was not a reliable indicator of Christian knowledge or practice (Nalle 1992, 126–27; Viñao Frago 1999, 62). Frequently, native Andeans charged with idolatry had received schooling in Spanish and Catholic doctrine (AAL, Hechicerías e Idolatrías, Leg. 1, Exp. 17, 1r; AAL, Hechicerías e Idolatrías, Leg. 2, Exp. 7, 1r; Polia Meconi 1999, 462).

42. "[Y]endo este declarante a decir missa al dicho pueblo, y aviendo gastado toda la mañana en traer por fuerza a el alguna gente antes de comensar la missa, quiso hacer Doctrina y hallando que los indios estaban ignorantes totalmente della, siendo algunos mui ladinos, le dixo al dicho don Juan este declarante que comensase el a enseñarlos, a que respondio no sauia" (AAL, Hechicerías e Idolatrías, Leg. 7, Exp. 13, 2r). Mills 1997, 185–89, provides a detailed account of Soclac's trial.

43. AAL, Hechicerías e Idolatrías, Leg. 7, Exp. 13, 9v, 19r.

44. AAL, Visitas Eclesiásticas, Leg. 19, Exp. 14, 4v; AAC, Colonial, XXXIX, 2, 31, 4r, 4v, 6r.

45. BNP, B 744, 5v.

46. "[N]o ay padre que no esconda su hijo ya que no uenga a el escuela visto que aunque sea abil letor, escriuano y cantor no se le haze mas graçia o franqueza que a el mas rustico mitaio, sino que a tasa, tambo y mita de minas todos pasan" (ACE, "Diligencias," 78r). In 1593, the Franciscan friars voiced a similar complaint to the Crown about the royal administrators in the province of Jauja: "The secular authorities of these provinces have forced the said Indians to do personal service, particularly in the province of Jauja, saying that only boys under the age of eighteen can be cantors, and the ones who are eighteen remain uneducated and cannot read or assist Mass, let alone sing or play instruments, and for this reason, they stop celebrating the divine office with solemnity; moreover, the Indians do

not want to enroll their children in school because once they turn eighteen, they are forced to do personal service" ([L]as Justiçias de esas proui.as an compelido a los tales Indios a que acudan a los Seruiçios personales y particularmente en la proui.a de Xauxa diçiendo que los muchachos que no llegan a diez y ocho años uastan para cantores y que los de esta edad por ser muchachos incapaçes aun no sauen leher ni ayudar a misa quanto y mas tañer y cantar y a esta causa se dexan de çelebrar con solenidad los offiçios diuinos y los indios no quieren poner a sus hijos al escuela uiendo que llegados a los diez y ocho años an de ser compelidos a los seruiçios personales) (ASFL, Reg. I-9, Núm. 2, Exp. 10, 328r).

47. "[L]e mando que aquellas llamas y ofrendas se las sachrificase al ydolo yanaurau para que su hijo don Alonso que actualmente lo tenia en el colegio del Sercado aprendiendo a leer y escrebir saliese buen letrado y assi mesmo pudiese conseguir el oficio de casique y gobernador" (AAL, Hechicerías e Idolatrías, Leg. 3, Exp. 11, 37v).

48. AAL, Hechicerías e Idolatrías, Leg. 2, Exp. 7, 35v–36r. Mannheim (1991, 52) argues that in pre-Hispanic times, boundaries between native languages were rigid, and individuals did not use language to achieve social advancement, whereas in colonial times Spanish formed part of a "prestige system" that allowed for social mobility and higher language status.

49. AGI, Quito, 8, R. 25, N. 92; AGI, Quito, 9, R. 2, N. 13.

50. AAL, Cedulario, Tomo II, 549r–v, 565r–566v.

51. "[Y]o no estoy persuadido para mi a que esta obra sea mia principalmente sino de los muchos indios del Cuzco a quienes yo he repreguntado y aueriguado con ellos cada vocablo, y de ellos lo he sacado, assi ellos son los principales autores desta obra" (González Holguín [1608] 1952, 8). González Holguín (1607, 4r) also praised his Indian coauthors in the prologue of his 1607 grammar of the Quechua language. The 1591 synod of Cuzco called for the recruitment of Indians to help prepare catechisms in native languages (Cuzco 1591, cap. 4, BNP, A 568, 4r–v).

52. AGN, Testamentos de Indios, Leg. 1, s.f.

53. AAL, Testamentos, Leg. 21, Exp. 5A, 30r; AAL, Capítulos, Leg. 11, Exp. 1, 12v. Burga [1988] 2005, 364, documents this family library.

54. "[N]o conviene que a estos reinos se traigan libros profanos y de mal exemplo porque lo recibiran los yndios que muchos van ya sabiendo leer" (Levillier 1921–1925, 5:284, cited in Estenssoro Fuchs 2003, 120).

55. Lima III, actio 3, cap. 37, Vargas Ugarte 1951–1954, 1:358.

56. Cerrón-Palomino (2003) studies the autobiographical text of Francisco Tito Yupanqui, the sixteenth-century indigenous sculptor of the Virgin of Copacabana, which the missionary chronicler Alonso Ramos Gavilán transcribed in his *Historia del celebre santuario de Nuestra Señora de Copacabana* (1621). Rivarola (1985) analyzes the impact of Quechua phonology, grammar, and lexicon on the written Spanish of Joseph Sulcaguaman, found among the papers of a late seventeenth-century lawsuit in the region of Huancavelica.

57. AAL, Hechicerías e Idolatrías, Leg. 1, Exp. 11, 1r.

58. See AAL, Hechicerías e Idolatrías, Leg. 3, Exp. 10, 1r–v; AAL, Hechicerías e Idolatrías, Leg. 2, Exp. 7, 36r.

59. AAL, Hechicerías e Idolatrías, Leg. 2, Exp. 6, 16r–v.

60. AAL, Hechicerías e Idolatrías, Leg. 2A, Exp. 12, 175r–v.

61. AAL, Civiles, Leg. 83, Exp. 1.

62. "[A]cí no gusta que ayga escuela ni que sepa ler y escriuir, quiere que sean ynfieles ydúladras" (Guaman Poma [c. 1615] 1980, 728).

63. "The two most-used words in the whole notarial repertoire," notes Burns (2005a, 12) in her discussion of this drawing.

64. "[T]ubo otros muchos decípulos y an salido cristianos y ladinos prencipales, amigo de defender a los pobres" (Guaman Poma [c. 1615] 1980, 499).

65. "[N]o convenía que los indios supiesen leer ni escribir, porque el sabello no servía sino de poner capítulos a sus curas" (Arriaga [1621] 1999, 78).

66. Guaman Poma states: "[The parish priest] orders the indios ladinos out of his doctrina right away because, if they know how to read and write, they will file charges against him" ([A] los yndios ladinos luego le manda echar de su doctrina porque, ci saue leer y escriuir, le pondrá capítulos) ([c. 1615] 1980, 609).

67. Lima II, españoles 120, Vargas Ugarte 1951–1954, 1:239.

68. Burns (2005a, 7) cites Toledo's ordinance to limit the judicial writings of native alcaldes of local cabildos: "[T]hey shall not write, because they are to [administer justice] summarily" (Levillier 1921–1925, 8:312). Toledo restricted the native alcaldes' jurisdiction to civil lawsuits between Indians and ordered Spanish corregidores to hear legal cases involving caciques and disputes between native pueblos. Presumably, the native cabildo's summary judgments obeyed both European and Andean legal precedents, which indicates the viceroy's open-mindedness toward indigenous traditions of justice in the settling of conflicts at the local level.

69. Clanchy (1993) examines similar development of quotidian uses of written records, what he calls "practical or utilitarian literacy," among members of medieval England's lay society.

70. Cressy (1981, 105) defines "passive literacy" as the ability to read but not write and "active literacy" as the ability to read and write.

71. Sixteenth-century records of the Peruvian Inquisition document native uses of Spanish writing that alarmed ecclesiastical censors. The trial of the presbítero Gerónimo Rodríguez Zambrano, who oversaw the cartillas that native scribes prepared for Indian boys and girls in Cuzco, referenced the Indians writers' irreverent approach to the teachings of the catechism: "He found many [cartillas] that were badly written because in one it said 'hijos de yegua' (sons of mare) instead of 'hijos de Eva' (sons of Eve) and in other parts 'todo potroso' (all horselike) for 'todopoderoso' (all powerful), and in another cartilla it said in the second commandment 'el hijo madural tidos' (the mature son off-god) instead of 'el hijo

natural de Dios' (the natural son of God)" ([H]allo muchas dellas que estavan mal scriptas porque en una dezía por dezir hijos de Eva dezía hijos de yegua, y en otras partes por dezir todopoderoso dezía todo potroso, y ansí en una cartilla dezía en el segundo mandamiento que encarnó el hijo madural tidos por dezir el hijo natural de Dios) (AHN, Inquisición, libro 1027, 215r, cited in Estenssoro Fuchs 2003, 118–19).

72. "[S]e a de criarse cristiano ladino y, ci pudiere, sepa latín y leer, escriuir, contar y sepa ordenar peticiones y enterrogatorios para defensa de sus personas y de sus yndios y supgetos, bazallos, pobres de Jesucristo" (Guaman Poma [c. 1615] 1980, 785).

Chapter 2

1. "vivo exemplo de cristiandad y virtud para sus súbditos y los demás indios" ("Libro de la fundación" 1923, 796).

2. "[P]or la experiençia a mostrado no sabe la lengua gen.l del ynga ni menos ttiene colasion ni presentasion R.l[,] pues el ttienpo de ocho meses que administra no les predica en la dha lengua ni en la española en grabe perjuiçio y daño de los miserables yndios" (AAL, La Merced, Leg. 7, Exp. 42, 1r).

3. The cacique principal inherited from his grandfather portions of an estate consisting of numerous houses, farmland, thousands of livestock, religious artwork, and silver (BNP, B 784).

4. Heath and Laprade (1982), Mannheim (1991), and Durston (2007) examine the changes over time in Spanish colonial language policy and the attempts of European missionaries to translate Christian concepts into Quechua and other native languages.

5. The idea that divine favor descended on even the ignorant justified the sixteenth-century practice of baptizing Indians en masse with cursory religious instruction or none at all (Armas Medina 1953, 244–45; Vargas Ugarte 1953–1962, 226–27). America's first Christian missionaries believed that the Holy Spirit could inspire conversion through speech without explicit transference of doctrinal knowledge.

6. "[S]i unos pocos españoles, estando en patria extraña, no pueden con todo olvidar su propia lengua y aprender la extranjera . . . ¿en qué cabeza cabe que innumerables gentes tengan que olvidar la lengua de sus padres en su propia patria y usar sólo de un idioma extranjero que oyen raras veces y muy a disgusto?" (Acosta [1577] 1987, 2:63).

7. Lima I, naturales 1, Vargas Ugarte 1951–1954, 1:7; Lima I, naturales 6, Vargas Ugarte 1951–1954, 1:10.

8. Lima II, indios 32, Vargas Ugarte 1951–1954, 1:175–76; Lima II, indios 35, Vargas Ugarte 1951–1954, 1:177. Evidence of native-language catechisms from the first years of evangelization comes mainly by indirect reference. Quechua texts included the catechism and dialogues of the First Council; Juan de Betanzos's

Doctrina cristiana, vocabulario y confesionario; Francisco Churrón y Aguilar's *Cartilla, catecismo y sermones en la lengua general del Perú;* the catechism of Bishop Sebastián de Lartaún; Jodocus de Ricke's *Doctrina y sermones en lengua peruana;* Tomás de San Martín's *Catecismo doctrinal para los indios;* and Diego Ortiz's *Doctrina cristiana y sermones en lengua quichua* (Castillo Arroyo 1966, 49–51). Two surviving Quechua catechisms from that period are Pedro de Quiroga's "Modo breve de doctrinar los indios" ([c. 1563] 1992, 164–65) and Domingo de Santo Tomás's "Plática para todos los Indios" (in Santo Tomás [1560] 1995, 172–79). For a comprehensive bibliography of Quechua- and Aymara-language works of the colonial period, see Rivet and Créqui-Monfort 1951.

9. Lima II, indios 3, Vargas Ugarte 1951–1954, 1:161; Lima II, indios 53, Vargas Ugarte 1951–1954, 1:184. Parish assignments in the Archdiocese of Lima were awarded by *oposición,* a competitive oral examination in which priests had to demonstrate their skills in Latin and Quechua through explication of scriptural passages and the basic tenets of the Christian faith (García Cabrera 1997, 422).

10. Lima III, actio 2, cap. 6, Vargas Ugarte 1951–1954, 1:325.

11. "[P]ues no puede ser buen juez el que da sentencia en lo que no entiende" (Lima III, actio 2, cap. 16, Vargas Ugarte 1951–1954, 1:329).

12. Lima III, actio 2, cap. 31, Vargas Ugarte 1951–1954, 1:335–36; Lima III, actio 2, cap. 40, Vargas Ugarte 1951–1954, 1:339; Lima III, actio 4, cap. 17, Vargas Ugarte 1951–1954, 1:368. Ecclesiastical synods of the sixteenth and seventeenth centuries supported these decrees (Lima 1594, cap. 12, ACE, "Originales del Concilio Limense," 187v; Cuzco 1591, cap. 1, BNP, A 568, 2v–3v; Cuzco 1601, cap. 25, BNP, B 1675, 7r; Quito 1594, cap. 86, Campo del Pozo and Carmona Moreno 1996, 118; Quito 1594, cap. 87, Campo del Pozo and Carmona Moreno 1996, 118–19; Lima 1613, Lib. I, tit. vii, cap. 8, Lobo Guerrero and Arias de Ugarte [1613, 1636] 1987, 90–91; Arequipa 1638, Lib. II, tit. 10, cap. 3, BNP, B 1742, 166v–167r; Arequipa 1638, Lib. IV, tit. 3, cap. 15, BNP, B 1742, 253v–254v; La Paz 1638, Lib. I, tit. 7, cap. 2, Vega 1639, 25–26).

13. *RLI* 1841, Lib. I, tit. vi, ley 30, 1:50; *RLI* 1841, Lib. I, tit. xxii, ley 46, 1:156; see also Eguiguren 1951, 2:592–98. Despite his Castilianization policy, Toledo conceded that religious instruction required the use of native languages (Levillier 1921–1925, 8:115). On the history of the academic chairs in Quechua, see Castro Pineda 1963 and Meneses 1982.

14. Lima III, actio 2, cap. 3, Vargas Ugarte 1951–1954, 1:323.

15. Early modern theorists held that the confusion of languages at Babel and the dispersion of ancient peoples had provided the conditions for linguistic ambiguity and deviant forms of religion. They argued that if humans had lived together under one language, teaching successive generations their knowledge of God, ignorance of the divine never would have spread (MacCormack 1991, 221). In this view, the linguistic plurality observed in the Indies stood for paganism and digression from the oneness of the Christian faith.

16. "una enfermedad idolátrica hereditaria, . . . contraída en el mismo seno de la madre y criada al mamar su misma leche" (Acosta [1577] 1987, 2:255).

17. Santo Tomás ([1560] 1951, [1560] 1995) authored the first printed grammar and dictionary of the Quechua language, both published in Spain in 1560. Cerrón-Palomino (1995, xvi) has identified Santo Tomás's variant as a koine, or amalgam of dialects, similar to the language of the coastal region between Lima and Chincha.

18. "La imperfeccion o barbariedad, que ay en los que hablan corruptamente la lengua Quichua, no esta tanto en la conexion de las dicciones, quanto en la variedad de los vocablos, que son differentes de los que se vsan en el Cuzco, y algo toscos, tomados de sus ydiomas particulares, o del vso que comunmente rescibieron todos los que se llaman Chinchaysuyos" (*Doctrina christiana* [1584] 1985, 167).

19. "los que vsauan los Ingas, y señores, o . . . de otras naciones con quien tratan" (*Doctrina christiana* [1584] 1985, 167, cited in Mannheim 1991, 67). The collectively authored *Arte y vocabulario en la lengua general* (1586), also commissioned by the Third Council, featured select lexicon from the central provinces despite the council's disapproval of words used in this region (Cerrón-Palomino 1992, 221; Torero 1995, 16).

20. Few writers exalted the Cuzco language more fervently than El Inca Garcilaso. In the lengthy meditations on language that appear in his *Comentarios reales de los Incas* (1609, 1617), Garcilaso viewed the language of Cuzco as the Quechua standard. For him, the extent to which speakers obeyed the Third Council's norms marked the difference between proper and corrupt uses of Quechua (Cerrón-Palomino 1991).

21. "[L]a ciudad del Cuzco es el Athenas, que en ella se habla en todo el rigor y elegancia que se puede ymaginar, como la Ionica en Athenas, la Latina en Roma, el romance Castellano en Toledo, y assi es la lengua Quichua en el Cuzco" (Oré [1598] 1992, 144). Murúa ([1590] 2004, 128v) and Pérez Bocanegra (1631, s.f.) repeated this view.

22. "[Q]uanto mas distan desta ciudad, ay mas corrupcion y menos elegancia" (Oré [1598] 1992, 144).

23. "[L]os indios Puquinas, Collao, Urus, Yuncas y otras naciones, que son rudos y torpes, y por su rudeza aun sus propias lenguas hablan mal, cuando alcanzan a saber la lengua del Cozco, parece que echan de sí la rudeza y torpeza que tenían y que aspiran a cosas políticas y cortesanas, y sus ingenios pretenden subir a cosas más altas; finalmente se hacen más capaces y suficientes para recibir la doctrina de la fe católica" (Garcilaso [1609] 1960, 2:251).

24. Diego González Holguín attributed these values to the Inca language in his Spanish-Quechua dictionary ([1608] 1952, 375–76), and the investigator of idolatries Pablo de Prado reiterated the widespread belief that "on the coasts and in other regions . . . the general language is not spoken with the correctness and purity as it is in Cuzco" (en los Llanos, y otras partes . . . la lengua general no se

habla con la propiedad y pureza que en el Cuzco) (1641, s.f.; see also Roxo Mexía y Ocón 1648, s.f.).

25. BNP, F 219, 1r.

26. "[A]quella confusion y multitud de lenguas que los Incas con tanto cuidado procuraron quitar, ha vuelto a nacer de nuevo; . . . por lo cual . . . es imposible que los indios del Perú . . . puedan ser bien instruídos en la fe y en las buenas costumbres" (Garcilaso [1609] 1960, 2:249).

27. "[R]egían y gobernaban los Incas en paz y quietud todo su imperio, y los vasallos de diversas naciones se habían como hermanos porque todos hablaban una lengua" (Garcilaso [1609] 1960, 2:248). Acosta ([1577] 1987, 2:63, 65) and Solórzano Pereira (1648, 221) also viewed Inca language policy as a model for uniting colonized subjects.

28. Visitadores had the authority to punish public sins, including those of priests, and to receive legal grievances from parishioners (Ortiz de Salcedo 1691, 13v–14r, 150v–151r).

29. Duviols ([1971] 1977, 406) and Griffiths (1996, 149–50) also mention the ties between charges of idolatry and litigation against priests and the polarizing effect this had on native communities.

30. Catholic courts ruled on wide-ranging matters of canon law pertaining to benefices, tithes, sacraments, and marital disputes. Juan de Hevia Bolaños (1619, 24r, 27r, 158r) outlines the rights of laypersons to raise civil and criminal charges against priests in ecclesiastical tribunals.

31. Lima II, indios 6, Vargas Ugarte 1951–1954, 1:163; Lima II, indios 9, Vargas Ugarte 1951–1954, 1:164–65.

32. AAL, Capítulos, Leg. 1, Exp. 1, 2r–5r; AAL, Capítulos, Leg. 2, Exp. 16, 5r, 9v; AAL, Capítulos, Leg. 3, Exp. 11, 2v–4r; AAL, Capítulos, Leg. 4, Exp. 3, 3v–4r. Council decrees proscribing illegal economic activity include: Lima II, españoles 36, Vargas Ugarte 1951–1954, 1:118; Lima II, españoles 93, Vargas Ugarte 1951–1954, 1:143; Lima II, indios 17, Vargas Ugarte 1951–1954, 1:169; Lima III, actio 3, cap. 4, Vargas Ugarte 1951–1954, 1:344–45; Lima III, actio 3, cap. 5, Vargas Ugarte 1951–1954, 1:345.

33. AAC, Colonial, X, 3, 44, 1r; AAL, Capítulos, Leg. 5, Exp. 14, 2r, 6v; AAL, Capítulos, Leg. 14, Exp. 4, 1r–v; AAL, Capítulos, Leg. 15, Exp. 5, 1v; AAL, Capítulos, Leg. 16, Exp. 1, 1r, 3r, 44v–45r. Conciliar laws against forced offerings include: Lima II, indios 26, Vargas Ugarte 1951–1954, 1:173; Lima III, actio 2, cap. 13, Vargas Ugarte 1951–1954, 1:328; Lima III, actio 2, cap. 38, Vargas Ugarte 1951–1954, 1:338–39.

34. Lima II, indios 6, Vargas Ugarte 1951–1954, 1:163; Lima II, indios 9, Vargas Ugarte 1951–1954, 1:164–65; Lima III, actio 2, cap. 39, Vargas Ugarte 1951-1954, 1:339; Guaman Poma [c. 1615] 1980, 519.

35. Lima II, indios 7, Vargas Ugarte 1951–1954, 1:163–64; Lima III, actio 3, cap. 17, Vargas Ugarte 1951–1954, 1:351; Lima III, actio 3, cap. 18, Vargas Ugarte

1951–1954, 1:352; Lima III, actio 3, cap. 19, Vargas Ugarte 1951–1954, 1:352–53; Lima III, actio 3, cap. 24, Vargas Ugarte 1951–1954, 1:354.

36. "[A] llegado a tanto su mala orden de vivir[,] mal exemplo q. da a los naturales" (AAL, Capítulos, Leg. 3, Exp. 14, 4v). See also AAC, Colonial, LXXV, 4, 72, 6v–9v; AAC, Colonial, V, 1, 2, 2v; AAL, Capítulos, Leg. 3, Exp. 11, 2v, 4v–5r; AAL, Capítulos, Leg. 5, Exp. 14, 4v; AAL, Capítulos, Leg. 6, Exp. 1, 4v; AAL, Capítulos, Leg. 6, Exp. 6, 21r.

37. AAC, Colonial, V, 1, 2, 1v–2v; AAC, Colonial, XXXIX, 2, 31, 4v; AAL, Capítulos, Leg. 1, Exp. 6, 1r; AAL, Capítulos, Leg. 3, Exp. 11, 4v–5r; AAL, Capítulos, Leg. 16, Exp. 1, 44v.

38. AAL, Capítulos, Leg. 5, Exp. 14, 2v–3v; AAL, Capítulos, Leg. 6, Exp. 1, 4v, 8v; AGN, Tribunal Eclesiástico, Leg. 43, Cuad. 4, 12v.

39. AAL, Capítulos, Leg. 2, Exp. 16, 5r; AAL, Capítulos, Leg. 9, Exp. 9, 7r; AAL, Visitas Eclesiásticas, Leg. 15, Exp. 34, 4r; AAL, Visitas Eclesiásticas, Leg. 12, Exp. 6, 1r–v; BNP, B 744, 5v.

40. AAL, Hechicerías e Idolatrías, Leg. 3, Exp. 9, 3v, 15v. In 1664, Sarmiento investigated the local dispute over rights to Rupay Chagua's governorship (AAL, Hechicerías e Idolatrías, Leg. 5, Exp. 4, 23v, 31r, 32v, 34r, 39r).

41. "que estaua cansado de haçer tantos sacrifizios y gastar su rrecado en ellos sin hauerle dado plata ninguna" (AAL, Hechicerías e Idolatrías, Leg. 3, Exp. 9, 9v). Thanks are owed to Kenneth Mills for calling attention to this quotation from the trial record (personal communication, 10 May 2005).

42. According to Millones (1978, 269), the Spanish mandate was not enough to uphold the power of the caciques in the central sierra; therefore, native elites maintained influence by supporting the ancestral religious practices of the traditional *ayllus* (kin groups). Mills (1997, 41) argues that despite the isolation and anti-Christian posture of some huaca-ministers, most Andeans practiced traditional rites in ways that were intertwined with the activities of native parishes.

43. AAL, Visitas Eclesiásticas, Leg. 23, Exp. 30, 1r, 5r, 5v, 7r.

44. "[E]s de adbertir que el dicho don Rodrigo se firma en la dicha petision Don Rodrigo de gusman Apo Rupaichagua[,] y este sobrenombre de Apo significa en la lengua natural de los indios el Señor de todo[,] y este sobrenombre de Apo no lo tiene de sus antepasados sino que el se lo a puesto[,] y no firma ordinariamente con el sino es cuando escribe a los indios de su repartimiento pero no cuando escribe a los coregidores y otras justicias[,] que indica malisia" (AAL, Visitas Eclesiásticas, Leg. 23, Exp. 30, 9r).

45. AAL, Visitas Eclesiásticas, Leg. 23, Exp. 30, 9v. Guaman Poma derided cacique parvenus, such as Don Juan Capcha, who falsely claimed spiritual status by appropriating the ancestral title "Apo" ([c. 1615] 1980, 791, see also 544). Dedenbach-Salazar Sáenz (1997, 198) examines the colonial meanings of the Quechua term.

46. BNP, B 1282, 1r, 2r–3r. Rupay Chagua's employment of the term *enemigo capital* (chief enemy) was not accidental. Hevia Bolaños (1619, 77r) references

Alfonso X of Castile's thirteenth-century ruling that banned "chief enemies" from testifying in trials. See also Martínez 1791, 3:213.

47. Studies have presented El Colegio del Príncipe's graduates as ultraorthodox Christians who identified unconditionally with the values of Spanish rule (Cárdenas Ayaipoma 1975–1976, 16), but their experience as criminal defendants in the tribunals of extirpation calls this stereotype into question. In contrast, Alaperrine-Bouyer (2007, 207–22) summarizes the litigious careers of several graduates of the colegio, including Rupay Chagua's. The various stances assumed by Rupay Chagua in his continual movement between Spanish and Andean society illustrates what Adorno has called "the multiple subject positions that the colonial subject seemed destined to take, not merely sequentially but most often simultaneously" (1991, 258).

48. The research of De la Puente Brunke (1998, 469 n. 31) shows that in that same year Rupay Chagua and several curacas of the central highlands sent a letter to the Spanish monarch in which they declared their loyalty to the Crown and denied the accusations of idolatry against them (AGI, Lima, 11).

49. "[E]stán tan naturalizados los conceptos errados, particularmente en los Chinchaysuyus, que ignoran los términos cusquenses por donde se tradujo la doctrina Xpiana" (Molina [1649] 1928, 85).

50. "pronunciando la lengua vnos mas gutturalmente q otros . . . o qtando letras o añadiendo, o mudando, . . . no guardan a vezes la perfecta construccion de las partes de la oracion, antes cometen algunos solecismos" (*Doctrina christiana* [1584] 1985, 167–68).

51. "[E]nseñan con muchos errores, trastrocando o mudando algunas palabras o letras, con que hacen muy diverso sentido" (Arriaga [1621] 1999, 72).

52. "[C]omo en el credo por decir Hucllachacuininta, que es la comunión o junta de los santos, decir Pucllachacuininta, que es la burla o trisca de los santos" (Arriaga [1621] 1999, 72).

53. Church and audiencia officials insisted that because native catechists were prone to doctrinal error, visitadores should examine them on their command of the catechism. See Huamanga 1629, Lib. I, tit. 1, const. 2, Torres 1970, 14; Arequipa 1638, Lib. IV, tit. 3, cap. 16, BNP, B 1742, 254v; León Pinelo 1661, 8v; Liñán y Cisneros c.1685, 56r.

54. "[P]ara sacar en linpio estas dichas historias ube tanto trauajo por ser cin escrito ni letra alguna, cino no más de quipos y rrelaciones de muchas lenguaxes ajuntando con la lengua de la castellana y quichiua ynga, aymara, poquina colla, canche, cana, charca, chinchaysuyo, andesuyo, collasuyo, condesuyo, todos los bocablos de yndios" (Guaman Poma [c. 1615] 1980, 11).

55. "[A]ssí mandó que los bestidos y traxes de cada pueblo fuesen defirentes, como en hablar, para conoçer porque en este tiempo no echavan de ver y conosçer a los yndios qué naçión y qué pueblo eran" (Pachacuti Yamqui [c. 1613] 1993, 198).

56. "[Q]ue en el dho pueblo [el testigo] oyo echar pregones de noche antes de hacer la fiesta de señor san Ju.o y corpus que no comiessen sal ni agi y[,] aunque no decian en su lengua general del ingua [sino que] vsaban de la materna [,] los mismos yndios [e] yndias le decian a este tt.o en la lengua general del ingua que mandaban los biejos y camachicos no comiesen sal ni agi y que era tiempo de mochar sus malquis" (AAL, Hechicerías e Idolatrías, Leg. 3, Exp. 11, 3v–4r, cited in Itier 1992, 1012–13).

57. "[Q]ue el dho cura no sabe bien la lengua general por cuya caussa se que-dan muchos yndios sin confesar[,] como no lo sabe no ara bien las confesiones ni tienen los yndios otra persona con quien puedan confesar[,] y que esta lengua es la que no sabe el dho cura la general de los yndios nuebamente conbertidos[,] porque la otra lengua general del ynga la sabe el dho cura muy bien y asi no se entiende sino en la lengua de los yndios cristianos nuebos" (AAL, Capítulos, Leg. 16, Exp. 1, 49r).

58. AAL, Visitas Eclesiásticas, Leg. 15, Exp. 34, 5r.

59. In 1702, at the end of Guevara's fifty-year missionary career, the cacique principal and alcalde of Chavín de Pariarca, Don Domingo Yupaxari, told church authorities that Guevara had met his pastoral obligations and "preached to his parishioners in the language" (AAL, Visitas Eclesiásticas, Leg. 16, Exp. 1, 3r).

60. Durston (2008, 56–59) discusses subtle points where mundane Quechua literature departed from Third Council linguistic standards.

61. Lima 1613, Lib. I, tit. ii, cap. 3, Lobo Guerrero and Arias de Ugarte [1613, 1636] 1987, 44; Lima 1636, Título de Constitutionibus, cap. 3, Lobo Guerrero and Arias de Ugarte [1613, 1636] 1987, 262.

62. "E visto en muchas partes, que hombres muy buenos lenguas (y yo soy vno déstos) no sólo no saben los errores de sus feligreses, pero ni entienden las palabras, y vocablos conque dizen" (Ávila 1648, 83).

63. Cuzco 1591, cap. 1, BNP, A 568, 2v–3v; Cuzco 1591, cap. 4, BNP, A 568, 4r–v.

64. BNP, F 219, 1r.

65. Arequipa 1638, Lib. I, tit. 1, cap. 5, BNP, B 1742, 71v–72r.

66. Quito 1594, cap. 3, Campo del Pozo and Carmona Moreno 1996, 72–73.

67. Oré's Guaraní text was a copy of the catechism by the Franciscan friar Luis Bolanos (Tibesar [1953] 1991, 128 n. 53). Medina (1904, 1:345–46) states that the first grammar and catechism of the Yunga language, now lost, was authored by Roque de Cejuela, the parish priest of Lambayeque, according to correspon-dence found in the Archive of the Indies. Alternative language publications also include Ludovico Bertonio's Aymara-language works (1612a, 1612b, 1612c), Luis de Valdivia's pastoral complements in Allentiac (1606, 1607a, 1607b), Antonio Ruiz de Montoya's Guaraní-language books of instruction (1639, 1640a, 1640b), and Pedro Marbán's Moja grammar and catechism (1702).

68. BNP, F 933.

69. Huerta stated his aim as follows: "[T]hough until now documents for speaking the Chinchaysuyu language have not been produced, in this grammar I will present a few so that the different ways of speaking in the two provinces are understood, the language of the Inca extending from Huamanga to the south and the Chinchaysuyu extending from there north to Quito" (Y aunque hasta aquí no se han enseñado documentos para hablar la lengua Chinchaysuyo, en este arte iré enseñando algunos para que se entienda la diferencia que hay de hablar entre las dos Provincias, que empiezan, la del inga desde Huamanga arriba, y la Chinchaysuyo desde allí abajo hasta Quito) ([1616] 1993, 18).

70. "uso y ejercicio de hablar con los indios chinchaysuyos" (AAL, Ordenaciones, Leg. 2, Exp. 31, cited in Durston 2002, 234; 2007, 127). Huerta's tenure as chair of Quechua at San Marcos was not without controversy. In 1620, the chief prosecutor of the Lima archdiocese, Antonio Rodríguez de la Cruz, accused him of neglecting his teaching duties and receiving payments from candidates in return for language certifications needed for native parish appointment (AAL, Criminales, Leg. 5, Exp. 18).

71. "[J]uzgo . . . que principalmente se han de predicar en este Arçobispado en que el vulgo habla la lengua Chinchaisuyu, es esta la mas genuina y mas corriente traduccion, y no la [lengua cuzqueña] que los cultos han introducido para que no los entienda el pueblo" (Avendaño 1649, s.f.). This sentiment culminated in 1700 with the publication of the second edition of the Jesuit priest Diego de Torres Rubio's Quechua grammar of 1619. The publication featured an appendix of Chinchaysuyu lexicon compiled by the Jesuit Juan de Figueredo and was reprinted in 1754 (Torres Rubio [1619, 1700] 1963; Cerrón-Palomino 1992, 222). A compendium of Quechua grammar for instructing priests in the "common language" of the northern regions of Quito and Maynas was also published in Lima around that time (Breve instrucción 1753).

72. "[N]o pueden entrar con ellos ningunos en competencia porque los de allá saben las lenguas, y costumbres de los Indios, sus ritos, y su capacidad, y gouierno en que no les pueden engañar: como auiendo ocultado en la prouincia de Lima, a los Prelados, y Curas las Idolatrias antiguas, se descubrieron aora por los Eclesiasticos nacidos en ellas, y Visitadores, que salen de ordinario a predicarles" (Ortiz de Cervantes 1620, 8r).

73. Solórzano Pereira (1648, 668–69), Velázquez de Ovando (c. 1658, 22v–23v), León Pinelo (1661, 3r), and Bolívar y de la Redonda (1667, 2r–3r) make the same argument in favor of Creole appointments.

74. A partial list of the mid-seventeenth-century works published in Lima consists of: Ávila (1648), Avendaño (1649), Jurado Palomino (1649), and Roxo Mexía y Ocón (1648). With the exception of Melgar (1691), the production of works in ecclesiastical Quechua waned after this time, but new editions of previous publications continued to be in high demand. A Spanish-Quechua reedition of the

Tercero catecismo (1585) was published following the Sixth Provincial Council of Lima (1772–1773), and, according to Barnes (1992, 67), the Third Council publications remained in use until the plenary council of Latin America of 1899. Despite their expressed opposition to the official Quechua, Avendaño and Molina complied in their sermonic texts with the Third Council's lexical and orthographic guidelines, perhaps due to the requirements of ecclesiastical censors (Cerrón-Palomino 1987, 89–90; Taylor 2001, 213).

75. "Sauiendo quatro palabras: 'Apomuy cauallo. Mana miconqui. Padreta ricunqui. Maymi soltera? Maymi muchachas? Apomoy dotrinaman,' no saue más" (Guaman Poma [c. 1615] 1980, 624). Translation of the Quechua by Jorge L. Urioste.

76. Don Gaspar de Arce's 1652 petition to the archbishop for appointment to the doctrina of Chavín de Pariarca was typical in this regard: "It has come to my attention that the parish of Chavín is vacant and edicts have been posted [about the vacancy], and in the best form that may be acceptable in law, I would like to compete for the said parish post on account of my linguistic expertise" (dijo que a mi notiçia es venido que la dotrina de chauin esta vaca y puesto editos a ella a la qual en la mexor forma que aya lugar en dr.o me opongo a la dha dotrina por ser lenguaraz) (AAL, Concursos, Leg. 4, Exp. 15, 6r). The Third Council required priests to learn Quechua, but allowed in extreme circumstances the appointment of priests who spoke only Spanish: "Those who know the language should be sought out for the doctrinas, and so that all priests learn the language, it is appropriate to encourage them with rewards of honors and privileges. However, when persons skilled in the language cannot be found, a priest still must be sent to the doctrina de indios, provided he is a person of good moral example" (Dévense procurar para las doctrinas personas que sepan la lengua, y para que todos la aprendan es justo animarlos con premios de honras y ventajas. Pero, quando no se halleren personas diestras en la lengua, no por eso se ha de dejar de enviar algún sacerdote para doctrina de indios con tal que sea persona de buena vida) (Lima III, actio 2, cap. 40, Vargas Ugarte 1951–1954, 1:339).

77. Rupay Chagua's case would also have benefited from church legislation of 1617 that gave the archbishop the right to suspend religious clergy for linguistic insufficiency or for refusing visitations of the juez ordinario (AGN, Tribunal Eclesiástico, Leg. 43, Cuad. 1, 1r–3v).

78. AAL, Capítulos, Leg. 2, Exp. 16, 5r.

79. "[D]ise ser cura de la dha doctrina sin hauer ni entender la lengua gen.l del ynga ni tener colasion ni canonica ynstitusion ni presentasion R.l para ello" (AAL, Capítulos, Leg. 21, Exp. 1, 33r).

80. AAL, Visitas Eclesiásticas, Leg. 12, Exp. 6; AAL, Capítulos, Leg. 6, Exp. 5.

81. "[P]or no saber la lengua con engaño mostraron a vs.a otro religiosso que la sabia y luego que vs.a passo se quedo en la dha Doctrina" (AAL, Orden de Santo Domingo, Leg. 1, Exp. 21, 1r).

82. AAL, Visitas Eclesiásticas, Leg. 9, Exp. 22, 1r.

83. "[Era] sufisiente de lengua y virtuoso que se ocupaua en predicarles y cate-quisarles la doctrina christiana a los yndios con mucho fruto" (AAL, La Merced, Leg. 7, Exp. 42, 1r). In addition, in 1664 Rupay Chagua defended the Mercedarian friar Juan de Espinosa Campo, who he claimed had been physically assaulted by a group of "depraved" native congregants (AAL, Criminales, Leg. 23, Exp. 11, 1r).

84. AAL, La Merced, Leg. 7, Exp. 42, 7r, 9r–12r, 13v.

85. Viceroy Melchor de Navarra y Rocafull's ordinances of 1685 upheld the duty of native governors and caciques principales to monitor parish priests in their treatment of the Indians and teaching of Christian doctrine (López y Mar-tínez 1685, 137).

86. Cornejo Polar (1994) examines native Andean writings and dramatic rep-resentations of the Spanish conquest of Cajamarca from colonial through mod-ern times, centering on how indigenous portrayals of the Inca's defeat evidence unresolved conflicts between Quechua orality and European written culture. Pachacuti Yamqui's attention to the problem of intercultural communication also deserves mention in this regard. The indigenous writer identified clerical igno-rance of native languages as a problem in colonial evangelization and criticized the priests of his day for their lack of linguistic training ([c. 1613] 1993, 268).

Chapter 3

1. An often cited example of the link between the imposition of books and the advance of colonialism can be found in the actions of Mexico's first bishop, Juan de Zumárraga, who oversaw the establishment of the printing press in Mex-ico and the destruction of painted manuscripts in the Mesoamerican archive of Texcoco (see Calvo 2003, 280).

2. Burns (2005a) examines the "making of indigenous archives" and its impact on the scribal culture of colonial Cuzco. For surveys of colonial sources on khipu practices, see Sempat Assadourian 2002 and Urton 2002.

3. Allen 2005 and Beyersdorff 2005 outline the renewed interest in khipu cul-ture in today's Andeanist scholarship, most notably that of the anthropologists Gary Urton and Frank Salomon.

4. Quilter and Urton 2002 features studies by scholars of various disciplines that question the theory that khipus recorded only numerical information.

5. Salomon (2004) and Estenssoro Fuchs (2003, especially 223–28) examine the ethnographic contexts in which knotted cords survived and operated along-side written documents.

6. "Demanera, que no saben lo que se confiessan, ni dizen, y ponen al Con-fessor en confusion, assi juzgando, como absoluiendo: y é hallado, que guar-dan semejantes ñudos, para otra confession, aunque la hagan de breue tiempo, ó para otro año. Y que los prestan, y dan a los que se an de confessar de nueuo,

. . . [e]nredandose en millares de errores, con estos quipos, y memorias" (Pérez Bocanegra 1631, 112–13).

7. "[C]uanto los libros pueden decir de historias, y leyes y ceremonias, y cuentas de negocios, todo eso suplen los quipos tan puntualmente, que admira" (Acosta [1590] 2002, 385).

8. In Toledo's vision, the municipal alcaldes would catalog the Indians' attendance at Mass with khipus (Levillier 1921–1925, 8:305–12).

9. AGI, Patronato, 231, N.7, R.8. Estenssoro Fuchs (2003, 217) and Sempat Assadourian (2002, 136–37) discuss Porres's instruction.

10. "[D]arselo por quipo al caçique porque no pretendan ygnorançia de lo que alli les obliga y manda" (AGI, Patronato, 231, N.7, R.8, 1r).

11. AGI, Patronato, 231, N.7, R.8, 5r–7v.

12. "[U]n indio curaca y viejo tenia en un cordel grande destos todo el calendario Romano y todos los sanctos y fiestas de guardar y me dio a entender como y de que manera lo sabia y que a un fraile muy curioso de mi horden los años pasados le auia dicho se lo leyese el calendario y que le diese a entender y que asi como el fraile se lo iba deziendo iba el asentando en su quipu y asi fue cosa de gran admiraçion ber de la manera que el buen viejo se entendia por el como si fuera por papel y tinta" (Murúa [1590] 2004, 77v).

13. "[D]alles las quatro oraçiones que son obligados a sauer, y mandamientos, por quipo, asi como lo rrezan por sus pausas, y silauas, y mandalles que ningun yndio biejo ni muchacho ande sin el tal quipo para que por alli sepan las dichas oraçiones y que siempre lo traigan consigo doquiera que fueren, aunque vayan afuera de sus tierras, para que tengan rregla de xpianos, y den rrazones de las dichas oraçiones donde se las preguntaren, y lo que cada oraçion quiere dezir" (AGI, Patronato, 231, N.7, R.8, 2r).

14. "[M]uchos hombres y mugeres y los niños y niñas andan todo el día con quipos como estudiantes que repiten liçión. Cuando llegamos aquí nos dezían los españoles que no avría remedio de traer los indios a la doctrina sino a palos" (transcribed in Egaña 1954–1986, 2:276, cited in Albó 1966, 417).

15. MacCormack 1989 traces this theme in the early Peruvian chronicles.

16. "Todo era hazer quipos p.q confessarse aprender lo q no sabian de la doctr.a confessarse, ayunar, y disciplinarse, y generalm.te attender cada vno ala saluacion de sus almas" (transcribed in Polia Meconi 1999, 273). Egaña (1954–1986, 2:252, 262) and Mateos ([1600] 1944, 2:101, 128) feature comparable Jesuit testimonies of confessional khipus.

17. "Y el yndio haga quipo de sus pecados. Y al yndio y a la yndia le enseñe cómo lo a de confesarse de cada pecado" (Guaman Poma [c. 1615] 1980, 630).

18. "Que los yndios dizen que no tomando zeniza a de comer carne en toda la quaresma y entran a deseplinarse por sus quipos. Le manda los camachicos y el quien se deseplina dizen que a de comer carne el Jueues Santo y para asotarse disen que a de estar muy borracho y a la misa an de yr por quipo y qüenta.

¡O qué mala enseñansa que le enseñan los mandones!" (Guaman Poma [c. 1615] 1980, 895).

19. Another example of the Andeans' unorthodox enactment of penitential rites can be found in a 1654 legal dispute involving the ethnic lords of Chavín de Pariarca, who challenged the Lima see's appointment of secular clergy in replacement of the Jesuit priests who had evangelized there for nineteen years (García Cabrera 1992, 45–46). The notables claimed that the new priests had increased the local tributary burden through illegal ventures, while ignoring their sacramental duties in the village and surrounding hamlets. As a result, "the work of the said Jesuit fathers, who achieved [the Indians' conversion] with their example and teachings, is ruined" (se malogra el trauajo de dhos padres de la comp.a que consiguieron [la conversión de los indios] con su exemplo y doctrina) (AAL, Capítulos, Leg. 16, Exp. 1, 2r–3v, 44r). During the lengthy trial deliberations, some witnesses testified that due to clerical negligence, Andean officials had assumed the role of spiritual directors. In the deserted subsidiary church of La Montaña, for instance, one parishioner, Jerónimo Chuchunimpa, came upon some black vestments and a biretta that the Jesuits had left behind. At the behest of the residents, he donned the garments, recruited his own team of native alcaldes and alguaciles, and sat dutifully upon the altar hearing confessions of indigenous penitents (266v–268r, 269v–270r, 275v).

20. "Lo primero, hijo mio, has de pensar bien tus peccados, y hazer quipo dellos: como hazes quipo, quando eres tambo camayo, de lo que das, y de lo que te deuen: assi haz quipo de lo que has hecho, contra Dios y contra tu proximo, y quantas vezes: si muchas, o si pocas. . . . Despues de auerte pesado, y hecho quippo de tus peccados por los diez mandamientos, o como mejor supieres, has de pedir a Dios perdon con mucho dolor de auelle offendido" *(Tercero catecismo* [1585] 1985, 482–83). English translation adapted from Harrison 2002, 268.

21. "[E]stos ñudos y señales . . . los tienen de muchos colores, para hazer diuision de los pecados, y el numero de los que an cometido, ó no" (Pérez Bocanegra 1631, 111).

22. "[D]e seis varas de cordel torcido y de trecho en trecho un hilo que lo atravesava y algunas señales de piedras o güesos o plumas, conforme a la materia del peccado que avía de confessar" (cited in Rappaport and Cummins 1998, 27 n. 20; Harrison 2002, 281).

23. "[A]cudían a las confesiones con muchas lágrimas y arrepentim.to y verdad, trayendo sus memoriales que llaman quipos, unos en hilo, otros en escrito y otros con rayas, lo mejor que podían, incitandose los unos a los otros" (Mateos [1600] 1944, 2:128).

24. "porque hay en todo este Reyno gran multitud de pueblos y gente, porque todo lo tenian puesto, con mucho orden y conçierto en sus quipus y cuerdas por donde ellos se entendían con la façilidad que nosotros en nuestra lengua por nuestro papel y tinta" (Murúa [1590] 2004, 77r).

25. "[P]orque en lugar de los libros los yndios han usado y usan unos como registros hechos de diferentes hilos, que ellos llaman quipos, y con estos conservan la memoria de su antigua superstición y ritos y ceremonias y costumbres perversas; procuren con diligencia los obispos que todos los memoriales o quipos, que sirven para su superstición, se les quiten totalmente a los yndios" (Lima III, actio 3, cap. 37, Vargas Ugarte 1951–1954, 1:358). English translation adapted from Harrison 2002, 268–69.

26. "que tanta razón ay de creer á sus antepassados, y á sus Quipos y memoriales, como á los mayores y antepassados de los Christianos y á sus Quillcas y escripturas" (Polo de Ondegardo [1559] 1906, 202). Murúa ([1590] 2004, 104r) made a similar pronouncement about the khipus' capacity to preserve the memory of idolatrous customs.

27. A native trial declaration of 1657 states that Andean dogmatists in the parish of San Juan de Machaca recorded with khipu the Indians' attendance at fasting and confession (AAL, Hechicerías e Idolatrías, Leg. 2A, Exp. 2, 7v).

28. Villagómez (1649, 54r, 63r) reprints Arriaga's instructions on the use of khipus (Galen Brokaw, personal communication, 14 September 2007).

29. AAL, Hechicerías e Idolatrías, Leg. 5, Exp. 2, 12r–v.

30. Cuzco 1591, cap. 11, BNP, A 568, 6r–v; Quito 1594, cap. 35, Campo del Pozo and Carmona Moreno 1996, 87–88; La Plata 1619, tit. 15, cap. 1, BNP, B 1673, s.f.; Arequipa 1638, Lib. II, tit. 2, cap. 2, BNP, B 1742, 121r–122r; Arequipa 1638, Lib. II, tit. 10, cap. 10, BNP, B 1742, 171v–172r; AAC, Colonial V, 1, 4, 6v. Following church visitation procedures, Andean parishes were required to display a *tabla* (board) with instructions in Spanish and the local native language for baptizing infants when necessary during the priest's absence (AAL, Visitas Eclesiásticas, Leg. 11, Exp. 15, 2r; BNP, B 1100, 42r). Errors in the performance of the sacrament could bring legal consequences, as occurred with Don Diego Yaruparia, the cacique principal of the north-central highland village of Santiago de Aija. In 1672, Yaruparia was prosecuted by the Church for orchestrating the baptism of an illegitimate child without authorization (BNP, B 612, 1v).

31. Cuzco 1591, cap. 4, BNP, A 568, 4r–v; Peña Montenegro [1668] 1985, 319–20, 371.

32. Lima II, españoles 13, Vargas Ugarte 1951–1954, 1:108; Lima II, indios 49, Vargas Ugarte 1951–1954, 1:182–83; Arequipa 1638, Lib. II, tit. 4, cap. 6, BNP, B 1742, 128v.

33. Cuzco 1591, cap. 4, BNP, A 568, 4r–v.

34. Lima III, actio 2, cap. 14, Vargas Ugarte 1951–1954, 1:270–71.

35. "Hallando quipos, donde algun indio, ó india que tu conoces, auia añudado sus pecados, para memoria de su confesion, as lo mirado, y por las colores de los ñudos, as fabricado los pecados que hizieron, y diuulgastelos, ú dixistelos a alguna persona? y dime por auerlo tu dicho siguiosele al indio, ó india, infamia

notable?" (Pérez Bocanegra 1631, 341). The charge of indiscretion made against interpreters of the sacrament was at times turned against the clergy itself. In the parish of Ambar, at the time when Pérez Bocanegra wrote his manual, the Andean ethnic lords accused their parish priest of publicizing the private matters of penitents in his weekly sermon address: "[The padre] has not even begun to confess the people, though there will not be many who confess with him, since he reveals the confession in his conversation and address and sermon, not to mention many other grave offenses" ([El padre] no a empesado a confesar la gente aunque no abra muchos que confiese con el por rrebelar la confiçion en su conbersasion y Platica y sermon y esto y otras muchas cosas grabes) (AAL, Capítulos, Leg. 6, Exp. 4, 3r).

36. "Esta quenta la tiene el yndio contador destos pueblos en su quipo" (AAL, Capítulos, Leg. 1, Exp. 9, 3r).

37. AAL, Capítulos, Leg. 1, Exp. 9, 96r.

38. "El dho cura apremia a los dhos yn.os desta su doctrina y a sus mandones a que le den gallinas pollos papas cocopa maiz diziendo que la tasa se lo manda dar forcando a los mandones de las parcialidades y si no lo hazen los manda castigar cruelmente de que desto el dho cura les deue restituyr mucha plata como constara por los quipos que tienen" (AAL, Capítulos, Leg. 3, Exp. 11, 4r).

39. The Spanish jurist Juan de Hevia Bolaños (1619, 96r) declared that ecclesiastical magistrates had the authority to admit or deny as evidence the extrajudicial accounting instruments presented before the court. Hevia Bolaños also stipulated procedures for sanctioning accountants for trial and verifying the accounts of ledger books against other accounting instruments (1619, 80r–80v, 83v–84r).

40. "[Q]ue el dho corregidor de orden que cada yndio de los que ffueren de tassa tome su quipo de lo que ouiere de pagar prq. entiendan q. no se les a de llevar mas tassa" (AGN, Derecho Indígena, Leg. 31, Cuad. 617, 10r).

41. "[C]ualesquier pleitos civiles y criminales que acaecieren entre indios, con que las causas que los indios truxeran con sus caciques o principales, civiles o criminales, las ponga por quipo el tocuirico" (Matienzo [1567] 1967, 51).

42. "[T]odo lo demás que se pudiere, que los indios suelen poner en Quipos, se ordena y manda que se reduzca á escritura por mano de dicho escribano, para que sea más cierto y durable, en especial en las faltas que tuvieren de doctrina y entradas y salidas de sacerdotes y ausencias que hicieren, y lo mismo en lo que tocare a los correjidores y sus tenientes y otras cosas particulares, que ellos suelen asentar en los dichos Quipos" (Levillier 1921–1925, 8:337–38, cited in Burns 2005a, 10).

43. "Yo no me atreveré á dar tal, i tan grande fee i autoridad á estos Quipos: porque he oido dezir á los que entiendan dellos, que es muy incierta, falaz, i intricada la forma de hazerlos, i de explicarlos. . . . [S]on Indios, cuya fee vacila, i assi tambien vacilará la explicacion que dieren remitida á sus Quipos" (Solórzano

Pereira 1648, 432, cited in Urton 1998, 430). Solórzano Pereira's commentary came in reference to tribute-restitution litigation of the 1570s against the heirs of the encomendero Alonso de Montemayor.

44. "si sauen el dho cura forsase a sus feligreses sobre las ofrendas por si o por sus fiscales o sacristanes o por otras personas cobrandolos por quipos" (AAL, Visitas Eclesiásticas, Leg. 11, Exp. 1, 2v).

45. AAL, Visitas Eclesiásticas, Leg. 11, Exp. 1, 15r.

46. "si saben q. el susodho [cura] haze fuerça a sus feligreses açerca de las offrendas de todos sanctos y las otras de fiestas solemnes de entre año cobrandolas por tassa quipos y padrones contra la bol.d de los yn.os" (AAL, Capítulos, Leg. 4, Exp. 3, 2r). Salomon (2004, 120) and Salomon and Spalding (2002, 2:861) have previously identified this reference to evidentiary khipus.

47. "[A]ndando en compañia del corregidor por las calles de vn pueblo llamado Atunxauxa, vimos vn Indio viejo, con vn grande maço de cuerdas de lana bien torcida y de diuersas colores en la mano, que ellos llaman Quipos, pues como este Indio viesse que el corregidor y yo le auiamos visto, procuró esconderse con su carga, mas no lo pudo hazer como pensaua, porque el corregidor lo llamó y preguntó de que eran tan largas quentas, el Indio turbado començo a variar, con lo qual acrescentó en el corregidor el desseo de saber lo que le preguntaua, y assi lo puso en termino de açotes y de cortarle el cabello (que es la mayor afrenta que se les puede hazer) el Indio vino a confessar diziendo, que aquel quipo con otros muy grandes que tenia, era la razon y cuenta que auia de dar al Inga quando boluiesse del otro mundo de todo lo que auia succedido en aquel valle en su ausencia: donde se yncluyan todos los Españoles que por aquel real camino auian passado, lo que auian pedido y comprado, todo lo que auian hecho assi en bien como en mal. El corregidor tomó y quemó sus quentas, y castigó al Indio" (Dávalos y Figueroa 1602, 151r, cited in MacCormack 1985, 458).

48. Estenssoro Fuchs (2003, 217) and Harrison (2002, 270) discuss the significance of *hucha,* the missionary Quechua term for sin, and how it emphasizes the countable aspect of church teachings on the topic of confession.

49. Church law had long established the sacrament of confession as an extension of juridical procedures. Starting in the thirteenth century, the Roman canon declared confession with a priest a requirement for the full sentencing of criminals, especially heretics (Peters 1985, 53–54), and the practice of imposing the sacrament on convicted offenders endured through early modern times, often under the threat of inquisitorial force (Hevia Bolaños 1619, 222r). Confession's dual purpose as a "system of discipline and consolation" (Tentler 1977, xvi), which aimed to correct wayward thought and behavior, on the one hand, and console the penitent and reaffirm community bonds, on the other, resulted in a sacramental rite that was filled with ambiguities. The correspondence between the juridical procedures of the Church and the methods of sacramental confession led to problems in the

practice of Indian ministry, for it endangered the bonds of trust that confessors had established with confessants. During the extirpation campaigns of the mid-seventeenth century, Jesuit priests voiced to the Lima see their disillusionment with the disciplinary methods of the visitadores de idolatrías. The inspectors allegedly prosecuted and punished religious offenders based on information conveyed in confessions, which complicated the Jesuits' efforts to encourage Indians to seek absolution for their sins (Vargas Ugarte 1963–1965, 2:135). Native parishioners also denounced priests who attempted to exceed the limits of their authority by converting the confessional into a site for legal denunciation. In 1630, the Indians of Ambar maintained that the priest Martín de Mena Godoy used information from a penitent's confession to file criminal charges of public scandal against the curaca Don Gaspar Rodríguez (AAL, Capítulos, Leg. 6, Exp.1, 4r).

50. "De manera, que cada hilo y ñudo les traía a la memoria lo que en sí contenía, a semejanza de los mandamientos o artículos de nuestra santa fe católica y obras de misericordia, que por el número sacamos lo que debajo de él se nos manda" (Garcilaso [1609] 1960, 2:205). According to Murúa ([1590] 2004, 77r–v), the ancient khipus recorded the virtues and vices of the Incas.

51. Durston's findings cast doubts on whether the Jesuits ever occupied Andahuaylillas, given that the royal grant was contingent upon Pérez Bocanegra's acceptance (Durston 2007, 339 n. 24).

52. "[H]azen muy malas cosas, diziendo, que el Padre ó los Padres con quien se an criado se las an enseñado" (Pérez Bocanegra 1631, 115).

53. "Acusaste ante qualquier juez, el peccado de otro, por odio que le tuuiesses? ó por vengarte de el, no pudiendo probar el delito de que le acusaste?" (Pérez Bocanegra 1631, 336–37).

54. "Antes que vaya el Indio, ó India penitente a los pies del Confesor, y Sacerdote, ya se á confessado con estas Indias, é Indios de todos los pecados" (Pérez Bocanegra 1631, 111).

55. "[D]espues de se auer confessado con el Sacerdote, van a tratar con estos Indios, lo que el Padre les dixo, y la penitencia que les dió. Haziendo burla del, diziendo, que no sabe preguntar al penitente, ó que no les entiende su lengua: y mofan de su manera de absoluer" (Pérez Bocanegra 1631, 113). Similarly, in 1617, the Indians of Santo Domingo de Tauca mocked Fray Lucas Mudarra's attempts to confess them in Quechua through excessive reliance on the published manual. Their accusation stated: "Father confesses the Indians only using books because he does not know how to speak the language" ([E]l dho Padre confiesa a los yndios por los libros por no sauer ablar la lenga [sic]) (AAL, Capítulos, Leg. 2, Exp. 16, 7v).

56. "[E]nseñarles á confessar conforme este Confessionario quitandoles aquellas cuentas, y ñudos; y quemandolos en su presencia. Y no darles el Sacramento de la Eucaristia, hasta tenerlos reduzidos, al buen orden de se confessar sin semejantes enredos, y defetos" (Pérez Bocanegra 1631, 114).

Chapter 4

1. "El escribir se debía enseñar juntamente con el leer a todos los mucha-chos, y . . . cuando siendo hombres de razón puedan, no sólo labrar las tierras, sino tener su cuenta para saber lo que dan y lo que reciben, y no hacerla de cabeza, rayando en la pared, con que se pueden engañar, y los engañan" (Covarrubias Orozco [1611] 1995, 496).

2. Osvaldo Pardo deserves credit for pointing out this element of Martínez de Ripalda's catechism (personal communication, 27 January 2008). The Arequipa synod of 1684 advocated the use of the Jesuit's work *(Constituciones synodales del Obispado de Arequipa* 1688, 37v).

3. Guaman Poma's attention to Spanish colonial discipline was not surpris-ing given the sentence of two hundred lashes and two-year banishment from Huamanga that he received after his unsuccessful bid to reclaim the lands of Chu-pas, which allegedly belonged to his family's estate (Adorno 1993, 75–76; 2007, 30).

4. Indigenous officials protested the harsh tortures that they endured from churchmen for minor oversights or even when dutifully complying with their obligations (AAL, Capítulos, Leg. 16, Exp. 1, 2r; AAC, Colonial, V, 1, 3, 2r). Fre-quently, charges of physical mistreatment involved situations in which parish officials did not produce the high allowances of community goods demanded of them (AAL, Capítulos, Leg. 2, Exp. 16, 4r; AAL, Capítulos, Leg. 3, Exp. 11, 3r, 4r; AAL, Capítulos, Leg. 15, Exp. 7, 1v). During church inspection tours, native assis-tants often reported the abuses of their parish minister to the visitador. How-ever, such testimony could lead to further beatings following the departure of the inspection team (AAL, Capítulos, Leg. 16, Exp. 1, 2v). A native lawsuit in the prov-ince of Huarochirí claimed that the local priest had caused a cacique's death. In 1619, the procurador Jerónimo Ortiz de Mena represented the Andean nobles of San Pedro de Casta, who asserted that Francisco de Galarza strangled and killed the cacique of Caranpoma because he was not able to compensate the priest for the lost tithes of recently deceased Indians (AAL, Capítulos, Leg. 3, Exp. 2, 2r).

5. "[D]omingo llasta[,] alcalde ordinario del pueblo de yamor[,] paresco ante Vs.a illustrisima [y] digo que el dho don Ju.o Celis me a hecho muy gran agrauio[,] asotandome en la capilla llamado cotopara en veinte asotes[,] amarrado en un arbol[,] . . . [y] en eso me a asotado y mas me [ha] asotado en el pueblo de cahacay otro treinta asotes[,] amarrado en el rollo[, y] el dia que fue domingo de rramos visito el dia con el padron a los in.os e in.as [y] por falta de los enfermos y coxos y mancos en eso m[e] a asota[do] treinta asotes y mas me a dado con la uara el que trae [el] alguacil y [la] quebro sobre de mi sin razón y otro mas coçes y pontillasos dentro de la iglesia con mano consagrada" (AAL, Capítulos, Leg. 9, Exp. 13, 6r).

6. AAL, Capítulos, Leg. 9, Exp. 13, 6r. Native accounts of clerical violence point to common routines of description. The 1654 complaint of Antonio Martínez Alca Guaman, *indio principal* of San Pedro de Ninacaca in the province of Tarma,

contains motifs that appear in Llasta's statement. By his own account, Martínez Alca Guaman was a high-standing member of the community, "a descendant of caciques," whose actions to defend Indians from the greed of Father Francisco Pérez de Tordesillas resulted in the latter's taking vengeance on him. In this case, Tordesillas had obliged the plaintiff's ailing uncle to sign a will bequeathing all his assets to the priest, which prompted the indio principal to have another drawn up. A series of verbal and physical humiliations, each punishment more brutal than the one before, followed the initial conflict. Eventually, the priest ordered his African slaves to sequester the cacique in the rectory. The slaves removed Martínez Alca Guaman's clothes, shackled his hands, bound him to a bench, whipped him more than one hundred times, cropped his hair, and left him without food or water. Death was narrowly avoided, thanks to the rescue of a Spanish lieutenant, and after an extended period of convalescence, the aggrieved recovered and asked for restitution: sixty heads of cattle he had lost during his incarceration, plus eight llamas that Tordesillas had stolen from him (AAL, Criminales, Leg. 18, Exp. 39, 2r–3r). Lastly, the plea derived not from "malice," but from a desire for justice, so that the priest's abuse of the parishioners would stop.

7. Confessional discipline is taken up in Barnes 1992 and Klor de Alva 1991, though studies in this vein abound. Clendinnen 1982 and Tedlock 1993 explore the well-documented topic of missionary violence in colonial Yucatan. Duviols [1971] 1977, 233–48, and Mills 1994 examine the Lima Church's theoretical restrictions on the use of coercion and the difficulty of their observance in the conduct of the extirpation-of-idolatries campaigns. Kamen 1984, 201–16, appraises the role of violence in Spanish Catholic society more generally.

8. Pardo 2006 investigates this question through study of the relationship between Franciscan friars and native subjects in colonial Mexico.

9. A report of one visitador's inspection of the parish books reads: "[T]hen the baptismal font was inspected, and the holy oils, and the books of the married, the baptized, and the deceased, which were found to be kept with the order and decency that the Holy Council and the synodal constitutions of this archbishopric mandate" ([L]uego se uissito la pila y santos olios y los libros de cazados, baptizados y muertos y se hallo con el orden y deçençia q. dispone el santo conçilio y constituçiones sinodales deste Arçobispado) (AAL, Capítulos, Leg. 4, Exp. 3, 1r).

10. The 1613 *Padrón de los indios que se hallaren en la ciudad de los Reyes del Pirú*, which Viceroy Juan de Mendoza y Luna commissioned for the purpose of counting Lima's indigenous population, is a prominent example of ladino bookkeeping. The native alcalde of Lima, Miguel Sánchez, assembled a team of native parish officials from throughout the city, which collaborated with the royal scribe, Miguel de Contreras, to compile a list of Indian subjects, indicating the parish, neighborhood, and domicile of each (BNM, 3032, 3r–v; see Contreras [1613] 1968).

11. AGI, Patronato, 231, N.7, R.8, 5v.

12. Lima II, indios 6 and 9, Vargas Ugarte 1951–1954, 1:241–42.

13. In the 1620s, Francisco de Ávila requested a benefice in the Lima archbishopric, citing the low income that he received from his dignitary post in the Cathedral of La Plata (Almansa c. 1620, 3r).

14. Governor Lope García de Castro granted labor and tribute exemptions to caciques and municipal council officials (Levillier 1921–1925, 3:126), and royal edicts and civil ordinances reiterated this order (*RLI* 1841, Lib. VI, tit. v, ley 18, 2:242; *RLI* 1841, Lib. VI, tit. v, ley 20, 2:242; Enríquez 1581, ASFL, Reg. I-13, Núm. 3, 227r; Toledo y Leiva 1641, ASFL, Reg. I-14, Núm. 5, 256v).

15. The Spanish Crown required Indian men between the ages of eighteen and fifty to give tribute through labor and payments of goods and money. Labor tribute occupied one-sixth of the adult population during six months of each year. Corregidores supervised the indigenous workforce, collected tax payments, and oversaw the forced redistribution of goods and merchandise at the local level (Spalding 1974, 116–17).

16. ASFL, Reg. I-11, Núm. 1, Exp. 81, 704v; Levillier 1921–1925, 8:359–60. Toledo's ordinance reads: "Each missionary priest should recruit an indio ladino with a yearly salary of two *abasca* suits and six *fanegas* of corn or potato flour, and twelve Castilian livestock, paid by the priest using community property" (Cada doctrinero debía buscar un indio 'ladino' con salario de dos vestidos de abasca y seis fanegas de maíz o chuño anuales, y doce carneros de Castilla, pagados por el doctrinero, a costa de los bienes de la comunidad) (transcribed in Eguiguren 1940–1951, 1:118). In 1641, Viceroy Pedro de Toledo y Leiva reissued the order to provide maestrescuelas with a yearly salary (ASFL, Reg. I-14, Núm. 5, 256v–257r).

17. AAL, Capítulos, Leg. 15, Exp. 5, 151v–152r.

18. AAL, Capítulos, Leg. 6, Exp. 6, 21v–22r.

19. "[L]os fiscales teniendo solo en esto el cuydado y no en el que [los indios] acudan a la dotrina" (AAL, Capítulos, Leg. 15, Exp. 7, 2r). For other complaints of priests' misuse of the padrón, see AAL, Criminales, Leg. 1, Exp. 40, 1r; AAL, Capítulos, Leg. 1, Exp. 4, 16v; AAL, Capítulos, Leg. 21, Exp. 1, 33v.

20. According to Sabine MacCormack, the book represented obedience to the colonial order from the perspective of native intermediaries such as Guaman Poma: "For books containing unalterable written and quotable texts lent weight to Spanish and Christian claims for dominance" (1989, 150).

21. "Y ancí andaua la tierra muy justa con temoridad de justicia y castigos y buenos egenplos" (Guaman Poma [c. 1615] 1980, 309).

22. Quito 1594, cap. 93, Campo del Pozo and Carmona Moreno 1996, 121–24.

23. "[P]uede proceder el eclesiástico contra legos de qualquier pecado para atraerlos a penitencia, y procurar librar su ánima de la muerte perpetua" (Hevia Bolaños 1619, 165r).

24. Lima III, actio 2, cap. 38, Vargas Ugarte 1951–1954,1:279–80; Lima III, actio 3, cap. 4, 5, 17, 18, 19, 24, Vargas Ugarte 1951–1954, 1:285–86, 291–93.

25. Parish priests were prohibited from administering corporal punishments, except with special permission from the bishop, whereas vicars and ecclesiastical magistrates had the right to dispense bodily punishments (Lima III, actio 4, cap. 8, Vargas Ugarte 1951–1954, 1:303–4). The Church in Spain took similar measures to reassert the clergy's sacred function (Kamen 1993, 212).

26. For secular and church law on the disciplinary role of native officials, see Toledo 1575, Levillier 1921–1925, 8:314; Loja 1596, const. 30, Campo del Pozo and Carmona Moreno 1996, 187–91; *Constituciones de los Frailes Menores* 1601, 21r; Franciscans 1619, 32v; *Constituciones desta Provincia* 1631, 53; Arequipa 1638, Lib. IV, tit. 7, BNP, B 1742, 272v–273v.

27. "[A]cabada la Missa se pone el cura reuestido a un lado de la puerta de la Iglesia con el manipulo en la mano, y el Fiscal a otro con un azote, y saliendo los Indios uno a uno le da a besar el manipulo, y ellos dan la limosna por fuerça" (cited in Frasso 1684, s.f.).

28. "con tanta crueldad que le dejaron las espaldas llagadas y llenas de sangre" (AAL, Capítulos, Leg. 1, Exp. 4A, 1r). For similar testimony of punishments at the hands of native fiscales, see AAL, Capítulos, Leg. 16, Exp. 1, 44v.

29. The *Tercero catecismo* ([1585] 1985, 661), Pérez Bocanegra (1631, 280–81), and Prado (1641, 102v) contain similar models of questioning.

30. La Plata 1619, tit. 6, cap. 6, BNP, B 1673, s.f.

31. AAL, Capítulos, Leg. 1, Exp. 9, 4v.

32. AAL, Capítulos, Leg. 4, Exp. 3, 3r, 4r–v; see also AAL, Capítulos, Leg. 1, Exp. 1, 2r.

33. "¿Por qué cauza quieren ser lengua del corregidor o del jues o de la becita de la santa madre yglecia o de rreuicitas o de los comenderos en las dichas prouincas? Por rrobar a los pobres yndios sus haciendas. Y de ello no hay rremedio" (Guaman Poma [c. 1615] 1980, 518).

34. AAL, Capítulos, Leg. 15, Exp. 5, 1v.

35. AAL, Capítulos, Leg. 9, Exp. 13, 2r.

36. "[D]e modo que sus fiscales no osan abisarle por no berle en su tierra y asi se an muerto los dhos yn.os sin conficion" (AGN, Tribunal Eclesiástico, Leg. 43, Cuad. 4, 13v).

37. "[S]oi tal gobernador y estoi sentado en el lugar que me toca con los casiques e yndios principales del dho pueblo y [el sacerdote] mandandome [que] ocupe la puerta de la yglessia para que no dexe salir della a ningunos yndios e yndias sino tan solamente a los que an ofrendado causando con lo dho grandes miedos y temores amedrentando con la gran colera y palabras q. les dize p.a que de esta suerte ninguno se atreua a uenir sin la dha ofrenda y dando motiuo con esto y mandarme leuantar de mi assiento siendo tal gobernador a que los yndios

uiendome puesto como portero en la puerta de la dha yglessia a que no me tengan el respecto que es justo y dandoles a entender que yo que los auia de defender ayudo al dho p.e fran.co pacho de herrera a que haga cosas que no se deuen hazer mayormente con gente tan pobre y miserable como son los dhos indios pues apenas pueden pagar la tasa y tributo a su encomendero y a otras personas" (AAL, Capítulos, Leg. 6, Exp. 5, 1v).

38. Internal disputes characterized Pacho de Herrera's ministry in Santa Ana de Tusi. Two years following Anicama's complaint, Pacho stood accused of beating the parish fiscales for revealing the priest's illicit relationships with women (AAL, Curatos, Leg. 20, Exp. 6, 1r–v).

39. *RLI* 1841, Lib. V, tit. ii, ley 3, 1:168; Lisson Cháves 1943–1948, 1:123.

40. Berman (1983, 199–224, 255–69) and Benton (2002, 33–45) elucidate the medieval origins of the ecclesiastical system of justice and the attending jurisdictional conflicts between secular and church authority. Weisser (1980) analyzes the competing justice systems in early modern Spain.

41. "[P]odrianse escusar los corregidores españoles que les son muy perjudiciales y costosos [a los indios]" (transcribed in Lisson Cháves 1943–1948, 2:273).

42. Lima II, indios 118, Vargas Ugarte 1951–1954, 1:219–20.

43. Spalding (1970, 656–57) reviews the functions of Toledo's cabildo de indios. Studies of the role of Indian town councils in the Spanish colonization of America include Bayle 1951, and, for colonial Mexico, Chevalier 1944, Gibson 1953, and Haskett 1991. No comprehensive study yet exists of Peru's native cabildos.

44. Levillier 1921–1925, 7:206–7, 8:43, 112, 114, 305–15, 362–63.

45. ASFL, Reg. I-11, Núm. 1, Exp. 81, 704v. In 1618, the Crown allowed priests to appoint no more than one fiscal, two or three cantors, and one sacristan in pueblos of at least one hundred inhabitants (*RLI* 1841, Lib. VI, tit. iii, ley 7, 2:229). However, Viceroy Toledo issued special provisions in response to the needs of certain parishes, as occurred in the Franciscan mission of San Antonio de Cajamarca. While Toledo maintained the stipulated limits on the number of native church officials in the pueblos surrounding Cajamarca, he consented to two additional alguaciles and four additional cantors for the parish, "since this was the principal town where more friars will attend [to the Indians]" (por ser el pueblo principal donde acudiran mas religiosos) (ASFL, Reg. I-11, Núm. 1, Exp. 81, 705r–v). Andean ethnic lords also wished to limit native parish employment. In 1607, the caciques principales of Andahuaylas, Don Juan Topa Guasco and Don Luis Tomay Guaraca, drafted a report on the district's native tributary population in response to a royal provision mandating laborers for the construction of the Jesuit school in Huamanga. Their survey of twelve pueblos discovered 112 church assistants in a total population of three thousand Indians. According to the caciques, the protected situation of the parish assistants, the high number of fugitive tributaries, and the demands of mine production in Huancavelica made it

impossible for them to provide the fifteen additional Indians requested for the Jesuit cause (BNP, B 28, 2r–3v). The greater tribute burden did not concern the corregidor Miguel Gerónimo de Cabrera, who ordered the caciques' incarceration until they produced the native tributaries (7r). In 1673, Don Francisco Solano Canis, cacique of the pueblo of Chongos, protested to the Lima church authorities when Father Antonio de Gutiérrez asked him to hand over eight tributaries for parish service: "I responded to him that I could not provide so many Indians, for I had all I could do to hand over three alguaciles and one fiscal" ([L]e Respondi que no podia ajustar a tantos yndios que harto hacia de darle tres alguaziles y un fiscal) (AAL, Capítulos, Leg. 21, Exp. 1, 1r). According to Solano, Gutiérrez reacted with force. The priest raided the cacique's home with a team of fiscales, and, not finding Solano, they dragged his wife by the hair to the public square and whipped her thirty times (1r).

46. ASFL, Reg. I-13, Núm. 3, 226v.

47. *RLI* 1841, Lib. VI, tit. iii, ley 15, 2:230; *RLI* 1841, Lib. VI, tit. iii, ley 16, 2:230.

48. Guaman Poma [c. 1615] 1980, 806, 808, 814, 816, 818, 820, 822, 825, 828.

49. AAL, Papeles Importantes, Leg. 2, Exp. 10, 1r. Disputes between church and secular authorities intensified in the late seventeenth century during the tenures of Archbishop Melchor de Liñán y Cisneros and Viceroy Melchor de Navarra y Rocafull. The conflict originated in the viceroy's secret order of 1684 to grant corregidores permission to investigate and report on the pastoral competence of priests and the crimes they committed against Indians. Liñán y Cisneros denounced the viceroy's illegal provision to the Crown, citing the clergy's ecclesiastical immunity. Frasso (1684), Liñán y Cisneros (c. 1685), and López y Martínez (1685) present both sides of the controversy.

50. Church laws prohibiting royal administrators from recruiting native parish officials for tributary labor and personal service include: Lima 1592, cap. 16, ACE, "Originales del Concilio Limense," 178v–179r; Quito 1594, cap. 35, Campo del Pozo and Carmona Moreno 1996, 87–88; Arequipa 1638, Lib. II, tit. 10, cap. 10, BNP, B 1742, 171v–172r.

51. For church laws on the appointment of parish officers, see Lima 1586, cap. 20, ACE, "Originales del Concilio Limense," 150r–159r; Lima 1588, cap. 21, ACE, "Originales del Concilio Limense," 162v; Cuzco 1591, cap. 37, BNP, A 568, 15r; Arequipa 1638, Lib. II, tit. 10, cap. 10, BNP, B 1742, 171v–172r; La Paz 1638, Lib. I, tit. 8, cap. 8, Vega 1639, 31.

52. In 1628, the Lima audiencia reprimanded the Franciscan friars of La Magdalena for enlisting twenty-four Indians for service in their parish and convent (ASFL, Reg. I-14, Núm. 3, 90r).

53. *Constituciones de los Frailes Menores* 1601, 21r; Franciscans 1619, 32v; *Constituciones desta Provincia* 1631, 53.

54. "Cómo los dichos padres de la dotrinas se pierden por meterse demás de lo que son al oficio de justicia. . . . [S]iendo beneficiado cura, y quiere ser corregidor" (Guaman Poma [c. 1615] 1980, 580).

55. On the authorized use of staffs by secular and ecclesiastical officials, see Hevia Bolaños 1619, 16v, and Ortiz de Salcedo 1691, 18v, 26v–27r.

56. AGI, Quito, 9, R.4, N.36, 2v.

57. "[L]os dichos padres de las dotrinas se meten en la eligión de los alcaldes y después de hecha, lo quita la uara de la justicia. Y lo da a quien le parese de su voluntad" (Guaman Poma [c. 1615] 1980, 600).

58. "[E]l dho don Ju.o Celis nro. cura hazen eliger alcaldes ordinarios asentando en el cauildo como si fuera corregidor con dezir ese quiero o este no quiero sin auer boto de boluntad de los in.os no mas de por su qrer" (AAL, Capítulos, Leg. 9, Exp. 13, 15v). Objections to the clergy's intrusion in the cabildo election process occurred in all regions of the Indies. In 1563, the audiencia of Guatemala complained to the Crown that "the religious clergy meddle in the cabildos of the Indian pueblos and they attempt to make the Indians of their liking the alcaldes, regidores, and other officials of the republic" (los religiosos . . . se entrometen en los Cabildos de los pueblos de Indios y procuran con ellos que se hagan alcaldes y regidores y otros oficiales de republica a los quellos quieren) (quoted in Bayle 1951, 22, cited in O'Phelan Godoy 1997, 27).

59. Church and civil administrators occasionally worked together to remove subversive parish leaders and install more dependable native assistants. In 1654, the cantor Juan Malqui of the parish of Chavín de Pariarca narrated an episode in which colonial authorities conspired to unseat the popularly elected alcalde: "In the election of alcaldes of the year 1654, though Bartolomé Guanca was elected as alcalde, the priest intervened and said that the corregidor had given the position to Domingo Xari, and he gave Xari the staff against the will of all the Indians, who had cast him off for being a troublemaking Indian" ([E]n la elecsion de los alcaldes del año de sinq.a y cuatro estando electo por alcalde por el cabildo B.me guanca entro el cura y dijo que el coregidor le abra mandado alcalde a domingo jari y le dio la bara contra la boluntad de todos los yndios a quien querian mal por ser yndio reboltoso) (AAL, Capítulos, Leg. 16, Exp. 1, 77v).

60. Ortiz de Salcedo 1691 and other manuals for ecclesiastical notaries provided templates for the recording of all proceedings and transactions of the church tribunals.

61. The oath of the deposing witness in colonial Peru typically initiated the legal testimony. This practice differed from the oath giving of medieval European folklaw, which came at the conclusion of the face-to-face confrontation between the disputing parties (Green 1999, 92; Frisch 2004, 91–94).

62. Spanish-speaking Andeans, identified in court documents as "ladinos," often testified in Quechua through interpreters, perhaps realizing that, beyond

the need to state events accurately, declarations without supporting mechanisms could be challenged.

63. Lima III, actio 3, cap. 6, Vargas Ugarte 1951–1954, 1:302.

64. The Third Council declared that, following the sacred canons, only the most "upright and God-fearing" Indians should offer sworn testimony before church magistrates, given that the majority of Andeans, being "so new in the faith," were especially vulnerable to enticements to perjure themselves (Lima III, actio 4, cap. 6, Vargas Ugarte 1951–1954, 1:302). This echoed the caution of Acosta ([1577] 1984, 1:583–85), who objected strongly to the requirement that Indians provide sworn testimony based on the supposed fragility of native judgment. Viceroy Toledo ordered secular judges to admit legal grievances as worthy of credit only if six Indian witnesses could attest to the charges (Solórzano Pereira 1648, 235). Toledo believed that after hearing several versions of the same events, Spanish judges could evaluate competing biases and develop a more credible picture of what actually occurred.

65. Burns (2005b) examines the conditions that accounted for legal truth through the study of scribal culture in the colonial Andes.

66. AAL, Capítulos, Leg. 9, Exp. 13, 10r, 18v. Don Rodrigo Flores Caja Malqui also used the alternative surnames "Flores Guayna Malqui," perhaps to emphasize his status as the son of Don Juan Flores Guayna Malqui, who served as cacique principal and governor of Santo Domingo de Ocros until his death in 1634. Burga ([1988] 2005, 362–69, 380–92) examines the lineage and career of Flores Caja Malqui from an ethnohistorical perspective, in relation to the interethnic conflicts that transpired in the central highlands in the seventeenth century.

67. AAL, Capítulos, Leg. 9, Exp. 13, 4r, 5r, 9r, 12r, 13r.

68. AAL, Ordenaciones, Leg. 4, Exp. 8, 2r–4r.

69. AAL, Visitas Eclesiásticas, Leg. 11, Exp. 12; AAL, Visitas Eclesiásticas, Leg. 11, Exp. 21.

70. AAL, Capítulos, Leg. 11, Exp. 12, 4v.

71. "[A]uiendose de ser castigados por causas y delitos que lo merescan, sea conforme los dhos delitos y con la correcçion que requiere el estado de cura" (AAL, Capítulos, Leg. 11, Exp. 21, 4r).

72. AAL, Criminales, Leg. 9, Exp. 31, 1r.

73. "[El testigo] dijo ques berdad que conose al dicho don Rodrigo desde muy pequeño y que save quel dicho agora quatro o sinco años poco mas o menos ocasionandose aser un selebre sacrificio al rayo que llaman comunmente Libiac[,] . . . para el efeto del dicho sacrifiçio y festejo que se le dispuso[,] don Rodrigo Caxamalqui bistio y adorno a los yndios principales . . . al uso gentilico con mantas y camisetas de cunbe eredados de sus antepasados[,] y que aci bestidos los enbio a un serro llamado Racian donde mataron entre estos y los demas que les siguieron onbres y mujeres un guanaco cuya carne repartieron entre si con serimonias

y rito jentilicos[,] ofreciendole primero al dicho rayo en orden a aplacar su yra y enojo que con ellos jusgaba que tenia" (AAL, Capítulos, Leg. 11, Exp. 1, 15r). García Cabrera 1994, 171–347, includes a transcription of Caja Malqui's trial.

74. AAL, Capítulos, Leg. 11, Exp. 1, 192r. See Lima II, indios 114, Vargas Ugarte 1951–1954, 1:216–17.

75. AAL, Capítulos, Leg. 11, Exp. 1, 152v–153v. Teruel had a distinguished career as an investigator of idolatries in the Lima archbishopric and authored a 1620 treatise on traditional Andean rituals and beliefs (Duviols 1983).

76. According to Kagan (1981, 5), early modern Castile was also governed by a mixture of intricate laws and competing legal authorities that litigants used to their profit. Benton (2004, 45 n. 15) has made this point for Spain and Spanish America in general.

77. AAL, Capítulos, Leg. 11, Exp. 1, 40r, 90v–92r.

78. Pardo (2006, 81) posits this idea for the administration of Indian justice in colonial Mexico. Comparing global regimes through history, Benton (2002, 15–18) describes in similar terms the perceptions of aboriginal intermediaries who participated in the juridical institutions of colonial societies.

79. AAL, Civiles, Leg. 67, Exp.1, 6r–v.

80. AAL, Capítulos, Leg. 5, Exp. 14, 2v; AAL, Capítulos, Leg. 6, Exp. 1, 4v, 8r.

81. "[N]uestro modo de negociar tan cobdicioso, muy raro es el hombre que no deua algo a otro. Y ama nos Dios tanto, y tiene nuestra deudas tan por suyas, que no quiere ser amigo de quien nos es mal enemigo, ni se quiere reconciliar con quien no nos quiere satisfacer" (Mercado 1569, 167r).

82. AAL, Civiles, Leg. 67, Exp. 1, 8r–v, 10r.

83. "[Q]ue le auer hecho este pedimiento el dicho don rrodrigo flores es por el odio y enemiga que siempre me ha tenido sin mas caussas que no auerle permitido entre en mi dotrina por el escandalo que en ella a caussado con sus superstiçiones y idolatrias de que le tengo echo caussas . . . de q. he hecho castigos generales y demostraçiones del entendimiento en conformidad de lo que tan sanctamente tiene buessa senoria ylustrisima mandado en su carta pastoral" (AAL, Civiles, Leg. 67, Exp. 1, 9r).

84. AAL, Civiles, Leg. 67, Exp. 1, 74v–75r.

85. AAL, Capítulos, Leg. 15, Exp. 7, 10r–v.

86. AAL, Capítulos, Leg. 15, Exp. 7, 12r–v.

87. "[P]ues de no aserce assi sera dar ocaçion a que por instantes se den nuevos pedimientos como Vm. lo tiene experimentado mayormente quando no bienen firmados del señor protetor fiscal o de algunos de sus abogados" (AAL, Capítulos, Leg. 15, Exp. 7, 12r).

88. AAL, Visitas Eclesiásticas, Leg. 2, Exp. 40.

89. This argument draws from Kamen's contention that in Counter-Reformation Spain, strong community spirit united parishioners to their priests: "Where the religious functionary is allotted a secular role normally alien to his

ritualistic activities, in Spain the communal tradition of Mediterranean societies assigned a crucial function to the priest and local clergy. It is perhaps unnecessary to emphasise that this role did not imply piety or even trust on the part of the parishioners" (1993, 214).

Chapter 5

1. Duviols ([1971] 1977, 180–85), Salomon (1991, 27), and Mills (1997, 29–31) include vivid descriptions of Ávila's capture of Pauccar and the auto-da-fé in Lima.

2. More recent investigators, building on Duviols's ([1971] 1977) diachronic examination of the pastoral ideologies and methods that competed for ascendancy in the course of the first campaigns, have posited native Andean religious practices as far less hidden or antagonistic as the missionary polemicists suggest. Mills (1997) and Estenssoro Fuchs (2003) argue against polarized conceptions of religion in the Andes that portray the cultural values and activities of European and indigenous groups as internally coherent and fixed through time. This line of research holds that Peru's clergy and native parishioners took part in a shared, albeit conflictive, religious history in which Andean and Catholic structures and behaviors comingled and influenced each other.

3. León-Portilla (1974, 20) mentions Indian converts who denounced idolatries in sixteenth-century Mexico.

4. A notable exception to the general omission of Indian-authored documents in published transcriptions is García Cabrera 1994, which includes writings by Agustín Capcha, the native fiscal of Ambar. The 2003 reprint of Duviols's 1986 edition of the campaigns omits several Indian-authored denunciations of the trial record.

5. Duviols ([1971] 1977, 176–203) divides the extirpation campaigns of the seventeenth century into three periods, which roughly coincide with the tenures of Archbishops Bartolomé Lobo Guerrero (1610–1621), Gonzalo de Campo (1625–1626), and Pedro de Villagómez (1641–1671). Though institutional support of extirpation waned at the end of the 1660s, Griffiths (1996) and Mills (1997) demonstrate that the Lima see's efforts to eradicate native religious practices continued, albeit at irregular intervals, until the mid–eighteenth century.

6. Pauccar was not only Ávila's powerful symbol in the crusade against idolatries, but also a key figure in the cura's attempt to gain the political favor of Lima's high clergy. Acosta Rodríguez (1987, 563) has documented that Ávila's repression of Andean religion began after the Indians of San Damián mounted charges of economic, sexual, and ministerial abuse against him, which suggests that Ávila, by committing to the cause of extirpation, aimed to overshadow the negative reports of his pastoral conduct. Four days after the auto-da-fé, the provisor Feliciano de Vega cleared Ávila of the capítulos the native litigants had brought, and before

long the priest assumed the high post of visitador de la idolatría. Ávila successfully convinced the ecclesiastical magistrate that it was his anti-huaca campaign that had turned the Indians against him, not the misuse of his office. Pérez Bocanegra claimed that priests in Cuzco denounced idolatries only to advance their careers: "By the mercy of God, there is little [idolatry] in this city of Cuzco, but there may be people who say there is, and they deceive Your Majesty King Philip our lord with the falsehood that there are idolatries, and they say it with their own interests and ambitions in mind, not because it actually exists" ([P]or la misericordia de Dios, no aya mucho desto en esta ciudad del Cuzco, y aya personas que digan, y engañen a su Magestad del Rey Don Felipe nuestro señor con falsedad, que ay idolatrias, dizenlo por sus intereses, y ambiciones y no porque aya) (1631, 126).

7. "[C]onviene que no sea indio, porque se han experimentado muchos inconvenientes, y yo he visto algunos muy graves, sino que sea persona diligente y de mucha confianza" (Arriaga [1621] 1999, 115).

8. AAL, Hechicerías e Idolatrías, Leg. 1, Exp. 11, 2r–6r; AAL, Hechicerías e Idolatrías, Leg. 2, Exp. 6, 10r; AAL, Hechicerías e Idolatrías, Leg. 4, Exp. 2, 14r–23v.

9. Prosecutions by native fiscales include: AAL, Hechicerías e Idolatrías, Leg. 1, Exp. 5; AAL, Hechicerías e Idolatrías, Leg. 1, Exp. 11; AAL, Hechicerías e Idolatrías, Leg. 2, Exp. 3; AAL, Hechicerías e Idolatrías, Leg. 2, Exp. 4; AAL, Hechicerías e Idolatrías, Leg. 2A, Exp. 7A; AAL, Hechicerías e Idolatrías, Leg. 2A, Exp. 1; AAL, Hechicerías e Idolatrías, Leg. 2A, Exp. 2; AAL, Hechicerías e Idolatrías, Leg. 3, Exp. 8; AAL, Hechicerías e Idolatrías, Leg. 3, Exp. 10; AAL, Hechicerías e Idolatrías, Leg. 3, Exp. 11; AAL, Hechicerías e Idolatrías, Leg. 4, Exp. 2; AAL, Hechicerías e Idolatrías, Leg. 4, Exp. 8; AAL, Hechicerías e Idolatrías, Leg. 4, Exp. 9; AAL, Hechicerías e Idolatrías, Leg. 4, Exp. 10; AAL, Hechicerías e Idolatrías, Leg. 4, Exp. 28. García Cabrera (1994) and Duviols (2003) have transcribed and published large portions of the prosecutions involving Don Juan Tocas and Agustín Capcha.

10. See AAL, Civiles, Leg. 83, Exp. 1, 3r–5r. Native fiscales also acted as language interpreters and catechists. The fiscal de la visita Thomas Guaman served in this capacity (Duviols [1971] 1977, 293). In 1646, Visitador Tomás de Espinoza recruited Guaman, the fiscal of Don Antonio Chupica's parish, San Francisco de Ihuari, to work as an interpreter on his extirpation campaign in Paccho (AAL, Hechicerías e Idolatrías, Leg. 2, Exp. 4, 10r, 16r, 18r; AAL, Hechicerías e Idolatrías, Leg. 2, Exp. 7, 5r; AAL, Hechicerías e Idolatrías, Leg. 2, Exp. 7A, 2r). After his service, Guaman returned to his work as a parish assistant. He surfaces in trial records of 1649 as a cantor who accompanied Licentiate Diego de Palma on his visita in the region of Checras (AAL, Capítulos, Leg. 14, Exp. 4, 126r, 127r, 131v). Ecclesiastical inspectors valued the contributions of native assistants such as Guaman, for fiscales de la visita knew the language and terrain of the region. Equally important, they were outsiders without affective bonds to the communities under the visita's scrutiny.

11. Francisco Ortiz de Salcedo (1691, 18v) delineates the broad judicial authority of the "fiscal de vara eclesiástica" to prosecute crimes before church magistrates.

12. Chupica began his studies at the colegio in 1623 ("Libro de la fundación" 1923, 801).

13. "[M]ando atento a que es delicto contra la fee catolica y no deber gossar de los prebilegios de la yglessia" (AAL, Hechicerías e Idolatrías, Leg. 2, Exp. 3, 4r–v). Chupica's assistants executed the directives, though the prisoners claimed that their arrest was for having refused the cacique's demand that they abandon their native village of Paccho and join his tributary workforce in San Francisco de Ihuari (AAL, Hechicerías e Idolatrías, Leg. 2, Exp. 4, 7r, 10v, 18r).

14. African interpreters participated in Damián de la Bandera's general visita in Huamanga of 1557 as well as in other ecclesiastical trials (Jiménez de la Espada 1965, 1:180; AAL, Capítulos, Leg. 14, Exp. 3, 418r).

15. The Second Council ordered the isolation of native dogmatists (Lima II, indios 107, Vargas Ugarte 1951–1954, 1:211–12), as did the Third Council (Lima III, actio 2, cap. 42, Vargas Ugarte 1951–1954, 1:340). In 1618, during the Lima see's first extirpation-of-idolatries campaign, Viceroy Borja authorized the construction of the Jesuit-run Casa de Santa Cruz (Arriaga [1621] 1999, 110, 148–49).

16. "[E]xaminó el visitador con grande disimulo quatro, o seis muchachos, y con algunas amenazas de açotes nos descubrieron unos diez y seis adoratorios, y doze dogmatizadores" (Villagómez 1649, 76v). Olaechea Labayen (1969, 242–47) and Trexler (1987, 549–73) discuss the role of Indian children in evangelization in colonial Mexico.

17. AAL, Hechicerías e Idolatrías, Leg. 1, Exp. 4, 2v.

18. Arriaga ([1621] 1999, 118, 122, 133) outlined the duties of local church personnel during the visita de idolatrías, which Villagómez (1649, 52v–53r) reiterated in his *Carta pastoral*. The Lima synod of 1613 ordered the recruitment of trial interpreters (Lima 1613, Lib. I, tit. vii, cap. 15, Lobo Guerrero and Arias de Ugarte [1613, 1636] 1987, 95). Typically, two Indians were chosen as interpreters at the start of idolatry investigations and trials.

19. "[Q]ue por tener sus ýdolos uacas y mochar a los demonios no quiere que lo sepa el dicho padre ni corregidor ni qualquier yndio ladino cristiano" (Guaman Poma [c. 1615] 1980, 908).

20. "El primero es ganar algún indio de razón, y a éste con grande secreto, ofreciéndoles grandes premios y que no lo sabrá persona viviente, persuadirle a que diga la huaca principal de su pueblo y el hechicero que la guarda, o lo más que supiere acerca de esto, y la primera vez contentarle y agradecelle, y aun pagalle lo poco que dijere" (Arriaga [1621] 1999, 124). Villagómez (1649, 63r–v) repeated Arriaga's guidelines for recruiting native elites.

21. "[V]encido pues el cacique fue facil vencer a los demás" (Carrera 1644, s.f.).

22. Novoa was one of Archbishop Villagómez's most active extirpators. A Creole priest educated in Quechua at the University of San Marcos, Novoa began

his career in 1643 as the beneficiary of Santa Ana de Sucha before moving to San Pedro de Ticllos in 1651, where he participated in his first idolatry trial before ascending to the posts of vicar general and visitador de la idolatría in Cajatambo (García Cabrera 1996, 14–19). Duviols 2003 contains transcriptions of ten investigations that Novoa led in Cajatambo in the mid-1650s and early 1660s as well as the visitador's *información de servicios* of 1664, which documents his discoveries in twenty-eight pueblos.

23. According to Cervantes (1994, 25–30), Acosta's treatment of Amerindian religiosity marked a Nominalist turn in explanations of idolatry worship that occurred after the Council of Trent, whereby missionary theorists emphasized the devil's power to exploit human thought and action over Thomist or naturalistic justifications, which viewed idolatry as a natural manifestation of humankind's aspiration toward the divine. Though recognizing the existence of native customs that did not conflict with Christianity, and the Indians' receptivity to Catholic teachings, Acosta could not explain the origin and perseverance of Amerindian religious expression that closely resembled the confession and Eucharistic sacraments. Like Church fathers before him, such as the Spanish theologians Martín de Castañega and Pedro Ciruelo, who associated diabolism with idolatry, Acosta believed the devil imitated the Creator and induced credulous followers to turn away from true belief and ritual (MacCormack 1991, 39–41, 269). In this view, Indian rites exhibited Satan's mimetic desire to found a counterchurch and steal the honor that belonged only to God. The Nominalist view contrasted with the arguments of Bartolomé de las Casas, who in his *Apologética historia sumaria* proposed a Thomist explanation of Amerindian religiosity. Las Casas ([1555–1559] 1967, 378–80) stated that idolatry touched all peoples in history and manifested humanity's natural inclination to seek the divine (Cervantes 1994, 31).

24. The second part of Avendaño's sermonario includes the reprint of twenty-two sermons of the *Tercero catecismo*.

25. Studies of the role of preaching in Peru's anti-idolatry campaigns are few. Duviols [1971] 1977, 341–69, Estenssoro Fuchs 1996, and Mills 1997, 189–204, provide the most insightful treatments.

26. "[D]igo que a llegado a mi notitia que todos los ssusosdhos [indios culpados en la prosecución de la visita] con gran desacato escandalo y poco temor de Dios nuestro señor faltando en todo a nuestra sancta fee catholica y apartatando [*sic*] de ella sin temor de la Real Justicia" (AAL, Hechicerías e Idolatrías, Leg. 3, Exp. 11, 1r). Duviols 2003, 325–476, supplies a lengthy transcription of the trial; Tocas's initial denunciation is not included.

27. "[V]iben en su primera Jentilidad guardando los rritos y ceremonias supresticiones [*sic*] adorando y dando culto a sus malquis cuerpos de Gentiles difuntos y otros ydolos lares y [piedras] llamados conepas al sol luna lucero de la mañana dos strellas pequenas que llaman chuchu color y a las siete estrellas que llaman siete cabrillas al mar rios remolinos grandes de vientos al Arco

Yris al paxoro que llaman yuyoc y en especial a Ydolo yanac tarqui vrao" (AAL, Hechicerías e Idolatrías, Leg. 3, Exp. 11, 1r).

28. Tocas's letters of denunciation in 1657 against the sorcerers of San Juan de Machaca and the idol ministers of San Francisco de Cochillas repeated the same claims. He alleged that both groups practiced ancient rituals and made sacrifices to natural marvels (sun, moon, stars, whirlwinds, rainbows), the remains of important ancestors, and idols of human creation (AAL, Hechicerías e Idolatrías, Leg. 2A, Exp. 1, 1r–v; AAL, Hechicerías e Idolatrías, Leg. 2A, Exp. 2, 1r). In this way, the native fiscal's writings prefigure the "denial of coevalness" that Johannes Fabian has identified as central, in modern anthropology, to the production of the European colonizers' descriptions of non-European subjects: "a persistent and systematic tendency to place the referent(s) of anthropology in a Time other than the present of the producer of anthropological discourse" (1983, 31).

29. Acosta ([1577] 1987, 2:427), Avendaño (1649, 36v, 44r, 65v), and Ávila (1648, 1:134–35, 185, 249, 460, 473, 512, 2:27, 47, 72) make the same contention.

30. "[Los indios guardan] a los malquis haciendoles sacrificios con sangre de llamas sebo coca y chic[h]a cuies dos vezes en diferentes ocasiones del año haciendo que se confiessen los yndios con los susosdhos y que ay en cinco dias a fin de adorar sus dhos ydolos pidiendoles salud y vi[da] quitando la adoracion y el culto debido a dios nuestro señor y dandosele a simulacros del demonio y a otros criaturas docmatiçando y enseñando al demas comun de yndios yndias no adoren a dios nuestro señor sino a sus ydolos y mal[quis]" (AAL, Hechicerías e Idolatrías, Leg. 3, Exp. 11, 1r).

31. "que el diablo lo auia engañado que lo callase" (AAL, Hechicerías e Idolatrías, Leg. 2, Exp. 4, 1v). Cervantes (1994, 47, 49, 53–54) analyzes the ways in which native peoples of colonial Mexico assimilated theories of diabolism to explain their traditional beliefs and ritual behaviors. Whereas for some Indians, the devil's power allowed them to conceive native religiosity in the terms that Christian missionaries provided, for others, the devil played the oppositional role of protecting and preserving ancient customs against the Spaniards' faith. Mills (1997, 227) contends that missionary ideas about the devil influenced native Andean religious approaches, but to a lesser degree than Cervantes suggests for native parishioners in Mexico. While demonic intervention provided Peru's Indians with an explanation for native religiosity, many continued to believe that regional divinities and spiritual forces consisted of both good and evil properties. For additional trial cases in which Indian defendants blamed "idolatry" on the devil's manipulative powers, see Griffiths (1996, 116–21).

32. AAL, Hechicerías e Idolatrías, Leg. 3, Exp. 8, 19v; AAL, Hechicerías e Idolatrías, Leg. 2A, Exp. 1, 1r; AAL, Hechicerías e Idolatrías, Leg. 2A, Exp. 2, 1r.

33. "[M]andamos que los que fuéredes cómplices o encubridores en las dichas idolatrías, seáis privados de vuestros oficios y azotados, y tresquilados y reservados a mita, y que no podáis ser alcaldes, fiscales, y alguaciles" (BNP, B 352, 17v).

34. AAL, Hechicerías e Idolatrías, Leg. 3, Exp. 11, 9v, 44r; Griffiths 1996, 187–88. Jesuit priests stated that Cajatambo's huaca priests rejected Spanish customs and preached the demise of Indians who had forsaken the regional divinities (Arriaga [1621] 1999, 61; Polia Meconi 1999, 388). During his 1644 trial in Paccho, the accused idolater Sebastián Rupay expressed the pressure that he faced from local ministers to participate in the traditional devotions: "The said ayllu leader scolded him, asking him how was it he refused to do as the other Indians, and if he was Spanish, after which he was persuaded to go with the others to venerate the said rock" ([L]e rriño el dho camachico diziendole que como se apartaua de lo que hazian los demas yn.os que si era El Español y le persuadio a que fueran a mochar a la dha piedra) (AAL, Hechicerías e Idolatrías, Leg. 2, Exp. 4, 25r).

35. AAL, Hechicerías e Idolatrías, Leg. 3, Exp. 11, 9v, 37r.

36. "[D]esde aquel dia y ora empeso a tener mejoria de su emfermedad y estando ya bueno fue este testigo a ber al dicho Hern.do hacaspoma a dalle las gracias porque ya tenia salud y le dijo: 'yayamic [padre] y señor mio bos sois gran sabio y doctor desidme quien me hiso este mal' y el dicho Hern.do hacaspoma le respondio disiendo: 'yo soy quien os hise emfermar porque me llebasteis a la yglesia por fuersa y a empellones y a todos los yndios en tiempo que estabamos ayunando a nuestros ydolos y guacas y mirad no lo agais otra bes porque os e de bolber haser el mesmo mal'" (AAL, Hechicerías e Idolatrías, Leg. 3, Exp. 11, 37v).

37. AAL, Hechicerías e Idolatrías, Leg. 3, Exp. 11, 40r.

38. "[C]omo este testigo era y es maestro de capilla andaba siempre con los curas y quando bolbia a su pueblo si era tiempo de dichos ayunos y comfesiones los dichos echiseros le despachaban un yndio para que le dijese que no entrase en el pueblo ni se juntase con ellos en dichos ayunos y sacrificios porque benia susio que disen raccha por aber estado con el dicho cura cantando y oficiando las misas y que por esta caussa no se juntase con ellos porque se enojarian los dichos malquis e ydolos y se perderian los dichos sacrificios y con esto no entraba de miedo porque no le matasen" (AAL, Hechicerías e Idolatrías, Leg. 2A, Exp. 2, 4v).

39. Native officials of extirpation sometimes refused duties that placed their local authority at risk. In 1672, Domingo Francisco del Castillo, the ecclesiastical judge and parish priest of Santiago de Aija, incited the rebellion of the local villagers when he investigated charges of incest and idolatry against the cacique principal Don Diego Yaruparia. Taking refuge in the church, the priest wrote to the Lima see to report the dangers he faced from the angry mob that sought revenge for his having jailed the cacique for religious crimes. Yaruparia had escaped from prison with the help of native allies and, in Castillo's words, "assembled the whole town, men and women alike, armed with stones, such that my life is in jeopardy" (juntando todo el pueblo asi Yndios como Yndias con sus piedras con que no tengo seguro de vidas) (BNP, B 612, 37r). When Castillo ordered his fiscal to arrest the cacique, the church assistant responded: "First I side with the

idolater and not my priest" (hasta el fiscal Yndio diciendole yo que lo prendiesse respondio que primero era el Ydolatra que no su cura) (BNP, B 612, 37v).

40. AAL, Hechicerías e Idolatrías, Leg. 2A, Exp. 2, 35v. Gareis (1999, 234) asserts that by 1639, the Casa de Santa Cruz had ceased to function, which suggests that Novoa may have utilized the empty threat due to the notoriety that the prison continued to have among the Indians. However, at a later date, Diego de León Pinelo (1661, 3v) noted the imperative of relocating Indian idolaters to Lima's house of reclusion, which calls Gareis's contention into question.

41. AAL, Hechicerías e Idolatrías, Leg. 3, Exp. 9, 8r, 14v–15v.

42. "[P]adre y Dios nro. tu que quitaste la salud a esta pobre dadle Vida y quitadle El Achaque" (AAL, Hechicerías e Idolatrías, Leg. 3, Exp. 9, 2r).

43. AAL, Hechicerías e Idolatrías, Leg. 3, Exp. 9, 2v.

44. AAL, Hechicerías e Idolatrías, Leg. 3, Exp. 9, 3v, 9r.

45. AAL, Hechicerías e Idolatrías, Leg. 3, Exp. 8, 44r; AAL, Hechicerías e Idolatrías, Leg. 3, Exp. 10, 2v, 15v; AAL, Hechicerías e Idolatrías, Leg. 3, Exp. 11, 5r, 10v, 71r–v.

46. Duviols 2003, 296–99, 304–8; AAL, Hechicerías e Idolatrías, Leg. 3, Exp. 10, 11r–21v.

47. AAL, Hechicerías e Idolatrías, Leg. 2A, Exp. 12, 1r–v. An irony of the Andeans' fervor in celebrating the body of Christ was how few received the sacrament of communion, as Carolyn Dean (1999, 1) has noted in her study of Corpus Christi in colonial Cuzco. The First Council (1551–1552) prohibited Indians from taking communion based on their neophyte status, unless they received special permission. The Second Council (1567) and Third Council (1582–1583) eased the prohibition, but parish priests commonly refused the Eucharist to native parishioners (Dean 1999, 1). Pardo (2004, 131–58) and Estenssoro Fuchs (2003, 228–33) examine the debate within the colonial Church over whether to administer the Eucharist to the Indians.

48. The donation of gifts and other forms of largesse constituted a key source of legitimation for the indigenous nobility of Inca and colonial times. By sponsoring public banquets, Andean lords exhibited their ability to look after the community's interests, which fortified in traditional terms the reciprocal dependence between them and native subordinates (see Spalding 2002, 68–69).

49. AAL, Hechicerías e Idolatrías, Leg. 2A, Exp. 12, 10v.

50. AAL, Hechicerías e Idolatrías, Leg. 2A, Exp. 12, 1v–4v.

51. Lima II, indios 74, Vargas Ugarte 1951–1954, 1:249. See also Liñán y Cisneros c. 1685, 55r–56r; Olavarrieta Medrano 1717, 23. Hevia Bolaños (1619, 162r) stated that ecclesiastical judges had the right to prosecute laypersons for wearing the vestments of priests.

52. Arriaga ([1621] 1999, 82) charged that native parish assistants placed small huacas in the Eucharist's processional float or hid them in the altar of the church.

Acosta ([1590] 2002, 347–50) alleged that in Mexico native elders used Corpus as a cover for ancient celebrations in honor of the deity Huitzilopochtli; they officiated processions, banquets, and ritual dances that culminated in the Indians' consumption of idols made of corn. See also Lima II, indios 95, Vargas Ugarte 1951–1954, 1:203–4.

53. "[P]oniendose boca abajo fingiendose muy viejo y que le temblaban las manos haziendo la ceremonia de consagrar lebanto el papel mostrandole al concurso" (AAL, Hechicerías e Idolatrías, Leg. 2A, Exp. 12, 4v).

54. Native satires of the clergy appear to have been widespread. Pérez Bocanegra (1631, 113) complained that Indians elders of Andahuaylillas poked fun at the way parish priests confessed and absolved, which for him evidenced an attempt to usurp the priests' sacramental role, and Guaman Poma satirized ([c. 1615] 1980, 623–26) the self-interested content and flawed speech of the clergy's Quechua sermons. Saignes (1993, 70) argues that it was common for Indians to caricature the Spanish of the colonizers in ritual drinking ceremonies as a way to compete with Catholic ministers for control of new linguistic registers and areas of knowledge.

55. AAL, Hechicerías e Idolatrías, Leg. 2A, Exp. 12, 35v, 8r–9r.

56. Burns takes this approach in her study of Peru's indigenous notaries: "A crucial first step in historicizing notarized sources is to recognize the agonistic principle and the templates according to which they were made" (2005b, 375).

57. "[S]eñalando asia el sanctissimo sacramento dixo el dho cura aquel señor que esta alli que nos esta jusgando ha permitido esto para que tenga castigo este mal Indio [Don Juan Rodríguez Pilco] y llorando este declarante le dixo el dho cura que callase la boca y no llorase que bien sabia que Don Joan auia tenido la culpa segun lo que le auian contado la noche antes y que fuese este declarante a su casa con el dho cura y si acaso le diesse algunos asotes los llebase por el amor de Dios" (AAL, Hechicerías e Idolatrías, Leg. 2A, Exp. 12, 39v).

58. AAL, Hechicerías e Idolatrías, Leg. 2A, Exp. 12, 40r.

59. The conflict between Ávila and the Indians of San Damián suggests that adjusting to the will of native elites was often necessary to secure from them a share of indigenous goods and labor. The mutual accusations between Ávila and the parishioners reveal the fragility of such arrangements (Acosta Rodríguez 1979, 1987). One year after the Indians alleged economic abuse and moral impropriety, Ávila denounced the idolatrous practices of his parishioners.

60. AAL, Hechicerías e Idolatrías, Leg. 2A, Exp. 12, 42r–43v. Salazar had become the parish priest of Ambar in 1657 after passing competitive examinations in Quechua and Catholic theology (AAL, Concursos, Leg. 4, Exp. 63). Additional records show that he was born in Huaura and received holy orders in 1648 after completing studies at Lima's Seminario Santo Toribio de Mogrovejo (AAL, Ordenaciones, Leg. 10, Exp. 56).

61. "[La prisión] fue por auer desamparado el pueblo el dho cura yendosse a passear aquella tarde quando deuiera estar atendiendo a los inconuenientes y peligros q. en semejantes dias de juntas ay en los pueblos de los indios" (AAL, Hechicerías e Idolatrías, Leg. 2A, Exp. 12, 98r).

62. "[L]os señores Inquisidores . . . no conosian de causas de los Indios, y que si el cura hiçiera alguna demostrasion en defensa de este testigo todos lo auian de capitular al dho cura" (AAL, Hechicerías e Idolatrías, Leg. 2A, Exp. 12, 5r).

63. AAL, Hechicerías e Idolatrías, Leg. 4, Exp. 2, 1r–v. García Cabrera 1994, 393–450, 453–72, includes transcriptions of Capcha's accusations of idolatry. The lengthy trial of Juana Mayguay also includes Capcha's second denunciation to Sarmiento regarding local ritual practices during the feast of Corpus Christi. The fiscal requested the imprisonment and punishment of Pablo Pilco Quispe, mayordomo of the confraternity of the Holy Sacrament, for his sponsoring the performance of ancient ritual dances during the Corpus celebrations of 1662 (AAL, Hechicerías e Idolatrías, Leg. 4, Exp. 2, 27r).

64. "A vuestra mersed pido y suplico se cerva de mandar que les condene en las penas del en que han encorrido . . . y que mi pague los derichos que mi combinen confurme a diricho que mi toca sobre que pido justisia y costos" (AAL, Hechicerías e Idolatrías, Leg. 4, Exp. 2, 1r).

65. AAL, Hechicerías e Idolatrías, Leg. 4, Exp. 8, 1r.

66. "[P]onerse a baylar con las mugeres cantando en sus lenguas alabandoles a los hombres por sus desendentes o cerros o punas desindo que fue nasidos de tal cerros o punas" (AAL, Hechicerías e Idolatrías, Leg. 4, Exp. 9, 1r). Acosta described the guacón as a dance whose masks and gestures were inspired by the devil: "Other dances were masked dances, which they call guacones, and the masks and their visages were purely of the devil" (Otras danzas eran de enmascarados, que llaman guacones, y las máscaras y su gesto eran del puro demonio) ([1590] 2002, 415).

67. AAL, Hechicerías e Idolatrías, Leg. 4, Exp. 10, 1r–v. The denunciations against female ministers for poisoning men recall Ruth Behar's (1989) research on trials of the Mexican Inquisition in which women healers allegedly infected the male spouses or lovers of clients through food contamination in order to make them less domineering, violent, or false-hearted.

68. AAL, Hechicerías e Idolatrías, Leg. 4, Exp. 8, 6r.

69. AAL, Amancebamiento, Leg. 5, Exp. 27, 30–38. Rivarola 2000 includes transcriptions of Capcha's criminal accusations of concubinage (see 77, 83, 85–86, 89, 91, 93, 95, 101–3, 105–7).

70. "[E]s justo que se castige para escarminto de muchos" (AAL, Amancebamiento, Leg. 5, Exp. 27, 1r).

71. AAL, Amancebamiento, Leg. 5, Exp. 31, 1r.

72. AAL, Amancebamiento, Leg. 5, Exp. 30, 1r; AAL, Amancebamiento, Leg. 5, Exp. 37, 1r; and AAL, Amancebamiento, Leg. 5, Exp. 34, 1r.

73. "no para el cervisio de Dios Señor, antes para ofenderle como tan mal chrestiano poco temeroso de Dios Noestro Señor" (AAL, Amancebamiento, Leg. 5, Exp. 38, 1r).

74. "[A]l qual su hijo lo hiso bautisar vn dia domingo como si fuira su mismo hijo ligitimo con musica de chirimias, hallandose presente en la puerta de la ygelisia el dicho Luis Gonsaga, de que se quedaron mas admirados todos los que no comiten tales pecados de lujuriosas" (AAL, Amancebamiento, Leg. 5, Exp. 35, 1r–v).

75. AAL, Amancebamiento, Leg. 5, Exp. 35, 1v–2r.

76. AAL, Civiles, Leg. 83, Exp. 1, 1r, 12r.

77. AAL, Hechicerías e Idolatrías, Leg. 4, Exp. 6, 3r.

78. AAL, Hechicerías e Idolatrías, Leg. 2A, Exp. 12, 42r, 98r.

79. AAL, Capítulos, Leg. 17, Exp. 3, 16r–v.

80. AAL, Criminales, Leg. 22, Exp. 6A, 1r.

81. "[D]esir que lo avia hechisado que dello se hallava enfermo con dolor de barriga que cogio de los cabellos a la dicha endia desindo a perra endia que vos mi abes hechisado" (AAL, Hechicerías e Idolatrías, Leg. 4, Exp. 28, 1r).

82. "[P]odiendo ampararme el dicho lic.do como sacerdote ministro de dios no la a hecho seno antes dando mano para que los demas seglares tengan lugar de perderme el respeto por ver que los mismos yclisyasticos mi trata mal querian lo mismo perderme el respeto por estar en sus bisios y pecados y quedarse sen castigar de sus malos custumbres de hacer poco caso a las justisias de su magestad y de los señores bisitadores que representan de la real persona del arsobispo mi señor" (AAL, Criminales, Leg. 22, Exp. 7, 1r).

83. AAL, Criminales, Leg. 22, Exp. 7, 1v.

84. AAL, Visitas Eclesiásticas, Leg. 11, Exp. 31, 1r–3v.

85. "[O]i disirle que ia le abia dicho que se fuera en pas de este dho pueblo porque lo alborotaba y abia tratado mal de palabra a Augustin Capcha siendo su ministro eclesiastico y que de ello estaba actualmente dando quenta por escrito a su Ss.a Ill.ma el Arsobispo su señor" (AAL, Visitas Eclesiásticas, Leg. 11, Exp. 31, 5r).

86. AAL, Hechicerías e Idolatrías, Leg. 3, Exp. 11, 128r–129r; AAL, Hechicerías e Idolatrías, Leg. 2A, Exp. 2, 59r–v; Griffiths 1996, 191–92. Duviols 2003, 468–75, 529–75, contains transcriptions of the allegations of Novoa's misconduct. Synodal constitutions ordered parish priests to care for the needs of visitadores and their assistants for up to six days of inspection and to protect Indians from undue economic burdens (Torres 1970, 52–53).

87. AAL, Hechicerías e Idolatrías, Leg. 2A, Exp. 2, 169r–172v; Griffiths 1996, 192–93.

88. AAL, Hechicerías e Idolatrías, Leg. 4, Exp. 4, 40v.

89. AAL, Visitas Eclesiásticas, Leg. 14, Exp. 18, 1r, 5r.

90. "[Y] las dhas priçiones y bejaziones es solo por uengar por este medio la paçion y odio que les tiene a estos miserables porque no juraron y conspiraron que Don Juan Rg.s Pilco gouern.or del dho repartim.to lo que les dicto el dho uissitador y el cura Liz.do Juan de Salazar" (AAL, Visitas Eclesiásticas, Leg. 11, Exp. 33, 1r–v).

91. AAL, Visitas Eclesiásticas, Leg. 11, Exp. 33, 17v, 46v.

92. Duviols ([1971] 1977, 409–10), Griffiths (1996, 193–94), and Mills (1997, 159) review the charges of 1665 that the cacique and governor of San Juan de Lampián, Don Cristóbal Pariasca, mounted against Sarmiento.

93. "[Q]ue permiti que los indios de mi repartimiento vsasen en sus vayles y danças de las vestiduras ecclesiasticas sin perjuiçio de mis derechos y defensas" (AAL, Hechicerías e Idolatrías, Leg. 2A, Exp. 12, 146r).

94. AAL, Hechicerías e Idolatrías, Leg. 2A, Exp. 12, 280r.

95. AAL, Hechicerías e Idolatrías, Leg. 2A, Exp. 12, 173r.

96. AAL, Hechicerías e Idolatrías, Leg. 2A, Exp. 12, 173v–174r.

97. "[L]e respondi al papel dicho con achaque de que tingo oblegasion y esta oc[u]pado con mis chacaras de papas" (AAL, Hechicerías e Idolatrías, Leg. 2A, Exp. 12, 175r).

98. "[Q]ue las bengansas no se debe pensar ne por la ymaginasyon porque las que son sera meresido al castigo eterno de dios" (AAL, Hechicerías e Idolatrías, Leg. 2A, Exp. 12, 175r).

99. AAL, Hechicerías e Idolatrías, Leg. 2A, Exp. 12, 176r.

100. AAL, Hechicerías e Idolatrías, Leg. 2A, Exp. 12, 368r.

101. Mills (1996) provides lucid analysis of this phenomenon using alternative examples from the Archivo Arzobispal de Lima's idolatry trial record.

Chapter 6

1. Griffiths (1996, 43–46) and Mills (1997, 157–64) examine numerous polemics related to the campaigns of extirpation in the Villagómez period.

2. Marzal (1983, 119–71) summarizes Padilla's memorial and the correspondence that followed.

3. "como ay experiencia, de que siempre salen semejantes pleitos defectuosos en la probança" (León Pinelo 1661, 7v).

4. Studies that address this area are, for Mexico, Borah 1983, Kellogg 1995, and Stavig 2000, and for Peru, Stern [1982] 1993, 114–37, Poloni-Simard 2005, and Mumford 2008, though the examples are legion. Mumford 2008, 9–13, reviews scholarship on the topic of native litigation in colonial Latin America.

5. The research of Taylor (1996, 396–423) on lawsuits against priests in eighteenth-century Mexico and that of Duviols ([1971] 1977) and Acosta Rodríguez (1979, 1987) on the legal dispute between Francisco de Ávila and the native parishioners of San Damián are noteworthy exceptions.

6. For studies of "protectors of the Indians" in colonial Spanish America, see Cutter 1986, Ruigómez Gómez 1988, Bonnett 1992, and De la Puente Brunke 2005.

7. Lima III, actio 3, cap. 3, Vargas Ugarte 1951–1954, 284–85.

8. In Mexico City, the Spanish government established the General Indian Court for the Indians' legal protection (Borah 1983), whereas in Lima the adjudication of prominent native lawsuits took place in the royal audiencia. Cobo's history of the founding of Lima states that in 1603 Viceroy Luis de Velasco inaugurated the "Juzgado de Indios" of the Cercado, whose presiding judge was the corregidor Don Joseph de Rivera (Cobo [1639] 1964a, 2:349–50). However, scarce mention of the court in the documentary record suggests that the initiative did not take hold.

9. AGI, Quito, 9, R. 1, N. 5, 1v; BNM, 2927, IV, 30, 166v–167r; BNM, 2989, 733, 812–13. The Spanish Crown also complained that due to the protectors' negligence, Indian plaintiffs filed lawsuits independently, many of the complaints reaching the Council of the Indies (AGI, Quito, 8, R. 25, N. 92, 3r; BNM, 2927, VI, 51, 227v).

10. "[H]a auido Procurador de Indios, nombrado por el Virrey, que apenas sabia firmar, y traia siempre vn muchacho para que escriuiesse" (Reinaga Salazar 1626, 9r).

11. De la Puente Brunke (2005, 238) cites Cornejo's denunciation of 15 June 1666 to the Spanish monarch: "[León Pinelo is] a dangerous man and very beholden to the affect of his dependents, and he has many in this city and relatives of his wife in this city and in Ica and Pisco, and it is my understanding that he does not see as he should to the protection of the Indians, and they complain, as they have to me many times, about his slow response to their requests for assistance and the many expenses and costs that he and his agent charge them" (hombre peligroso y que se lleva mucho del afecto de sus dependientes, que tiene muchos en esta ciudad, y deudos por la parte de la mujer en ella y en las de Ica y Pisco, con que tengo entendido que no cumple como debe con la protección de los indios, y ellos se quejan, y se me han quejado a mí muchas veces, así del mal despacho que les da, como de los muchos gastos y costas que les lleva él y su agente) (AGI, Lima, 280).

12. AAL, Capítulos, Leg. 18, Exp. 1, 1r.

13. See AAL, Civiles, Leg. 83, Exp. 1, 3r–5r.

14. "After [De la Cruz] turned for assistance to the protector and letrado of the Indians, [the protector] refused to make or sign [the list of charges], saying that [the protectors] were under no obligation to make the charges or sign them" ([A]cudiendo al protector y letrado de los naturales no los an querido hazer ni firmar diziendome que ellos no eran obligados hazer los capitulos ni firmarlos) (AAL, Capítulos, Leg. 2, Exp. 16, 1r).

15. "Don Hernando de la cruz Principal y natural del Pu.o de sancto domingo de tauca de la provincia de los conchucos Parezco ante Vsa. S.a yllustrissima querellando criminalm.te contra del l.do fray lucas mudarra cura y beneficiado

del dho mi pueblo y contando el caso y esta mi querella Premisas las solenidades del dr.o[,] digo que el sobredho con poco temor de Dios nro s.r y en grande deseruicio suyo y menosprecio de la just.a yglesiastica y daño de su conciencia en tiempo de seys meses poco mas o menos que es cura del dho mi pueblo y assi teniendo el dho padre obligacion asi por lo dispuesto por el sancto concilio prouincial y constituciones sinodales hechas por us.a ss.a yll.ma de mirar y tener mucho cuydado por nro. amparo y difensa y procurar por nro. aum.to y saluaçion con el cuydado y deligencia que se requiere no lo ha hecho" (AAL, Capítulos, Leg. 2, Exp. 16, 3r).

16. Hevia Bolaños defines *delito notorio:* "A notorious crime is one that is committed before the judge or in presence of the entire town or its majority or the number of persons that, depending on the place and time, bring it to the judge for ruling. [The judge] can initiate court proceedings without the accuser or accusation, confession of the offender, or any other formality or court order; [he can proceed] simply by questioning at least two witnesses who testify to the crime and its circumstances and notoriety and by summoning the accused so that he ask for pardon" (Delito notorio es, el que se comete ante el juez, ó en presencia de todo el pueblo, ó de la mayor parte del, o del numero de personas, que segun la calidad del lugar, y tiempo que lo induzca a arbitrio del juez. El qual en el puede proceder de oficio, sin preceder acusador, ni acusacion, ni confession del delinquente, ni otra solenidad, ni orden de juyzio, mas de solo examinado dos testigos por lo menos, que depongan del delito, calidad, y notoriedad suya, citando al reo, para que luego se descargue) (1619, 206v).

17. "A Vs.a S.a yll.ma pido y suplico humillmente sea seruido mandar tener estos capitulos por ciertos y verdaderos y mande que se remedie tantos agrauios asi mios como los demas caciques y principales y yndios e yndias de dho mi pue.o descargando la conciencia de Vs.a s.a dandonos un sacerdote que nos trate bien y de buena vida y que sepa predicar y dar buen exemplo con lengua general del ynga" (AAL, Capítulos, Leg. 2, Exp. 16, 11v).

18. Native plaintiffs expressed requests for reparations as a call for justice, in keeping with the Third Council's definition of rightful legal appeal (Lima III, actio 4, cap. 6, Vargas Ugarte 1951–1954, 1:363). A 1600 petition by native leaders in the parish of Chavín de Pariarca concludes: "[E]sta querella que açemos no es de maliçia sino por alcançar justicia" (AAL, Capítulos, Leg. 1, Exp. 1, 1r).

19. For native lawsuits that reference canon law, see AAC, Colonial, X, 3, 44, 1r; AAL, Capítulos, Leg. 1, Exp. 1, 1r; AAL, Capítulos, Leg. 3, Exp. 2, 2r; AAL, Capítulos, Leg. 3, Exp. 11, 4r; AAL, Capítulos, Leg. 6, Exp. 6, 21v, 22r; AAL, Capítulos, Leg. 8, Exp. 2, 4v, 5v; AAL, Capítulos, Leg. 9, Exp. 13, 2r, 2v; AAL, Capítulos, Leg. 14, Exp. 4, 1r; AAL, Capítulos, Leg. 15, Exp. 7, 1v; AAL, Capítulos, Leg. 16, Exp. 1, 2r, 3r; AGN, Tribunal Eclesiástico, Leg. 43, Cuad. 4, 11r, 11v, 12r.

20. "yendo contra lo probeydo por el sancto concilio"; "siendo mandado por el sancto concilio y constituciones por Vs.a S.a yllustrissima"; "el dho Padre

haze contra lo dispuesto por las constituciones y sinodales"; "siendo mandado por las constituciones synodales de Vs.a S.a" (AAL, Capítulos, Leg. 2, Exp. 16, 5r, 9r, 9v, 10v).

21. The constitutions of Lobo Guerrero's 1613 synod declared that religious clergy needed the see's approval to minister in native parishes and authorized visitadores to dismiss friars for linguistic ignorance, pastoral neglect, or economic abuse; for sentencing, visitadores had orders to refer lawbreaking friars to the accused's provincial (Lima 1613, Lib. 1, tit. 7, cap. 25, Lobo Guerrero and Arias de Ugarte [1613, 1636] 1987, 100). Lima's audiencia supported the Church's plan to limit the autonomy of regular clergy in filling parish vacancies (Ribera 1621), but not surprisingly, these directives faced the opposition of the religious orders. Peru's Franciscans, for example, claimed the "special privileges" of religious clergy, meaning that language training and supervision of friars was internal to the orders and exempt from the inspections and rulings of the secular Church (Franciscans 1619, 26v–27r; *Constituciones desta Provincia* 1631, 49). Provincial congregations defied the authority of bishops and the viceroy by appointing friars to native parish posts without proper linguistic examination or title (Lavallé 1993, 63). However, Trent had granted diocesan authorities rights of inspection, leaving certain sanctions to the discretion of religious superiors (Torres 1970, 56), and the Crown required secular and religious clergy to obtain royal license for parish assignments (*Constituciones synodales del Obispado de Arequipa* 1688, 55v–56r).

22. "Pido y sup.co mande darnos sacerdote clerigo y no frayle porque . . . agora dize el Padre mudarra que el no es clerigo sino frayle y que tiene combento y su perlado y que aca no ay quien conozco" (AAL, Capítulos, Leg. 2, Exp. 16, 11v).

23. AGI, Contratación, 5346, N. 2, 8v; AGI, Pasajeros, L.9, E. 4181.

24. "[Y] no es justo que diga el padre por ser capillan del señor virrey como lo dize siempre que se a de salir con todo y que no nos ha de oyr Vs.a s.a yll.ma" (AAL, Capítulos, Leg. 2, Exp. 16, 11v).

25. "[N]o consiente que se entremeta Just.a sino el solo con su fiscal la administra" (AAL, Capítulos, Leg. 4, Exp. 3, 3r). See also AAL, Capítulos, Leg. 9, Exp. 13, 15v; AAL, Capítulos, Leg. 20, Exp. 9, 2v, 3v.

26. "[E]ra ladino, sauía leer y escriuir y sauía las hordenanzas y el Santo Concilio y cienpre le rrespondía al padre dotrinante y al encomendero y al corregidor y al tiniente y a los mayordomos de el encomendero" (Guaman Poma [c. 1615] 1980, 586). The chronicler repeatedly extolled canon and royal laws as tools for the defense of native peoples (see Guaman Poma [c. 1615] 1980, 232, 448–49, 493, 528, 579–80, 585, 600, 604, 612, 622, 656, 665, 673–74, 679, 693, 701–2, 877, 892, 895, 910, 958, 966–67, 982, 987, 999, 1125–26).

27. "[D]e no hazernos Just.a Pido se me de testimonio para acudir a que me la haga el Rey nro. s.r y su Real audiençia" (AAL, Capítulos, Leg. 2, Exp. 16, 11v).

28. AAL, Testamentos, Leg. 15, Exp. 8, 38v.

29. "[D]espues de puesto el nombre del actor dira, como mejor aya lugar de derecho. . . . Luego se pone otra clausula diziendo, me querello y demando, o pongo demanda a fulano. . . . Despues desto luego se ha de narrar el hecho breue, y claro. . . . Luego se sigue, y pone otra clausula que dize: Pido a V.m. auida mi relacion por verdadera. . . . Luego se sigue otra clausula, que dize, Condene, la qual sirue de conclusion. . . . Luego se sigue otra clausula, que dize: Y el oficio de V. merced imploro. . . . Luego se dize: Y pido justicia. . . . Tras esta clausula se pone otra que dize: Y las costas protesto. . . . La vltima clausula es. Y juro, &c. no ser de malicia. . . . Y [este juramento] se ha de hazer en qualquiera demandas, acusaciones, denunciaciones, excepciones, oposiciones, y otras peticiones semejantes en que se requiera, assi antes como despues de la contestacion, y en todas causas profanas, y Eclesiasticas" (Hevia Bolaños 1619, 55v–57v).

30. Ortiz de Salcedo's template for grievances begins: "In such-and-such place, etc., before N. etc., and before me the public notary and witnesses, appeared the prosecutor N. to denounce criminally N. because the aforementioned, with little fear of God Our Lord and in great burden to his soul and conscience, and in disregard of justice, has done such-and-such a thing, etc., which has caused much scandal and rumor" (En tal parte, &c. ante el señor N. &c. y ante mi el presente Notario publico, y testigos, pareció presente N. Fiscal, y denunció criminalmente de N. porque el susodicho con poco temor de Dios N. Señor, y en gran cargo de su anima, y conciencia, y en menosprecio de su justicia, ha hecho tal cosa, &c. de que se ha causado mucho escandalo, y murmuracion) (1691, 65v–66r).

31. For a discussion of the Lima Church's concerns about unfit clergy, see Mills 1996, 187–90.

32. "1. Prim.a mente si conosen al dho cura y de que tp.o asta p.te y si saue la lengua g.l del ynga. / 2. si sauen q. el dho cura aya sido negligente en la administraçion de los s.tos sacramentos y si por su caussa se ha muerto algunos de los y.os de su curato o alguna criatura sin bautismo. / 3. yten si sauen que el dho cura dixo la doctrina Christiana como estaba obligado los domingos y fiestas miercoles y viernes por su persona con sobrepeliç puesta. . . . / 12. yten si sauen q. el dho cura proçedio con el exemplo que deue. . . . / 17. yten si el dho cura hiziese algunos agrauios o malos tratamientos a sus feligreses quitandoles sus haziendas o siruiendose de ellos sin pagarles su trauajo. . . . / 26. yten si el dho cura hubiese fecho alguna ausençia deste benef.o sin dexar saçerdote aprobado en ella" (AAL, Visitas Eclesiásticas, Leg. 11, Exp. 1, 2r–3r).

33. Adorno ([1986] 2000, li–liii; 2007, 39) has noted that the types of data gathered from colonial inspections tours are evident throughout the chronicle of Guaman Poma.

34. According to Schoeck (1983, 276), lawyers of Renaissance Europe studied primarily the forensic rhetoric that pertained to the courtroom and, to a lesser degree, deliberative rhetoric (the art of persuading future action in political

assemblies) and epideictic rhetoric (the art of assigning praise or blame for past events in public councils).

35. "[Q]ue se remedie por lo que toca al descargo de la conciencia de Vs.a S.a" (AAL, Capítulos, Leg. 2, Exp. 16, 3r).

36. "You are not to receive any petition from the said Indians but rather, having informed yourself of what they intend to claim, write on their behalf an account with lists of charges, declaring therein the said Indians' request, so that I can respond to them and provide [judgment]; in this way, you will advocate in the interest of the said Indians with less volume of petitions and papers" ([N]o recibireis peticion ninguna de los dichos naturales, sino que informado de lo que pretendieren pedir, les hagais unas relaciones por capítulos, declarando en ellas el pedimento de los dichos indios, para que yo responda á ellas y provea, de manera que con ménos volúmen de peticiones y papeles vos pidais lo que conviniere á los dichos naturales) (Levillier 1921–1925, 8:289).

37. Burns (2005b, 365–66) makes this point in her discussion of the collusion between indigenous notaries and native elites. Many Andeanist scholars have argued the same; Burns (2005b, 365–66 n. 67) cites the examples of Spalding (1984) and Stern ([1982] 1993).

38. AAL, Capítulos, Leg. 2, Exp. 16, 26r–28r.

39. "[Y]ten el dho Padre siendo sacerdote castigo cruelm.te a domingo poma mango Principal y a don al.o cargua rupai y a Rodrigo cargua yaure y a pedro guanca Poma y a martin jurado y a don pablo cargua yaure y a augustin cargua namba y a Juan gua[nca?] yanai[,] acotaron con su mano el mismo porque el dho padre en todas cosas se haze uerdugo con tal condicion que tiene en ser cruel a todos los dhos Principales sin causa ninguna porque no los embiaron sus cauallos presto a las estancias llamada quichis y quillca[,] treynta cauallos por treynta fanigas de trigo para su grangeria es publico y notorio" (AAL, Capítulos, Leg. 2, Exp. 16, 4v).

40. "[M]ande Vs.a s.a recebir ynformacion que estoi presto de dar aqui porque ay muchos yndios que se an uenido huyendo por no poder sufrir tantos trauajos y vejaciones" (AAL, Capítulos, Leg. 2, Exp. 16, 11v).

41. AAL, Capítulos, Leg. 2, Exp. 16, 3r–4r

42. "[H]ize dejacion de el oficio de fiscal mayor porq. es tan cruel y de tal mala condicion que ya no lo podia sufrir por uengarse con qualquier achaque ha hecho en mi mil castigos como es notorio" (AAL, Capítulos, Leg. 2, Exp. 16, 4r).

43. Adorno ([1986] 2000, 57–79) examines Guaman Poma's strategy of using the rhetorical weapons of ecclesiastical speech against the colonizers themselves.

44. "[L]as obejuelas deste Pueblo estamos desparramados todos Por abernos espantado quien por nosotros abia de mirar con sus malos tratamientos y exemplos" (AAL, Capítulos, Leg. 6, Exp. 4, 3r).

45. "diziendo mas que el diablo se lo lleuase a el a los demas yndios porque eran capitulantes" (AAL, Capítulos, Leg. 6, Exp. 1, 4r).

46. "diçiendo que Podia hacerlo Por ser el Papa y rrey deste pue.o y que el pro-bisor de lima era nada para el ni el señor arçobispo podia quitar su dotrina" (AAL, Capítulos, Leg. 6, Exp. 4, 3r). The charge that the local priest declared himself to be "pope" and "king" appears in other trials as well (see AAL, Capítulos, Leg. 6, Exp. 1, 5r; AAL, Criminales, Leg. 24, Exp. 16, 5v).

47. Adorno has identified in Guaman Poma's chronicle eighty references to the sin of pride, "his common term of comparison for the Spaniards" ([1986] 2000, 72, 159 n. 13).

48. Stone (2004) and Firbas (2006) posit the concept of collective authorship as fundamental to the understanding of colonial textuality and its mechanisms of production.

49. "La petición que se da al juez o al señor para recuerdo de algún negocio" (Covarrubias Orozco [1611] 1995, 747).

50. "[E]stando en vna comission, que las mismas peticiones que le avian dado los indios contra vn doctrinero se las avia dado al doctrinero" (Padilla [1657] 1966, 394).

51. AAL, Visitas Eclesiásticas, Leg. 11, Exp. 12; AAL, Visitas Eclesiásticas, Leg. 23, Exp. 17A. Contradicting the statements of San Agustín de Cajacay's native capitulantes, Garavito stated that Celis fulfilled his office "with complete Christian integrity, personally teaching the catechism in the native language and Castilian in which all the Indians are very learned" (con toda linpiesa y christiandad enseñando por su persona la dotrina christiana en lengua de yndio y castellana en la qual [los indios] estan uien ynstruidos) (AAL, Visitas Eclesiásticas, Leg. 11, Exp. 12, 6r).

52. "Sirvase V.M. de apiadarse (como es sin duda lo hará) destos sus pobres y miserables vasallos, poniendo remedio en sus desdichas, de suerte que le ten-gan con effecto y que no se quede solo en terminos de mandarlo, para que no sea cierto lo que pocos dias ha le dijo vn casique de Tarama a su dotrinero, 'Ha Padre y qué caro nos cuesta este Nuestro evangelio,' que fuera menos mal si procu-rasemos como es justo que le tuviessen, que Dios Nuestro Señor que ve y no olvida sus persecuciones, se servirá de alzar el azote de las calamidades de la Monarchia de V.M. y de restituirla a su antigua paz y grandeza y de dar a V.M. la vida y suc-cesion que la christiandad ha menester" (Padilla [1657] 1966, 419).

53. Examples of the clergy's retaliation abound. Two cases are the litigation of 1631 between the caciques principales of Santa Ana de Tusi and Pedro del Campo (AAL, Capítulos, Leg. 6, Exp. 6, 1v; AAL, Capítulos, Leg. 8, Exp. 2, 3v–4r, 5r), and the 1655 lawsuit brought by Don Tomás Pantaleón against the Franciscan friar Alonso de la Vega in the parish of Luringuanca (AAL, Hechicerías e Idolatrías, Leg. 3, Exp. 7, 1r–3r).

54. "[P]ediendo justicia contra el padre los caciques prencipales y los yndios, luego el padre le leuanta testimonio y dize que son hicheseros y amansebados y le leuanta otras cosas muy feas" (Guaman Poma [c. 1615] 1980, 606).

55. Lima II, indios 114, Vargas Ugarte 1951–1954, 1:216–17; Lima II, españoles 120, Vargas Ugarte 1951–1954, 1:239; Lima III, actio 4, cap. 6, Vargas Ugarte 1951–1954, 1:363. Negative images of native litigants also appear in the Third Council's confession manual and sermon collection *(Confessionario* [1585] 1985, 223, 229; *Tercero catecismo* [1585] 1985, 582–92). Harrison (1994, 143) observes that native-language catechisms used the Quechua noun *hucha* (the act of speaking disapprovingly of a lord) to signify both "pecado" (sin) and "pleito" (lawsuit). The semantic ties between the Christian concept of sin, traditional Andean notions of defiance of authority, and lawsuits underscore the authors' proscriptive attitudes toward native legal activity.

56. "Si te quieres hazer immortal, hazte pleito Eclesiastico" (Solórzano Pereira 1648, 564). *Arbitristas* of seventeenth-century Spain denounced the growing power of legal agents who enriched themselves to the detriment of the poor (Fernández Navarrete [1626] 1982, 334–35; Saavedra Fajardo [1640] 1659, 180–81). Spanish nobles also saw popular education as a threat to the traditional social order; they feared the emergence of an unproductive "republic of letters" in which commoners pursued study in order to secure posts as government functionaries instead of providing the manual labor needed to sustain the economy. Diego de Saavedra Fajardo summarized this position: "Learned and glib vassals always love novelties, slander the government, challenge the prince's resolutions, awaken the masses, and incite them to rebellion" (Los Vasallos muy discursistas, y scientificos aman siempre las novedades, calumnian el gobierno, disputan las resoluciones del Principe, despiertan el Pueblo, y le solevan) ([1640] 1659, 650; see also Fernández Navarrete [1626] 1982, 359–60).

57. Lima 1613, Lib. 1, tit. 8, cap. 1, Lobo Guerrero and Arias de Ugarte [1613, 1636] 1987, 103–5; Lima 1613, Lib. 5, tit. 1, Lobo Guerrero and Arias de Ugarte [1613, 1636] 1987, 197.

58. *Constituciones synodales del Obispado de Arequipa* 1688, 88r–v; Torres 1970, 54–55.

59. AAL, Capítulos, Leg. 13, Exp. 8, 1r.

60. AAL, Capítulos, Leg. 13, Exp. 8, 56r–61r.

61. AAL, Capítulos, Leg. 14, Exp. 3, 376r–v, 380r–v.

62. "[L]os que suelen hacer esto no son los buenos christianos (si bien entre esta gente ay muy pocos) sino los malos, y no los malos comoquiera, sino los peores, y siendo los unos y los otros tan inclinados y faciles en leuantar falsos testimonios y en testificarlos con juramento es evidentemente mucho mayor el peligro de la honrra de los curas" (AAL, Capítulos, Leg. 15, Exp. 4, 28r).

63. AAL, Visitas Eclesiásticas, Leg. 22, Exp. 8; AAL, Visitas Eclesiásticas, Leg. 22, Exp. 12.

64. AAL, Capítulos, Leg. 15, Exp. 4, 29r.

65. "[N]o quedara en pie cura de los que hacen debidamente su oficio y muchos de los indios y aun estoy por decir casi todos no cessaran de capitularlos asta hallar cura a su modo" (AAL, Capítulos, Leg. 15, Exp 4, 34r).

66. AAL, Visitas Eclesiásticas, Leg. 22, Exp. 15, 8r.

67. AAL, Hechicerías e Idolatrías, Leg. 3, Exp. 15, 2v.

68. The protector general chose to confront the archbishop when moral or political conditions favored legal action. In 1657, at the start of León Pinelo's mandate, the protector wrote an appeal to Villagómez on behalf of the Indian Francisco de Rivera of the pueblo Santiago de Maray, who had fled the parish to Lima in order to escape the persecution of Father Bartolomé Jurado Palomino and obtain legal protection (AAL, Curatos, Leg. 28, Exp. 10, 3r).

69. "He enviado continuamente visitadores, los que mejor me han parecido, para extirpar las idolatrías, que han hecho cuanto se ha podido, y con todo eso son tan malos algunos de los indios (particularmente algunos de sus caciques) que . . . procuran capitular a los mismos visitadores, como hoy están tres de ellos capitulados maliciosamente con evidencia a lo que yo puedo entender, y no se habían descubierto tanto en su malicia como ahora que han tomado esta avilantez so capa de favor que quieren atribuirse que les hace don Juan de Padilla, alcalde de corte de esta Real Audiencia" (AGI, Lima, 59; transcribed in Marzal 1983, 222).

70. AAL, Hechicerías e Idolatrías, Leg. 3, Exp. 11, 23v–24r, 52r–v; Griffiths 1996, 196.

71. AAL, Visitas Eclesiásticas, Leg. 11, Exp. 1, 5r.

72. AAL, Concursos, Leg. 2, Exp 44; AAL, Visitas Eclesiásticas, Leg. 1, Exp. 30; AAL, Visitas Eclesiásticas, Leg. 2, Exp. 16; AAL, Curatos, Leg. 1, Exp. 30. The catalog of the Hechicerías e Idolatrías section of the Archivo Arzobispal de Lima lists a dossier of proceedings against Mudarra that took place in Chacas in 1643, titled "Causa que hace Joan Canes contra el licenciado fray Lucas Mudarra, cura de San Martín de Chacas," which is now missing from the collection (Gutiérrez Arbulú 1993, 110).

73. AAL, Curatos, Leg. 42, Exp. 4.

74. Lima II, indios 9, Vargas Ugarte 1951–1954, 1:164–65.

75. AAL, Capítulos, Leg. 1, Exp. 4, 135r.

76. Echoing Guaman Poma, the native leaders in Collana in the province of Cajatambo stated in 1626: "Your Excellency, we the poor, who God has so burdened, suffer without solace, without legal protection, and without remedy" ([Y]lustricimo s.or los pobres que tanto encargo Dios padesemos sin consuelo sin amparo y sin rremedio) (AAL, Capítulos, Leg. 5, Exp. 4, 12r). In 1654, the native governor Pedro Xari in the parish of Chavín de Pariarca concluded his grievance against Francisco de Guevara with resignation: "It may very well be that we do not attain justice, for we are 'pobres miserables' and without anyone to take up for us

besides the protection of Your Mercy" ([P]odra ser no alcansar jus.a por ser unos pobres miserables no tener quien buelua por nosotros mas quel amparo de vmd) (AAL, Capítulos, Leg. 16, Exp. 1, 62r).

77. "[S]e deciden luego Mejor le está al litigante vna condenacion, despachada brevemente, que vna sentencia favorable, despues de aver litigado muchos años. . . . Que restitucion puede esperar el desposeido, si primero le an de despojar tantos?" (Saavedra Fajardo [1640] 1659, 184–86).

78. Similarly, Adorno (1991, 247–48) has observed that Guaman Poma praised the ecclesiastical visita as an institution but criticized the abusive practices of Spanish inspectors.

79. "[D]e executar in totum las cedulas del aliuio de los Indios, se siguiera, que totalmente faltaran obradores en los minerales, y cessara la saca de metales, y no se pudieran ajustar embios, ó conducciones anales, que se hazen a V.M. de donde pende el bien publico" (Velázquez de Ovando c. 1658, 33v).

80. Clifford has underscored the interactive dimension of identity formation in ethnographic situations: "Stories of cultural contact and change have been structured by a pervasive dichotomy: absorption by the other *or* resistance to the other. A fear of lost identity, a Puritan taboo on mixing beliefs and bodies, hangs over the process. Yet what if identity is conceived not as a boundary to be maintained but as a nexus of relations and transactions actively engaging a subject? The story or stories of interaction must then be more complex, less linear and teleological" (1988, 344). Wyss (2000, 29–30) cites this passage in examining the manifold patterns of acculturation of Christian Indians in early North America.

Bibliography

Archives Consulted

AAC	Archivo Arzobispal del Cuzco (Cuzco)
AAL	Archivo Arzobispal de Lima (Lima)
ACE	Archivo del Cabildo Eclesiástico (Lima)
AGI	Archivo General de Indias (Seville)
AGN	Archivo General de la Nación (Lima)
AHN	Archivo Histórico Nacional de Madrid (Madrid)
ASFL	Archivo de San Francisco de Lima (Lima)
BNM	Biblioteca Nacional de Madrid (Madrid)
BNP	Biblioteca Nacional del Perú (Lima)

Print Sources

Acosta, José de. [1577] 1984, 1987. *De procuranda indorum salute*. Edited by Luciano Pereña. 2 vols. Madrid: Centro Superior de Investigaciones Científicas.

Acosta, José de. [1590] 2002. *Historia natural y moral de las Indias*. Edited by José Alcina Franch. Madrid: Dastin.

Acosta Rodríguez, Antonio. 1979. "El pleito de los indios de San Damián (Huarochirí) contra Francisco de Ávila, 1607." *Historiografía y Bibliografía Americanistas* 23:3–33.

Acosta Rodríguez, Antonio. 1982. "Religiosos, doctrinas y excedente económico indígena en el Perú a comienzos del siglo XVII." *Histórica* 6, no. 1: 1–34.

Acosta Rodríguez, Antonio. 1987. "Francisco de Ávila: Cusco 1573 (?)–Lima 1647." In *Ritos y tradiciones de Huarochirí*, edited and translated by Gerald Taylor, pp. 551–616. Lima: Instituto de Estudios Peruanos, Instituto Francés de Estudios Andinos.

Adorno, Rolena, ed. 1982. *From Oral to Written Expression: Native Andean Chronicles of the Early Colonial Period*. Syracuse, N.Y.: Maxwell School of Citizenship and Public Affairs, Syracuse University.

Adorno, Rolena. 1991. "Images of *Indios Ladinos* in Early Colonial Peru." In *Transatlantic Encounters: Europeans and Andeans in the Sixteenth Century*, edited by Kenneth J. Andrien and Rolena Adorno, pp. 232–70. Berkeley: University of California Press.

Adorno, Rolena. 1993. "The Genesis of Felipe Guaman Poma de Ayala's *Nueva corónica y buen gobierno.*" *Colonial Latin American Review* 2, nos. 1–2: 53–92.

Adorno, Rolena. 1994. "The Indigenous Ethnographer: The 'Indio Ladino' as Historian and Cultural Mediation." In *Implicit Understandings: Observing, Reporting, and Reflecting on the Encounters Between Europeans and Other Peoples in the Early Modern Era,* edited by Stuart B. Schwartz, pp. 378–402. Cambridge, U.K.: Cambridge University Press.

Adorno, Rolena. 1999. "Novedades en el estudio actual de la cronística peruana: Las Casas, Guaman Poma y el padre Oliva." In *Actas del Primer Congreso Internacional de Peruanistas en el Extranjero.* Edited by José Antonio Mazzotti. Cambridge, Mass.: Harvard University. Available from http://www.fas.harvard.edu/~icop/rolenaadorno.html.

Adorno, Rolena. [1986] 2000. *Guaman Poma: Writing and Resistance in Colonial Peru.* Austin: University of Texas Press.

Adorno, Rolena. 2007. *The Polemics of Possession in Spanish American Narrative.* New Haven, Conn.: Yale University Press.

Alaperrine-Bouyer, Monique. 2007. *La educación de las elites indígenas en el Perú colonial.* Lima: Instituto Francés de Estudios Andinos, Instituto Riva-Agüero, Pontificia Universidad Católica del Perú, Instituto de Estudios Peruanos.

Albó, Xavier. 1966. "Jesuitas y culturas indígenas. Perú 1568–1606. Su actitud. Métodos y criterios de aculturación." *América Indígena* 26, nos. 3 and 4: 249–308, 395–446.

Alfonso X, el Sabio. [c. 1265] 1587. *Siete partidas.* Valladolid, Spain: Diego Fernández de Córdoba.

Allen, Catherine J. 2005. "Knot-Words or Not Words." *Anthropological Quarterly* 78, no. 4: 981–96.

Almansa, Bernardino de. c. 1620. *Por parte del Dean y Cabildo de la Santa Iglesia de la ciudad de la Plata, Prouincia de los Charcas en el Reyno del Pirú, en razon de las Prebendas que se quieren proueer, se suplica a V.M. se sirua de considerar lo siguiente.* Madrid (?): n.p.

Álvarez, Bartolomé. [1588] 1998. *De las costumbres y conversión de los indios del Perú. Memorial a Felipe II (1588).* Edited by María del Carmen Martín Rubio, Juan J. R. Villarías Robles, and Fermín del Pino Díaz. Madrid: Ediciones Polifemo.

Armas Medina, Fernando de. 1953. *Cristianización del Perú (1532–1600).* Seville: Escuela de Estudios Hispano-Americanos.

Arriaga, Pablo José de. [1621] 1999. *La extirpación de la idolatría en el Pirú.* Edited by Henrique Urbano. Cuzco: Centro de Estudios Regionales Andinos "Bartolomé de las Casas."

Arte y vocabulario en la lengua general del Perú llamada Quichua, y en la lengua Española. [1586] 1604. Lima: Antonio Ricardo.

Ascher, Marcia, and Robert Ascher. 1981. *Code of the Quipu: A Study in Media, Mathematics, and Culture.* Ann Arbor: University of Michigan Press.

Avendaño, Fernando de. 1649. *Sermones de los misterios de nuestra santa fe católica en lengua castellana y la general del Inca.* Lima: Jorge López de Herrera.

Ávila, Francisco de. 1648. *Tratado de los evangelios que nuestra madre la Iglesia nos propone en todo el año desde la primera dominica de Adviento hasta la última missa de difuntos, santos de España, y añadidos en el nuevo rezado. Explicase el Evangelio, y se pone un sermon en cada uno en las lenguas castellana, y general de los indios deste Reyno del Perú, y en ellos donde da lugar la materia se refutan los errores de la gentilidad de dichos indios.* 2 vols. Lima: n.p.

Ávila, Francisco de. [1608] 1904. *Relación que yo, el doctor Francisco de Ávila, presbítero, cura y beneficiado de la ciudad de Huánuco, hice por mandado del señor Arzobispo de los Reyes.* In *La imprenta en Lima (1584–1824),* vol. 1, by José Toribio Medina, pp. 386–89. Santiago, Chile: José Toribio Medina.

Ávila, Francisco de. [1648] 1918. "Prefación al libro de los sermones, o homilías en la lengua castellana y la índica general quechhua." In *Informaciones acerca de religión y gobierno de los incas,* edited by Horacio H. Urteaga, pp. 57–98. Lima: Sanmartí.

Barnes, Monica. 1992. "Catechisms and *Confessionarios:* Distorting Mirrors of Andean Societies." In *Andean Cosmologies Through Time,* edited by Robert V. H. Dover, Katherine E. Seibold, and John H. McDowell, pp. 67–94. Bloomington: Indiana University Press.

Bartolomé Martínez, Bernabé. 1995. "Las escuelas de primeras letras." In *Historia de la acción educadora de la Iglesia en España,* vol. 1, edited by Bernabé Bartolomé Martínez, pp. 612–30. Madrid: Biblioteca de Autores Cristianos.

Bartra, Enrique T. 1967. "Los autores del catecismo del Tercer Concilio Limense." *Mercurio Peruano* 470:359–72.

Bayle, Constantino. 1951. "Cabildos de indios en la América Española." *Missionalia Hispanica* 8, no. 22: 5–35.

Behar, Ruth. 1989. "Sexual Witchcraft, Colonialism, and Women's Powers: Views from the Mexican Inquisition." In *Sexuality and Marriage in Colonial Latin America,* edited by Asunción Lavrín, pp. 178–206. Lincoln: University of Nebraska Press.

Benton, Lauren. 2002. *Law and Colonial Cultures: Legal Regimes in World History, 1400—1900.* Cambridge, U.K.: Cambridge University Press.

Benveniste, Émile. [1969] 1985. "The Semiology of Language." In *Semiotics: An Introductory Anthology,* edited by Robert E. Innis, pp. 228–46. Bloomington: Indiana University Press.

Berman, Harold. 1983. *Law and Revolution: The Formation of the Western Legal Tradition.* Cambridge, Mass.: Harvard University Press.

Bertonio, Ludovico. 1612a. *Confessionario muy copioso en dos lenguas, aymara y española.* Juli, Peru: Francisco del Canto.

Bertonio, Ludovico. 1612b. *Libro de la vida y milagros de Nuestro Señor Jesucristo en dos lenguas, aymara y romance.* Juli, Peru: Francisco del Canto.

Bertonio, Ludovico. 1612c. *Vocabulario de la lengua aymara.* Juli, Peru: Francisco del Canto.

√Beyersdorff, Margot. 2005. "Writing Without Words/Words Without Writing: The Culture of the Khipu." *Latin American Research Review* 40, no. 3: 294–311.

Bolívar y de la Redonda, Pedro de. 1667. *Memorial informe y discurso legal, historico, y politico al Rey nuestro señor en su Real Consejo de Camara de las Indias, en favor de los españoles, que en ellas nacen, estudian, y sirven, para que sean preferidos en todas las provisiones eclesiasticas, y seculares, que para aquellas partes se hizieren.* Madrid: Mateo de Espinosa y Arteaga.

Bonnett, Diana. 1992. *Los protectores de naturales en la audiencia de Quito, siglos XVII y XVIII.* Quito: Facultad Latinoamericana de Ciencias Sociales, Abya-Yala.

Boone, Elizabeth Hill, and Walter D. Mignolo, eds. 1994. *Writing Without Words: Alternative Literacies in Mesoamerica and the Andes.* Durham, N.C.: Duke University Press.

Borah, Woodrow. 1970. "Juzgado General de Indios del Perú o Juzgado Particular de Indios de El Cercado de Lima." *Revista Chilena de Historia del Derecho* 6:129–42.

Borah, Woodrow. 1983. *Justice by Insurance: The General Indian Court of Colonial Mexico and the Legal Aides of the Half-Real.* Berkeley: University of California Press.

Bouwsma, William. 1990. *A Usable Past: Essays in European Cultural History.* Berkeley: University of California Press.

√Bouza Álvarez, Fernando. [1999] 2004. *Communication, Knowledge, and Memory in Early Modern Spain.* Translated by Sonia López and Michael Agnew. Philadelphia: University of Pennsylvania Press.

Breve instrucción, o arte para entender la lengua comun de los Indios, segun se habla en la provincia de Quito 1753. Lima: Plazuela de San Cristóbal.

Brundage, James A. 2008. *The Medieval Origins of the Legal Profession: Canonists, Civilians, and Courts.* Chicago: University of Chicago Press.

Burga, Manuel. [1988] 2005. *Nacimiento de una utopía: Muerte y resurrección de los incas.* 2d ed. Lima: Universidad Nacional Mayor de San Marcos, Universidad de Guadalajara.

Burke, Peter. 1987. "The Uses of Literacy in Early Modern Italy." In *The Social History of Language,* edited by Peter Burke and Roy Porter, pp. 21–42. Cambridge, U.K.: Cambridge University Press.

Burns, Kathryn. 1999. *Colonial Habits: Convents and the Spiritual Economy of Cuzco, Peru.* Durham, N.C.: Duke University Press.

Burns, Kathryn. 2005a. "Making Indigenous Archives: The Quilcay Camayoc of Colonial Cuzco." Paper presented at the Latin American Library of Tulane University, New Orleans, 6 April.

Burns, Kathryn. 2005b. "Notaries, Truth, and Consequences." *American Historical Review* 110, no. 2: 350–79.

Cahill, David. 1984. "*Curas* and Social Conflict in the *Doctrinas* of Cuzco, 1780–1814." *Journal of Latin American Studies* 16:241–76.

Calancha, Antonio de la. [1638] 1974. *Corónica moralizada del orden de San Agustín en el Perú con sucesos ejemplares en esta monarquía.* Edited by Ignacio Prado Pastor. Lima: Universidad Nacional Mayor de San Marcos.

Calvo, Hortensia. 2003. "The Historiography of the Book in Early Spanish America." In *Book History,* vol. 6, edited by Ezra Greenspan and Jonathan Rose, pp. 277–305. University Park: Pennsylvania State University Press.

Campo del Pozo, Fernando, and Félix Carmona Moreno, eds. 1996. *Sínodos de Quito 1594 y Loja 1596 por Fray Luis López de Solís.* Madrid: Editorial Revista Augustiniana.

Campo y de la Reinaga, Nicolás Matías del. 1673. *Flores peruanas, historicas, politicas, iuridicas, recogidas en tres memoriales.* Madrid: Mateo de Espinosa y Arteaga.

Cárdenas Ayaipoma, Mario. 1975–1976. "El Colegio de Caciques y el sometimiento ideológico de los residuos de la nobleza aborigen." *Revista del Archivo General de la Nación* 4–5:5–24.

Cárdenas Bunsen, José Alejandro. 1998. "La redacción de la *Nueva corónica y buen gobierno.*" Tesis de licenciatura, Pontificia Universidad Católica del Perú, Lima.

Carrera, Fernando de la. 1644. *Arte de la lengua yunga de los valles del Obispado de Truxillo del Peru, con vn confessionario, y todas las oraciones christianas, traducidas en la lengua, y otras cosas.* Lima: Joseph de Contreras.

Castiglione, Caroline. 2005. *Patrons and Adversaries: Nobles and Villagers in Italian Politics, 1640–1760.* Oxford, U.K.: Oxford University Press.

Castillo Arroyo, Javier. 1966. *Catecismos peruanos en el siglo XVI.* Cuernavaca, Mexico: Centro Intercultural de Documentación.

Castillo Gómez, Antonio. 2001. "Entre public et privé: Stratégies de l'écrit dans l'Espagne du Siècle d'Or." *Annales HSS* 56:803–29.

Castro Pineda, Lucio. 1963. "La cátedra de lengua quechua en la Catedral de Lima." *Nueva Corónica* 1:136–47.

Celestino, Olinda, and Albert Meyers. 1981. *Las cofradías en el Perú: Región central.* Frankfurt: Vervuert.

Cerrón-Palomino, Rodolfo. 1987. "Unidad y diferenciación lingüística en el mundo andino." *Lexis* 9, no. 1: 71–104.

Cerrón-Palomino, Rodolfo. 1991. "El Inca Garcilaso o la lealtad idiomática." *Lexis* 15, no. 2: 133–78.

Cerrón-Palomino, Rodolfo. 1992. "Diversidad y unificación léxica en el mundo andino." In *El quechua en debate: Ideología, normalización y enseñanza*, edited by Juan Carlos Godenzzi, pp. 205–35. Cuzco: Centro de Estudios Regionales Andinos "Bartolomé de las Casas."

Cerrón-Palomino, Rodolfo. 1995. "Estudio introductorio." In *Grammatica o arte de la lengua general de los indios de los reynos del Peru* (1560), by Domingo de Santo Tomás, edited by Rodolfo Cerrón-Palomino, pp. vii–lxvi. Cuzco: Centro de Estudios Regionales Andinos "Bartolomé de las Casas."

Cerrón-Palomino, Rodolfo. 2003. *Castellano andino: Aspectos sociolingüísticos, pedagógicos y gramaticales*. Lima: Pontificia Universidad Católica del Perú, Cooperación Técnica Alemana.

Cervantes, Fernando. 1994. *The Devil in the New World: The Impact of Diabolism in New Spain*. New Haven, Conn.: Yale University Press.

Chartier, Roger. 1994. *Libros, lecturas y lectores en la edad moderna*. Madrid: Alianza Editorial.

Chevalier, François. 1944. "Les municipalités indiennes en Nouvelle Espagne, 1520–1620." *Anuario de Historia del Derecho Español* 15:352–86.

Clanchy, Michael T. 1993. *From Memory to Written Record: England 1066–1307*. 2d ed. Oxford, U.K.: Blackwell.

Clendinnen, Inga. 1982. "Disciplining the Indians: Franciscan Ideology and Missionary Violence in Sixteenth-Century Yucatan." *Past and Present* 94:27–48.

Clifford, James. 1988. *The Predicament of Culture: Ethnography, Literature, and Art*. Cambridge, Mass.: Harvard University Press.

Cobo, Bernabé. [1639] 1964a. *Fundación de Lima*. In *Obras del P. Bernabé Cobo de la Compañía de Jesús*. Edited by Francisco Mateos. 2 vols. Madrid: Ediciones Atlas (Biblioteca de Autores Españoles).

Cobo, Bernabé. [1653] 1964b. *Historia del Nuevo Mundo*. In *Obras del P. Bernabé Cobo de la Compañía de Jesús*. Edited by Francisco Mateos. 2 vols. Madrid: Ediciones Atlas (Biblioteca de Autores Españoles).

Confessionario para los curas de indios. [1585] 1985. In *Doctrina christiana y catecismo para instrucción de indios* (1584), edited by Luciano Pereña, pp. 189–332. Madrid: Consejo Superior de Investigaciones Científicas.

Constituciones de los Frailes Menores desta Provincia de los Doze Apostoles del Piru. 1601. Lima: Antonio Ricardo.

Constituciones desta Provincia de los Doze Apostoles del Piru. 1631. Lima: Geronymo de Contreras.

Constituciones synodales del Obispado de Arequipa, hechas y ordenadas por el ilustrissimo y reuerendissimo señor doctor don Antonio de Leon su obispo, del consejo de su Magestad, en la synodo diocessana que celebro año de 1684. 1688. Lima: Joseph de Contreras.

Constituciones synodales establecidas por el Illustrissimo Señor Doctor Don Augustin Rodriguez Delgado, del Consejo de su Magestad, obispo de la ciudad de Nuestra Señora de la Paz, para el govierno eclesiastico, y regimen sacro-político de su obispado. 1739. Lima: n.p.

Contreras, Miguel de. [1613] 1968. *Padrón de los indios de Lima en 1613.* Introduction by Noble David Cook. Transcription by Mauro Escobar Gamboa. Lima: Universidad Nacional Mayor de San Marcos, Seminario de Historia Rural Andina.

Cornejo Polar, Antonio. 1994. *Escribir en el aire: Ensayo sobre la heterogeneidad socio-cultural en las literaturas andinas.* Lima: Editorial Horizonte.

Covarrubias Orozco, Sebastián de. [1611] 1995. *Tesoro de la lengua castellana o española.* Edited by Felipe C. R. Maldonado. Madrid: Editorial Castalia.

Cressy, David. 1981. "Levels of Illiteracy in England, 1530–1730." In *Literacy and Social Development in the West: A Reader,* edited by Harvey J. Graff, pp. 105–24. Cambridge, U.K.: Cambridge University Press.

Cummins, Tom, and Joanne Rappaport. 1998. "The Reconfiguration of Civic and Sacred Space: Architecture, Image, and Writing in the Colonial Northern Andes." *Latin American Literary Review* 26, no. 52: 174–200.

Cutter, Charles R. 1986. *The Protector de Indios in Colonial New Mexico, 1659–1821.* Albuquerque: University of New Mexico Press.

Dávalos y Figueroa, Diego de. 1602. *Primera parte de la Miscelanea austral.* Lima: Antonio Ricardo.

Davis, Natalie Zemon. 1987. *Fiction in the Archives: Pardon Tales and Their Tellers in Sixteenth-Century France.* Stanford, Calif.: Stanford University Press.

Dean, Carolyn. 1999. *Inka Bodies and the Body of Christ: Corpus Christi in Colonial Cuzco, Peru.* Durham, N.C.: Duke University Press.

Decoster, Jean-Jacques, ed. 2002. *Incas e indios cristianos: Elites indígenas e identidades cristianas en los Andes coloniales.* Cuzco: Centro de Estudios Regionales Andinos "Bartolomé de las Casas," Instituto Francés de Estudios Andinos, Asociación Kuraka.

Dedenbach-Salazar Sáenz, Sabine. 1997. "La terminología cristiana en textos quechuas de instrucción religiosa en el siglo XVI." In *Latin American Indian Literatures: Messages and Meanings,* edited by Mary H. Preuss, pp. 195–209. Lancaster, Calif.: Labyrinthos.

De la Puente Brunke, José. 1998. "'Los vasallos se desentrañan por su rey': Notas sobre quejas de curacas en el Perú del siglo XVII." *Anuario de Estudios Americanos* 55, no. 2: 459–73.

De la Puente Brunke, José. 2005. "Notas sobre la audiencia de Lima y la 'protección de los naturales' (siglo XVII)." In *Passeurs, mediadores culturales y agentes de la primera globalización en el mundo ibérico, siglos XVI–XIX,* edited by Scarlett O'Phelan Godoy and Carmen Salazar-Soler, pp. 231–48. Lima: Pontificia Universidad Católica del Perú, Instituto Riva-Agüero, Instituto Francés de Estudios Andinos.

Díaz Rementería, Carlos J. 1977. *El cacique en el virreinato del Perú.* Seville: Universidad de Sevilla.

Doctrina christiana y catecismo para instrucción de indios. [1584] 1985. Edited by Luciano Pereña. Madrid: Consejo Superior de Investigaciones Científicas.

Durston, Alan. 2002. "El *Aptaycachana* de Juan de Castromonte: Un manual sacramental quechua para la sierra central del Perú (ca. 1650)." *Boletín del Instituto Francés de Estudios Andinos* 31, no. 2: 219–92.

Durston, Alan. 2007. *Pastoral Quechua: The History of Christian Translation in Colonial Peru, 1550–1650.* Notre Dame, Ind.: University of Notre Dame Press.

Durston, Alan. 2008. "Native-Language Literacy in Colonial Peru: The Question of Mundane Quechua Writing Revisited." *Hispanic American Historical Review* 88, no. 1: 41–70.

Duviols, Pierre. [1971] 1977. *La destrucción de las religiones andinas (conquista y colonia).* Translated by Albor Maruenda. Mexico City: Universidad Autónoma de México.

Duviols, Pierre. 1979. "Datation, paternité et idéologie de la 'Declaración de los quipucamayos a Vaca de Castro' (Discurso de la descendencia y gobierno de los Ingas)." In *Les cultures ibériques en devenir: Essais publiés en hommage à la mémoire de Marcel Bataillon (1895–1977)*, pp. 583–91. Paris: Singer-Polignac.

Duviols, Pierre. 1983. "El contra idolatriam de Luis de Teruel y una versión primeriza del mito de Pachacámac-Vichama." *Revista Andina* 1, no. 2: 385–92.

Duviols, Pierre, ed. 2003. *Procesos y visitas de idolatrías: Cajatambo, siglo XVII.* 2d ed. Lima: Instituto Francés de Estudios Andinos, Pontificia Universidad Católica del Perú.

Egaña, Antonio de, ed. 1954–1986. *Monumenta peruana.* 8 vols. Rome: Monumenta Historica Societatis Iesu.

Eguiguren, Luis Antonio. 1940–1951. *Diccionario histórico cronológico de la Real y Pontificia Universidad de San Marcos y sus colegios.* 3 vols. Lima: Imprenta Torres Aguirre.

Eguiguren, Luis Antonio. 1951. *La universidad en el siglo XVI.* 2 vols. Lima: Universidad Nacional Mayor de San Marcos.

Espinoza Soriano, Waldemar. 1960. "El alcalde mayor indígena en el virreinato del Perú." *Anuario de Estudios Americanos* 17: 183–300.

Estenssoro Fuchs, Juan Carlos. 1996. "Les pouvoirs de la parole. La prédication au Pérou: De l'évangélisation à l'utopie." *Annales HSS* 51, no. 6: 1225–57.

Estenssoro Fuchs, Juan Carlos. 2003. *Del paganismo a la santidad: La incorporación de los indios del Perú al catolicismo, 1532–1750.* Translated by Gabriela Ramos. Lima: Instituto Francés de Estudios Andinos, Pontificia Universidad Católica del Perú.

Fabian, Johannes. 1983. *Time and the Other: How Anthropology Makes Its Object.* New York: Columbia University Press.

Fernández Navarrete, Pedro. [1626] 1982. *Conservación de monarquías y discursos políticos.* Edited by Michael D. Gordon. Madrid: Instituto de Estudios Fiscales.

Firbas, Paul. 2006. "Textos y textualidad en los estudios coloniales." *Latin American Research Review* 41, no. 3: 222–37.

Foucault, Michel. 1977. *Language, Counter-memory, Practice: Selected Essays and Interviews by Michel Foucault.* Edited by Donald F. Bouchard. Translated from the French by Donald F. Bouchard and Sherry Simon. Ithaca, N.Y.: Cornell University Press.

Franciscans. Provincia de los Doce Apóstoles (Perú). 1619. *Información en derecho en defensa de la exempcion absoluta que las religiones tienen de los ordinarios, y la especial de que los dotrinantes religiosos no sean por ellos visitados de costumbre ni examinados en el idioma.* Lima: Francisco Lasso.

Frasso, Pedro. 1684. *Consulta y parecer del señor don Pedro Frasso, oidor de esta Real Audiencia de los Reyes, y assessor general del govierno, al exc.mo señor don Melchor de Navarra y Rocafull, del Consejo de Estado de Su Magestad, virrey y capitán general del Perú, Tierra Firme y Chile, sobre las dudas que se han movido en la inteligencia del despacho para remediar el excesso con que los curas y dotrineros cobran de los indios derechos prohibidos por concilios, sinodales y cédulas reales.* Lima: n.p.

Frisch, Andrea. 2004. *The Invention of the Eyewitness: Witnessing and Testimony in Early Modern France.* Chapel Hill: University of North Carolina Press.

García Cabrera, Juan Carlos. 1992. "Chavín de Pariarca en el siglo XVII: Un documento sobre una doctrina de la Compañía de Jesús." *Boletín del Instituto Riva-Agüero* 19:45–64.

García Cabrera, Juan Carlos, ed. 1994. *Ofensas a Dios: Pleitos e injurias: Causas de idolatrías e hechicerías. Cajatambo, siglos XVII–XIX.* Cuzco: Centro de Estudios Regionales Andinos "Bartolomé de las Casas."

García Cabrera, Juan Carlos. 1996. "¿Por qué mintieron los indios de Cajatambo? La extirpación de idolatrías en Hacas entre 1656–1665." *Revista Andina* 14, no. 1: 7–52.

García Cabrera, Juan Carlos. 1997. "Oposiciones a parroquias y doctrinas: El catálogo de la sección Concursos, Archivo Arzobispal de Lima, siglos XVII–XIX." *Revista Andina* 15, no. 2: 421–91.

Garcilaso de la Vega, El Inca. [1609, 1617] 1960. *Comentarios reales de los Incas.* In *Obras completas del Inca Garcilaso de la Vega.* Edited by Carmelo Sáenz de Santa María. 4 vols. Madrid: Ediciones Atlas (Biblioteca de Autores Españoles).

Gareis, Iris. 1999. "Repression and Cultural Change: The 'Extirpation of Idolatry' in Colonial Peru." In *Spiritual Encounters: Interactions Between Christianity and Native Religions in Colonial America,* edited by Nicholas Griffiths and Fernando Cervantes, pp. 230–54. Lincoln: University of Nebraska Press.

Garland Ponce, Beatriz. 1994. "Las cofradías de Lima durante la colonia: Una primera aproximación." In *La venida del reino: Religión, evangelización y cultura en América, siglos XVI–XX*, coordinated by Gabriela Ramos, pp. 199–228. Cuzco: Centro de Estudios Regionales Andinos "Bartolomé de las Casas."

Gibson, Charles. 1953. "Rotation of Alcaldes in the Indian Cabildo of Mexico City." *Hispanic American Historical Review* 33, no. 2: 212–23.

González Echevarría, Roberto. [1990] 1998. *Myth and Archive: A Theory of Latin American Narrative*. Durham, N.C.: Duke University Press.

González Holguín, Diego. 1607. *Gramática y arte nueva de la lengua general de todo el Perú, llamada lengua Quichua, o lengua del Inca*. Lima: Francisco del Canto.

González Holguín, Diego. [1608] 1952. *Vocabulario de la lengua general de todo el Perú llamada lengua quichua o del Inca*. Edited by Raúl Porras Barrenechea. Lima: Universidad Nacional Mayor de San Marcos.

Goody, Jack. 1977. *The Domestication of the Savage Mind*. Cambridge, U.K.: Cambridge University Press.

Green, Richard Firth. 1999. *A Crisis of Truth: Literature and Law in Ricardian England*. Philadelphia: University of Pennsylvania Press.

Griffiths, Nicholas. 1996. *The Cross and the Serpent: Religious Repression and Resurgence in Colonial Peru*. Norman: University of Oklahoma Press.

Guaman Poma de Ayala, Felipe. [c. 1615] 1980. *El primer nueva corónica y buen gobierno*. Edited by John V. Murra and Rolena Adorno. Quechua translations by Jorge L. Urioste. Mexico City: Siglo Veintiuno.

Gutiérrez Arbulú, Laura. 1993. "Índice de la sección hechicerías e idolatrías del Archivo Arzobispal de Lima." In *Catolicismo y extirpación de idolatrías: Siglos XVI–XVIII*, coordinated by Gabriela Ramos and Henrique Urbano, pp. 105–36. Cuzco: Centro de Estudios Regionales Andinos "Bartolomé de las Casas."

Hanke, Lewis. 1949. *The Spanish Struggle for Justice in the Conquest of America*. Philadelphia: University of Pennsylvania.

Hanke, Lewis. 1959. *Aristotle and the American Indians: A Study in Race Prejudice in the Modern World*. London: Hollis and Carter.

Harrison, Regina. 1994. "The Theology of Concupiscence: Spanish-Quechua Confessional Manuals in the Andes." In *Coded Encounters: Writing, Gender, and Ethnicity in Colonial Latin America*, edited by Francisco Javier Cevallos-Candau, Jeffrey A. Cole, Nina M. Scott, and Nicomedes Suárez-Araúz, pp. 135–50. Amherst: University of Massachusetts Press.

Harrison, Regina. 2002. "Pérez Bocanegra's *Ritual formulario*: Khipu Knots and Confession." In *Narrative Threads: Accounting and Recounting in Andean Khipu*, edited by Jeffrey Quilter and Gary Urton, pp. 266–90. Austin: University of Texas Press.

Haskett, Robert. 1991. *Indigenous Rulers: An Ethnohistory of Town Government in Colonial Cuernavaca*. Albuquerque: University of New Mexico Press.

Heath, Shirley Brice, and Richard Laprade. 1982. "Castilian Colonization and Indigenous Languages: The Cases of Quechua and Aymara." In *Language Spread: Studies in Diffusion and Social Change,* edited by Robert L. Cooper, pp. 118–47. Bloomington: Indiana University Press.

Hevia Bolaños, Juan de. 1619. *Curia filipica.* Madrid: Viuda de Alonso Martín.

Higgins, Antony. 2000. *Constructing the Criollo Archive: Subjects of Knowledge in the Bibliotheca Mexicana and the Rusticatio Mexicana.* West Lafayette, Ind.: Purdue University Press.

Huerta, Alonso de. [1616] 1993. *Arte de la lengua quechua general de los yndios de este reyno del Piru.* Edited by Ruth Moya and Eduardo Villacís. Quito: Proyecto Educación Bilingüe Intercultural, Corporación Editora Nacional.

Infantes, Víctor. 1998. *De las primeras letras: Cartillas y doctrinas españolas de los siglos XV y XVI.* Salamanca, Spain: Ediciones Universidad de Salamanca.

Itier, César. 1991. "Lengua general y comunicación escrita: Cinco cartas en quechua de Cotahuasi-1616." *Revista Andina* 9, no. 1: 65–107.

Itier, César. 1992. "La tradición oral quechua antigua en los procesos de idolatrías de Cajatambo." *Boletín del Instituto Francés de Estudios Andinos* 21, no. 3: 1009–51.

Jiménez de la Espada, Marcos, ed. 1965. *Relaciones geográficas de Indias.* 3 vols. Madrid: Ediciones Atlas (Biblioteca de Autores Españoles).

Jouve Martín, José Ramón. 2005. *Esclavos de la ciudad letrada: Esclavitud, escritura y colonialismo en Lima (1650–1700).* Lima: Instituto de Estudios Peruanos.

Jurado Palomino, Bartolomé, trans. [1643] 1649. *Declaración copiosa de las cuatro partes más essenciales y necessarias de la doctrina christiana [compuesta por el cardenal Roberto Belarminio].* Lima: Jorge López de Herrera.

Kagan, Richard L. 1981. *Lawsuits and Litigants in Castile, 1500–1700.* Chapel Hill: University of North Carolina Press.

Kamen, Henry. 1993. *Crisis and Change in Early Modern Spain.* Aldershot, U.K.: Variorium.

Karttunen, Frances. 1994. *Between Worlds: Interpreters, Guides, and Survivors.* New Brunswick, N.J.: Rutgers University Press.

Kellogg, Susan. 1995. *Law and the Transformation of Aztec Culture, 1500–1700.* Norman: University of Oklahoma Press.

Klor de Alva, J. Jorge. 1991. "Colonizing Souls: The Failure of the Indian Inquisition and the Rise of Penitential Discipline." In *Cultural Encounters: The Impact of the Inquisition in Spain and the New World,* edited by Mary Elizabeth Perry and Anne J. Cruz, pp. 3–22. Berkeley: University of California Press.

Konetzke, Richard, ed. 1953. *Colección de documentos para la historia de la formación social de Hispanoamérica, 1493–1810.* 2 vols. Madrid: Consejo Superior de Investigaciones Científicas.

Las Casas, Bartolomé de. [1555–1559] 1967. *Apologética historia sumaria.* Edited by Edmundo O'Gorman. Mexico City: Universidad Nacional Autónoma de México.

Lavallé, Bernard. 1993. *Las promesas ambiguas: Ensayos sobre el criollismo colonial en los Andes.* Lima: Pontificia Universidad Católica del Perú, Instituto Riva-Agüero.

Lease, Gary. 1996. "Denunciation as a Tool of Ecclesiastical Control: The Case of Roman Catholic Modernism." *Journal of Modern History* 68, no. 4: 819–30.

León Pinelo, Diego de. 1661. *Mandó que se imprimiesse este escrito el Excelent.mo señor Conde de Alva de Aliste, y de Villaflor, grande de Castilla, virrey destos Reynos del Peru, en la Iunta, que se ha formado, por cedula de Su Magestad, de 21 de setiembre de 1660 años.* Lima: n.p.

León-Portilla, Miguel. 1974. "Testimonios nahuas sobre la conquista espiritual." *Estudios de Cultura Náhuatl* 9:11–36.

Leuridan Huys, Johan. 1997. *José de Acosta y el origen de la idea de misión: Perú, siglo XVI.* Cuzco: Centro de Estudios Regionales Andinos "Bartolomé de las Casas."

Levillier, Roberto, ed. 1921–1925. *Gobernantes del Perú: Cartas y papeles, siglo XVI.* 8 vols. Madrid: Sucesores de Rivadeneyra.

"Libro de la fundación del colegio de los hijos de caciques." 1923. *Inca* 1, no. 4: 779–883.

Liñán y Cisneros, Melchor de. c. 1685. *Ofensa, y defensa de la libertad eclesiastica.* Lima (?): n.p.

Lisson Cháves, Emilio, ed. 1943–1948. *La Iglesia de España en el Perú.* Seville: n.p.

Loayza, Jerónimo de. [1545] 1951–1954. "Instrucción de la orden que se a de tener en la doctrina de los naturales." In *Concilios limenses (1551–1772)*, vol. 2, edited by Rubén Vargas Ugarte, pp.139–48. Lima: Tipografía Peruana.

Lobo Guerrero, Bartolomé, and Fernando Arias de Ugarte. [1613, 1636] 1987. *Sínodos de Lima de 1613 y 1636.* Madrid and Salamanca: Consejo Superior de Investigaciones Científicas, Instituto de Historia de la Teología, Universidad Pontificia de Salamanca.

Locke, Leland L. 1923. *The Ancient Quipu, or Peruvian Knot Record.* New York: American Museum of Natural History.

Lockhart, James. 1968. *Spanish Peru (1532–1560): A Colonial Society.* Madison: University of Wisconsin Press.

Lockhart, James. 1972. *The Men of Cajamarca: A Social and Biographical Study of the First Conquerors of Peru.* Austin: University of Texas Press.

Lockhart, James. 1992. *The Nahuas after the Conquest: A Social and Cultural History of the Indians of Central Mexico, Sixteenth Through Eighteenth Centuries.* Stanford, Calif.: Stanford University Press.

Lockhart, James, ed. and trans. 1993. *We People Here: Nahuatl Accounts of the Conquest of Mexico.* Berkeley: University of California Press.

Lockhart, James. 1999. *Of Things of the Indies: Essays Old and New in Early Latin American History.* Stanford, Calif.: Stanford University Press.

Lohmann Villena, Guillermo. 1957. *El corregidor de indios en el Perú bajo los Austrias.* Madrid: Ediciones Cultura Hispánica.

Lohmann Villena, Guillermo. 1961. "En torno de Juan de Hevia Bolaños: La incógnita de su personalidad y los enigmas de sus libros." *Anuario de Historia del Derecho Español* 31:121–61.

López y Martínez, Juan Luis. 1685. *Discurso iuridico, historico-politico, en defensa de la jurisdicion real: Ilustracion de la prouision de veinte de febrero del año passado de 1684.* Lima: n.p.

Loza, Carmen Beatriz. 1998. "Du bon usage des *quipus* face à l'administration coloniale espagnole (1550–1600)." *Population* 53, nos. 1–2: 139–59.

Luján Muñoz, Jorge. 1981. "La literatura notarial en España e Hispanoamérica, 1500–1820." *Anuario de Estudios Americanos* 38:101–16.

MacCormack, Sabine. 1985. "'The Heart Has Its Reasons': Predicaments of Missionary Christianity in Early Colonial Peru." *Hispanic American Historical Review* 65, no. 3: 443–66.

MacCormack, Sabine. 1989. "Atahualpa and the Book." *Dispositio* 14, nos. 36–38: 141–68.

MacCormack, Sabine. 1991. *Religion in the Andes: Vision and Imagination in Early Colonial Peru.* Princeton, N.J.: Princeton University Press.

Mannheim, Bruce. 1991. *The Language of the Inka since the European Invasion.* Austin: University of Texas Press.

Mannheim, Bruce. 1992. "The Inka Language in the Colonial World." *Colonial Latin American Review* 1, nos. 1–2: 77–108.

Marbán, Pedro. 1702. *Arte de la lengua moxa, con su vocabulario y cathecismo compuesto.* Lima: Joseph de Contreras.

Martínez, Manuel Silvestre. 1791. *Librería de jueces.* 10 vols. Madrid: Benito Cano.

Martínez de Ripalda, Jerónimo. 1591. *Doctrina christiana con una exposicion breue.* Burgos, Spain: Philippe de Iunta.

Marzal, Manuel M. 1983. *La transformación religiosa peruana.* Lima: Pontificia Universidad Católica del Perú.

Mateos, Francisco, ed. [1600] 1944. *Historia general de la Compañía de Jesús en la provincia del Perú.* 2 vols. Madrid: Consejo Superior de Investigaciones Científicas.

Matienzo, Juan de. [1567] 1967. *Gobierno del Perú.* Edited by Guillermo Lohmann Villena. Lima: Institut Français D'Études Andines.

Medelius, Mónica, and José Carlos de la Puente Luna. 2004. "Curacas, bienes y quipus en un documento toledano (Jauja, 1570)." *Histórica* 28, no. 2: 35–82.

Medina, José Toribio. 1904. *La imprenta en Lima (1584–1824).* Vol. 1. Santiago, Chile: José Toribio Medina.

Meléndez, Juan de. 1681. *Tesoros verdaderos de las Yndias en la historia de la gran provincia de San Juan Bautista del Perú.* Rome: Nicolas Angel Tinassio.

Melgar, Estaban Sancho de. 1691. *Arte de la lengua general del Ynga llamada Quechua*. Lima: Diego de Lyra.

Meneses, Teodoro L. 1982. "Cuatricentenario de la cátedra de quechua en San Marcos." In *Aula quechua*, edited by Rodolfo Cerrón-Palomino, pp. 237–46. Lima: Ediciones Signo.

Mercado, Thomas de. 1569. *Tratos y contratos de mercaderes y tratantes discididos y determinados*. Salamanca: Mathias Gast.

Metcalf, Alida C. 2005. *Go-Betweens and the Colonization of Brazil, 1500–1600*. Austin: University of Texas Press.

Mignolo, Walter D. 1989. "Literacy and Colonization: The New World Experience." In *1492–1992: Re/Discovering Colonial Writing*, edited by René Jara and Nicholas Spadaccini, pp. 51–96. Minneapolis: University of Minnesota Press.

Mignolo, Walter D. 1995. *The Darker Side of the Renaissance: Literacy, Territoriality, and Colonization*. Ann Arbor: University of Michigan Press.

Millones, Luis. 1978. "Religión y poder en los Andes: Los curacas idólatras de la sierra central." In *Etnohistoria y antropología andina*, edited by Marcia Koth de Paredes and Amalia Castelli, pp. 253–73. Lima: Centro de Proyección Cristiana.

Mills, Kenneth. 1994. "The Limits of Religious Coercion in Mid-colonial Peru." *Past and Present* 145:84–121.

Mills, Kenneth. 1996. "Bad Christians in Colonial Peru." *Colonial Latin American Review* 5, no. 2: 183–218.

Mills, Kenneth. 1997. *Idolatry and Its Enemies: Colonial Andean Religion and Extirpation, 1640–1750*. Princeton, N.J.: Princeton University Press.

Mills, Kenneth. 2007. "The Naturalization of Andean Christianities." In *The Cambridge History of Christianity*, vol. 6, edited by R. Po-Chia Hsia, pp. 508–39. Cambridge, U.K.: Cambridge University Press.

Molina, Diego de. [1649] 1928. "Sermones de la cuaresma en lengua quechua." In "Un libro interesante," by Carlos Romero. *Revista Histórica* 9, no. 1: 51–87.

Monterroso y Alvarado, Gabriel de. 1566. *Practica civil y criminal e instruccion de escrivanos*. Valladolid, Spain: Francisco Fernández de Córdova.

Montesinos, Fernando de. [1642] 1906. *Anales del Perú*. Madrid: Gabriel L. y del Horno.

Mumford, Jeremy Ravi. 2008. "Litigation as Ethnography in Sixteenth-Century Peru: Polo de Ondegardo and the Mitimaes." *Hispanic American Historical Review* 88, no. 1: 5–40.

Murúa, Martín de. [c. 1611] 2001. *Historia general del Perú*. Edited by Manuel Ballesteros Gaibrois. Madrid: Dastin.

Murúa, Martín de. [1590] 2004. *Códice Murúa: Historia y genealogía de los reyes incas del Perú del padre mercedario Fray Martín de Murúa*. Edited by Juan M. Ossio. Madrid: Testimonio Compañía Editorial.

Nalle, Sara T. 1992. *God in La Mancha: Religious Reform and the People of Cuenca, 1500–1650*. Baltimore: Johns Hopkins University Press.

Nebrija, Antonio de. [1492] 1992. *Gramática de la lengua castellana*. Madrid: Ediciones de Cultura Hispánica.

Nussdorfer, Laurie. 1993. "Writing and the Power of Speech: Notaries and Artisans in Baroque Rome." In *Culture and Identity in Early Modern Europe (1500–1800): Essays in Honor of Natalie Zemon Davis*, edited by Barbara B. Diefendorf and Carla Hesse, pp. 103–18. Ann Arbor: University of Michigan Press.

Olaechea Labayen, Juan B. 1962. "Los colegios de hijos de caciques a raíz de los terceros concilios provinciales de Lima y México." *Missionalia Hispanica* 19:109–13.

Olaechea Labayen, Juan B. 1969. "Participación de los indios en la tarea evangélica." *Missionalia Hispanica* 26:241–56.

Olavarrieta Medrano, Miguel de. 1717. *Recuerdo de las obligaciones del ministerio apostólico en la cura de las almas*. Lima: Diego de Lyra.

Olsen, David R. 1994. *The World on Paper: The Conceptual and Cognitive Implications of Writing and Reading*. Cambridge, U.K.: Cambridge University Press.

O'Malley, John W. 1993. *The First Jesuits*. Cambridge, Mass.: Harvard University Press.

O'Phelan Godoy, Scarlett. 1997. *Kurakas sin sucesiones: Del cacique al alcalde de indios (Perú y Bolivia, 1750–1835)*. Cuzco: Centro de Estudios Regionales Andinos "Bartolomé de las Casas."

Oré, Luis Jerónimo de. [1598] 1992. *Symbolo catholico indiano*. Edited by Antonine Tibesar. Lima: Australis.

Ortiz de Cervantes, Juan. 1620. *Informacion en favor del derecho que tienen los nacidos en las Indias a ser preferidos en las prelacias, dignidades, canongias, y otros beneficios eclesiasticos, y oficios seculares de ellas*. Madrid: Viuda de Martín Alonso.

Ortiz de Salcedo, Francisco. 1691. *Curia eclesiástica*. Pamplona, Spain: Juan Micón.

Pachacuti Yamqui Salcamaygua, Juan de Santacruz. [c. 1613] 1993. *Relación de antigüedades deste reyno del Pirú*. Edited by Pierre Duviols and César Itier. Cuzco: Institut Français d'Études Andines, Centro de Estudios Regionales Andinos "Bartolomé de las Casas."

Padilla, Juan de. [1657] 1966. "Memorial de D. Juan de Padilla." In *Historia general del Perú: Virreinato (1596–1689)*, vol. 3, by Rubén Vargas Ugarte, pp. 391–420. Lima: Editor Carlos Milla Batres.

Pagden, Anthony. [1982] 1986. *The Fall of Natural Man: The American Indian and the Origins of Comparative Ethnology*. Cambridge, U.K.: Cambridge University Press.

Pardo, Osvaldo F. 2004. *The Origins of Mexican Catholicism: Nahua Rituals and Christian Sacraments in Sixteenth-Century Mexico*. Ann Arbor: University of Michigan Press.

Pardo, Osvaldo F. 2006. "How to Punish Indians: Law and Cultural Change in Early Colonial Mexico." *Comparative Study of Society and History* 89:79–109.

Peña Montenegro, Alonso de la. [1668] 1985. *Itinerario para párrocos de indios, en que se tratan las materias mas particulares tocantes a ellos para su buena administracion.* Guayaquil, Ecuador: Ediciones Corporación de Estudios y Publicaciones.

Pérez Bocanegra, Juan. 1631. *Ritual formulario e institución de curas.* Lima: Geronymo de Contreras.

Peters, Edward. 1985. *Torture.* New York: Blackwell.

Pidal, Pedro José, and Miguel Salvá, eds. [1842–1895] 1964–1975. *Colección de documentos inéditos para la historia de España.* 113 vols. Madrid: La Viuda de Calero.

Platt, Tristan. 2002. "'Without Deceit or Lies': Variable *Chinu* Readings during a Sixteenth-Century Tribute-Restitution Trial." In *Narrative Threads: Accounting and Recounting in Andean Khipu,* edited by Jeffrey Quilter and Gary Urton, pp. 225–65. Austin: University of Texas Press.

Polia Meconi, Mario, ed. 1999. *La cosmovisión religiosa andina en los documentos inéditos del Archivo Romano de la Compañía de Jesús (1581–1752).* Lima: Pontificia Universidad Católica del Perú.

Polo de Ondegardo, Juan. [1559] 1906. "Instrucción contra las ceremonias y ritos que usan los indios conforme al tiempo de su infidelidad." *Revista Histórica* 1, no. 1: 192–231.

Poloni-Simard, Jacques. 2005. "Los indios ante la justicia: El pleito como parte de la consolidación de la sociedad colonial." In *Máscaras, tretas y rodeos del discurso colonial en los Andes,* edited by Bernard Lavallé, pp. 177–88. Lima: Instituto Francés de Estudios Andinos, Pontificia Universidad Católica del Perú, Instituto Riva-Agüero.

Prado, Pablo de. 1641. *Directorio espiritual en la lengua española, y quichua general del Inga.* Lima: Jorge López de Herrera.

Quilter, Jeffrey, and Gary Urton, eds. 2002. *Narrative Threads: Accounting and Recounting in Andean Khipu.* Austin: University of Texas Press.

Quiroga, Pedro de. [c. 1563] 1992. *Coloquios de la verdad.* Edited by Daisy Rípodas Ardanaz. Valladolid, Spain: Instituto de Cooperación Iberoamericana, Casa-Museo Colón, Seminario Americanista de la Universidad de Valladolid.

Rama, Ángel. [1984] 1996. *The Lettered City.* Translated by John Charles Chasteen. Durham, N.C.: Duke University Press.

Ramos Gavilán, Alonso. 1621. *Historia del celebre santuario de Nuestra Señora de Copacabana, y sus milagros e invencion de la Cruz de Carabuco.* Lima: Geronymo de Contreras.

Rappaport, Joanne. 1994. "Object and Alphabet: Andean Indians and Documents in the Colonial Period." In *Writing Without Words: Alternative Literacies in Mesoamerica and the Andes,* edited by Elizabeth Hill Boone and Walter D. Mignolo, pp. 271–92. Durham, N.C.: Duke University Press.

Rappaport, Joanne, and Tom Cummins. 1998. "Between Images and Writing: The Ritual of the King's *Quillca.*" *Colonial Latin American Review* 7, no. 1: 7–32.

Recopilación de leyes de los reinos de las Indias. 1841. 4 vols. Madrid: Boix.

Reinaga Salazar, Juan de la. 1626. *Memorial discursivo sobre el oficio de protector general de los indios del Pirú.* Madrid: Imprenta Real.

Restall, Matthew. 1997. *The Maya World: Yucatec Culture and Society, 1550–1850.* Stanford, Calif.: Stanford University Press.

Restall, Matthew. 2003. "A History of the New Philology and the New Philology in History." *Latin American Research Review* 38, no. 1: 113–34.

Ribera, Luis de. 1621. *Memorial que se dio por parte de Don Luys de Ribera a su Magestad, en su Real Consejo de Indias, sobre quitar las doctrinas y curatos que administran Frayles en el Reyno del Pirú, y darlas á Clerigos aprouados.* Madrid (?): n.p.

Rivarola, José Luis. 1985. *Lengua, comunicación e historia del Perú.* Lima: Editorial Lumen.

Rivarola, José Luis. 2000. *Español andino: Textos bilingües de los siglos XVI y XVII.* Frankfurt, Madrid: Vervuert, Iberoamericana.

Rivet, Paul, and Georges de Créqui-Monfort. 1951. *Bibliographie des langues aymará et kicua.* Vol. 1. Paris: Institut d'Ethnologie.

Romero, Carlos. 1928. "Un libro interesante." *Revista Histórica* 9, no. 1: 51–87.

Roxo Mexía y Ocón, Juan. 1648. *Arte de la lengua general de los indios del Perú.* Lima: Jorge López de Herrera.

Ruigómez Gómez, Carmen. 1988. *Una política indigenista de los Habsburgo: El protector de indios en el Perú.* Madrid: Ediciones de Cultura Hispánica.

Ruiz de Montoya, Antonio. 1639. *Tesoro de la lengua guaraní.* Madrid: Juan Sánchez.

Ruiz de Montoya, Antonio. 1640a. *Arte y vocabulario de la lengua guaraní.* Madrid: Juan Sánchez.

Ruiz de Montoya, Antonio. 1640b. *Catecismo de la lengua guaraní.* Madrid: Diego Díaz de la Carrera.

Saavedra Fajardo, Diego de. [1640] 1659. *Idea de un principe politico christiano, representado en cien empresas.* Amsterdam: J. Janszoon.

Saignes, Thierry. 1993. "Borracheras andinas: ¿Por qué los indios ebrios hablan en español?" In *Borrachera y memoria: La experiencia de lo sagrado en los Andes,* edited by Thierry Saignes, pp. 43–71. Lima: Hisbol, Instituto Francés de Estudios Andinos.

Saignes, Thierry. 1999. "The Colonial Condition in the Quechua-Aymara Heartland (1570–1780)." In *The Cambridge History of the Native Peoples of the Americas,* vol. 3:2, *South America,* edited by Frank Salomon and Stuart B. Schwartz, pp. 59–137. Cambridge, U.K.: Cambridge University Press.

Salomon, Frank. 1991. "Introduction: The Huarochirí Manuscript." In *The Huarochirí Manuscript: A Testament of Ancient and Colonial Andean Religion,* edited and translated by Frank Salomon and George L. Urioste, pp. 1–38. Austin: University of Texas Press.

Salomon, Frank. 2004. *The Cord Keepers: Khipus and Cultural Life in a Peruvian Village.* Durham, N.C.: Duke University Press.

Salomon, Frank, and Karen Spalding. 2002. "Cartas atadas con quipus: Sebastián Francisco de Melo, María Micaela Chinchano y la represión de la rebelión de Huarochirí de 1750." In *El hombre y los Andes: Homenaje a Franklin Pease G.Y.,* vol. 2, edited by Javier Flores Espinoza and Rafael Varón Gabai, pp. 857–70. Lima: Pontificia Universidad Católica del Perú.

Salomon, Frank, and George L. Urioste, eds. and trans. [c. 1608] 1991. *The Huarochirí Manuscript: A Testament of Ancient and Colonial Andean Religion.* Austin: University of Texas Press.

Sampson, Geoffrey. 1985. *Writing Systems: A Linguistic Introduction.* Stanford, Calif.: Stanford University Press.

Santo Tomás, Domingo de. [1560] 1951. *Lexicon, o vocabulario de la lengua general del Peru.* Lima: Universidad Nacional Mayor de San Marcos.

Santo Tomás, Domingo de. [1560] 1995. *Grammatica o arte de la lengua general de los indios de los reynos del Peru.* Edited by Rodolfo Cerrón-Palomino. Cuzco: Centro de Estudios Regionales Andinos "Bartolomé de las Casas."

Schoeck, Richard J. 1983. "Lawyers and Rhetoric in Sixteenth-Century England." In *Renaissance Eloquence: Studies in the Theory and Practice of Renaissance Rhetoric,* edited by James J. Murphy, pp. 274–91. Berkeley: University of California Press.

Scott, James C. 1985. *Weapons of the Weak: Everyday Forms of Peasant Resistance.* New Haven, Conn.: Yale University Press.

Sempat Assadourian, Carlos. 2002. "String Registries: Native Accounting and Memory According to the Colonial Sources." In *Narrative Threads: Accounting and Recounting in Andean Khipu,* edited by Jeffrey Quilter and Gary Urton, pp. 119–50. Austin: University of Texas Press.

Silverblatt, Irene. 1987. *Sun, Moon, and Witches: Gender Ideologies and Class in Inca and Colonial Peru.* Princeton, N.J.: Princeton University Press.

Solano, Francisco de. 1975. "El intérprete: Uno de los ejes de la aculturación." In *Estudios sobre política indigenista española en América: Terceras jornadas americanistas de la Universidad de Valladolid,* vol. 1:265–78. Valladolid, Spain: Universidad de Valladolid.

Solórzano Pereira, Juan de. 1648. *Política indiana.* Madrid: Diego Díaz de la Carrera.

Spalding, Karen. 1970. "Social Climbers: Changing Patterns of Mobility among the Indians of Colonial Peru." *Hispanic American Historical Review* 50, no. 4: 645–64.

Spalding, Karen. 1973. "*Kurakas* and Commerce: A Chapter in the Evolution of Andean Society." *Hispanic American Historical Review* 53, no. 4: 581–99.

Spalding, Karen. 1974. *De indio a campesino: Cambios en la estructura social del Perú colonial.* Lima: Instituto de Estudios Peruanos.

Spalding, Karen. 1984. *Huarochirí: An Andean Society under Inca and Spanish Rule*. Stanford, Calif.: Stanford University Press.

Spalding, Karen. 2002. "La otra cara de la reciprocidad." In *Incas e indios cristianos: Elites indígenas e identidades cristianas en los Andes coloniales,* edited by Jean-Jacques Decoster, pp. 61–78. Cuzco: Centro de Estudios Regionales Andinos "Bartolomé de las Casas," Instituto Francés de Estudios Andinos, Asociación Kuraka.

Stavig, Ward. 2000. "Ambiguous Visions: Nature, Law, and Culture in Indigenous-Spanish Land Relations in Colonial Peru." *Hispanic American Historical Review* 80, no. 1: 77–111.

Stern, Steve J. [1982] 1993. *Peru's Indian Peoples and the Challenge of Spanish Conquest: Huamanga to 1640*. Madison: University of Wisconsin Press.

Stock, Brian. 1983. *The Implications of Literacy: Written Language and Models of Interpretation in the Eleventh and Twelfth Centuries*. Princeton, N.J.: Princeton University Press.

Stone, Cynthia L. 2004. *In Place of Gods and Kings: Authorship and Identity in the Relación de Michoacán*. Norman: University of Oklahoma Press.

Street, Brian V. 1984. *Literacy in Theory and Practice*. Cambridge, U.K.: Cambridge University Press.

Szemiński, Jan. 1987. *Un kuraca, un dios y una historia: Relación de antigüedades deste reyno del Pirú por Don Joan de Santa Cruz Pacha Cuti Yamqui Salca Maygua*. Jujuy, Argentina: Antropología e Historia 2.

Taylor, Gerald, ed. and trans. [1987] 1999. *Ritos y tradiciones de Huarochirí*. Lima: Instituto Francés de Estudios Andinos, Banco Central de Reserva del Perú, Universidad Particular Ricardo Palma.

Taylor, Gerald. 2000. "Lengua general y lenguas particulares en la antigua provincia de Yauyos." In *Camac, camay y camasca y otros ensayos sobre Huarochirí y Yauyos,* pp. 35–69. Cuzco: Centro de Estudios Regionales Andinos "Bartolomé de las Casas."

Taylor, Gerald. 2001. "Un sermón en quechua de Diego de Molina (Huanuco, 1649)." *Boletín del Instituto Francés de Estudios Andinos* 30, no. 2: 211–31.

Taylor, William B. 1996. *Magistrates of the Sacred: Priests and Parishioners in Eighteenth-Century Mexico*. Stanford, Calif.: Stanford University Press.

Tedlock, Dennis. 1993. "Torture in the Archives: Mayans Meet Europeans." *American Anthropologist* 95, no. 1: 139–52.

Tentler, Thomas N. 1977. *Sin and Confession on the Eve of the Reformation*. Princeton, N.J.: Princeton University Press.

Tercero catecismo y exposición de la doctrina christiana por sermones. [1585] 1985. In *Doctrina christiana y catecismo para instrucción de indios,* edited by Luciano Pereña, pp. 333–777. Madrid: Consejo Superior de Investigaciones Científicas.

Tibesar, Antonine S., and Nicolás López. 1971. "The Lima Pastors, 1750–1820: Their Origins and Studies as Taken from Their Autobiographies." *The Americas* 28, no. 1: 39–56.

Torero, Alfredo. 1995. "Acerca de la lengua chinchaysuyo." In *Del siglo de oro al siglo de las luces: Lenguaje y sociedad en los Andes del siglo XVIII,* coordinated by César Itier, pp. 13–31. Cuzco: Centro de Estudios Regionales Andinos "Bartolomé de las Casas."

Torre Revello, José. 1960. "Las cartillas para enseñar a leer a los niños en América española." *Thesaurus* 15:214–34.

Torres, Julio, ed. 1970. *Constituciones synodales del obispado de Guamanga (Perú), 1629.* Cuernavaca, Mexico: Centro Intercultural de Documentación.

Torres Rubio, Diego de. [1619, 1700] 1963. *Arte de la lengua quichua, con las adiciones que hizo P. Juan de Figueredo.* Edited by Luis A. Pardo. Cuzco: Editorial H. G. Rozas.

Townsend, Camilla. 2006. *Malintzin's Choices: An Indian Woman in the Conquest of Mexico.* Albuquerque: University of New Mexico Press.

Trexler, Richard C. 1987. *Church and Community, 1200–1600: Studies in the History of Florence and New Spain.* Rome: Edizioni di Storia e Letteratura.

Urioste, Jorge L. 1980. "Estudio analítico del quechua en la *Nueva Corónica*." In *El primer nueva corónica y buen gobierno* (c. 1615), by Felipe Guaman Poma de Ayala, edited by John V. Murra and Rolena Adorno, Quechua translations by Jorge L. Urioste, pp. xx–xxxi. Mexico City: Siglo Veintiuno.

Urton, Gary. 1998. "From Knots to Narratives: Reconstructing the Art of Historical Record Keeping in the Andes from Spanish Transcriptions of Inka *Khipus*." *Ethnohistory* 45, no. 3: 409–38.

Urton, Gary. 2002. "An Overview of Spanish Colonial Commentary on Andean Knotted-String Records." In *Narrative Threads: Accounting and Recounting in Andean Khipu,* edited by Jeffrey Quilter and Gary Urton, pp. 3–25. Austin: University of Texas Press.

Valdivia, Luis de. 1606. *Arte y gramática general de la lengua que corre en todo el reyno de Chile.* Lima: Francisco del Canto.

Valdivia, Luis de. 1607a. *Confessionario breve en la lengua allentiac.* Lima: Francisco del Canto.

Valdivia, Luis de. 1607b. *Doctrina christiana y cathecismo en la lengua allentiac.* Lima: Francisco del Canto.

Valtón, Emilio, ed. 1947. *El primer libro de alfabetización en América: Cartilla para enseñar a leer, impresa por Pedro Ocharte en México, 1569.* Mexico City: Antigua Librería Robredo.

Vargas Ugarte, Rubén, ed. 1951–1954. *Concilios limenses (1551–1772).* 3 vols. Lima: Tipografía Peruana.

Vargas Ugarte, Rubén. 1953–1962. *Historia de la Iglesia en el Perú.* 5 vols. Lima and Burgos: Imprenta Santa María and Imprenta de Aldecoa.

Vargas Ugarte, Rubén. 1963–1965. *Historia de la Compañía de Jesús en el Perú.* 4 vols. Burgos: Imprenta de Aldecoa.

Vargas Ugarte, Rubén. 1966. *Historia general del Perú: Virreinato (1596–1689).* Vol. 3. Lima: Editor Carlos Milla Batres.

Varón Gabai, Rafael. 1982. "Cofradías de indios y poder local en el Perú colonial: Huaraz, siglo XVII." *Allpanchis* 17, no. 20: 127–46.

Vega, Feliciano de. 1639. *Constituciones synodales del obispado de la ciudad de Nuestra Señora de La Paz, en el Perú.* Lima: Geronymo de Contreras.

Vega Bazán, Estanislao de. 1656. *Testimonio auténtico de una idolatría muy sutil que el demonio avia introducido entre los indios.* Lima: Julian Santos.

Velázquez de Ovando y Zárate, Gutierre. c. 1658. *Memorial por via de desceptacion, para su magestad de nuestro Rey, y señor Felipe Quarto, en fauor de los naturales originarios benemeritos de las prouincias indianas, assi españoles, como indios.* Madrid (?): n.p.

Villagómez, Pedro de. 1649. *Carta pastoral de exortación e instrucción contra las idolatrías de los indios del Arçobispado de Lima.* Lima: Jorge López de Herrera.

Viñao Frago, Antonio. 1999. "Alfabetización y primeras letras (siglos XVI–XVII)." In *Escribir y leer en el siglo de Cervantes,* compiled by Antonio Castillo Gómez, pp. 39–84. Madrid: Gedisa.

Weisser, Michael. 1980. "Crime and Punishment in Early Modern Spain." In *Crime and the Law: The Social History of Crime in Western Europe since 1500,* edited by V. A. C. Gatrell, Bruce Lenman, and Geoffrey Parker, pp. 76–96. London: Europa Publications Limited.

Wood, Stephanie. 2003. *Transcending Conquest: Nahua Views of Spanish Colonial Mexico.* Norman: University of Oklahoma Press.

Wyss, Hilary E. 2000. *Writing Indians: Literacy, Christianity, and Native Community in Early America.* Amherst: University of Massachusetts Press.

Yannakakis, Yanna. 2008. *The Art of Being In-Between: Native Intermediaries, Indian Identity, and Local Rule in Colonial Oaxaca.* Durham, N.C.: Duke University Press.

Yrolo Calar, Nicolás de. 1605. *Primera parte de la politica de escrituras de Nicolas de Yrolo Calar, natural de Cadiz.* Mexico City: Diego López Dávalos.

Index

Acas: extirpation of idolatries in, 129, 139, 141–45, 147; linguistic situation in, 60; litigation in, 158, 191

Achacata, Gerónimo de, 30

Acosta, José de: and clerical reform, 120, 130, 174; on corporal punishment of Indians, 111; on idolatry, 139–40, 142, 236n23, 237n29; on indigenous fiestas and rituals, 150, 240n52, 241n66; on indigenous languages, 46; on indigenous nobility, 20–21, 138–39; on interpreters in confession, 88; on khipus, 75, 79–80, 81; on legal testimony by Indians, 231n64; and linguistic policy, 45, 211n27; on native lawsuits, 185–86; and Third Provincial Council works, 3, 22, 46–47, 140–41; on writing's civilizing power, 200n5

Adorno, Rolena, 4–5, 133, 181

alcaldes, of cabildo: in confession manuals, 113; corporal punishments for, 103, 105 fig. 12; cruelty of, 113; duties of, 76–77, 117–18, 119 fig. 15, 218n8; jurisdiction of, 207n68

alcaldes, of parish. See fiscales, of parish

Alfonso X, el Sabio, 30, 129, 166, 213n46

alguaciles, of cabildo: in confession manuals, 113; duties of, 117

alguaciles, of parish, 19–20

Álvarez, Bartolomé, 13–15, 26, 41, 172

Ambar: litigation in, 148–49, 151–57, 159, 161, 179, 221n35, 223n49

Andahuaylillas: church of, 98 fig. 11; confession in, 73, 240n54; legal dispute over, 97–98, 223n51

Archive, concept of the, 11–12, 71, 100, 130–31, 194

Arias de Ugarte, Hernando: and litigation in Cajatambo, 104, 121, 124, 128; on Quechua requirement for clergy, 63; synodal constitutions, 22

Arriaga, Pablo José de: on Andean religion, 140, 143; and assistants of extirpation, 135, 138, 235n18; on catechesis, 140–41; and education of indigenous nobility, 28; on khipus, 87; on parish assistants, 3, 57–58, 239n52

Atahualpa, 7, 14, 18, 79

attorneys. See legal agents

Avendaño, Fernando de: and central Quechua, 64–65; on idolatry ministers, 237n29; on khipu specialists, 89; sermons of, 62, 140, 215–16n74, 236n24; visita in Cajatambo of, 126

Ávila, Francisco de: and Cuzco
Quechua, 63; on idolatry ministers, 237n29; and litigation in San
Damián, 89–90, 113, 233–34n6,
240n59; on parish assistants, 3; petitions for benefice, 226n13; sermons
of, 62–63, 140; visita in Huarochirí
of, 132–34, 138–39, 144, 158

Barzana, Alonso de, 49
Benton, Lauren, 193
Benveniste, Émile, 85, 86
Bertonio, Ludovico, 30
Bolívar y de la Redonda, Pedro de, 65,
215n73
Borja y Aragón, Francisco de, 42, 171,
235n15
Bouwsma, William, 192
Brundage, James, 170–71
Burns, Kathryn, 93, 107

cabildo de indios: in Ambar, 155–56,
159; of Chincheros, 118 fig. 14; election of officers, 117; and electoral
conflict, 121, 171, 230nn58–59; founding of, 77; and litigation, 168; and
parish administration, 117–18, 120.
See also cabildo officers
cabildo officers: corporal punishments
for, 103; duties of, 76–77, 109, 117;
as legal agents, 166, 176–77; privileges of, 109, 226n14; ties to Andean
religion, 147. See also alcaldes, of
cabildo; alguaciles, of cabildo; mayordomos; notary-khipukamayuqs;
regidores
caciques: in Guaman Poma, 40; and
legal testimony, 122; as monitors of
clergy, 217n85; as parish assistants,
20; privileges of, 198n8, 226n14;
traditional base of authority, 212n42.
See also nobility, indigenous

Caja Malqui, Rodrigo Flores. See
Flores Caja Malqui, Rodrigo
Cajamarca, 7, 14, 18, 79, 217n86
Calancha, Antonio de la, 83
Campo y de la Reinaga, Nicolas Matías
del, 182
cantors: duties of, 19
Capcha, Agustín, 6, 134, 135, 153–54,
158, 159; gives testimony of false
Mass, 148–51; literacy of, 32, 35 fig.
5, 36; local opposition to, 151–53,
156–57, 160–61; prosecutions of debts
by, 156; prosecutions of idolatry by,
154–55, 241n63; prosecutions of sexual misconduct by, 155–56
Carhuas, Sebastián, 135; literacy of,
31–32, 33 fig. 3
Carrera, Fernando de la, 63, 138
cartillas de leer, 21, 207–8n71
Caruachin, Hernando, 53, 146–47
Castromonte, Juan de, 64
catechesis: and arithmetic, 102; contents of, 21–24; early attempts of,
18–19; in indigenous languages, 45;
with khipus, 78–79, 81, 84, 96; native
opposition to, 28, 205–6n46; and
primary letters, 18, 21; results of, 25,
27–28; in visitas, 140
causas de capítulos. See petitions, of
grievance
causas de idolatrías. See idolatry, prosecutions of
Celis de Padilla, Juan: and extirpation-of-idolatries campaigns, 129;
and litigation, 104, 106, 114, 123–30;
and jurisdiction, 106, 120–21; visita
report on, 184, 249n51
central Quechua: in Guaman Poma,
59; in parishes, 57, 60–61; support
for, 64–66, 215n71; and Third Provincial Council, 47–48
Cerrón-Palomino, Rodolfo, 31, 50

ordination, indigenous, 10, 199n18

Oré, Luis Jerónimo de, 28, 48, 63, 214n67

Ortiz de Cervantes, Juan, 65

Ortiz de Salcedo, Francisco, 173, 175

Pachacuti Yamqui Salcamaygua, Juan de Santacruz, 5, 11, 15, 147, 195, 198n9; on books, 16; on indigenous languages, 58–59; on linguistic ignorance of the clergy, 217n86

Padilla, Juan de: memorial of, 163–64, 166, 182, 184–85; as protector of Indians, 160, 190

padrones: and fiscal exploitation, 94, 109–10, 113–14; in native lawsuits, 53, 127–28, 155; *Padrón de los indios que se hallaren en la ciudad de los Reyes*, 108 fig. 13, 225n10; in parish administration, 103–4, 106–7, 109–10

Pardo, Osvaldo, 120

parish assistants: alleged corruption of, 113–14; appointment of, 116–17, 120, 201n13, 202n14, 228–29n45; autonomy of, 88–89, 97, 99–100, 149, 219n19; and civil jurisdiction, 116, 120–21; clerical mistreatment of, 104, 114–15, 152, 178–79, 224n4, 228n38; corporal punishments for, 111; disciplinary function of, 112–13; duties of, 10–11, 19–20; as economic functionaries, 103, 107, 109, 115–16; hierarchy of, 20; and legal testimony, 122; native opposition to, 113, 144–46; privileges of, 19, 109; and record keeping, 71, 106–7; and sacramental rites, 88, 220n30; ties to Andean religion, 147, 239n52. *See also* alguaciles, of parish; cantors; fiscales, of parish; maestrescuelas; sacristans

parishes: founding of, 19; and Spanish-Creole conflict, 65. *See also* Lima, archdiocese; Lima, audiencia

parish priests: "bad example" of, 52–53; books of, 22; and fiscal exploitation, 52, 109, 113–15; language requirement for, 46, 67; linguistic ignorance of, 42–43, 60–61, 65–67, 217n86; and oposiciones, 209n9, 216n76; pastoral neglect of, 53; and problem of native lawsuits, 38; and relations with indigenous nobility, 152–53; satires of, 66, 150, 240n54; and secular jurisdiction, 115–16, 120–21, 171–72, 230nn58–59; sources of income for, 52, 107, 109; use of corporal punishment by, 104, 106, 110–12, 124, 152

Patiño, Francisco, 137

Pauccar, Hernando, 132–34, 139

Peña Montenegro, Alonso de la, 199n18

Pérez Bocanegra, Juan, 62; on confession with khipus, 73, 75, 83, 97, 99–100; and conflict with Jesuits, 97–98, 223n51; on Cuzco Quechua, 210n21; on idolatry, 140, 234n6; on intermediaries, 3, 88–89, 99, 240n54; on maintenance of padrones, 107; and native litigation, 98–99; on Spanish in Cuzco, 27

petitions, of grievance: authorship of, 32, 176–77, 180–81; "bad priests" in, 130, 178–80; charge of linguistic ignorance in, 67–68, 170; compared to memoriales, 165, 182, 184–85; composition of, 121–22, 168–69, 180–81; disputes of jurisdiction in, 126–27, 171–72; and extirpation-of-idolatries campaigns, 6, 51; and formularies, 172–74; legal formulae in, 169–71; procedures for filing, 52, 122; reference to law in, 68, 171–72; rhetorical aspects of, 175–76, 178–80, 224–25n6; types of charges in, 52–53; and visita reports, 174–75

Philip II, 46, 167